# WOMEN IN COMBAT

Report to the President

# WOMEN IN COMBAT

## Report to the President

**Presidential Commission on the Assignment
of Women in the Armed Forces**

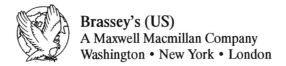

Brassey's (US)
A Maxwell Macmillan Company
Washington • New York • London

Brassey's (US)

*Editorial Offices*
Brassey's (US)
8000 Westpark Drive
First Floor
McLean, Virginia 22102

*Order Department*
Brassey's Book Orders
c/o Macmillan Publishing Co.
100 Front Street, Box 500
Riverside, New Jersey 08075

Brassey's (US) is a Maxwell Macmillan Company. Brassey's books are available at special discounts for bulk purchases for sales promotions, premiums, fund-raising, or educational use through the Special Sales Director, Macmillan Publishing Company, 866 Third Avenue, New York 10022.

**Library of Congress Cataloging-in-Publication Data**

United States. Presidential Commission on the Assignment of Women in
　　the Armed Forces.
　　　Women in Combat: report to the President / Presidential
　　Commission on the Assignment of Women in the Armed Forces.
　　　　　p.　cm.
　　　ISBN 0-02-881097-X (hardcover)　ISBN 0-02-881091-0 (softcover)
　　　1. Women in Combat—United States.　I. Title.
　　UB418.W56U58　1993
　　355.4'082—dc20
　　　　　　　　　　　　　　　　　　　　　　　　　　　　　　93-26786
　　　　　　　　　　　　　　　　　　　　　　　　　　　　　　CIP

10 9 8 7 6 5 4 3 2 1

Printed in the United States of America

The Presidential Commission on the Assignment of Women in the Armed Forces was established by Public Law 102-190, Dec. 5, 1991, for the purpose of assessing the laws and policies restricting the assignment of servicewomen and of making findings, conclusions and recommendations on such matters. The Commission is a bipartisan body whose members were appointed by the President in consultation with Congress.

**An AUSA Book**

The Association of the United States Army, or AUSA, was founded in 1950 as a not-for-profit organization dedicated to education concerning the role of the U.S. Army, to providing material for military professional development, and to the promotion of proper recognition and appreciation of the profession of arms. Its constituencies include those who serve in the Army today, including Army National Guard, Army Reserve, and Army civilians, and the retirees and veterans who have served in the past, and all their families. A large number of public-minded citizens and business leaders are also an important constituency. The Association seeks to educate the public, elected and appointed officials, and leaders of defense industry on crucial issues involving the adequacy of our national defense, particularly those issues affecting land warfare.

In 1988 AUSA established within its existing organization a new entity known as the Institute of Land Warfare. Its purpose is to extend the educational work of AUSA by sponsoring scholarly publications, to include books, monographs, and essays on key defense issues, as well as workshops and symposia. Among the volumes chosen for designation as "An AUSA Institute of Land Warfare Book" are both new texts and reprints of titles of enduring value that are no longer in print. Topics include history, policy issues, strategy, and tactics. Publication as an AUSA Book does not indicate that the Association of the United States Army and the publisher agree with everything in the book, but does suggest that the AUSA and the publisher believe this book will stimulate the thinking of AUSA members and others concerned about important issues.

# The Presidential Commission on the Assignment of Women in the Armed Forces

Robert T. Herres, Gen, USAF (Ret.)
Chairman

Mary E. Clarke, MG, USA (Ret.)
Samuel G. Cockerham, BG, USA (Ret.)
Elaine Donnelly
Thomas V. Draude, BGen, USMC
Mary M. Finch, CPT, USA
Wm. Darryl Henderson, PhD
James R. Hogg, ADM, USN (Ret.)
Newton N. Minow
Charles C. Moskos, PhD
Meredith A. Neizer
Kate Walsh O'Beirne
Ronald D. Ray
Maxwell R. Thurman, GEN, USA (Ret.)
Sarah F. White

# Commission Staff

## W. S. Orr
*Executive Director*

## General Counsel

Robert J. Moore, Esq.
*General Counsel*

Kelly Carlson, Esq.

Mary Ann Hook, Esq.

Sarah E. Scanlon

## Research and Analysis

Kathleen Robertson, J.D., PhD
*Director of Research and Analysis*

Maj Charles B. Johnson, USMC

S. Elizabethe Bogart

Stephen J. Brophy

Maj Katherine L. Brown, USAF

Mark A. Byrd

William W. S. Chipman

William F. Delaney

Peter Dolgenos

CPT (P) Mary P. Fletcher, USA

Richard E. Goldberg

J. David Kuo

Richard A. Love

CDR (sel) Edward J. Marcinik, PhD, USN

Stephen C. Matthews

LCDR (sel) Ruth Ann Mohr, USN

John T. Winkler

## Office of the Chairman

Col Kerry Green, USAF
*Executive Assistant to the Chairman*

Misty K. Hook

## Communications and Congressional Affairs

Magee Whelan
*Director of Communications and Congressional Affairs*

D. Bryce Hallowell

Kevin Kenneth Kirk

R. Cort Kirkwood

Holly Faith Lanoux

Mary Clark Linbeck

## Operations and Administration

William D. Duhnke III
*Director of Operations and Administration*

Rafael E. Fagundo

LTJG Harry J. Hirschman, USNR

Elizabeth A. Keller

Sarah Livingston

Jacqueline D. McKimmy

J. Morgan Whitacre

## Interns

John W. Boling, Jr.

Joseph P. Hill, Jr.

Michael V. Matson

Christopher E. Myers

Kevin A. Ring

Paul W. Rogers

Elizabeth L. Rosenblatt

Stephanie L. Sierakowski

# TABLE OF CONTENTS

# LETTER OF TRANSMITTAL

# PRESIDENTIAL COMMISSION ON THE ASSIGNMENT OF WOMEN IN THE ARMED FORCES

November 15, 1992

*Chairman*
Robert T. Herres

*Commissioners*
Mary E. Clarke
Samuel G. Cockerham
Elaine Donnelly
BGen Thomas V. Draude
CPT Mary M. Finch
Wm. Darryl Henderson
James R. Hogg
Newton N. Minow
Charles C. Moskos
Meredith A. Neizer
Kate Walsh O'Beirne
Ronald D. Ray
Maxwell R. Thurman
Sarah F. White

*Staff Director*
W. S. Orr

The President
The White House
Washington, D.C. 20500

Dear Mr. President:

On behalf of the Presidential Commission on the Assignment of Women in the Armed Forces, we are pleased to submit our final report containing a review of existing laws and policies and our recommendations for the future assignment of women in the Armed Forces.

For the past eight months, the Commission has undertaken a research study to assess the assignment of servicewomen. The Commission reviewed historical and current writings on the subject and invited the opinions of all interested Americans, resulting in over 11,000 letters. In hearings held across the country, we received testimony from a wide range of people including members of the U.S. House of Representatives and Senate, authorities on cultural and religious issues, and scientific and medical experts. We studied the extensive foreign military experiences relevant to women in the military. We heard the views of retired and active duty members of the U.S. Armed Forces, from junior enlisted to flag and general officer. The Commission conducted three surveys on the role of women in the military, one of the American public, one of a cross-section of military personnel and another of retired flag and general officers.

After studying this extensive amount of information and conducting days of intense and vigorous debate, the Commission defined the 17 critical issues relevant to this matter and subsequently voted on recommendations for each.

Today, the Commission respectfully submits this report comprised of recommendations, findings and conclusions. We are confident our work has met our obligations as defined in Public Law 102-190, Sec. 543. We expect that this report will assist you and the Congress in establishing sound policy regarding the utilization and assignment of women in the U.S. Armed Forces.

Respectfully,

Robert T. Herres
General, USAF (Ret.)
Chairman

Mary E. Clarke
Major General, USA (Ret.)

Samuel G. Cockerham
Brigadier General, USA (Ret.)

Elaine Donnelly

Thomas V. Draude
Brigadier General, USMC

Mary M. Finch
Captain, USA

Willliam Darryl Henderson, PhD
Colonel, USA (Ret.)

James R. Hogg
Admiral, USN (Ret.)

Newton N. Minow

Charles C. Moskos, PhD

Meredith Neizer

Kate Walsh O'Beirne

Ronald D. Ray

Maxwell R. Thurman
General, USA (Ret.)

Sarah F. White

# INTRODUCTION

# INTRODUCTION

More than 40,000 American military women served their country with courage, honor and distinction in the Persian Gulf. Their performance, along with that of their male counterparts, met the highest standards of military professionalism during a watershed period in our nation's history. In light of the experience of that war, the citizens of our country became engaged with the complex and emotional issue of whether U.S. women should serve in the combat arms or in other direct combat positions within the U.S. military.

In the aftermath of the Persian Gulf War, Congress focused on the repeal of existing combat exclusion laws. In the House Armed Services Committee debate of the 1992 Defense Authorization Act, Representative Patricia Schroeder (D-CO) offered an amendment to repeal the restrictions on women flying combat aircraft. The legislation was ultimately passed by the House of Representatives. During the floor debate of the Senate's version of the Defense Authorization Act, Senators Edward Kennedy (D-MA) and William Roth (R-DE) introduced an amendment to repeal restrictions on women flying combat aircraft. Prior to a vote on the Kennedy-Roth Amendment, Senators Sam Nunn (D-GA), Chairman of the Senate Arms Services Committee; John Warner (R-VA), Ranking Minority Member of the Committee; John McCain (R-AZ) and John Glenn (D-OH) offered an amendment to create a commission to study the legal, military and societal implications of amending the exclusionary laws. Senator McCain cautioned that to adopt the Kennedy-Roth Amendment would be to "rush ahead without proper study and a national consensus." By creating a commission, he said, "we will be able to make the kind of judgment which will give the American people what they want. We will find the best way to both defend this Nation's national security interests, and provide equality for women in all ranks and military specialties."

The Defense Authorization Act became Public Law 102-190 on December 5, 1991. Both Senate amendments were included in the law: one repealed the combat exclusionary provision relating to female Naval aviation officers and the exclusion of women from assignment in the Air Force to duty in aircraft engaged in combat missions; and the other amendment established the Presidential Commission on the Assignment of Women in the Armed Forces. Upon enactment of the statute, Defense Secretary Richard Cheney said that he would wait until the Commission issued its recommendations before deciding whether to modify the Services' policies as a result of the repeal of the exclusionary provisions.

The Commission's enabling statute requires it to "assess the laws and policies restricting the assignment of female servicemembers" and to make recommendations to the President by November 15, 1992. (Sec. 542 (a); 543, P.L. 102-190) The President is responsible for providing a copy of the Commission's report to Congress, along with his comments and recommendations, by December 15, 1992. (Sec. 543 (c), P.L. 102-190)

Congress specifically directed the Commission to make recommendations on: (i) whether existing law and policies restricting the assignment of servicewomen should be retained, modified or repealed; (ii) what roles servicewomen should have in combat; (iii) the appropriate transition process if servicewomen are given the opportunity to be assigned to combat positions; and (iv) whether special conditions and different standards should apply to servicewomen than apply to servicemen performing similar roles in the Armed Forces. (Sec. 543(b)(2), P.L. 102-190)

## STATUTORY AND POLICY RESTRICTIONS

The sole exclusion law in effect during the Commission's tenure was 10 U.S.C. 6015, which, as amended, prohibits the Navy and Marine Corps from assigning women to duty on vessels engaged in combat missions, other than as aviation officers as part of an air wing or other air element assigned to such a vessel. It also prohibits the assignment of women to other than temporary duty on other vessels of the Navy except hospital ships, transports and vessels of a similar classification not expected to be assigned combat missions. In addition to the law governing Navy and Marine Corps assignments, all Services have policies and/or regulations which restrict the assignment of women from combat positions.

The Department of Defense (DoD) does not have a directive or regulation that excludes women from combat positions but does utilize a Risk Rule policy which governs the assignment of women to non-combat positions in each of the Services. The rule was devised to standardize positions closed to women in the Services. Each Service has interpreted the Risk Rule according to its mission requirements in an effort to evaluate whether a non-combat position should be open or closed to women.

## COMMISSION RESEARCH METHODOLOGY

The research methodology was guided by a standard and philosophical underpinning of objectivity, thoroughness and well-supported analysis. As mandated by its enabling statute, the Commission "conduct[ed] a thorough study of duty assignments available for female servicemembers; examine[d] studies already completed concerning duty assignments for female servicemembers" and conducted additional research required to assess the laws and policies restricting the assignment of servicewomen. (Sec. 542 (a), (b), P.L. 102-190) Resources included DoD documents, reports from a variety of research and educational organizations, books, articles, testimony and fact-finding trips. The Commission divided the research topics among four panels, and each Commissioner was assigned to one panel. Panel charters were created and an issue-tracking process was developed to ensure that all significant issues, as identified within the law as well as by the Commission, were addressed by one or more of the panels.

The major products that evolved from the research included literary reviews, research materials organized by major issues and panel reports which were transmitted to the

Commission. The Commission approved 386 findings which are itemized in Appendix C, referenced within the panel reports, and incorporated under the issues. Other significant research projects included the professional administration of two polls conducted by The Roper Organization, one of the public and one of the military. In addition, a survey was conducted of 6,109 retired flag and general officers from all of the Armed Services.

## THE REPORT

Through extensive research and deliberations, the Commission developed issues pertinent to the examination of the assignment of women in the Armed Forces. The Commission defined an issue as "a question, the answer to which will result in a recommendation to be included in the Commission report and may necessitate further administrative or legislative action." The majority of the issues confronted by the Commission were drawn from the mandate provided in section 543 of the Commission's enabling statute. Other issues were developed by the Commission out of concern over quotas, occupational requirements and standards, family considerations, cultural values, and conscription. The recommendations for the President and Congress are based on the Commission findings drawn from testimony, reports, site visits, other avenues of research and the experience of Commissioners.

This report includes 17 issues and corresponding recommendations which the Commission believes to be central to the review of policies and law associated with the assignment of women in the Armed Forces. The rationale for all findings supporting the recommendations is contained herein.

The report also provides for the expression of alternative views by five Commission members. Additionally, the report provides for Commissioners to express their independent views on the issues relevant to the Commission's work. The Commission is confident that its work will serve both the President and the Congress in formulating and implementing future policy and law on the assignment of women in the Armed Forces of the United States.

# I.
# ISSUES
# and
# RECOMMENDATIONS

## A: QUOTAS AND GOALS

*Should a DoD-wide policy be established regarding the use of quotas or goals to influence gender-related personnel policies, e.g., recruitment, promotion, retention and assignment? If so, what should that policy be?*

**Recommendation:** *DoD should establish a policy to ensure that no person who is best qualified is denied access on the basis of gender to an assignment that is open to both men and women. As far as it is compatible with the above policy, the Secretary of Defense should retain discretion to set goals that encourage the recruitment and optimize the utilization of women in the Services, allowing for the requirements of each Service.*

In the course of the deliberations, the Commission found situations where quotas used by some of the Services had become discriminatory. In these cases, it appeared that special influences were creating situations in which better qualified persons were denied assignments. In addition, it was found that some Services have recruiting quotas, while others do not.

The Commission identified this issue to ensure that the Armed Forces select the best qualified people for positions, particularly those filled on a competitive basis. Faced with how best to recruit, promote, retain and assign women in the Services, the Commission decided that the most important criterion is an individual's qualification for any given assignment. It was argued that special gender quotas would work against the military's interest in identifying the most qualified person to fill each position.

The effectiveness of every combat and support unit hinges upon having the most qualified person in every position. Use of quotas fosters the perception of discrimination and sexual harassment. In addition, morale and cohesion of the military could be jeopardized if quotas allow less qualified individuals to fill roles for which others are more qualified.

The Commission recommends a policy to ensure that no person who is best qualified is denied an assignment on the basis of gender. The Commission also believes that the Secretary of Defense is in the best position to appreciate the overall needs of the Services and, therefore, should have the latitude to establish goals to encourage the recruitment and optimize the utilization of women in order to enhance the readiness of the Armed Forces of the United States.

*Commission Vote*

| | |
|---|---|
| *Yes:* | 9 |
| *No:* | 6 |
| *Abstention:* | 0 |

1

## Relevant Findings

*The findings relevant to this issue are listed below. These findings are referenced in Appendix C. The first number refers to the panel. For example, 1.5 is a Panel 1 finding.*

| | | | |
|---|---|---|---|
| 1.71 | 2.6.1I | 4.19 | 4.28 |
| 1.104 | 2.6.3C | 4.20 | |
| 1.105 | 2.6.4H | 4.21 | |
| 1.106 | 2.6.4I | 4.22 | |
| 1.125 | 4.17 | 4.24 | |
| 1.129 | 4.18 | 4.27 | |

## B: VOLUNTARY v. INVOLUNTARY DUTY

*Should special conditions and different standards apply to servicewomen than apply to servicemen performing similar roles in the Armed Forces in the area of voluntary (women) versus involuntary (men) assignment policies?*

**Recommendation:** *The Services should adopt gender-neutral assignment policies, providing the possibility of involuntary assignment of any qualified personnel to any position open to them.*

The Commission formulated this issue in response to information obtained from survey results regarding attitudes of assignment policies and to the Commission's statutory mandate to provide recommendations on "[w]hether special conditions and different standards should apply to females than apply to males performing similar roles in the Armed Forces." (Sec. 543(b)(2)(D), P.L. 102-190) Commissioners focused on the area of assignment policies because of its direct influence on military effectiveness and readiness.

Men can be involuntarily assigned to any position in the Service, and women can be involuntarily assigned to any position open to them based on the needs of the Services. The Armed Forces have never had a "voluntary assignment policy." Such a concept would hinder combat readiness and effectiveness, especially in an era which necessitates a readily deployable force.

The Commission concluded that a policy implementing special standards, set-asides, or privileges for one gender would be contrary to the interests of both sexes and the military. The weight of evidence presented to the Commission, in hearings, through research, and on fact-finding trips, suggests that servicemen and servicewomen should be treated as equals in those areas where women are not restricted by law or policy. The Commission also heard in testimony that, if the combat exclusions are eliminated, women should be involuntarily assigned to combat positions on the same basis as their male counterparts. Commissioners believed that if women were assigned to positions on a voluntary basis and men were assigned involuntarily, animosity between the genders would occur and cohesion could suffer as a result.

The Commission also considered the legal implications of a policy which assigns men and women on a different basis according to gender. The legal analysis indicates such a policy may not be constitutional under the Due Process Clause of the Fifth Amendment.

Based on the possible impact on military effectiveness, readiness and morale, the Commission recommends the Services adopt gender-neutral assignment policies that provide involuntary assignment of any qualified persons to any available position open to them in peace or war.

3

## Commission Vote

| | |
|---|---|
| Yes: | 10 |
| No: | 2 |
| Abstention: | 3 |

## Relevant Findings

*The findings relevant to this issue are listed below. These findings are referenced in Appendix C. The first number refers to the panel. For example, 1.5 is a Panel 1 finding.*

| | | | | | |
|---|---|---|---|---|---|
| 1.76 | 1.126 | 2.1.4 | 2.1.6B | 2.2.2A | 3.9 |
| 1.83 | 1.127 | 2.1.4A | 2.1.7 | 2.2.3 | 3.10 |
| 1.86 | 1.130 | 2.1.4B | 2.2.1 | 2.2.3A | 3.11 |
| 1.95 | 2.1.1 | 2.1.5 | 2.2.1A | 2.2.3B | 3.12 |
| 1.106 | 2.1.2 | 2.1.6 | 2.2.1B | 2.3 2.4 | 3A1 |
| 1.110 | 2.1.3 | 2.1.6A | 2.2.2 | 3.5 | 3A2 |

| | | | |
|---|---|---|---|
| 3A3 | 3.17 | 4.5 | 4.14 |
| 3A6 | 3.20 | 4.7 | 4.18 |
| 3.13 | 3.29 | 4.10 | 4.25 |
| 3.14 | 3.31 | 4.11 | |
| 3.15 | 3.32 | 4.12 | |
| 3.16 | 4.1 | 4.13 | |

## C: FITNESS/WELLNESS STANDARDS

*Should special conditions and different standards apply to servicewomen than apply to servicemen performing similar roles in the Armed Forces in the area of general physical fitness requirements for purposes of wellness?*

***Recommendation: The Services should retain gender-specific physical fitness tests and standards to promote the highest level of general fitness and wellness in the Armed Forces of the United States, provided they do not compromise training or qualification programs for physically demanding combat or combat support MOSs.***

The major concern to the Commission on this issue focused on determining the purpose of general fitness standards for the military. Should they be related to general health and wellness or should they be related to occupational requirements? Wellness can be defined as the capacity to achieve optimal quality of life. Wellness includes positive mental, social and physical behaviors which result in optimal health. Physical fitness can be defined as having a sufficient level of muscular strength, muscular endurance, cardiorespiratory capacity, and flexibility to accomplish a day's work without undue fatigue and the ability to perform required physical activities at desired levels.

The Commission believes the main purpose of military physical fitness programs is to promote good health and wellness and that *general* fitness standards should not be linked to specific occupations. A gender-neutral standard will unfairly subject most women to standards which are unrealistic for general fitness and will not be challenging for the majority of military men. A study that investigated whether women could meet the same physical fitness standards as men addressed this question. Study findings revealed that only 21 women of 623 tested (3.4 percent) achieved a score equal to the male mean score on the Army Physical Fitness Test. Only seven percent of women could perform 60 push-ups while 78 percent of men could achieve this score.

A high level of fitness is considered to be vitally important to the military to ensure a healthy and fit force. The basic intent of current fitness standards is to challenge the individual to train and become fit. The best way to achieve this goal is to adjust standards by gender and age. The Commission recognizes the categorical physical difference between men and women in the areas of upper body strength/endurance and cardiorespiratory capacity and agrees that general physical fitness standards should be age and gender-specific. An age and gender-neutral test is not compatible with physiological differences between individuals of different ages and sexes.

## Commission Vote
| | |
|---|---|
| *Yes:* | *12* |
| *No:* | *0* |
| *Abstention:* | *1* |

## Relevant Findings
*The findings relevant to this issue are listed below. These findings are referenced in Appendix C. The first number refers to the panel. For example, 1.5 is a Panel 1 finding.*

| | |
|---|---|
| 2.1.1 | 2.2.1B |
| 2.1.2 | 2.2.2 |
| 2.1.3 | 2.2.2A |
| 2.1.4A | 2.2.3B |
| 2.2.1 | 2.2.4 |
| 2.2.1A | |

# D: OCCUPATIONAL PHYSICAL REQUIREMENTS

*Should the Services establish and implement specific occupational, muscular strength/endurance, and cardiovascular capacity requirements where they are relevant to the duties of each specialty?*

***Recommendation: The Services should adopt specific requirements for those specialties for which muscular strength/endurance and cardiovascular capacity are relevant.***

This issue is significant to the Commission because, although many specialties require substantial physical capabilities, only the Air Force has occupational strength standards in place. Without strength testing, it is possible that personnel could be assigned to occupational specialties they could not perform, or they could sustain injuries by exceeding their capabilities. Although this is not a gender issue per se, it is under consideration because of the importance for all military personnel to meet occupational requirements of all relevant specialties.

Recognizing the importance of determining occupational requirements, the Services have conducted research in this area. For example, the Army made a concerted effort in the early 1980s to design a physical testing system which would match individual physical capacities to the demands of each relevant specialty. Unfortunately, the Military Entrance Physical Strength Capacity Test (MEPSCAT) was never used as intended. It was used only as a recruiting guidance tool, and was later eliminated all together. The Commission found that the MEPSCAT system failed because of disagreement about whether standards should reflect peacetime or wartime requirements. The Commission finds no evidence that the occupational classification process has changed since then, and this has become an increasing concern in the military, as women continue to enter physically demanding non-traditional occupations.

The Commission believes that the tendency of the Services to use greater numbers of women in physically demanding specialties creates the need to match individual capacities with occupational demands. The Commission recommends the development of gender-neutral standards for military occupation specialty qualifications commensurate with specialty demands. These standards will differ from general fitness standards for good health addressed by the Commission in Issue C. Commissioners were influenced in their decision by the results of the Roper survey. This survey asked military personnel whether physical standards for each combat assignment should reflect the demands of that assignment on a gender-neutral basis, 70 percent of the military strongly agreed, and another 17 percent agreed. Only 12 percent of military respondents disagreed with this statement to any degree.

*Commission Vote*
| | |
|---|---|
| *Yes:* | *9* |
| *No:* | *4* |
| *Abstention:* | *2* |

7

## Relevant Findings

*The findings relevant to this issue are listed below. These findings are referenced in Appendix C. The first number refers to the panel. For example, 1.5 is a Panel 1 finding. In addition, the Commission approved 25 findings offered by individual Commissioners. These are numbered 1-25 and are also referenced in Appendix C.*

| | | | | | |
|---|---|---|---|---|---|
| 1.39 | 1.130 | 2.1.4B | 2.1.6B | 2.2.2A | 2.54B |
| 1.76 | 2.1.1 | 2.2.1B | 2.1.7 | 2.2.3 | 3A6 |
| 1.106 | 2.1.2 | 2.1.5 | 2.2.1A | 2.2.3A | 3.20 |
| 1.110 | 2.1.3 | 2.1.6 | 2.2.1B | 2.2.3B | 3B1 |
| 1.126 | 2.1.4 | 2.1.6A | 2.2.2 | 2.2.4 | |
| 6 | 8 | 15 | 22 | | |

## E: BASIC TRAINING STANDARDS

*Should special conditions and different standards apply to servicewomen than apply to servicemen performing similar roles in the Armed Forces in the area of basic training?*

**Recommendation: *Entry level training may be gender-specific as necessary. Each advanced training program should be classified according to the military specialties to which it is principally dedicated, or to which it supplies personnel. Training programs which are dedicated to combat specialties shall be governed by policies which are consistent with laws and policies regarding the use of women in combat.***

One primary issue of concern to the Commission is whether physical fitness standards for basic training should be related to wellness or occupational physical requirements (See Issues C and D). The Commission believes that the main purpose of basic training is to provide enlistees a basic indoctrination to the military. Physical demands of occupational specialties pertain to advanced training for each enlistee following basic training. The Commission recommends that basic physical training standards be established for purposes of achieving general fitness; no attempt should be made to align physical demands of occupational specialties until trainees have been assigned to those specialties and advanced training begins.

Commissioners visited five training installations and observed different types of basic and unit training. In general, they found that almost all gender-integrated training was the same for both sexes. The Commission finds that in certain training situations, physiological differences between the sexes warrant different standards. As an example, integrated training for Navy recruits is being conducted on an experimental basis at the Recruit Training Center, Orlando, FL. Recruit training is the same for men and women, including all physical training. The Navy physical training test, however, has different standards for men and women, by age groups.

The Commission considered the consequences of establishing gender-neutral standards for basic training. Testimony from several experts indicated that implementing gender-neutral standards would lead to dramatic increases in rates of injury and attrition among women. For example, studies involving Army recruits indicate women are at a higher risk for exercise-induced injuries than men. Compared to men, women had a 2.13 times greater risk for lower extremity injuries and a 4.71 times greater risk for stress fractures. The men sustained 99 days of limited duty due to injury while women incurred 481 days of limited duty.

The existence of different, gender-specific physical fitness training standards in basic training is acceptable to the majority of Commissioners. The Commission recognizes the basic physiological gender differences and the need of the Services to accommodate these differences. The Commissioners also recognize the Services should have the flexibility to establish physical standards for specialties (See Issue D).

9

## Commission Vote

| | |
|---|---|
| *Yes:* | *8* |
| *No:* | *6* |
| *Abstention:* | *1* |

## Relevant Findings

*The findings relevant to this issue are listed below. These findings are referenced in Appendix C. The first number refers to the panel. For example, 1.5 is a Panel 1 finding.*

| | | | |
|---|---|---|---|
| 1.86 | 2.41D | 2.6IJ | 3.20 |
| 1.110 | 2.42B | 2.6.2F | |
| 2.41 | 2.42C | 2.6.3D | |
| 2.41A | 2.43 | 2.6.4J | |
| 2.41B | 2.44 | 2.6.4J | |
| 2.41C | 2.6IJ | 3A6 | |

## F: PRE-COMMISSIONING STANDARDS

*Should special conditions and different standards apply to servicewomen than apply to servicemen performing similar roles in the Armed Forces in the area of pre-commissioning training?*

**Recommendation: Military pre-commissioning training may be gender-normed in as much as post-commissioning training is designed specifically for individual specialties, combat, combat support and combat service support.**

As in Issue E, the Commission examined whether physical fitness standards should be related to wellness or occupational requirements in the area of pre-commissioning training. Pre-commissioning education and training includes the Service Academies, Officer Candidate Schools, and Reserve Officer Training Corps (ROTC) programs which prepare officers for commissions in the Armed Forces. Commissioners discovered through fact-finding trips to training facilities and through testimony before the Commission that virtually all pre-commissioning training is the same for both men and women. However, there are significant differences in the area of physical training standards. For example, at the United States Military Academy at West Point both men and women cadets must complete an indoor obstacle course test (IOCT), but the standards for the obstacle course are gender-specific. The test is designed to evaluate a cadet's muscular strength/endurance, flexibility, agility, and coordination. The IOCT consists of 10 obstacles and the average completion time is approximately 2:50 (min:sec) for men and 4:05 (min:sec) for women. Men must score 3:20 or better to pass; while women must score 5:30 or better. Additional illustrative examples were found in other pre-commissioning programs.

The criteria by which the military may determine if different standards are acceptable for training are: 1) Does the different standard compromise the men's training? 2) Does the different standard detract from realistic training for the women? The Commission finds that different standards are acceptable in pre-commissioning training, because the purpose of the training is to promote physical fitness, educate and evaluate an officer candidate; these standards are not designed for occupational requirements. Based on the Commission's recommendations on Issues C and D, general fitness standards for pre-commissioning training may be gender-normed and post-commissioning training for individual specialties, combat, combat support and combat service support should be gender-neutral.

*Commission Vote*
*Yes:*        *10*
*No:*          *4*
*Abstention:*  *1*

11

## *Relevant Findings*

*The findings relevant to this issue are listed below. These findings are referenced in Appendix C. The first number refers to the panel. For example, 1.5 is a Panel 1 finding.*

| | |
|---|---|
| 1.76 | 2.24B |
| 1.83 | 2.5.1 |
| 1.86 | 2.5.4 |
| 1.126 | 2.5.4B |
| 2.41B | 3A6 |
| 2.42A | 3.20 |

## G: GENDER-RELATED OCCUPATIONAL STANDARDS

*Should special conditions and different standards apply to servicewomen than apply to servicemen performing similar occupational roles in the Armed Forces in the area of muscular strength/endurance and cardiovascular capacity?*

***Recommendation: The Services should adopt gender-neutral muscular strength/endurance and cardiovascular capacity requirements for those specialties for which they are relevant.***

The issue was considered by the Commission because individual capabilities must match occupational strength requirements to maintain military effectiveness. The Commission acknowledges the need to establish specialty-related strength standards to ensure the quality of the U.S. Armed Forces. There is a strong consensus among Commissioners that standards for all military specialties open to women should not differentiate on the basis of gender. The Commission agrees that strength standards would benefit the military by matching only physically qualified people, men or women, to physically demanding specialties.

During testimony, servicemembers expressed great concern that women would not be able to perform physically demanding tasks in a combat environment. The Commission addressed the issue of physiological gender differences. Testimony from physiologists indicated that women, in general, are shorter, weigh less, have less muscle mass and have a greater relative fat content than men. In terms of military significance, women are at a distinct disadvantage when performing military tasks requiring a high level of muscular strength and aerobic capacity, due to their lower muscle mass and greater relative fat mass. The dynamic upper torso muscular strength of women is approximately 50 to 60 percent that of men, while their aerobic capacity is approximately 70 to 75 percent that of men. Thus it is important that specialty-related standards not be gender-normed.

As Issue D determined, the Services should adopt specific requirements for those specialties for which muscular strength/muscular endurance and cardiovascular capacity are relevant. The Commission believes this concept should be applied to men and women where relevant. The consensus of the Commission is that the anticipated benefits from using a gender-neutral system based on specialty-related performance requirements in an operational environment are greater productivity and efficiency, as well as lower injury rates.

*Commission Vote*
*Yes:*       *14*
*No:*        *0*
*Abstention:*   *0*

13

## *Relevant Findings*

*The findings relevant to this issue are listed below. These findings are referenced in Appendix C. The first number refers to the panel. For example, 1.5 is a Panel 1 finding.*

| | | | | |
|------|--------|-------|--------|-------|
| 1.39 | 2.1.1 | 2.1.5 | 2.2.1B | 2.2.4 |
| 1.76 | 2.1.2 | 2.1.6 | 2.2.2 | 2.54B |
| 1.106 | 2.1.3 | 2.1.6A | 2.2.2A | 3A6 |
| 1.110 | 2.1.4 | 2.1.6B | 2.2.3 | 3.20 |
| 1.126 | 2.1.4B | 2.1.7 | 2.2.3A | 3B1 |
| 1.130 | 2.2.1B | 2.2.1A | 2.2.3B | |

## H: PARENTAL AND FAMILY POLICIES

*Should DoD policies, e.g., recruitment, retention, child care, and deployment policies, regarding single and dual-service parents be revised? What effect do policies on the assignment of servicewomen have upon military families, children, and the larger American society?*

*Recommendation: During and after U.S. involvement in the Gulf War, the American public and military community expressed extreme disapproval of the deployment of single mothers/fathers due to the possible effect on the children left behind. The Commission recommends that DoD review its policies and either adopt new policies or better implement current policies to reflect concerns of the public and military communities. Specifically, the Commission recommends that DoD consider the following alternatives:*

*1. DoD should adopt a waivable policy that single parents with custodial care of children up to two years of age must accept assignment to a nondeployable position, if available, or be discharged from the Service with the opportunity to re-enter the Service without loss of rank or position.*

*2. For those single parents who have children older than two years and those parents who have been out for two years, they must have an approved and reliable child care package to re-enter the Service.*

*3. In dual-service families, only one parent should be allowed to serve in a deployable position.*

*4. Single parents with custody of children under school age should not be allowed to deploy.*

*5. Single parents should not be permitted to join the Armed Forces (current situation).*

*6. Spouses of military parents should not be allowed to enter the Service.*

*7. One parent in a dual-service couple should be forced to separate from the Service.*

*8. In order to reduce the number of children subjected to prolonged separation or the risk of becoming orphans during deployment, long-term DoD policies regarding the recruitment, deployment and retention of single and dual-service parents should be revised on a phased-in basis. Such policies should allow for voluntary or involuntary discharges at the discretion of local commanders, or reasonable incentives for separation. They may also include waivers by local commanders in certain circumstances.*

*In order to avoid severe separation, child care and deployability problems at a time of mobilization, all family care plans must be regularly reviewed and evaluated by local commanding officers, with consideration given to the relationship of the potential caregiver to the child(ren) of deployable parents. Failure to ensure full compliance with family care requirements may constitute grounds for administrative or disciplinary action.*

The Commission, as the recommendation implies, views this as an important, but complex issue. Unless DoD develops a sound array of policies to deal with this issue, problems and difficulties will affect the military readiness of the Armed Forces. The Commission noted that a bill was introduced in the U.S. House of Representatives to exempt certain members of the Armed Forces from duty assignments in a combat zone or areas of imminent danger which would result in separating those members from their minor children. This bill would have affected one parent of dual-parent households and all single parents with minor children. Subsequently, the Deputy Secretary of Defense issued a policy to authorize military mothers a four-month deferment from duty away from their home station after childbirth. The policy also affords the same four-month deferment for a member of a military couple or single member after adoption of a child.

The American public and military faced the problems of deploying large numbers of single and dual-service parents for the first time during the Persian Gulf War. During that war, about 32,000 children of single parent households were separated from their parents and nearly 5,000 children were separated from their dual-service parents, who were deployed to the combat theater. Those children are a fraction of the children of existing single parent and dual-military couple families. Many experts testified before the Commission that problems in current military family policy must be addressed before another armed conflict involving U.S. forces puts tens of thousands of American children at risk of losing their parent(s).

There are 76,000 single parents and 46,000 dual military parents on active duty in the military, comprising 6.5 percent of the active force. Women comprise a disproportionate segment of single parents. Although they comprise 11.2 percent of the active duty force (211,296 out of 1,894,911), women make up 34.7 percent of single parents (26,419 out of 76,238). Moreover, 12.5 percent of the women serving on active duty are single parents (26,419 out of 211,296), while only 2.9 percent of the men serving on active duty are single parents (49,819 out of 1,683,615).

Results of polls conducted by the Commission indicate that the vast majority of the public and the military were concerned about the effect on children whose parents are deployed in the event of war. Sixty-nine percent of the public surveyed believed that a single woman with young child(ren) should not serve in a direct combat position, while 48 percent of those surveyed said a man so situated should not serve in direct combat positions. In the same survey, 55

16

percent of the respondents stated that, in the case of dual military parents, the wife should be exempt from direct combat. Two percent said the husband should be exempt, and 14 percent believed both members should be exempt from direct combat. Seventy-two percent of military personnel believe a single woman with children should not be assigned to combat, while 48 percent believe a single man with children should not be so assigned. Fifty-four percent of military respondents did not believe a married woman with children should be assigned to combat, while 14 percent felt that a married man with children should not be so assigned. Regarding dual military parents with young children, 65 percent of military respondents felt that the wife of such a couple should be exempt from direct combat.

Although recent directives from the Office of the Secretary of Defense (OSD) aim to strengthen the requirements and enforcement of Dependent Care Plans, DoD reports a significant number of deployable service members do not have workable plans. For example, a Navy study published in 1992 found that less than 50 percent of single and dual service parents had a current Dependent Care Plan. In a 1991 spot check within the Navy, less than 25 percent of Navy personnel were in compliance with dependent care certificate requirements.

Testimony from civilian child development specialists indicated that young children separated from their parents are vulnerable to emotional and psychological difficulties that include anxiety, depression and insecurity. As a general observation, the younger the child, the worse the effects of long-term separation from parents. Some experts emphasized the role of the mother and stressed the importance of a secure attachment between parent and infant in the earliest months of a child's life. Expert testimony and literature almost universally cited the period from birth to three years as the most critical and vulnerable in the child's life -- a period during which even the best substitute care may not alleviate the devastating effects of a long-term separation from a single parent or both parents in a two-parent family.

Some argue that DoD compensation and child care policies may have the unintentional effect of increasing the number of children of military families who are at risk of being separated for long periods of time from their deployable parents. However, such influences were not verified; therefore, the Commission offers no recommendations in this regard other than to suggest careful consideration of the relevant ramifications should this actually be the case.

The need for sound policies governing single and dual service parents is evident to the majority of the Commission. Deciding *what* to recommend, however, was a task more difficult to accomplish. Some of the Commission's recommendations, made in good faith, may result in undesirable consequences to those affected by divorce or death of a spouse. The Commission believes that the problems of childcare associated with deploying parents are complex. Therefore, the Commission recommends policy alternatives for these issues and believes that the Military Departments and DoD are best positioned to review present policies and determine future policies regarding these issues.

17

*Commission Vote on Current Policies of*                              *Vote on Effects of Current*
*Recruitment, Retention, Child Care and Deployment Policies*          *Assignment Policies*

| | | | |
|---|---|---|---|
| *Yes:* | *9* | *Yes:* | *15* |
| *No:* | *0* | *No:* | *0* |
| *Abstention:* | *1* | *Abstention:* | *0* |

## Relevant Findings

*The findings relevant to this issue are listed below. These findings are referenced in Appendix C. The first number refers to the panel. For example, 1.5 is a Panel 1 finding.*

| | | | | |
|---|---|---|---|---|
| 3.6 | 3 25 | 3.37 | 3.42 | 3.49 |
| 3.7 | 3.27 | 3.38 | 3.44 | 3.51 |
| 3.8 | 3 31 | 3.39 | 3.45 | 3.54 |
| 3.22 | 3.34 | 3.40 | 3.46 | 3.55 |
| 3.23 | 3.35 | 3.41 | 3.47 | |
| 3.24 | 3.36 | 3.42 | 3.48 | |

# I: PREGNANCY AND DEPLOYABILITY POLICIES

*Should DoD rules regarding pregnancy, excluding deployability of servicewomen, be retained, modified or rescinded?*

*Should special conditions and different standards apply to servicewomen than apply to servicemen performing similar roles in the Armed Forces regarding deployability?*

*Should servicewomen who become pregnant continue to serve in deployable positions?*

*Should comparable restrictions on deployability be applied to servicemen?*

*Recommendation: The Commission reviewed the rules regarding pregnancy and found no specific areas of concern other than the problems associated with deployability and lost time; these problems are addressed in a separate issue. However, DoD should review rules regarding pregnancy to ensure consistency and force readiness.*

*Comparable deployability standards for each Service should be adopted by DoD and should be applied on a gender-neutral basis with exceptions for pregnancy.*

*A pregnant servicewoman should not be assigned to or remain in a position with a high probability of deployment. The Commission suggests that deployability for purposes of implementing such a policy be defined in terms of probabilities; a deployment-probability-designation coding system could be established to determine which positions have the higher probabilities of deployment and thus would be subject to restrictions under the recommended policy. Comparable restrictions should be applied to other servicemembers based on projected amount of time an individual will be unable to fulfill normal duties of his/her position because of injury, etc.*

Much attention was focused on pregnancy throughout the Commission's tenure because of its impact on readiness, deployability and cohesion in the Armed Forces. Additionally, the Commission formulated this issue in response to its statutory mandate to provide recommendations on "[w]hether special conditions and different standards should apply to females than apply to males performing similar roles in the Armed Forces." (Sec. 543(b)(2)(D), P.L. 102-190). This issue was addressed in hopes of creating an equitable system where women are not the subject of discrimination due to pregnancy, and where men with lengthy, but not acute injuries are treated similarly. As with all other issues, the overriding concern was military effectiveness.

The Commission found the Services' and DoD policies addressing pregnancy are adequate except for those regarding deployability. The annual service pregnancy rates for 1990 were as follows: Army: 11.9 percent (officers and enlisted); Navy: 13.4 percent (enlisted only);

Air Force: 4.8 percent (officers), 8.1 percent (enlisted); Marine Corps: 3.0 percent (officers), 8.7 percent (enlisted).

The Commission finds that deployability standards, in all circumstances other than pregnancy, need to be standardized. Non-deployability due to commander discretion on the sole basis of gender should not be permitted. A key to military readiness is that all members, male and female, will deploy with their units. Such a policy prevents the discrimination the Commission heard occurred during the Persian Gulf War, where individual commanders refused to deploy women for no reason other than their gender.

According to testimony and survey research presented to the Commission, the pregnancy rate at the onset of the Persian Gulf War significantly affected the deployability of some units. The Commission also found that the non-deployability rate for women was three times greater than that of men, largely due to pregnancy.

In a report released on August 31, 1992, the General Accounting Office (GAO) found that a number of active and reserve personnel were unable to deploy for the Persian Gulf War. The causes of nondeployability ranged from incomplete training to varying medical conditions and personnel problems. GAO reported that the "Department of Defense said nondeployables were not considered a serious problem because the Services were able to replace them with other personnel. Nevertheless, available data indicates the number of nondeployables was sizeable." Regarding lost time, women have a lower rate than men when pregnancy and postpartum convalescent leave are excluded. When including these factors, however, women have approximately four times as much lost time as men.

To deal with the concern over deployability, the Commission recommends the development of a deployment-probability-designation coding system to distinguish those areas where a pregnant woman can serve during pregnancy, and those areas where her pregnancy would have an adverse affect on the unit. Likewise, the Commission recommends that men who suffer debilitating injuries for an equivalent period of time should be treated in the same manner.

*Commission Vote on Pregnancy*
*Yes:*　　　　8
*No:*　　　　0
*Abstention:*　2

*Commission recommendation on deployability adopted without objection.*

20

## _Relevant Findings_

_The findings relevant to this issue are listed below.  These findings may be referenced in Appendix C.  The first number refers to the panel.  For example, 1.5 is a Panel 1 finding._

| | | | | | |
|---|---|---|---|---|---|
| 1.59 | 2.3.2B | 2.3.5 | 2.6.3B | 3.8 | 3.24 |
| 1.69 | 2.3.3 | 2.3.5A | 2.6.3D | 3A6 | 3.25 |
| 2.3.1A | 2.3.3A | 2.5.4B | 2.6.4E | 3B1 | 3.40 |
| 2.3.1B | 2.3.3B | 2.6.1GH | 2.6.4J | 3.20 | 3.41 |
| 2.3.2 | 2.3.4 | 2.6.1J | 3.6 | 3.22 | 3.52 |
| 2.3.2A | 2.3.4A | 2.6.2F | 3.7 | 3.23 | 3.53 |

3.54
3.55
3.58
3D1
3D2

## J: COMBAT ROLES FOR WOMEN

*In view of American military history, experience of war, and religious and cultural values, should the U.S. under any circumstances assign any servicewomen to any combat position, on land, at sea, or in the air?*

***Recommendation: Yes. Military readiness should be the driving concern regarding assignment policies; there are circumstances under which women might be assigned to combat positions.***

The American experience -- military, religious, and cultural -- and how that relates to the role of women in direct combat was of great interest to the Commission. American history is replete with examples of women defending the nation with courage and dedication, and as the Persian Gulf War experience indicated, there are women who, today, serve in combatant positions. Testimony from sociologists, ethicists, moralists, theologians, and clergy indicated that the U.S. is a country with a diverse set of beliefs and varied heritages. After eight months of consideration, the Commission decided that the "American experience" does not preclude assigning capable women to direct combat positions for which they are qualified.

It was noted by the Commission in examining the assignment of women to combat positions that women, although precluded from combat assignments by law and policy, are currently serving in combat positions in Air Force missile silos, in Army air defense units, and in other combat service support roles where they are exposed to enemy fire. To assess attitudes regarding women's roles in the military, the Commission conducted an extensive poll of public and military attitudes. The public survey revealed that the views of Americans on women in combat are as diverse as their backgrounds. The Commission's public poll on women in the military revealed that while the public is almost evenly split on the concept of women in direct combat generally; when asked about specific assignments such as combatant vessels and aircraft, they support the assignment of women to some combat roles.

One of the strongest sociological arguments in favor of women in combat focused on selecting the best qualified person for a position, regardless of gender. A number of witnesses, Members of Congress and senior military women advanced the belief that women should not be barred from any position in the military unless there is convincing evidence that they cannot meet the occupational demands. Testimony revealed maintained that the burden should be on those who would continue gender-based classifications. Other witnesses stated that placing the best qualified person in a specialty requires servicemembers should be judged as individuals -- not as white or black, not as Italian or Greek or Jewish and not as men or women -- they should be treated as individuals, and not members of groups.

Many other witnesses testified that the demand for full integration of women in the Armed Forces is about the advancement of a particular vision of culture and society that advocates gender-neutrality. A number of people testified that no human society has ever intentionally used female soldiers in extended combat except in cases of national survival. They viewed that placing women in combat arms as a reckless act when there are sufficient numbers of qualified men available to serve in those positions.

Theological testimony was received from representatives of a wide range of different religions and denominations. Among the major religious establishments in the U.S., none has adopted a position regarding women being assigned to combat positions on the basis of theology. The Commission concludes that although the U.S. has an undeniably strong religious heritage, it is not one that speaks clearly on the issue of women in combat.

There was general agreement among theologians, Catholic, Lutheran, Baptist, Jewish and Episcopalian that the military's policies should not unduly infringe upon the rights of the family. Similarly, there was a strong concern that in an effort to defend the country, the nation's internal values not be diminished. The conclusions varied as some stated that women should not be assigned to these positions under any circumstances, while others distinguished assignment between air, sea and land combat. Still others believed that, as long as American women must accept broad societal responsibilities, they have the right to be represented in all aspects of the military, including ground combat.

A great effort was made by the Commission to determine the attitudes of the public toward women in direct combat and the effect of such assignment on the public. Its review of the diverse testimony reveals no thread from which a definitive position can be drawn that would preclude roles for women in combat. As evident by the Commission's recommendations on air, sea and land direct combat positions, a majority of Commissioners believe that under some circumstances, American society not only allows, but actually encourages and approves the further integration of women into combat roles.

*Commission Vote*
*Yes:*         *8*
*No:*          *1*
*Abstention:*  *1*

*Relevant Findings*
*The findings relevant to this issue are listed below. These findings are referenced in Appendix C. The first number refers to the panel. For example, 1.5 is a Panel 1 finding.*

| | | | | | |
|------|-------|------|------|------|------|
| 1.11 | 2.5.5 | 3A9  | 3.22 | 3.39 | 3.63 |
| 1.12 | 3.5   | 3A10 | 3.23 | 3.40 | 3.64 |
| 1.15 | 3.9   | 3A13 | 3.24 | 3.41 | 4.2  |
| 1.21 | 3.10  | 3A14 | 3.25 | 3.59 | 4.5  |
| 1.25 | 3.11  | 3A15 | 3.27 | 3.60 | 1.36 |
| 1.28 | 3.12  | 3A16 | 3.37 | 3.61 | 3A8  |

23

# K: GROUND COMBAT

*Should the existing service policies restricting the assignment of servicewomen with respect to ground combat MOS/specialties be retained, modified, rescinded, or codified?*

***Recommendation: The sense of the Commission is that women should be excluded from direct land combat units and positions. Further, the Commission recommends that the existing service policies concerning direct land combat exclusions be codified. Service Secretaries shall recommend to the Congress which units and positions should fall under the land combat exclusion.***

The issue of whether to retain, modify, rescind, or codify the policies restricting the assignment of women in ground combat specialties was statutorily required to be considered by the Commission. In addressing the issue, the Commission found the effectiveness of ground units to be the most significant criterion.

American military women are prohibited by Service policies that preclude them from serving in direct ground combat positions. Current policy excluding women from ground combat is based, in part, on Congressional intent to preclude women from serving in combat aircraft or on combatant ships. The specialties that fall under the exclusion may be grouped into four major areas: infantry, armor, artillery, and combat engineers, all of which require a soldier to be prepared to fight in direct, close-quarters combat.

Through testimony and trips, the Commission heard and observed that the daily life of the ground soldier in combat circumstances is one of constant physical exertion, often in extreme climatic conditions with the barest of amenities and the inherent risks of injury, capture and death. The Commission learned that despite technological advances, ground combat has not become less hazardous and physically demanding.

The evidence before the Commission clearly shows distinct physiological differences between men and women. Most women are shorter in stature, have less muscle mass and weigh less than men. These physiological differences place women at a distinct disadvantage when performing tasks requiring a high level of muscular strength and aerobic capacity, such as hand-to-hand fighting, digging, carrying heavy loads, lifting and other tasks central to ground combat.

The Commission also heard from women of tremendous physical ability who expressed a desire to serve in the ground combat arms. There is little doubt that some women could meet the physical standards for ground combat, but the evidence shows that few women possess the necessary physical qualifications. Further, a 1992 survey of 900 Army servicewomen showed that only 12 percent of enlisted women and ten percent of the female noncommissioned officers surveyed said they would consider serving in the combat arms.

The Commission considered the effects that women could have on the cohesion of ground combat units. Cohesion is defined as the relationship that develops in a unit or group where: (1) members share common values and experiences; (2) individuals in the group conform to group norms and behavior in order to ensure group survival and goals; (3) members lose their personal identity in favor of a group identity; (4) members focus on group activities and goals; (5) members become totally dependent on each other for the completion of their mission or survival; and (6) members must meet all standards of performance and behavior in order not to threaten group survival. The evidence clearly shows that unit cohesion can be negatively affected by the introduction of any element that detracts from the need for such key ingredients as mutual confidence, commonality of experience, and equitable treatment. There are no authoritative military studies of mixed-gender ground combat cohesion, since available cohesion research has been conducted among male-only ground combat units.

One research study reviewed by the Commission indicates that the following are areas where cohesion problems might develop:

1.  Ability of women to carry the physical burdens required of each combat unit member. This entails an ability to meet physical standards of endurance and stamina.
2.  Forced intimacy and lack of privacy on the battlefield (e.g. washing, bathing, using latrine facilities, etc.).
3.  Traditional Western values where men feel a responsibility to protect women.
4.  Dysfunctional relationships (e.g. sexual misconduct).
5.  Pregnancy.

Of these, the prospect of sexual relationships in land units in direct combat with the enemy was considered to be dysfunctional and would encumber small unit ground combat leaders, noncommissioned officers, lieutenants and captains, in carrying out their military missions.

Ground combat incurs a high risk of capture by the enemy. The Commission's review of our nation's recent wars with respect to POWs suggests that potential enemies may not accord respect for the Geneva Convention and customary rules related to protection of prisoners. During our nation's major wars in this century, except Vietnam, the number of POWs has been greatest from the ground forces, the next largest number from downed aircraft and the least number from Navy ships. The Commission heard testimony from DoD representatives and POWs who indicated that the mistreatment of women taken as POWs could have a negative impact on male captives.

The Commission's enabling statute required examination of public attitudes toward the assignment of women in the military. Several surveys were conducted to determine what the American public and military attitudes were toward women in ground combat. The results of these surveys indicate that members of the military are strongly against women serving in all branches of ground combat, while the public has mixed views on service in different ground

25

combat specialties. The Roper survey of the American public showed that 57 percent of the American public polled said that women should not be assigned to the infantry, and 52 percent were against women in Marine infantry. However, 58 percent of the public surveyed were in favor of assigning women to both artillery and armor positions.

The Roper military poll reported that 74 percent of the military members surveyed did not think women should serve in the infantry, 72 percent rejected the idea of women in Marine infantry, 59 percent opposed women in tank crews, and 54 percent did not want women to serve in the artillery. When the same question was asked of military personnel who had actually served in the ground combat arms, the numbers increased to 83 percent against women in the infantry, 83 percent against women serving in Marine infantry, 71 percent against women in armor, and 64 percent against women in artillery.

Several countries have placed women in ground combat units with little success. Historically, those nations that have permitted women in close combat situations (the Soviet Union, Germany and Israel) have done so only because of grave threats to their national survival. After the crisis passed, each nation adopted policies which excluded the employment of women in combat. In more current times, the Commission learned that countries that have tested integrating women in ground combat units have found those tests unsuccessful.

The Commission also considered the effect on registration and conscription if women were allowed in ground combat units. In 1981, the Supreme Court upheld the male-only registration provision of the Military Selective Service Act, 50 U.S.C. App. 453, against a due process equal protection challenge from men who claimed that it was discriminatory because it required men, but not women, to register for the draft. The Court's opinion rested on the following argument: the purpose behind the registration requirement is to create a pool of individuals to be called up in the event of a draft; a draft is used to obtain combat troops; women are prevented, through law and policy, from serving in combat positions in any of the four Services; therefore, men and women are dissimilarly situated in regard to the registration requirement and it is permissible to treat them differently.

The Commission reviewed the assignment of draftees in our most recent conflicts, and according to statistics provided by DoD, 98 percent of draftees went to the Army during Vietnam, 95 percent during Korea and 83 percent during World War II. Because a draft is used to obtain combat troops and historically most draftees go into the Army, it can be deduced that the draft is used primarily to obtain a pool of ground combat troops. The Commission considered the possibility that lifting the ground combat exclusion pertaining to women may undermine the justification used by the Supreme Court to uphold the constitutionality of the all-male draft, because women would be eligible to serve in the positions which are filled through conscription.

The case against women in ground combat is compelling and conclusive. The physiological differences between men and women are most stark when compared to ground combat tasks. This is underscored by the evidence that there are few women, especially enlisted women, interested in serving in ground combat specialties. The overriding importance of small unit cohesion to ground military success, and the unknown but probably negative effect that the presence of women would have in those units were of critical concern to most Commissioners. Several polls revealed in most convincing terms that the public and military, especially the military people most familiar with its rigors, were fundamentally opposed to women in ground combat. The weight of international experience with women in ground combat units provides no conclusive evidence supporting the assignment of women in ground combat units. Finally, the legal implications of lifting the ground combat exclusion policy for the possible registration and conscription of women for ground combat were considered. The current ground combat exclusion policies, which are derived from Congressional intent to restrict the assignment of women in other Services, would be vulnerable if the remaining statute was repealed. The Commission therefore recommends that the ground exclusion policies be enacted into law for consistency and as sound public policy.

*Commission Vote*

| | |
|---|---|
| *Yes:* | *10* |
| *No:* | *0* |
| *Abstention:* | *2* |

*Relevant Findings*
*The findings relevant to this issue are issue below. These findings may be referenced in Appendix C. The first number refers to the panel. For example, 1.5 is a Panel 1 finding. In addition, the Commission approved 25 findings offered by individual Commissioners. These are numbered 1-25 and are also referenced in Appendix C.*

| | | | | | |
|---|---|---|---|---|---|
| 1.6 | 1.23 | 1.30 | 1.88 | 1.117 | 1.1 |
| 1.9 | 1.2 | 1.39 | 1.89 | 1.118 | 2.1.4A |
| 1.11 | 1.26 | 1.56 | 1.90 | 1.119 | 2.1.4B |
| 1.12 | 1.27 | 1.80 | 1.9 | 1.120 | 2.1.5 |
| 1.14 | 1.28 | 1.81 | 1.97 | 1.121 | 2.1.6 |
| 1.16 | 1.29 | 1.87 | 1.110 | 1.129 | 2.2.3A |
| | | | | | |
| 2.4.2 | 2.5.5 | 3.5 | 3A6 | 3.26 | 3B3 |
| 2.4.2A | 2.6.2 | 3.11 | 3.13 | 3.27 | 3.54 |
| 2.5. 1 | 2.6.2B | 3.12 | 3.16 | 3.29 | 3.55 |
| 2.5.3 | 2.6.2.F | 3A3 | 3.17 | 3.31 | 4.7 |
| 2.5.4 | 2.6.3 | 3A4 | 3.20 | 3.32 | 4.11 |
| 2.5.4B | 2.6.3.D | 3A5 | 3.21 | 3B1 | 4.13 |
| | | | | | |
| 6 | 18 | 10 | | | |
| 8 | 22 | 11 | | | |
| 9 | 15 | 13 | | | |

# L:  COMBAT AIRCRAFT

*Should the existing service policies restricting the assignment of servicewomen with respect to aircraft be retained, modified, rescinded, or codified?*

***Recommendation***:  ***In view of the evidence gathered by this Commission with regard to the potential consequences of assigning women to combat positions, current DoD and Service policies with regard to Army, Air Force and Navy aircraft on combat missions should be retained and codified by means of the re-enactment of Sec. 8549 of Title 10, U.S. Code which was repealed by Public Law 102-190, Sec. 531 for the Air Force, and re-enactment of the provisions of 10 U.S.C. sec. 6015 prohibiting women from assignment to duty on aircraft engaged in combat missions, which was repealed by Public Law 102-190 for the Navy, and codification of Army policy.***

Congress repealed 10 U.S.C. 8549 and amended provisions of 10 U.S.C. 6015 removing statutory restrictions of women aviators to fly combat aircraft.  These actions and the strong performance of U.S. servicewomen in the Persian Gulf War warranted the Commission to develop a recommendation on the integration of women into combat aircraft.

During the discussion of the assignment of women to combat aircraft, this issue more than any other raised the question of "can versus should?"  Although the evidence presented indicates that women are capable of flying and competing with men in combat aviation assignments, the Commission finds that concerns over cohesion and women as prisoners of war (POWs) were more persuasive and voted to recommend retention and codification of the Service's policies prohibiting the assignment of women to combat aircraft.

The Commission heard testimony from former POWs of the Vietnam War and one of the female POWs of the Persian Gulf War.  The record of brutal treatment of POWs at the hands of the Vietnamese is incontrovertible.  Iraq mistreated male POWs and indecently assaulted one U.S. woman POW.

Many experts and former POWs testified that the presence of women might cause additional morale problems for male prisoners.  In Survival, Evasion, Resistance, and Escape (SERE) training, evidence indicates that men will try to protect women, to the detriment of the unit.  The experience of foreign countries with women as POWs (the Soviet Union and Germany during WWII) also suggests that it would be detrimental to the military and the society.  Some military experts and historians told the Commission that one of the major reasons for the exclusion of women from combat in Israel was the fear that female POWs would dishearten the Israeli people in wartime.  The majority of Commissioners believe that the assignment of women to combat aircrews would inevitably require women aviators to conduct routine combat missions penetrating hostile air space over enemy territory, with the inherent risks of shoot-down, escape, evasion and capture.

A majority of Commissioners also believe that the introduction of women into air combat squadrons would disrupt the cohesion of their units, resulting in a lower quality force. Commissioners' views on the subject are contentious, as evidenced by the extremely close vote in favor of retaining and codifying the Services' existing prohibition against assigning women to fly combat aircraft. For several years, the U.S. military has had mixed gender aircraft squadrons, yet many men who have positive feelings about working with women in a non-combat unit, still believe women should not be integrated into air combat units. Across all Services, men in air combat units were against women entering those units. According to the Commission's worldwide survey of the U.S. military, 69 percent of all pilots (Air Force, Navy and Marines) believed that women should not be assigned to combat aircraft.

The Commission finds that there is no evidence in its review of scientific literature that defines a physiological basis to categorically restrict women from selection opportunity for combat aviation. In a number of informal studies measuring the capability of men and women aviators to withstand the rigors of flight, no information was found suggesting that women were at any kind of disadvantage vis-a-vis men. However, there are also concerns among several Commissioners that the effects of repetitive high G-stresses on aviators, both male and female, have not been adequately investigated under all relevant conditions.

The potential for pregnancy among female aviators was considered. The Commission found that there are suitable provisions by each of the Services to restrict pregnant pilots from flying. The Commission also found that active duty female pilots have negligible pregnancy rates and thus the Commission discerned that pregnancy is not a major problem with regard to the pilotage issue.

The one vote margin by which this issue was resolved illustrates the deeply divided views that exist on the assignment of women to combat aircraft. Uncertainties about the ramifications of physiologically-driven performance differences, unit cohesion effects and the proportionately high probability of exposure to POW status were the major factors driving the exclusion recommendation.

*Commission Vote*
*Yes:*        *8*
*No:*         *7*
*Abstention:*  *0*

## *Relevant Findings*

*The findings relevant to this issue are listed below. These findings are referenced in Appendix C. The first number refers to the panel. For example, 1.5 is a Panel 1 finding.*

| | | | | | |
|---|---|---|---|---|---|
| 1.8 | 1.46 | 1.52 | 1.122 | 2.1.7 | 2.3.6 |
| 1.18 | 1.47 | 1.53 | 1.136 | 2.3.1A | 2.4.3 |
| 1.41 | 1.48 | 1.57 | 2.1.2 | 2.3.1B | 2.5.1 |
| 1.43 | 1.49 | 1.73 | 2.1.4A | 2.3.2A | 2.5.3 |
| 1.44 | 1.50 | 1.80 | 2.1.4B | 2.3.3 | 2.5.3C |
| 1.45 | 1.51 | 1.85 | 2.1.6A | 2.3.3A | 2.5.4 |

| | | | | | |
|---|---|---|---|---|---|
| 2.5.4B | 2.6.1GH | 2.6.4A | 3.9 | 3.14 | 3.31 |
| 2.5.5 | 2.6.1J | 2.6.1J | 3A1 | 3.20 | 3.32 |
| 2.6.1B | 2.6.2D | 2.6.3D | 3A4 | 3.21 | 3B1 |
| 2.6.1C | 2.6.3A | 2.6.4J | 3A5 | 3.26 | 3B3 |
| 2.6.1D | 2.6.3B | 2.6.4A | 3A6 | 3.27 | 3.35 |
| 2.6.1F | 2.6.3D | 3.5 | 3.13 | 3.29 | 3.36 |

| | | |
|---|---|---|
| 3.52 | 4.7 | 4.29 |
| 3.53 | 4.10 | 4.1 |
| 3.54 | 4.11 | 4.2.5 |
| 3.55 | 4.13 | |
| 3D2 | 4.22 | |
| 4.6 | 4.27 | |

## M: COMBATANT VESSELS

*Should the combatant vessel exclusions (law and policy) be retained, modified, or rescinded/repealed? Should the current policy be modified to conform with existing law?*

**Recommendation: Repeal existing laws and modify Service policies for servicewomen to serve on combatant vessels except submarines and amphibious vessels.**

The Commission concludes that the current Navy law governing assignment of servicewomen is inconsistent because it allows women to serve as aviation officers aboard Navy ships, but prohibits their assignment to combatant ships in any other capacity. The law, 10 U.S.C. 6015, currently reads:

> The Secretary of the Navy may prescribe the kind of military duty to which such women members may be assigned and the military authority which they may exercise. However, women may not be assigned to duty on vessels engaged in combat missions (other than as aviation officers as part of an air wing or other air element assigned to such a vessel) nor may they be assigned to other than temporary duty on vessels of the Navy except hospital ships, transports, and vessels of a similar classification not expected to be assigned combat missions.

Since the late 1970s, women have served aboard tenders and service craft. In 1987, they began service in Combat Logistic Force (CLF) ships, which supply the combatant vessels, and in 1991, they began service aboard training frigates, all with no apparent changes in readiness or effectiveness. During that time, the Navy has accrued over 14 years of data regarding women's performance in the seagoing operational environment. The experiences of over 40,000 women, both officers and enlisted, serving in traditional and non-traditional billets and ratings on 66 ships, were a valuable resource for the Commission.

There are few differences between combatant and non-combatant ships in relation to physical strength tasks, with the possible exception of the flight decks of aircraft carriers. Many of the duties women perform on CLF and training ships are the same as those on a combatant ship. In general, men as a group perform better than women on military tasks requiring heavy lifting, carrying, pushing and pulling efforts. While there is a significant overlap in task performance between the sexes, debate over the importance of physical strength on ships continues to be an issue. The Commission generally believes that it is very important that women be integrated in accordance with the Commission's recommendations on Issues D and G, which emphasize the significance of meeting strength, endurance and cardiovascular requirements.

The Commission is well aware of the realities and dangers of serving at sea. Navy ships generally deploy for months at a time, are crowded and have few amenities. Space is at a premium aboard all Navy ships, especially in living facilities. Most ships have dozens of people berthing in one small compartment. Most ships require berthing modifications to accommodate the assignment of women, the cost of which varies greatly depending on the ship class. The Commission found that the costs can range from $66,000 to $4 million per ship. (See Issue P for costs by ship class.) Some argue that these costs waste dollars in a time of shrinking defense budgets.

Submarines are the most confined and crowded and would be the most difficult ships to modify. Modifying an SSN-688 attack or SSBN ballistic missile submarine to accommodate enlisted females could cost as much as $1 million per submarine depending on the number and mix of women assigned. Certain amphibious ships present serious habitability difficulties due to lack of complete privacy given that berthing areas of the embarked Marines are necessarily collocated with public passageways.

Opponents of assigning women to combatant vessels argue that women are incapable of excelling at physically demanding shipboard tasks. Research corroborates that many women have problems performing some of the training tasks related to the physically demanding shipboard tasks of damage control, like fire fighting, flood limitation, and emergency evacuation of wounded. However, 200 women performed well in an actual firefighting emergency aboard a Navy ship in 1988.

The Navy has no specific studies on mixed-gender crew cohesion. The Commission notes that there has been no comparative study showing that gender integration makes Navy ships equally or more efficient than all-male crews. Ship performance in the Navy is regularly rated on the basis of readiness criteria by inspection teams external to the command, and gender-integrated ships perform as well as those with only men.

Commissioners also are concerned with readiness problems that might occur because of pregnancy. While pregnancy is discussed in full in Issue I, the Navy's annualized pregnancy rate among enlisted members is 13.4 percent. The current Navy rule, which precludes pregnant women from deploying, has been a successful policy on the ships to which women are presently assigned.

The statute creating the Commission required examination of public attitudes toward the assignment of women in the military. Two surveys were conducted to determine what American public and military attitudes were toward women serving aboard combatant ships. When asked in the national public survey whether women should be assigned to combat ships, 83 percent of the public surveyed said that women should be assigned. Among those who had prior military experience, 72 percent said that women should be assigned to combatant ships. The results of the military poll showed that in today's Navy, 73 percent of those surveyed felt that women should be allowed to serve on combatant ships. In fact, one-half of Navy respondents felt that women should be required to serve on combatant ships.

The experience of gender integration in foreign navies was also studied by the Commission during its trips to Canada and Europe. Several European countries are at different stages of integrating women into surface combatant ships, and all countries visited reported they are continuing to integrate women in their respective navies.

The Commission notes that the U.S. Coast Guard has successfully integrated all ship classes and places no restrictions upon women regarding their number or the occupational specialties in which they serve.

The Commission recommends that the combatant vessel exclusion law (10 U.S.C. 6015) be repealed, with the exception of submarines and amphibious vessels. The contributions that women sailors have made on Navy support ships over the past 14 years were a major factor in the Commission's recommendation supporting opening combatant ships to women. Women's outstanding performances have resulted in a more capable force, and, during the process, changed traditional attitudes within the Navy. The Commission believes that women are well qualified for sea service. Their presence, it was successfully argued, will increase the military effectiveness of the Navy's surface warships.

*Commission Vote*

| | |
|---|---|
| *Yes:* | *8* |
| *No:* | *6* |
| *Abstention:* | *1* |

*Relevant Findings*
*The findings relevant to this issue are listed below. These findings may be referenced in Appendix C. The first number refers to the panel. For example, 1.5 is a Panel 1 finding.*

| | | | | | |
|---|---|---|---|---|---|
| 1.7 | 1.75 | 1.129 | 2.1.4A | 2.3.5 | 2.5.3A |
| 1.13 | 1.93 | 1.133 | 2.1.4B | 2.3.5A | 2.5.3B |
| 1.18 | 1.94 | 2.1.1 | 2.1.6 | 2.3.6A | 2.5.3C |
| 1.22 | 1.95 | 2.1.2 | 2.2.3A | 2.4.4 | 2.5.4 |
| 1.71 | 1.109 | 2.1.3 | 2.3.2 | 2.5.1 | 2.6.4B |
| 1.74 | 1.95 | 2.1.4 | 2.3.2B | 2.5.3 | 2.6.4C |

| | | |
|---|---|---|
| 2.6.4FG | 3A5 | 3B3 |
| 2.6.4J | 3A6 | 3.52 |
| 2.6.5 | 3.13 | 3.53 |
| 3.5 | 3.20 | 4.22 |
| 3.10 | 3.29 | 4.23 |
| 3A4 | 3B1 | 4.27 |

## N: SPECIAL OPERATIONS

*Should existing policies restricting the assignment of servicewomen with respect to Special Operations Forces be retained, modified, rescinded or codified?*

*Recommendation:* **Retain the existing policies.**

Current rules which exclude the assignment of women from Special Operations Forces are entirely derivative of other exclusionary policies and law. Nevertheless, the Commission feels that it should specifically address Special Operations Forces, in light of their growing importance in the spectrum of military activity. Special Operations Forces conduct some of the most dangerous and physically demanding operations undertaken by the military. Women are currently excluded from these positions by policies of the respective Services. Special Operations often involve small groups infiltrating deep behind enemy lines to gather information or destroy important targets. The physical demands of Special Operations training alone would be, with rare exception, beyond the ability of women.

The Commission heard testimony from men serving in Special Operations units, and visited the United States Special Operations Command Headquarters (USSOC) in Tampa, FL, and the Navy Special Warfare Command in Coronado, CA. The Commission conducted two national surveys which helped show how the public and military felt about this issue. Fifty-nine percent of the public surveyed felt women should be assigned as members of the Special Forces operating behind enemy lines, while 66 percent of the military surveyed felt women should not be members of the Special Operations Forces.

The negative effect on small unit cohesion was echoed by all of the Special Operations witnesses as a reason not to assign women to Special Operations Forces. In order to be effective, Special Operations Forces rely on strong small unit cohesion to the same or higher degree than their counterparts in the infantry. The fragile nature of bonding and its relationship to disciplined bravery in the presence of fear was recognized by the Commission as being endangered by the presence of women and consequently by men's reactions to them.

The question of whether women can physically fly aircraft used in Special Operations was never challenged. Women currently fly Air Force cargo aircraft, such as the C-130 Hercules, and Army helicopters like the UH-60 Blackhawk, which are used in Special Operations. Women are excluded from flying Special Operations missions in these aircraft because of Service policies. In Special Operations, these aircraft are used for missions which entail a high risk of being shot down over hostile territory. Therefore, the pilots who fly Special Operations must be prepared to evade capture or risk becoming a prisoner of war (POW). A physically fit Special Operations Forces team evading capture could be slowed down and possibly caught if held back by the presence of a woman pilot possessing less physical strength and endurance. The Commission found that these risks are incompatible with effective operations. Similarly, the fact that many of our potential enemies do not always observe the Geneva Convention provisions that Americans do, coupled with the unknown effects of introducing women into the POW environment, convinced the Commission that Special Operations Forces should not be opened to women, even if it means the most qualified person is not in the cockpit.

*Commission Vote*
*Yes:*          *14*
*No:*           *0*
*Abstention:*   *0*

*Relevant Findings*
*The findings relevant to this issue are listed below.  These findings are referenced in Appendix C.  The first number refers to the panel.  For example, 1.5 is a Panel 1 finding.*

| | | | | | |
|---|---|---|---|---|---|
| 1.6  | 1.23  | 1.30  | 1.88  | 1.117 | 2.1.4A |
| 1.9  | 1.2   | 1.39  | 1.89  | 1.118 | 2.1.4B |
| 1.11 | 1.26  | 1.56  | 1.90  | 1.119 | 2.1.5 |
| 1.12 | 1.27  | 1.80  | 1.9   | 1.120 | 2.1.6 |
| 1.14 | 1.28  | 1.81  | 1.97  | 1.121 | 2.2.3A2. |
| 1.16 | 1.29  | 1.87  | 1.110 | 1.129 | 4.2 |

| | | | | | |
|---|---|---|---|---|---|
| 2.4.2A | 2.6.2   | 3.11 | 3.13 | 3.27 | 3.54 |
| 2.5. 1 | 2.6.2B  | 3.12 | 3.16 | 3.29 | 3.55 |
| 2.5.3  | 2.6.2.F | 3A3  | 3.17 | 3.31 | 4.7 |
| 2.5.4  | 2.6.3   | 3A4  | 3.20 | 3.32 | 4.11 |
| 2.5.4B | 2.6.3.D | 3A5  | 3.21 | 3B1  | 4.13 |
| 2.5.5  | 3.5     | 3A6  | 3.26 | 3B3  | 4.22 |

## O: RISK RULE

*Should the DoD "Risk Rule," which reduces servicewomen's risk of injury, death or capture be retained, modified, rescinded, or codified?*

***Recommendation: Retain the DoD Risk Rule as currently implemented. Navy policies which implement the Risk Rule should be modified to reflect the changes made in Issue M.***

In light of the experiences of the Persian Gulf War, where some U.S. military women were employed in positions which exposed them to direct combat, the Commission believes the Risk Rule was an important issue to address.

The DoD Risk Rule was developed in 1988 to help standardize the Services' assignment of women with regard to possible deployment to hostile areas. Each Service interprets the Risk Rule according to its mission requirements using it to evaluate whether a non-combat position should be closed to women. The rule states:

> Risks of direct combat, exposure to hostile fire, or capture are proper criteria for closing non-combat positions or units to women, when the type, degree, and duration of such risk are equal to or greater than the combat units with which they are normally associated within a given theater of operations. If the risk of non-combat units or positions is less than comparable to land, air or sea combat units with which they are associated, they should be open to women. Non-combat land units should be compared to combat land units, air to air and so forth.

The Commission discovered some confusion over the purpose of the Risk Rule. It is not intended to prevent women from serving in combat, but to reduce the probability that women will be exposed to direct land combat inadvertently. The Commission concludes that because the line between direct combat and support units is sometimes blurred, the Risk Rule provides the best mechanism available for maintaining consistency in assignment policies and integrity of the relationship between support and direct land combat units. Therefore, the Commission recommends that the Risk Rule be retained with appropriate modifications made to reflect the Commission's recommendation to allow women to be assigned to most combatant ships.

*Commission Vote*
| | |
|---|---|
| *Yes:* | *9* |
| *No:* | *4* |
| *Abstention:* | *2* |

## *Relevant Findings*

*The findings relevant to this issue are listed below. These findings may be referenced in Appendix C. The first number refers to the panel. For example, 1.5 is a Panel 1 finding.*

| | | |
|-----|------|------|
| 1.1 | 1.7  | 1.18 |
| 1.2 | 1.8  | 1.19 |
| 1.3 | 1.9  | 1.20 |
| 1.4 | 1.14 | 3.43 |
| 1.5 | 1.16 | 3.5  |
| 1.6 | 1.17 | 3.13 |

## P: TRANSITION PROCESS

*What transition process is appropriate if servicewomen are to be given the opportunity to be assigned to combat positions in the Armed Forces?*

***Recommendation: The integration process should be accomplished in an orderly fashion and without undue haste. Any necessary modifications to vessels, equipment, and facilities should be done during the normal course of maintenance in a fashion that minimizes cost. Additionally, the integration process should be consistent with the Commission's recommendations on Issues D and G.***

In an effort to guide DoD with the implementation of the Commission's recommendations to open the majority of combatant vessels to women and to establish and prescribe criteria for endurance, physical strength and training, the Commission recommends the transition process occur in an orderly fashion and without undue haste. Specifically, the Commission believes that any necessary modifications to vessels, equipment and facilities should be done during the normal course of maintenance in a fashion that minimizes cost. The Navy should consider specific occupational, muscular, strength/endurance and cardiovascular capacity requirements throughout the integration process, consistent with the Commission's recommendations in Issues D and G.

The Commission notes that space is limited on all Navy ships, especially for living facilities. Most ships will require berthing modifications to accommodate the assignment of women, a cost which will vary greatly depending on the ship class. The Commission finds costs will range from $66,000 to $4 million per ship. Costs of modifying surface combatants, as estimated by the Navy, are as follows:

| Class | # of Women | Cost |
|---|---|---|
| CGN 38 (Guided Missile Cruiser - Nuclear) | 18 | $135,000.00 |
| CGN 36 | 20 | $160,000.00 |
| DD 963 (Destroyer) | 23 | $ 80,000.00 |
| FFG 7 (Guided Missile Frigate) | 29 | $305,000.00 |
| FFT (Training Frigate) | N/A | $500,000.00 |
| DDG 993 (Guided Missile Destroyer) | 38 | $ 80,000.00 |
| CG 16 (Guided Missile Cruiser) | 35 | $190,000.00 |
| CG 26 | 35 | $200,000.00 |
| CG 47 (Aegis Missile Cruiser) | 43 | $150,500.00 |
| DDG 51 (Guided Missile Destroyer) | 22 | $ 80,000.00 |
| AOE 1 (Fast Combat Support Ship) | 42 | $240,000.00 |
| AOE 6 | 30 | $104,000.00 |
| AOR 1 (Replenishment Oiler) | 33 | $115,000.00 |

| Class | # of Women | Cost |
|---|---|---|
| MCM 1 (Mine Countermeasures Ship) | 20 | $114,300.00 |
| MHC 51 (Mine Countermeasures Ship) | 19 | $ 66,000.00 |
| AGF (Miscellaneous Command Ship) | 51 | $291,500.00 |

The cost to modify an aircraft carrier has been estimated to be $2 million to $4 million.

Although the Commission's enabling statute asked the Commission to consider testing of women for combatant positions, a conscious decision not to conduct tests was made due to the time constraints of the Commission's existence. The Commission believed that testing, if done properly, would require more time and resources than were available. With regard to setting and implementing occupational standards and modifying vessels, the Commission wants to provide the broadest possible latitude to DoD and the respective Services, with the understanding that the changes will be addressed in a timely manner.

*Commission Vote*
*Yes:*      *11*
*No:*      *3*
*Abstention:*    *1*

*Relevant Findings*
*The findings relevant to this issue are listed below. These findings may be referenced in Appendix C. The first number refers to the panel. For example 1.5 is a Panel 1 finding.*

| | | | |
|---|---|---|---|
| 1.78 | 1.110 | 2.6.4B | 4.23 |
| 1.79 | 1.132 | 2.6.4B | 4.29 |
| 1.93 | 1.133 | 4.14 | |
| 1.94 | 1.134 | 4.18 | |
| 1.95 | 2.4.1C | 4.21 | |
| 1.107 | 2.6.4B | 4.22 | |

## Q: CONSCRIPTION

*Should women be required to register for and be subject to conscription under the Military Selective Service Act: (a) on the same basis as men, if women are provided the same opportunity as men for assignment to any position in the Armed Forces; (b) on the same basis as men, if women in the Armed Forces are assigned to combat positions only as volunteers; or (c) on a different basis than men if women in the Armed Forces are not assigned to combat positions on the same basis as men?*

*Recommendation: Women should not be required to register for or be subject to conscription. (Covers sub-issues a-c.)*

The Commission was directed by its enabling statute to consider the legal and policy implications of certain conscription scenarios. For this reason, and because of concern regarding the effect of changes in combat exclusion law and policies on women's current exemption from conscription and registration obligations, the Commission decided to provide the President and Congress with a recommendation on this subject.

Currently, the Military Selective Service Act (MSSA or Act) provides authority to the President to require qualified men to register for the draft. Congress would have to amend the Act to require women to register.

The issue of conscription was discussed throughout the Commission's tenure. In the final vote, there was an overwhelming consensus among the Commissioners that women should not be drafted. The Commission adopted a blanket recommendation against imposing any requirements on women with regard to conscription, regardless of the assignments for which they are eligible in the Armed Forces. It determined that important government interests exist which are substantially related to excluding women from draft registration, e.g., the military effectiveness of our land combat forces.

In Rostker v. Goldberg, 453 U.S. 57 (1981), the U.S. Supreme Court held that a male-only draft registration requirement was constitutional because the primary purpose of registration was to acquire a "pool of combat troops," and women were not eligible for combat assignments. The Commission found that excluding women from ground combat positions by statute or policy may be consistent with the Court's ruling in Rostker. Women's eligibility for combatant vessel assignments, therefore, would not appear to affect their utility in a draft situation as long as they remain excluded from ground combat positions and, therefore, would not affect the constitutionality of the all-male draft.

These findings influenced the Commissioners' approach to issues regarding assignment policies. For example, there was a proposal to modify the recommendation that was ultimately adopted by the Commission with respect to conscription to include a statement that current

40

assignment policies should not be modified in ways that might create a legal risk that women's exemption from the draft might be successfully challenged and repealed. Additionally, during the debate on whether ground combat specialties should be opened to women, the Commission discussed enacting the existing exclusion policies associated with direct ground combat into law to provide an additional barrier to any amendment of the MSSA to provide for the conscription of women. Leaving discretion to open ground combat roles to women with DoD would entail a risk that the existing exclusion policies would be incrementally rescinded over time. Congress should prohibit women from serving in direct land combat positions (See Issue K); in so doing, the need for female conscription is obviated.

## Commission Vote
Yes:            11
No:              3
Abstention:      0

## Relevant Findings
*The findings relevant to this issue are listed below. These findings are referenced in*
*Appendix C. The first number refers to the panel. For example, 1.5 is a Panel 1 finding.*

| | | | | |
|---|---|---|---|---|
| 1.1 | 1.7 | 1.18 | 4.1 | 4.11 |
| 1.2 | 1.8 | 1.19 | 4.2 | 4.13 |
| 1.3 | 1.9 | 1.20 | 4.5 | 4.22 |
| 1.4 | 1.14 | 3.43 | 4.6 | 4.23 |
| 1.5 | 1.16 | 3.5 | 4.7 | 4.27 |
| 1.6 | 1.17 | 3.13 | 4.10 | 4.29 |

# II.
# ALTERNATIVE VIEWS

*Submitted by:*

Samuel G. Cockerham
Elaine Donnelly
Sarah F. White
Kate Walsh O'Beirne
Ronald D. Ray

# PRESIDENTIAL COMMISSION ON THE ASSIGNMENT
# OF WOMEN IN THE ARMED FORCES

November 15, 1992

*rman*
ert T. Herres

*missioners*
y E. Clarke
uel G. Cockerham
e Donnelly
n Thomas V. Draude
Mary M. Finch
Darryl Henderson
es R. Hogg
ton N. Minow
les C. Moskos
edith A. Neizer
Walsh O'Beirne
ald D. Ray
well R. Thurman
h F. White

*Director*
. Orr

The Honorable George Herbert Walker Bush
President of the United States of America
Washington, D.C.

Dear Mr. President:

It has been a great honor to serve on the Presidential Commission on the Assignment of Women in the Armed Forces. After careful consideration of the testimony the Commission heard and the research it conducted, we are pleased to present you with this Alternative View Section of the Commission's report, which outlines the basis for a consistent position opposed to the use of American women in combat.

We believe the importance of this issue demands an alternative perspective be presented for your consideration, and we appreciate the opportunity to state our views clearly in this section. At the same time, we join our fellow Commissioners in endorsing many recommendations we believe will enhance the Armed Forces with sound military policies affecting both men and women.

Mr. President, our statements and recommendations are prompted by our primary concern for the continuing strength, readiness, and military efficiency of our Armed Forces. The Commission record is solid and compelling, and we hope this section will prompt you, the Congress and future decision makers to consider this historic record in the formulation of wise policies that will continue to support the American military as the finest in the world.

Samuel G. Cockerham

Kate Walsh O'Beirne

Elaine Donnelly

Ronald D. Ray

Sarah F. White

*1001 Pennsylvania Avenue, NW, Suite 275N, Washington, DC 20004-2505    Tel: 202-376-6905    Fax: 202-376-6925*

# SECTION II -- ALTERNATIVE VIEWS

# THE CASE AGAINST WOMEN IN COMBAT

## EXECUTIVE SUMMARY

### Background

In its historic deliberations, the Presidential Commission has addressed some of the most controversial and sensitive issues facing the military, American women and our country. At the conclusion of eight months of research, hearings and fact-finding trips, the signers of this section believe it is important to set out and summarize the considerable testimony and evidence gathered by the Commission that supports continuing America's long-standing exemption of women from combat duty.

Decisions on the principle questions before the Commission -- whether American women should be assigned to combat on land, at sea or in the air -- involved a wide variety of issues and concerns. They include the history and nature of war, physiology, psychology, sociology, family and cultural values, the legal consequences of a change in the law, and most importantly, the overarching, classic concerns of the military itself: combat readiness, unit cohesion and military effectiveness -- defined as the ability to deter aggression and if necessary, to fight and win wars.

Addressing these issues led the Commission to focus on, evaluate and determine the military significance of the many differences between the sexes and the ultimate purpose and mission of the Armed Forces. Secretary of Defense Richard Cheney restated the focus of the American military on March 26, 1992:

> [I]t's important for us to remember that what we are asked to do here in the Department of Defense is to defend the nation. *The only reason we exist is to be prepared to fight and win wars* [emphasis added]. We're not a social welfare agency. We're not an agency that's operated on the basis of what makes sense for some member of Congress' concern back home in the district. This is a military organization. Decisions we make have to be taken based upon those kinds of considerations and only those kinds of considerations.

### A Question of Priorities

COL Bryan D. Brown, USA, Commander 1/160th Special Operations Aviation Regiment (Airborne), Ft. Campbell, KY, spoke for many of the service members who testified before the Commission at hearings or out in the field:

> I in no way doubt the female officers' and soldiers' bravery, dedication, or capability, but I do believe their assignment would not enhance the combat capability of the 160th.

43

To many, COL Brown's statement would seem to present a contradiction. If female officers and soldiers offer bravery, dedication and capability, shouldn't they be assigned to combat on the same basis as men? Shouldn't we be looking for the best qualified individuals for the job, regardless of gender?

But this approach -- focusing on the best or most capable *individual* -- fails for a very basic military reason. In combat training and in war, an individual's desires, interests or career aspirations are totally subordinated to the accomplishment of the military mission. Strengthening the capability of combat units is the essence of military readiness. Moreover, for the military as a whole to function as a capable fighting force, each unit, from the smallest up, must operate cohesively and in harmony with other units.

The key question in preparing to win and survive in combat is not what is best for the *individual*, but what is best for the *unit* and the military as a whole. This is why the Commission spent considerable time seeking and evaluating testimony and studies on unit cohesion, including the expert work of Commissioner Darryl Henderson.

## *Military Service v. Civilian Employment*

The fundamental issue before the Commission is whether and in what specific ways the assignment of women to combat would affect the combat capability of the United States to wage war. If the military were substantially the same as a civilian employer, a decision to promote equal opportunity as the primary goal would have been easy to make.

Civilian society forbids employment discrimination. But the military, in building fighting units, must be able to choose those most able to fight and win in battle. There is good reason for this. In a combat unit serving on land, at sea or in the air, the inability of any member of the group to perform at levels demanded by the battlefield can present a direct risk to the lives of others and to the accomplishment of the military mission.

This is one of several reasons why the Armed Forces differ in many important respects from civilian employers, including police forces that preserve order close to home. It is a separate society governed by a different set of rules and regulations because its principle purpose is to fight and win wars. While civilian workers operate on a "9 to 5" schedule, units in combat operate 24 hours-a-day, seven-days-a-week. For the deployed American fighting man, there is no home and family waiting at the end of the day. The home is where the soldier stands to face the enemy. Good order and discipline are crucial for morale, survival and victory in battle.

Even in peacetime, continuous deployments and training prepare our military to confront violence worldwide. Successfully waging war under difficult conditions imposes extraordinary demands upon service members. These include surrendering a great deal of personal freedom and identity, the obligation in many cases to deploy worldwide on short notice, and the ultimate risk of injury, capture or death in the line of duty.

The duties, obligations and life and death struggles that are inherent considerations of combat assignments rarely come into question in civilian life. Military units must be able to function effectively over protracted periods of time against an equally determined enemy. A military unit at maximum combat effectiveness is a military unit least likely to suffer casualties. Winning in war is often only a matter of inches, and unnecessary distraction or any dilution of that combat effectiveness puts the mission and lives in jeopardy. Risking the lives of a military unit in combat to provide career opportunities or accommodate the personal desires or interests of an individual, or group of individuals, is more than bad military judgment. It is morally wrong.

Service members are encouraged to pursue opportunities and career enhancements in the Armed Forces, limited only by the needs and good of the Service. But when it comes to combat assignments, the needs of the military must take precedence over all other considerations, including the career prospects of individual service members. The military service is not a corporation, and being a soldier, sailor or airman is more than just a job. Civil society protects individual rights, but the military, which protects civil society, must be governed by different rules.

That is why Congress and the courts have held that Title VII of the Civil Rights Act of 1964, which ensures all individuals are treated equally before the law with respect to civilian employment, does not apply to the military profession. No less than seven major Supreme Court decisions are distilled in the these words from Goldman v. Weinberger:

> [T]he military is, by necessity, a specialized society [separate] from civilian society.... 'The military must insist upon a respect for duty and a discipline without counterpart in civilian life,' in order to prepare for and perform its vital role.... The essence of the military service 'is the subordination of the desires and interests of the individual to the needs of the service.'

The history of the courts deferring to the judgment of military leaders on matters affecting the Armed Forces is one of the most consistently upheld principles of constitutional law. Furthermore, serving in the military is a privilege and sometimes an obligation, conferring neither the right to serve nor the right to avoid service [see Kennedy v. Mendoza-Martinez 372 U.S. 144 (1963)].

Some have suggested the issue before the Commission is a civil rights issue comparable to racial integration of the Armed Forces in 1948. That analogy fails for several reasons. Dual standards are not needed to compensate for the physical differences between racial groups, but they are needed where men and women are concerned. A proud history as successful warriors exists among men of different races, but not among women.

History also shows that the Soviet Union, which in desperation deployed women to fight during the darkest days of World War II, rescinded that action when their national survival was no longer at stake. By contrast, as the Commission found in the course of its international fact-finding trip, countries that have repealed combat exemption policies in recent years, such as Canada, Denmark and the Netherlands, have done so for reasons of equal opportunity. After the trip, the Commission learned these nations recognize that assigning women to combat specialties might adversely affect combat readiness and effectiveness.

But the United States is not Canada or Denmark. Retired Army General Norman Schwarzkopf, former Commander of Operations Desert Shield and Desert Storm, spoke for many Americans when he declared, "Decisions on what roles women should play in war must be based on military standards, not women's rights."

## The Alternative View

An objective review of the body of research and testimony before the Commission reveals that although some witnesses argued that including women would improve combat effectiveness, the case for unprecedented change was most often framed as the "right" or "equal opportunity" of individuals to serve in all positions they desire regardless of military need.

Those skeptical about assigning women to combat, however, primarily have focused on the needs of the military and combat effectiveness, as well as deep-seated cultural and family values millions of Americans hold and are still teaching their children. As one Commissioner put it, those values can be summed up in one simple phrase: Good men respect and defend women.

A reasonable conclusion against assigning women to combat is drawn not from any *single* factor in the Commission's record, but from the *cumulative* body of evidence suggesting such assignments would adversely affect military readiness, cohesion and effectiveness.

Although some have argued that adverse affects and additional burdens on combat units are justified on grounds of equal opportunity, virtually no one has argued they are justified by military necessity. Centuries of military experience should not be disregarded if the burden of proof has not been met. It is not up to the skeptics to disprove a case that has not been made.

This is why the Commission voted, on two out of three major issues, to maintain the exemption with respect to the assignment of women to close combat in ground troops, combat aviation, amphibious ships and submarines. The signers of this section maintain, however, that the Commission's limited support for the assignment of women to some combatant ships is *inconsistent* with the other major recommendations the Commission submitted for the consideration of the President.

The purpose of this section is to emphasize areas of agreement with recommendations that call for sound military policies that enhance -- or at the very least do not detract from -- the strength, cohesiveness and readiness of combat units.

## *Conclusion*

Congress charged this Commission with examining all aspects of the role of women in the military, which kept in mind the past, present and future in its research and deliberations.

The Commission did just that, providing a comprehensive record for future researchers and historians. Its work will provide insights and guidance for policymakers and elected officials for years to come. It remains to be seen whether policy makers will objectively assess the Commission's comprehensive record, or make personnel decisions disregarding the facts the Commission has pulled together. The signers of this section weighed those facts, and came to an unavoidable conclusion:

The proponents of assigning women to combat have not made their case.

The Commission heard no compelling evidence that the military *needs* women to fight its wars. Demographically, the military does not face a manpower shortage that would demand a radical change in settled American law, policy and custom.

The case for assigning women to combat fails for the very basic reason that it is grounded principally in the concept of equal opportunity, which is an important American value. When national security is at stake, however, the need to maintain a strong military must take precedence over concerns about equal opportunity.

The American people must bear in mind that the advocates of women in combat are asking the military to conduct an experiment meaningful only under wartime conditions. Judging from the experience of other countries and the evidence presented to this Commission, it would be an experiment fraught with immense risks and foreseeable consequences, which is why it is incumbent on the supporters of women in combat to meet a high burden of proof for their case, particularly when lives are at stake.

As Commissioner Charles Moskos said in a short statement to the Commission:

> You raised a question, Mr. Chair, where the burden of proof should lie. Other things being equal, you say, well, then let equal opportunity triumph. Well, most of the evidence that we've heard here -- and there will be some debate about the degree -- is that mixed-gender units, particularly as it [sic] gets closer to the combat area, have lower deployments rates, higher attrition, less physical strength, more sexual activity, higher costs, et cetera, et cetera.

It would seem to me the burden of the proof would be on the side of saying equal opportunity is
of such significance that we're going to override some of these costs.

Those costs are a series of consequences and problems that will ultimately result from
ignoring the nature of war and the military significance of the differences between men and
women. No one problem will degrade the military's ability to fight and win wars, its one and
only mission. Rather, an accumulation of problems, such as those Commissioner Moskos
described, will have a devastating impact on combat readiness, unit cohesion and military
effectiveness. Yet supporters of women in combat argue it will be worth the costs.

The facts suggest otherwise. A compelling body of evidence and personal testimony
reveals a variety of consequences and problems that might result from assigning women to
combat positions. The proponents of women in combat argue that "leadership" is the answer.
Unfortunately, the Commission learned, leadership did not solve these problems during the Gulf
War. The unstated but very real argument of some Commission witnesses was that the military
must pay any price and bear any burden to promote equal opportunities and career progression
for an ambitious few.

But military policies must be based on actual experience and sound judgment, not
doctrinaire notions of sexual equality unsupported by human experience and history. By
necessity, the military must be free to pursue policies aimed at maximizing combat readiness,
unit cohesion and military effectiveness.

The Commission learned that assigning women to combat would adversely affect these
critical components of a successful military. It would leave women exposed to the possibility
of involuntary assignment to combat and conscription. Most importantly, it would overturn two
centuries of settled law and military policy based on deeply held and commonly shared cultural
assumptions defining how men should treat women. Lastly, the Commission learned the military
does not need women in combat units.

The Armed Forces should not assign women to combat.

# COMMISSION ISSUES

## ISSUE A: QUOTAS AND GOALS

*Should a DoD-wide policy be established regarding the use of quotas or goals to influence gender-related personnel policies, e.g., recruitment, promotion, retention and assignment? If so, what should that policy be?*

**MAJORITY RECOMMENDATION:** *DoD should establish a policy to ensure that no person who is best qualified is denied access on the basis of gender to an assignment that is open to both men and women. As far as it is compatible with the above policy, the Secretary of Defense should retain discretion to set goals that encourage the recruitment and optimize the utilization of women in the Services, allowing for the requirements of each Service. (Adopted: Y:9 N:6)*

### Overview

Concur with the first sentence of the Majority Recommendation; object to the second. Testimony before the Commission shows that military personnel think affirmative action, quotas and goals are inappropriate and unfair, particularly if qualifying standards are compromised to reach the quota or the goal. To be consistent with the first directive, the Secretary of Defense should also establish a DoD-wide policy ending the use of gender-related quotas, goals or set-asides in the formulation of recruitment, assignment, pre-commissioning or retention policies.

### *Discussion Points*

*       There is no compelling legal reason to enact quotas and goals; Title VII of the Civil Rights Act of 1964 has not been applied to the military because of its special purpose and relationship to important government interest. (Panel 4 Report/CF 4.6)

*       The Commission heard no evidence of serious or systematic discrimination against women serving in non-combat positions in the military. To the contrary, DoD figures show that the Armed Forces are promoting women officers and enlisted at similar or faster rates than men based on time in service at the time of promotion. (Panel 4 Report/CF 4.24)

*       Neither military readiness nor military necessity demands the use of quotas. A colloquy between Commissioner O'Beirne and MGen Jack Wheeler, Commander of the Army Recruiting Command (14 July, Chicago) shows that the absence of quotas will not affect the readiness of the Army:

COMMISSIONER O'BEIRNE: And then just one final question for the General. Thank you all so much. Would it pose either a military readiness problem or a combat effectiveness problem for the Army if the number of women in uniform dropped from 11 percent to, say, six or seven percent? Would that have a negative impact on overall performance of the Army?

GENERAL WHEELER: I would think, in response to your question, Commissioner O'Beirne, what would cause that policy to come into effect -- in other words, if it was dictated, I don't think it would -- if your question is, would it cause a readiness problem, if they were replaced in time with MOS-qualified individuals, the answer is no. But I think that it would be -- I mean, what would be the perception of such a policy? In other words, what --

COMMISSIONER O'BEIRNE: I guess, General, I'm saying, if there weren't a quota, an affirmative policy trying to recruit women -- if that didn't exist and, as a result, the number of women in uniform in the Army dropped from, say, 11 percent down to six or seven, would that pose a readiness or effectiveness problem for the Army?

GENERAL WHEELER: I would have to say that the short answer would be no, and the reason for it is because if we were not recruiting young women, we would probably be recruiting young men.

*      Goals and quotas add to personnel costs:

-- The Army presented evidence to the Commission that it cost 50 percent more to recruit women than men. (CF 4.17)

-- Women leave the service at a faster rate than men. Except for the Army, retention rates are lower for females than males. Commissioners attending a Command briefing at the Paris Island Marine Corps Recruit Depot learned that "attrition rates prior to completion of contract...is 36 percent for men, 50 percent for women." (CF 4.21/Parris Island Trip Report, page 2)

*      Quotas and goals will impose pressures to make decisions based on political considerations rather than military necessity. In 1991, Canada's Human Rights Tribunal, acting on complaints of discrimination, ordered the military to drop tests to evaluate combat units in which women would be serving with men. (CF 3)

*      At the Naval Academy, Commissioners learned that Navy pilot billets are reserved for women at the time of service selection in the senior year. These positions cannot be claimed by men unless women pass them by. Thus, even lower ranking women can claim the reserved positions over male midshipmen of higher class standing. (USNA Trip Report)

50

## ISSUE B:  VOLUNTARY V. INVOLUNTARY DUTY

*Should special conditions and different standards apply to servicewomen than apply to servicemen performing similar roles in the Armed Forces in the area of voluntary (women) versus involuntary (men) assignment policies?*

**MAJORITY RECOMMENDATION:** *The Services should adopt gender-neutral assignment policies, providing for the possibility of involuntary assignment of any qualified personnel to any position open to them.* (Adopted:  Y:10 N:2 A:3)

### Overview

<u>Concur with Majority Recommendation as adopted.</u>  Navy policy allows the involuntary assignment of women to noncombatant vessels. According to DoD, "When applying for enlistment, the service woman completes an 'enlistment statement of understanding,' in which she indicates the understanding that she may be ordered to sea duty aboard a non-combatant ship."

Gender neutral assignment and current policy will mean women must be involuntarily assigned to combatant ships if they are open to women. Sen. John Warner (R-Va.), a member of the Senate Armed Services Committee and former Secretary of the Navy, told the Commission on June 25:

> If this Commission should find that the facts -- and I repeat the facts -- that support the view that women are fully capable of performing combat duty, I believe that it will be very difficult to describe a proper public purpose to be served by a policy that would then permit women to be assigned to such duties only if they volunteer to such duty.

*******************

## ISSUE C:  FITNESS/WELLNESS STANDARDS

*Should special conditions and different standards apply to servicewomen than apply to servicemen performing similar roles in the Armed Forces in the area of general physical fitness requirements for purposes of wellness?*

**MAJORITY RECOMMENDATION:** *The Services should retain gender-specific physical fitness tests and standards to promote the highest level of general fitness and wellness in the Armed Forces of the United States, provided they do not compromise training or qualification programs for physically demanding combat or combat support MOSs.* (Adopted:  Y:12 N:0 A:1)

### Overview
<u>Concur with the Majority Recommendation as adopted.</u>

51

## ISSUE D: OCCUPATIONAL PHYSICAL REQUIREMENTS

*Should the Services establish and implement specific occupational, muscular strength/endurance and cardiovascular capacity requirements where they are relevant to the duties of each specialty?*

**MAJORITY RECOMMENDATION:** *The Services should adopt specific requirements for those specialties for which muscular strength/endurance and cardiovascular capacity are relevant. (Adopted: Y:9 N:4 A:2)*

### Overview

Concur with Majority Recommendation as adopted. However, adopting the recommendation will likely require an ambitious, complicated testing program that would be unnecessary if women are not introduced into strenuous combat MOSs.

With respect to positions currently open, women should be assigned only to physically demanding occupations if they can demonstrate the ability to perform all necessary tasks under emergency or combat situations as well as in peacetime.

*******************

## ISSUE E: BASIC TRAINING STANDARDS

*Should special conditions and different standards apply to servicewomen than apply to servicemen performing similar roles in the Armed Forces in the area of basic training?*

**MAJORITY RECOMMENDATION:** *Entry level training may be gender-specific as necessary. Each advanced training program should be classified according to the military specialties to which it is principally dedicated, or to which it supplies personnel. Training programs which are dedicated to combat specialties shall be governed by policies which are consistent with laws and policies regarding the use of women in combat. (Adopted: Y:8 N:6 A:1)*

### Overview

Concur with the Majority Recommendation as adopted. MGen Gene Deegan, Commanding General at the Parris Island Marine Corps Recruit Depot, told the Commission, "If I were to maintain the same intensity for [women in training as] the male recruits, I would have a very difficult time recruiting any females, and if my recruiting mission remained the same, I would fail in my recruiting mission."

## ISSUE F: PRE-COMMISSIONING STANDARDS

*Should special conditions and different standards apply to servicewomen than apply to servicemen performing similar roles in the Armed Forces in the area of pre-commissioning training?*

**MAJORITY RECOMMENDATION:** *Military pre-commissioning training may be gender-normed in as much as postcommissioning training is designed specifically for individual specialties, combat, combat support and combat service support. (Adopted: Y:10 N:4 A:1)*

### Overview

<u>Concur with the Majority Recommendation as adopted with reservations.</u> An important issue brought to the Commission was the impression among servicemen that grades are awarded under a different standard, giving unfair advantages to women at the expense of men. This impression creates morale problems and may lead to inappropriate expressions of resentment. The GAO's survey on sexual harassment at the service academies found that most incidents described as sexual harassment were related to complaints about dual standards.

To reduce this problem, scoring in precommissioning training should truthfully reflect any adjustment for gender or be recorded separately for men and women. In addition, scores adjusted for gender should not be used to determine class rank or standing.

*********************

## ISSUE G: GENDER-RELATED OCCUPATIONAL STANDARDS

*Should special conditions and different standards apply to servicewomen than apply to servicemen performing similar occupational roles in the Armed Forces in the area of muscular strength/endurance and cardiovascular capacity?*

**MAJORITY RECOMMENDATION:** *The Services should adopt gender-neutral muscular strength/endurance and cardiovascular capacity requirements for those specialties for which they are relevant. (Adopted: Y:14 N:0 A:0)*

### Overview

<u>Concur with the Majority Recommendation as adopted.</u> Regardless of the military occupation specialties to which women are assigned, the Services must not compromise qualifying standards to accommodate physiological differences between men and women.

## ISSUE H: PARENTAL AND FAMILY POLICIES

*Should DoD policies, e.g., recruitment, retention, child care and deployment policies, regarding single and dual-service parents be revised? What effect do policies on the assignment of servicewomen have upon military families' children and the larger American society?*

**MAJORITY RECOMMENDATION:** *During and after U.S. involvement in the Gulf War, the American public and military community expressed extreme disapproval of the deployment of single mothers/fathers due to the possible effect on the children left behind. The Commission recommends that DoD review its policies and either adopt new policies or better implement current policies to reflect concerns of the public and military communities.*

*Specifically, the Commission recommends that DoD consider the following alternatives:*

*1. DoD should adopt a waivable policy that single parents with custodial care of children up to two years of age must accept assignment to a non-deployable position, if available, or be discharged from the Service with the opportunity to re-enter the Service without loss of rank or position.*
*2. For those single parents who have children older than two years and those parents who have been out for two years, they must have an approved and reliable child care package to re-enter the Service.*
*3. In dual-service families, only one parent should be allowed to serve in a deployable position.*
*4. Single parents with custody of children under school age should not be allowed to deploy.*
*5. Single parents should not be permitted to join the Armed Forces (current situation).*
*6. Spouses of military parents should not be allowed to enter the Service.*
*7. One parent in a dual-service couple should be forced to separate.*
*8. In order to reduce the number of children subjected to prolonged separation or the risk of becoming orphans during deployment, long-term DoD policies regarding the recruitment, deployment and retention of single and dual-service parents should be revised on a phased-in basis. Such policies should allow for voluntary or involuntary discharges at the discretion of local commanders, or reasonable incentives for separation. They may also include waivers by local commanders in certain circumstances. (Adopted: Y:9 N:0 A:1)*

*In order to avoid severe separation, child care and deployability problems at a time of mobilization, all family care plans must be regularly reviewed and evaluated by local commanding officers, with consideration given to the relationship of the potential caregiver to the child(ren) of deployable parents. Failure to ensure full compliance with family care requirements may constitute grounds for administrative or disciplinary action. (Adopted: Y:15 N:0 A:0)*

# Overview

Concur with the opening paragraph of the Majority Recommendation. Favor Option 8 over Option 1. Dissent from Option 2, which does not resolve the problem. The need for parental supervision and attachment does not subside or decrease at the age of two years.

With respect to Option 4, in the interest of unit readiness and cohesion, the issue must be addressed before the order to deploy is given. DoD should favorably review Recommendations 3, 5, 6 and 7. Also Concur with final paragraph.

In addressing this issue, the Commission was concerned about the number of children left behind by parents who deployed to the Persian Gulf during Operations Desert Shield and Storm. In addition to the pain of separation from their parents, the children were at risk of becoming orphans if the war had been prolonged with large numbers of casualties.

One dramatic expression of opinion measured in the Commission's Roper Poll of the public was the nation's clear opposition to single mothers going to war. In addition, a broad-based group of Americans representing organizations such as the U.S. Catholic Conference, United Auto Workers and the National Women's Political Caucus voiced this sentiment in a strongly written appeal to Secretary of Defense Cheney in February 1991. The writers said they were "concerned that current military personnel policies regarding deployment may cause serious harm to dependent children in single parent and dual-military families." (CF 3.22, 3.6)

The Commission clearly responded to this strong public sentiment, recognizing that family responsibilities may not be conducive to or compatible with military service.

## *Discussion Points*

\* Dr. Jay Belsky, a psychologist at Penn State University, told the Commission on June 9 that the needs of the children must be addressed:

> [T]o voluntarily send off single parents or both parents, and psychologically, from the child's perspective, abandon them, I contend is immoral, and nobody has the right in a nation that's not being attacked to do that. And I guarantee you that if the children were up here, they would tell you that loud and clear.

> In fact, one of the things I'm struck by when we have the issues of children and the issues of careers, and typically female careers posed against each other, we have this new emergent language of child development. All we hear about is their resilience. Lost is a language of vulnerability.

And I contend to you, every time you hear resilience spoken, you will hear simultaneously, really, a driving motivation, which is an adult's career development.

Children have feelings right there on the surface. Sure, they can learn to steel themselves. Sure, they can learn not to feel it. Sure, they can learn to be tough. But there are huge costs associated with that.

\*       A colleague, Dr. Brenda Hunter, agreed, elaborating on the pain of separation and its potential harmful effects on children:

[H]ow does separation from a parent affect children? Separation from parents, whether for weeks or months is serious business. Parental love, as translated into physical and emotional accessibility, is the anchor that holds a child to life, to paraphrase Sophocles.

Children depend on their parents for physical and emotional supplies. When a parent is absent for a prolonged period of time, children become angry and experience acute anxiety, fearing the present and the imagined future.

Moreover, when the family structure is threatened, a child's psychological development is also threatened.

Loss of a parent, either to death or prolonged separation, strikes a blow to a child's developing sense of trust and self esteem....

If separation is painful and difficult for young children, what about its effect on mother... Pediatrician T. Berry Brazleton has said that, 'When mothers know they must leave their babies for either full-time employment or war, they retreat and withdrawal emotionally. They withdraw,' he said, 'not because they don't care, but because it hurts to care.'

Along this same line, Bowlby suggested that if mothers are separated from their young children over a long period of time, their feelings of maternal love are apt to cool. Hence, not only would the young child become detached possibly from mother, either temporarily or for longer, but the mother's feelings of love would wane as well.

We are tampering with something profoundly elemental in human development when we think about separating mothers from their young children for any reason, and the cost of the separation may be high, not only for individuals, but for society as well.

*******************

## ISSUE I: PREGNANCY AND DEPLOYABILITY POLICIES

*Should DoD rules regarding pregnancy, excluding deployability of servicewomen, be retained, modified or rescinded? Should special conditions and different standards apply to servicewomen than apply to servicemen performing similar roles in the Armed Forces regarding deployability? Should servicewomen who become pregnant continue to serve in deployable positions? Should comparable restrictions on deployability be applied to servicemen?*

**MAJORITY RECOMMENDATION:** *The Commission reviewed the rules regarding pregnancy and found no specific areas of concern other than the problems associated with deployability and lost time; these problems are addressed in a separate issue. However, DoD should review rules regarding pregnancy to ensure consistency and force readiness. (Adopted: Y:8 N:0 A:2) Comparable deployability standards for each Service should be adopted by DoD and should be applied on a gender neutral basis with exceptions for pregnancy. (Adopted without objection)*

*A pregnant servicewoman should not be assigned to or remain in a position with a high probability of deployment. The Commission suggests that deployability for purposes of implementing such a policy be defined in terms of probabilities; a deployment-probability-designation coding system could be established to determine which positions have the higher probabilities of deployment and thus would be subject to restrictions under the recommended policy. Comparable restrictions should be applied to other servicemembers based on projected amount of time an individual will be unable to fulfill normal duties of his/her position because of injury, etc. (Adopted without objection)*

## Overview

Concur with the first paragraph of the Majority Recommendation as adopted, with the understanding that current policy will continue to restrict pregnant women from being deployed. However, more study is needed to determine the effects on an unborn child of G-force, radiation and other hazardous substances such as hydraulic fluids and toxic fumes.

Concur with the first sentence of the second paragraph as adopted: pregnant women should not be assigned to or remain in a position with a high probability of deployment. The issue here centers on the adverse affects of losing a unit leader at a time of deployment -- a concern that applies to both men and women because prolonged separation, regardless of the reason, negatively affects unit readiness and cohesion. The Commission was concerned about pregnant women in positions of leadership who were not or would not be available to deploy with their units to the Gulf War.

## *Discussion Points*

\*	According to the Roper Poll of the Military, "56 percent of those who were deployed in Desert Shield/Desert Storm with mixed gender units reported that women in their unit became pregnant just prior to or while deployed in the Gulf." Forty six percent of that group reported that pregnancies had a negative impact on unit readiness, and 59 percent reported a negative impact on morale. (CF 1.69)

\*	Nondeployability briefings before the Commission showed that women were three times more nondeployable than men, primarily due to pregnancy, during Operations Desert Shield and Storm. According to Navy CAPT Martha Whitehead's testimony before the Commission, "the primary reason for the women being unable to deploy was pregnancy, that representing 47 percent of the women who could not deploy...." (CF 16, 17, 1.59, 1.69(b), 3.54)

**Overall percentages for Desert Shield/Desert Storm non-deployability by service are indicated below.** (Cumulative Report over eight month period [Panel Three Report] )

|              | % Male | % Female | Comparison Factor |
|--------------|--------|----------|-------------------|
| ARMY         | 2.7    | 9.0      | 3.3X              |
| NAVY         | 1.5    | 5.6      | 3.7X              |
| AIR FORCE    | 1.8    | 6.4      | 3.5X              |
| MARINE CORPS* | 8.8   | 26.3     | 3.9X              |

\*      Between August 1989 and August 1991, voluntary and involuntary discharge figures for the "convenience of the government" (including such categories as hardship/dependency, pregnancy/childbirth and parenthood) were roughly twice as high among women as among men. (CF 2) See chart below (CF 6).

**Involuntary and voluntary separations for convenience of government**

|                                              | FY89  | FY90  | FY91  |
|----------------------------------------------|-------|-------|-------|
| Chapter 5 Parenthood (Involuntary Separation) |       |       |       |
| Male                                         | 33    | 42    | 152   |
| Female                                       | 87    | 85    | 610   |
| Total                                        | 120   | 127   | 762   |
| Chapter 6 Parenthood (Voluntary Separation)  |       |       |       |
| Male                                         | 272   | 338   | 281   |
| Female                                       | 609   | 765   | 982   |
| Total                                        | 881   | 1,103 | 1,263 |
| Chapter 8 Pregnancy                          | 2,136 | 2,351 | 2,651 |

\*      The Commission's recommendation suggests a complicated coding system that would not solve this problem.

## ISSUE J:  COMBAT ROLES FOR WOMEN

*In view of American military history, experience of war, and religious and cultural values, should the United States under any circumstances assign any servicewomen to any combat position, on land, at sea or in the air?*

**MAJORITY RECOMMENDATION:** *Yes.  Military readiness should be the driving concern regarding assignment policies; there are circumstances under which women might be assigned to combat positions.* (*Adopted:  Y:8 N:1 A:1*)

### Overview

Do not concur with the Majority Recommendation as adopted. The assignment of women to combat could be justified *only* in the most dire emergency where the nation's very survival is at risk and there is no reasonable alternative.  Absent these conditions, there is no military need at any time to assign women to combat.  The social, religious and cultural arguments against women in combat were pervasive themes in the testimonies of witnesses who represented all walks of life and all ranks of the military.  Many argued if women are assigned to combat to fight this nation's wars, the resulting damage to American culture and society would be monumental and irreversible.

### *Discussion Points*

The Commission recognized early in its series of meetings that this issue is not easily compartmentalized into quantifiable data and bureaucratic structures.  This by no means makes the question less important than others.

The Commission heard a great deal of testimony that women can fly fighter aircraft, perform some jobs on combat ships and in some rare cases meet the arduous physical demands of ground combat specialties in a peacetime environment.  The Commission also heard from a number of witnesses who said deeply held American values, which are based on commonly shared cultural and religious convictions, would not support or accept sending women into direct combat.  (CF 3A16, 3A17)

Thus, the question is whether the American people would view it as right and proper to assign women to the combat arms and whether they would support the decision of the President to do so.  Notwithstanding the significant strides women have made in the civilian world, assigning women to combat would be taking egalitarianism to an unprecedented extreme. As David Horowitz, President of the Center for the Study of Popular Culture, told the Commission in August:

> [P]lacing women in harm's way and training them to kill one-on-one is not a mere extension of women working outside the home.... As a layman, I can tell you, without statistics and without detailed reporting from the field, that American ability to wage war has already been seriously weakened by the deployment of relatively large numbers of women troops to an overseas

battlefield, even without sending them into combat. Who does not remember the poignant stories done in lavish detail on network TV of children left behind by their mothers deployed to the Persian Gulf, and in some cases, mothers and fathers.... The result is that an American president is now under pressure to win a war in four days or lose the war at home....

Cultural values, such as respect for women and the mutual responsibility of men and women to preserve a civilized order in sexual and family relationships, are crucial in any discussion of the appropriate role of women in the military. In the view of many of our witnesses and the overwhelming majority of an estimated 13,000 Americans who wrote to the Commission, assigning women to combat would be a fundamental departure from sound American and military values.

The essence of the question is whether we as a society should continue to encourage men to respect, protect and defend women. As one Commissioner observed, "right now millions of American mothers are raising their sons to protect and defend women." A policy of assigning women to combat would clearly be inconsistent with these ongoing cultural practices. In other words, the successful integration of women into combat units could occur only if we as a society undergo a cultural change discouraging men from protecting women.

This is why some members of the Commission felt compelled to seriously examine the cultural implications of training women in combat skills and subjecting them, as a matter of government policy, to the experience of direct combat and the known risks associated with capture. Such a policy would signify that we as a society are willing to tolerate (and even encourage through combat training) deliberate violence against women.

The issue of violence against women was crystallized when former prisoners of war appeared before the Commission, including one of two women captured during Operation Desert Storm. Testimony about the indecent assault of one of the women drew further attention to POW training programs already in place that "desensitize" male POWs to the brutalization of women with whom they may be held captive. An interview with trainers at the Survival, Evasion, Resistance and Escape training center at Fairchild Air Force Base (CF 1.45- 1.52) uncovered a logical but disturbing consequence of assigning women to combat:

> If a policy change is made, and women are allowed into combat positions, there must be a concerted effort to educate the American public on the increased likelihood that women will be raped, will come home in bodybags, and will be exploited. The consequence of not undertaking such a program would be large scale disillusionment with the military should the United States get in a protracted military engagement.

Ironically, some people argue that assigning women to combat will curb sexual harassment, a problem that drew national attention in connection with the scandalous incident involving naval aviators and women officers attending the Tailhook convention. One of the most disturbing aspects of Tailhook was that other male officers did not intervene to protect and defend those women, a disturbing sign of a breakdown of American values that must be repaired, not worsened, by government policy.

The Commission heard no evidence that assigning women to combat or altering our cultural values will stop sexual harassment and violence against women. As Dennis Prager argued in the Los Angeles hearings on August 6, "the only thing that helps any bad thing people do is values.... If a man is a decent man, he doesn't harass a woman." The only way to stop sexual harassment against women, he averred, is "to raise good men."

Good men respect and defend women. Women should not be required, as the price of equality, to sacrifice this fundamental principle that governs a civilized order. Permitting women in combat is egalitarianism of a different order than providing opportunities for them to become doctors, lawyers and members of the U.S. Senate.

Assigning women to combat would require reordering our cultural values and dismissing the experience of human and military history. As Allan Carlson, President of the Rockford Institute, told the Commission at its hearings in Chicago:

> From history this Commission can draw another lesson. No significant human society since the dawn of the historical record has ever, with any degree of success, intentionally used organized female soldiers in real extended combat, let alone forcibly conscripted its young women and young mothers and pressed them into combat positions. The possible few exceptions have been among peoples under great military or political stress, and they either disappeared from the stage of history or they quickly abandoned the approach. Viewed in historical terms, it would be an act of reckless hubris for this country now to go down that path.

********************

## ISSUE K:  GROUND COMBAT

*Should the existing service policies restricting the assignment of servicewomen with respect to ground combat specialties be retained, modified, rescinded or codified?*

**MAJORITY RECOMMENDATION:** *The sense of the Commission is that women should be excluded from direct land combat units and positions. Further, the Commission recommends that the existing service policies concerning direct land combat exclusions be codified. Service Secretaries shall recommend to the Congress which units and positions should fall under the land combat exclusion. (Adopted: Y:10 N:0 A:2)*

61

# Overview

Concur with the Majority Recommendation as adopted.  Based on the testimony presented to the Commission, the exclusion policy should continue to include multiple launch rocket systems and field artillery units.  Despite technological advances, ground combat is no more refined, no less barbaric and no less physically demanding than it has been throughout history.  The ground combatant relies heavily on his physical strength and mental toughness for survival.

## *Discussion Points*

### *The Nature of Modern Combat*

\*      LTG Binford Peay, Army Deputy Chief of Staff for Operations and Plans, testified to the Commission about modern combat:

> In fact, technology has made today's battlefield a more lethal, violent, shocking and horrific place than it has ever been.  Paradoxically, the last war may have, to external audiences and the uninitiated, appeared clean and very easy.  We need only to contemplate for a single moment man's inhumanity to his fellow man and the irrational nature of ethnic conflicts today to get an appreciation that the face of battle has not changed.  It is just that we recently have not been involved in the horror as it passes before us on the nightly news....

\*      Sgt Maj Harold Overstreet, USMC, told the Commission what ground combat involves on a personal level:

> We say, 'Combat is combat is combat.'  I'm here to tell you, it is not.  First of all, I'm here to tell you that it is one thing to be in a combat area; it's another thing to be in a combat area and to have rounds coming in on you.  It's even another thing to send rounds down range.  But it's a little bit different when you know that you are the guy that is going to have to seek out, close with, and do whatever it takes to the enemy.  You.  You're going to go out there and confront him, one on one.  You realize that this is no game, there is no second place, and if you are second place, you don't come back.
>
> It's a little bit different situation than just working or refueling or resupplying in a combat area, to go out and seek out....
>
> That's what I would like to explain to you now:  engaging the enemy.  For just a moment, I have -- I would like to retrograde and go back to Vietnam in 1967, and for this engagement I have selected a Marine which most of you know, who has credibility with you and you with him.

Sgt Maj Overstreet went on to describe what he had experienced in Vietnam. Although the language is graphic, his testimony was an important reminder of the nature of close combat:

> In 1967, the Republic of Vietnam, Operation Union 2, Companies of India and Mike Company of Third Battalion, Fifth Marines, had made contact with a North Vietnamese regiment.  Now,

bear in mind, this is two Marine companies that has run into a North Vietnamese regiment. No sooner than they had made contact than six NVA soldiers come dashing right through the lines, and where did they come dashing through to? To the young company commander by the name of Captain Stackpole, and his radio operator. They ended up in the same fighting hole as he did.

Well, obviously, they had just got there. There was really not much of a fighting hole at all, because it was just a little scooped-out area, a place in defalade (phonetic) there they had selected to fight from.

Well, when six NVA soldiers show up in your fighting position, there is not a lot of time to negotiate. So, immediately, Captain Stackpole pulled his .45 and shot the first two coming into his position. They fell in the hole.

About the time they fell in the hole, there's four other individuals in the hole with he and his radio operator. While they're thrashing around in the mud and the blood and the fog of battle, Captain Stackpole loses his pistol. Now, what does he do? With arms and legs and AK-47s thrashing around all over the area, he pulls his K-bar knife, the only thing that he could find at the time. He pulls his K-bar and finally gets a hold of one of the NVA, sticks him in the groin, and rips him all the way to his appetite.

While thrashing around, he grabs a hold of the third one, cuts his throat. At the same time, the radio operator cleaves the next one in the head with an E-tool, and Captain Stackpole then stabbed the sixth one to death in the fighting hole.

Now, that does take a little bit of upper body strength; it does take a little bit of aggressiveness, as you can obviously see.

## Physical Strength Factors

\*       All branches of the Armed Forces play an important role in determining the outcome of ground combat, but the ground combat soldier, the tip of the spear, faces unique challenges and demands normally not imposed on the soldier in combat support and combat service support roles.

\*       The Commission heard an abundance of expert testimony about the physical differences between men and women that can be summarized as follows:

 -- Women's aerobic capacity is significantly lower, meaning they cannot carry as much as far as fast as men, and they are more susceptible to fatigue. (CF 2.1.3, 2.1.4, 2.1.4A, 2.1.4B)

 -- Women are shorter, have less muscle mass and weigh less than men, placing them at a distinct disadvantage when performing tasks requiring a high level of muscular strength and aerobic capacity, like ground combat. (CF 2.1.1)

 -- Women are also at a higher risk for exercise-induced injuries than men, with 2.13 times greater risk for lower extremity injuries, and 4.71 times greater risk for stress fractures. (CF 2.1.5)

\*       In his testimony before the Commission, Dr. William Gregor, LTC, USA, (Ret.), a military science professor at the University of Michigan, elaborated on the following differences:

-- In terms of physical capability, the upper five percent of women are at the level of the male median.  (CF 1.39)

-- This means that in the very physically demanding ground combat environment, as a unit extends the physical envelope of its members, the men have room to improve, whereas the women have already reached the upper end of their limits. (CF 1.39)

-- The average 20-to-30 year-old woman has the same aerobic capacity as a 50 year-old man.  (CF 1.39)

\*       Marine Corps Staff Sergeant Barry Bell, who served as a combat engineer during Operation Desert Storm, illustrated these points in his testimony before the Commission:

My rucksack when I went in weighed 75 pounds.  And I walked 12 miles from the border to the mine field.... If you're not in peak physical condition during this type of environment, you're not going to be able to perform.  And, unfortunately, we weren't in peak physical condition.  During the six months prior to going in, we did PT, we did try to get in some semblance of shape, but we did not get to the point where we are at now, and it kicked our butts...we were bent over, our backs were killing us.  The weight was just way too heavy for us, let alone a female Marine or female soldier.....Physically, they are just unable to do it.  If we were almost unable to do it, I know we would have a hard time pulling the female Marines up to where we were at.  Physically, they are just not capable of performing everything we are able to do, and I think that's one of the major concerns here.

\*       Army and Marine Desert Storm combat veterans who testified on Air-Land battle doctrine at the Los Angeles hearings said women should not be assigned to ground combat. Army LTC Douglas Tystad, an M-1 tank commander, told the Commission:

My view of it is that the physiological requirements, the strength requirements, are extreme.  The stress over time, stamina is required.

In my experience, limited though it may be, I've met very few women that I believed could handle the stress, coupled with the physical requirements that we have.

At this level, you are down at what the military psychologists and sociologists call the primary group.  A crew is a primary group, and we believe that in combat motivation you fight for the primary group.  And the group is only as good as its weakest member....

\*       After extensive research, Canada has found little evidence to support the integration of women into ground units.  Of 103 Canadian women who volunteered to join infantry units, only one graduated the initial training course.  (CF 1.76, 2.5.4B)  The Canadian experience

64

corroborates the testimony of LTC Gregor, who said the odds of selecting a woman matching the physical size and strength of the average male are more than 130-to-1.

*Readiness, Cohesion and Effectiveness*

*       Introducing women into ground combat units could have an adverse affect on unit cohesion. The lower stamina and endurance of women is already established. In the likely situation that women were unable to carry their full load without male assistance, unit cohesion would suffer. Furthermore, lack of privacy in combat units could result in cohesion problems when normal and widely accepted standards of personal modesty must routinely be sacrificed to military necessity. (CF 2.5.4)

*       Lt Col Stephen Smith, a Gulf War mechanized infantry commander, told the Commission in Los Angeles:

> By introducing women, even women who have the physical capability to lift the rucksacks, walk the distances, raise the hatches, load the TOW missiles, break the track on those vehicles and put it back together again, you are still introducing into that equation other factors that weren't there before: sexual jealousies, intentions, our own social or moral values come into play, and they make more difficult that job of that commander who is forward.

> It has been said that in combat the important things are simple, and the simple things are difficult. We are making this more difficult by doing that. This is not Olympic diving. We do not get extra credit for adding an extra degree or an added degree of difficulty.

> I believe that women in those squads would reduce the combat effectiveness of those squads, and I think we would pay for that in casualties.

*       Research done by Commissioner Henderson and other cohesion experts shows units lacking discipline and cohesion suffer excess casualties and perhaps even defeat. (CF 2.5.5)

*Legal Issues*

*       As defined by Title 10 U.S. Code Sec. 3062, the "Army shall be organized, trained and equipped primarily for prompt and sustained combat incident to operations on land."

*       Another important consideration is the impact placing women in combat units would have on the legal status of women and a compulsory draft for military service. In Rostker v. Goldberg, the Supreme Court determined that the purpose of the draft was to raise combat soldiers, and because women could not serve in those units, the government could exempt them from registering for the draft. Thus, if women are placed in combat specialties, they might be

subject to the draft because the equal protection clause of the Constitution will apply to the military and the courts may have no choice but to mandate it. (CF 4.1, 4.3, 4.7)

* Barring an act of Congress, women are not in jeopardy of conscription as long as women are exempt from combat duty. Introducing them into any combat situation invites a myriad of predictable legal challenges with unforeseen and perhaps irreversible consequences for American women, society and the military. (CF 4.3, 4.4, 4.7)

*International Issues*

* According to the Panel One Report on international issues, the only modern nation that had actually used women in combat units is the former Soviet Union because at the time their national survival in World War II demanded it. Despite reports of a number of women in all branches of its military, the Soviet Union virtually eliminated women from its Armed Forces after the war, assigning those who remained to traditional roles of medicine, communications and administration. Before the Soviet Union's breakup, women made up only 0.7% of its active force, second smallest of any country studied by the Commission. (CF 1.112 through 1.123)

*Retired Flag Officer Survey*

* According to the Commission's survey of all known retired Flag Officers, 76 percent (attack helicopters) to 90 percent (infantry) opposed the assignment of women to the different ground combat specialties. Within the two Services with ground combat specialties, the figures were basically higher: between 74 percent and 92 percent of Army Generals surveyed opposed such assignments as did 90 percent to 99 percent of Marine Generals. (Appendix D/CF 2.5.5)

*******************

## ISSUE L: COMBAT AIRCRAFT

*Should the existing Service policies restricting the assignment of servicewomen with respect to aircraft be retained, modified, rescinded or codified?*

**MAJORITY RECOMMENDATION:** *In view of the evidence gathered by this Commission with regard to the potential consequences of assigning women to combat positions, current DoD and Service policies with regard to Army, Air Force and Naval aircraft on combat missions should be retained and codified by means of the re-enactment of Section 8549 of Title 10, U.S.C. which was repealed by Public Law 102-190, Sec. 531 for the Air Force, and re-enactment of the provisions of 10 U.S.C. sec. 6015 prohibiting women from assignment to duty on aircraft engaged in combat missions, which was repealed by Public Law 102-190 for the Navy, and codification of Army policy. (Adopted: Y:8 N:7 A:0)*

# Overview

<u>Concur with the Majority Recommendation as adopted.</u>  Some women who fly combat aircraft in non-combat missions testified before the Commission.  Indications are that some women can fly them quite well under non-combat conditions. Flying combat aircraft, however, transcends the question of peacetime capability.  Some of the issues associated with women in air combat include the increased probability of becoming a POW, readiness, cohesion, morale and effectiveness problems associated with pregnancy, and physiological/aeromedical problems that may reduce the flexibility of assignments of women in combat aircraft.

## *Discussion Points*

### *The Nature of Air Combat*

\*        Combat fighter pilots testified to the difference between *flying* and *fighting* an aircraft.

--   Air Force LtGen Buster Glosson, who was responsible for much of the air campaign strategy and its daily execution in the Gulf War, told the Commission:

There are those who say technology has removed the personal demands and the horrors of combat.  That is just simply not true.  To me, the air combat arena comes down, as I said, to stamina and cohesion.

One, stamina is fairly straightforward to deal with from an Air Force point of view.  From a medical standpoint, it can either be accomplished or it can't.  And so we don't think that there is very much room for subjective judgment in that arena, and we are not trying to instill any.

But the common perception of a combat air mission -- to plan the mission to the target, brief with a wingman, fly an hour or two, 15 minutes of intense being fired at and avoidance of the ordnance -- avoidance of the threat, deliver your ordnance and return and have the rest of the day off -- is simply a misconception.

The physical demands encompassed in this area are tremendous.  The high speeds of the modern aircraft, as a result of technology, the high rates of turn that require the high instantaneous G loads that literally makes your body shake or may put you in G lock, as we call it, when you lose consciousness, that we have to deal with all the time -- the current requirement for sustaining consciousness is strength and endurance, and to us that is overall stamina.

The jury is out on what the final verdict will be on that issue, but, like I said, it should not be a problem for either you or I; it should be black and white.

Let me share a personal example in the Gulf war.  The 14th Air Division, which I was the commander, had about 800 fighters in it.  The F-15Cs at Ta'if that I was asking -- at Tabuk, I'm sorry, that I was asking to fly missions over and around Baghdad, those young men were flying seven- to nine-hour missions, of which about 70 percent of the time was in hostile territory.

Now, let's think about that from the standpoint of something we all can relate to.  Think about getting on an airplane at Dulles Airport, flying to Frankfurt, Germany, sleeping for eight hours,

67

and coming back this way, sleeping for eight hours and going back again, every day, day after day after day.

-- Air Force Col Richard F. Jones, Chief of Flight Medicine at the Air Force surgeon general's office told the Commission:

[T]here are some differences in combat versus non-combat aviation.... [C]ombat aviation differs predominantly in the one area, in my mind, and that is that the combat pilot has to fly, fight and win.

-- Navy LT John Clagett, a Top Gun instructor, told the Commission at hearings in Los Angeles:

[Y]es, we do have women flying F-18s today, and that is a fact. They are certainly not flying the F-18s that any of us have flown in the fleet or out in the combat missions. To compare the missions that they are doing today to what we are doing is like comparing driving on the L.A. Freeway to driving in the Indianapolis 500. It's just not the same.

We are out there max performing the greatest airplane in the world every day, or attempting to. The women are not asked to do that. That is not their job. They have not been trained in the missions that we have been trained in. They have not performed the missions we have been performing.

And I just really object to the news or whatever coming out and saying, 'Oh, they're already doing that job.' That's not true. Yes, they are flying F-18s. They're not flying combat mission F-18s, you know, and to put them in the same role is just ludicrous.

-- Fellow panel member, Capt Patrick Cooke, USMC, agreed:

The second area that I would like to address is, due to the advancement in technology that we have witnessed throughout the years, a lot of people would like to refer to aerial combat as being a long-range game, where we have long-range missiles, and we are talking about mileage there, where you can probably kill your opponent, but in actuality it's a game of inches, and, again, the outcome of that game is life or death.

What I mean by inches is, as you pick up an opponent, deep at your six o'clock, doing 550-plus knots, or miles an hour, and you look over your shoulder, and he has launched a missile at you, the only thing that you can do to save your life is to break back, or turn back into that threat, to neutralize him as best you can.

Now, I know that somebody is going to try to do some studies where they put people in a centrifuge and just sit them there and say, 'Let's see how many Gs that you can pull,' but I doubt there is going to be any simulation to see whether somebody is going to be able to, A, look over their shoulder while they are doing that under the high G force, and also work the switchology of the aircraft.

And I said it was a game of inches; while doing that high G maneuver over your shoulder, still maintaining a tally-ho on the enemy, and potentially reversing the roles, you still have to have the physical capability under that high G situation to get the first weapon off on that opponent should there be a role reversal, and that's where the game of inches comes in. Not only do you have to be able to pull hard on the pole and make that maneuver, but you have to do it with visual acuity, while maintaining sight of your opponent and ensuring that your weapons system is on him before it's on you.

## *The Prisoner of War Question*

*       Allowing women to fly combat missions would dramatically increase the probability the United States would have women become prisoners of war. In Vietnam and Operation Desert Storm, the great majority of POWs were combat aviators. Col John Ripley, USMC, told the Commission in June, "When that airplane, with its female pilot, returns to earth or collides with earth or she must bailout of it, she is no longer a female pilot; she is now a victim."

> -- *Into the Mouth of the Cat* , a book about Air Force Medal of Honor recipient
> and Vietnam POW Lance Sijan, countered the notion that combat aviation is safe
> and clean:

> In the short time it took him [Sijan] to parachute to earth, he would travel from the relative
> security of the twentieth century's most advanced military technology to a jungle where the rules
> and conduct of combat had not undergone any major alteration since Neolithic times.

*       Aside from being shot down and taken prisoner, women may also face the likelihood of being used as ground troops when the need arises. According to Louis Morton, who wrote the official Army history of the Philippines campaign in *The Fall of the Philippines,* the Japanese destroyed two-thirds of the American planes (the 21st and 34th Pursuit Squadrons) in the Philippines on December 8, 1941, forcing fighter pilots and ground crews to fight as combat infantry during the fall of Bataan and Corregidor.

*       If assigned to combat positions on an equal basis, women aviators would have the responsibility to rotate into Air Liaison Officer (ALO) positions with Army ground units. According to Air Force Capt Ron Gaulton, who flew A-10s in the Gulf War:

> [W]hen Desert Storm kicked off, [some pilots] were immediately sent down to the 24th Infantry
> Division...and were shipped over, and they spent the entire Shield/Storm on the ground with the
> forward forces, and those were the guys that actually directed the A-10 strikes in.... So they lived
> out of the Army, they're right on the front lines, and they are...for all intents and
> purposes...Army people.

*       Pilots meeting with Commissioners at Nellis Air Force Base said that if women are exempt from rotation into ALO positions because ground combat restrictions forbid it, morale problems are likely to surface among male pilots.

*       The presence of women would increase morale problems for male prisoners, as well as their vulnerability should the enemy torture women prisoners to coerce cooperation from the men, as highly decorated American aviators who spent years of captivity in Vietnam, told the Commission. Two American aviators who were POWs in Vietnam said hearing the screams of women would have made their captivity all the more difficult. Air Force Col Fred Cherry, who

spent seven-and-a-half years in a North Vietnamese prison camp said:

> I am certain had the cries and screams and being next door to my fellow prisoners being tortured and given the rope treatment and the bamboo beatings and the rubber straps -- I'm sure I would -- it would have affected [me] more severely had that been a woman, rather than a man.

-- Added Air Force Col Norman McDaniel, another POW:

> There is no doubt in my mind that it would make a difference...there is no question in my mind, I would certainly lean toward giving the enemy something if I knew they were raising hell with a fellow female prisoner.

*        Instructors at the SERE school for pilots have observed a protective response among men when a female trainee was threatened. A survey at the school also noted that were a female POW to become pregnant, there would be a negative impact on morale and discipline in the POW camp. (SERE Commission Testimony of June 8/CF 1.50)

*        Likewise, the impact of brutal treatment on American women POWs could likely have a far more demoralizing effect on the American public than similar treatment on male prisoners. The Commission found that Germany amended its constitution after World War II because women who served on the Eastern Front were so horribly brutalized as POWs. As LTC William Bryan, USA, told the Commission:

> My point of view is that if you do that [allow women to fly attack helicopters], you set up a conflict of values, of American society, particularly how men view women, family values, religious values, those kinds of things. And I think that ultimately, at least near term, would result in reduced effectiveness in combat.....But I am not prepared to see America's mothers and daughters paraded down the streets of Baghdad and subjected to abuse, when it's not necessary. Now those are my values as an American citizen.

## Cohesion

*        Unit cohesion is another concern. For several years the United States has had mixed-gender aircraft units, yet many men who have positive feelings about working with women in a noncombat unit still believe women should not be in combat units. (CF 2.5.1, 2.5.3, 2.5.4, 2.5.5)

*        Combat aviators who testified before the commission expressed deep concern that assigning women to their units would seriously erode cohesion. One pilot talked about the unique requirements in combat squadrons for direct, confrontational ready room exchanges to improving tactical skills and making everyone safer in combat. Those necessary exchanges could not and would not occur in mixed gender combat squadrons. (CF 2.5.3C)

-- Top Gun pilot LT John Clagett presented the views of 23 fellow instructors:

> Of the 23 instructors we have at Top Gun, I'll just tell you that I think we have 21 of them that

decided that they wanted to sign this paper, and we'll give this to the panel, and it pretty much falls along with being a JO. I'm going to say that it mainly is the lieutenants out there, and the captains in the Marine Corps, that are screaming that, 'No, we don't want this to happen.' And our big reason for it is that we need to have those units act as units.

When you are out there in your fleet squadron, it is very important that you act as one, and you believe and you share your experiences with each and every member, and you expect a lot out of that person, and you have to act as a unit. And if you can't do that -- and we don't believe you can act as a unit unless you keep it the way it is, where it's the bonding -- it's that intangible, the bonding, that makes a squadron good, better, and we don't believe you can have that go on if we have females in aviation.

-- Navy aviator LT Tom Downing agreed:

So my feeling is that if you put women into these combat units that are primarily all male right now, is that not only do combat aviators or naval aviators or infantrymen or artillery officers -we function differently when in fact we are amongst all men, when we are with external women, women who are external to the group, and also when there are women integrated into the group, and I think that goes across society.

Men in general will act differently amongst men. They will act differently when women are involved. And I think the penalty that you pay when you put a woman into that particular unit is going to decrease the overall effectiveness of that unit to go out there and actively engage the enemy and kill people.

And I think that is the bottom-line issue, because physically, yes, it is demanding. You will be able to -- there are women out there who can fly the jets. I'm sure of it. There's probably women out there that can lift more weights, maybe pull more G than I can, but interaction amongst the combat unit, which we are -- fighter aviation and attack aviation is to go out and actively kill the enemy.

The cohesion involved there is what makes winners, and I think if women are put into that situation, that is going to decrease the overall effectiveness.

*       The Commission heard no evidence that placing women in combat squadrons will increase combat efficiency. With the current drawdown, some pilots are placed in non-flying assignments for one-to-three years until combat aircraft become available.

*       Potential pregnancy of female aviators must be considered. It costs the Air Force $3 million to train one pilot for fighters or bombers. The cost to retrain aviators who have been off flying status ranges from $70,000 (helicopters) to $247,847 (fighter pilots). (Panel Two Report [page 118]/CF 2.6.1GH)

*       The Commission also found that the Air Force restricts assignment status for six weeks after childbirth, which translates into more than nine months away from flying combat aircraft. (CF 2.3.3A, 2.3.3B) As noted earlier, the prolonged absence of a pregnant aviator from a combat unit will likely affect readiness, unit cohesion and morale.

*       The Commission found that pregnant females may not fly in ejection seat aircraft, which

71

encompasses all fighters and fighter-bombers.  (CF 2.3.2A and 2.3.3A)

*Retired Flag Officer Survey*

\*        According to the Commission's survey of all known retired flag officers, 71 percent opposed the assignment of women to combat aircraft.  For Services that possess fighter/bomber aircraft, 72 percent of Air Force generals opposed combat aircraft assignments for women, as did 71 percent of Navy admirals, and 83 percent of Marine Corps generals.  (Appendix D/CF 2.5.5)

*******************

## ISSUE M:  COMBATANT VESSELS

*Should the combatant vessel exclusions (law and policy) be retained, modified or rescinded/repealed?  Should the current policy be modified to conform with existing law?*

**MAJORITY RECOMMENDATION:** *Repeal existing laws and modify service policies for servicewomen to serve on combatant vessels except submarines and amphibious vessels. (Adopted:  Y:8 N:6 A:1)*

### Overview

<u>Dissent from Majority Recommendation that women be assigned to combatant ships except for amphibious ships and submarines.</u>

The Commission's recommendation to assign women to some combatant vessels is inconsistent with its recommendations regarding aircraft, ground combat and Special Forces. The basic arguments against assigning women to other combat specialties are equally valid with respect to combatant vessels; e.g., nondeployability, pregnancy, cohesion, physical strength, risk of capture and legal issues regarding the possibility of conscripting women.

Those who would assign women to combatant ships are suggesting that this policy can be justified by political expediency rather than the needs of the military. This proposition creates an inherently unstable situation that could unravel the principle on which other exemptions are based, including exemption from the draft. It is not enough to exempt women from service on amphibious ships and submarines because such an exemption, if enacted into policy or law, cannot long stand. The Majority Recommendation is not only inconsistent but also imprudent and irresponsible. (CF 4.1 through 4.30)

## Discussion Points

### Involuntary Assignment

*       As noted earlier, current Navy policy is to involuntarily assign women to non-combatant vessels. It would be inconsistent with current Navy policy to assign women only on a voluntary basis to combatant ships. In fact, logic and the law may require mandatory assignments.

*       In answer to a Commission request, the Navy replied that the availability of non-traditional shipboard assignments open to women exceeds the current demand. Furthermore, "recruiting statistics indicate that the propensity among female applicants is still toward the shore-intensive rating." (Nov. 9 OSD response)

### Combatants v. Noncombatants

*       Advocates of assigning women to combat ships base their arguments on the performance of women in normal peacetime operating conditions on noncombatant ships. But that case cannot be made convincingly. As VADM Dudley Carlson, former National Security Advisor and Chief of Navy Personnel, told the Commission in September:

> You know, a combat ship is built to go in harm's way, and a logistics support ship, like a tender - - the *Cape Cod*, for instance, is tied up to a pier. It's a building, it's a factory, and it sits there - - they may get underway three or four times a year and go out, and the rest of the time, it's, you know, an 8:00 to 5:00 kind of job. And those ships have a lot of women on board, and they do a great job. And a lot of those women are single parents.

### Readiness, Cohesion and Effectiveness

*       The physical rigors of some Navy specialties do not preclude some servicewomen from qualifying for them, even though serious questions arise about physically strenuous and potentially dangerous battle drill and emergency functions that must be performed by an entire crew, regardless of individual specialties. In answer to a question from Commissioner Moskos about the comparative abilities of women to fight fires aboard ships, VADM Carlson replied:

> Sure and they are going to fight the fire. But to knowingly put them in a hostile combat environment in which their physical competence may make a difference in savings someone's life or losing a life, then I want to go with the more capable, physical person.... I'm talking about the environment, fighting the ship, as opposed to steaming it at sea. If you're going to take the ship into hostile combat and seek out the enemy, then I think you ought to have the most capable people in the crew you can have.

\*       The Robertson and Trent study of 1985, as reported by Panel Two (Page 39), "found significant male/female differences in emergency shipboard task performance." While clear majorities of women (more than 90 percent in some cases) failed to meet the physical standards for eight critical shipboard tasks, virtually all the men passed (in most cases 100 percent).

*Habitability Concerns and Interpersonal Relationships*

\*       Though most combatants are home-based on the East or West coasts, their peacetime schedules routinely involve six- to seven-month deployments at sea.

\*       The issues involved in a long deployment aboard the confines of a ship are more than unit cohesion and ship morale. They include privacy for both the men and women, (particularly aboard amphibious ships and submarines), fraternization and sexual harassment in close quarters, family morale and child care issues associated with mothers and single parents who might routinely deploy for more than six months in peacetime, not to mention wartime.

\*       The same deployment and habitability problems on amphibious ships and submarines will appear in the long deployments (normally at least six months) that are routine for other surface combatants as well.

-- In a letter to the Commission following a visit to two submarines stationed at Naval Station Norfolk,  VADM G.H. Chiles, Jr., USN, expressed serious concern that life aboard submarines might become more difficult if women are assigned.

-- Commissioners who visited an amphibious ship at the 32nd Street Naval Base in San Diego reported that separate berthing compartments for women  might not be sufficient to preserve privacy on board most amphibious ships, primarily because some corridors which women would have to walk through in order to get to work areas are lined with curtained sleeping bunks.  Separate berthing areas reserved for the temporary use of Marines would present the same problem.

*Lost Time and Non-deployability*

\*       The Commission found that whereas women are 11.2 percent of the total force, they make up 34.7 percent of the Navy's single parents. ( CF 3.35) The Navy's Desert Storm non-deployability briefing to the Commission revealed a "1.5 percent nondeployable rate for men and a 5.6 percent nondeployable rate for women," mostly due to pregnancy.  Other Commission findings reinforce this nondeployability rate. For instance, "nine or ten percent of Navy women are pregnant at any one time." (CF 5)

*The Hazards of Serving at Sea*

\*      In at least two areas, earlier arguments against women flying combat missions reinforce arguments against their assignment to combat ships. As with air combat, women at sea might quickly find themselves thrust into circumstances where physical strength means the difference between life and death. Likewise, the POW issue, extensively addressed with respect to women flying combat aircraft, applies to women at sea.

> -- According to Samuel Eliot Morison's *History of US Naval Operations in World War II,* the crew of a naval vessel must also face hazards other than direct combat. On July 30, 1945, a Japanese submarine sank the heavy cruiser *USS Indianapolis*. Of 1,199 crewmen, roughly 800 successfully abandoned ship. Only 316 survived three-and-a-half days in the water. The others died of exposure or were killed by sharks.

> -- When the North Koreans captured the *USS Pueblo* in 1968, they unmercifully tortured the crewmen until they were released. Its commander, Lloyd Bucher, wrote to the Commission to voice his opposition to the assignment of women to combatant ships.

*Legal Issues*

\*      Repeal of the exemption regarding Navy combat ships might undermine any legal case that women should not be subjected to conscription based on the argument that men and women are not similarly situated. The Navy conscripted men during World War II. (CF 4.7)

\*      Assigning women to combat ships suggests men and women are similarly situated -- meaning both men and women will be assigned to combat -- which could conceivably undermine the legality of exempting women from involuntary assignment to ground combat or conscription. (CF 4.3)

\*      The Commission's recommendation is inconsistent with Issue Q. Because the exemption of women from the draft is inextricably tied by legal precedent to their exemption from combat duty, the only way to avoid the risk of losing that draft exemption is to embrace a consistent policy against assigning women to any combat military occupation specialty.

\*      Furthermore, assigning women to one type of combatant vessel, while exempting them from others, creates an inherently unstable situation unlikely to withstand political pressure for further change, scrutiny by the courts or legal challenges on grounds of equal opportunity.

\*      It is necessary to understand that although the Commission has not called for the assignment of women to submarines and amphibious ships, legal changes put in motion by partial repeal of the combat exclusion law could make the distinction unsupportable.

75

*Retired Flag Officers Survey*

\*       According to the Commission's survey of all known retired flag officers, 76 percent opposed the assignment of women to combat ships.  Specifically, 77 percent of Navy admirals and 90 percent of Marine Corps generals opposed assigning women to combatant ships. (Appendix D/CF 2.5.5)


*******************

## ISSUE N:  SPECIAL OPERATIONS

*Should existing policies restricting the assignment of servicewomen with respect to Special Operations Forces be retained, modified, rescinded or codified?*

**MAJORITY RECOMMENDATION:  Retain the existing policies.**  *(Adopted: Y:14 N:0 A:0)*

### Overview

Concur with Majority Recommendation as adopted.  Special Operations demonstrate the brutal nature of warfare at its most basic dimension.  Special Operations Forces depend on the close integration of air, ground and sea components, rigorous training, cohesion and team building. Testimony from RADM Raymond Smith, Commander of the Naval Special Warfare Command and Army GEN Carl Stiner, Commander in Chief of the U.S. Special Operations Command, was unequivocal:  "Because of unparalleled physical demands and forced intimacy, even in training, women would degrade the readiness, cohesion and effectiveness of the Special Forces."


*Discussion Points*

\*       Testimony from RADM Smith:

We make no compromises in SEAL training, because there are no compromises in the missions we conduct....

This, I believe, is the crux of the issue.  Would the integration of females in a SEAL platoon improve our combat effectiveness?  My belief is that such an integration would reduce our combat effectiveness....

[T]he main point is that life in the SEALs involves the closest of personal and physical contacts.... So how would a female impact a platoon...?

The impact of sex at this age and under this type of environment will be overwhelming. Just as parents normally separate brothers and sisters when reaching puberty, parents knowing the power of sex at that age, even among siblings, we in the SEALs would be confronted with young men and women living together under even closer conditions than brothers and sisters.

One or two 19-year-old females introduced into a group of 19- to 26-year-old men, all of whom are involved in highly stressful physical training, extremely close from an interpersonal aspect, will result, in my opinion, in romantic or sexual relationships....

I might add that I recognize that a woman might not have any interest in developing a personal relationship, but my experience in life tells me that men, being what we are, will in fact complicate this issue. Sex in males is the most powerful drive at a young age, and whether, in a given situation, a man or a woman initiates the relationship is irrelevant. All that is relevant is that it will happen, and when it does, it will create within a SEAL platoon a distraction, at best, and a romantic or fraternizing situation, at worst, but ultimately male and female personal relationships will reduce our combat effectiveness.

\*     Excerpt of trip report, including office call to GEN Stiner:

General Stiner indicated to Commissioner Cockerham that he was against the idea of changing policy so that women could be assigned to combat specialties.... The General's opposition concerned crossing the barriers of combat in the assignment of women and the impact that would have within the military and within his Command.

The General pointed to the training requirements, physical demands, and mental endurance of combat as limiting factors on the integration of women further into the military. 'The physical demands of special operation training alone would be beyond all but a rare exception.'

The General stated that *'there is no question that introducing women in special operations combat units, including aviation, will most definitely degrade combat readiness'* [emphasis added].

The General indicated he had concerns about the issue of women in combat specialties in regards to increased sexual activity, fraternization and unit cohesion.... He indicated the wives of soldiers may not fully understand the military's rationale for forcing men in close quarters to

women over a long periods of time. 'The performance of soldiers can often be a function of the support wives give them as they serve this difficult profession.'

When asked if aviation pilot specialties should be an exception to the present policy that restrict women, the General said 'all our missions are combat missions...the risk of death and capture are probably at least as high in our aviation...the level of air and ground synchronization makes all fields of combat equally difficult, integrated and dependent.'

## ISSUE O:  RISK RULE

*Should the DoD "Risk Rule," which reduces servicewomen's risk of injury, death, or capture, be retained, modified, rescinded or codified?*

**MAJORITY RECOMMENDATION:** *Retain the DoD "Risk Rule" as currently implemented. Navy policies which implement the risk rule should be modified to reflect the changes made in Issue M.  (Adopted:  Y:9 N:4 A:2)*

### Overview

Concur with the first sentence of the Majority Recommendation as adopted.  A consistent position against the assignment of women to combat requires retaining and enforcing the DoD Risk Rule.  It also demands exempting women from assignment to combat vessels.

********************

## ISSUE P:  TRANSITION PROCESS

*What transition process is appropriate if servicewomen are to be given the opportunity to be assigned to combat positions in the Armed Forces?*

*MAJORITY RECOMMENDATION:  The integration process should be accomplished in an orderly fashion and without undue haste.  Any necessary modifications to vessels, equipment and facilities should be done during the normal course of maintenance in a fashion that minimizes cost.  Additionally, the integration process should be consistent with the Commission's recommendations on Issues D and G.  (Adopted:  Y:11 N:3 A:1)*

### Overview

Concur with the Majority Recommendation as adopted.

78

## ISSUE Q:  CONSCRIPTION

*Should women be required to register for and be subject to conscription under the Military Selective Service Act:*

> *(a)  on the same basis as men, if women are provided the same opportunity as men for assignment to any position in the Armed Forces?*

> *(b)  on the same basis as men, if women in the Armed Forces are assigned to combat positions only as volunteers?*

> *(c)  on a different basis than men if women in the Armed Forces are not assigned to combat positions on the same basis as men?*

**MAJORITY RECOMMENDATION:**  *Women should not be required to register for or be subject to conscription.  (Covers a-c)  (Adopted:  Y:11 N:3 A:0)*

### Overview

<u>Concur with Majority Recommendation as adopted.</u>  However, the legal precedent exempting women from conscription is based on the recognition that men and women are not "similarly situated," i.e., men are assigned to combat and women are not.  Partial repeal of the exemption regarding Navy combat ships might undermine that precedent and leave women vulnerable to conscription should Congress reinstate the draft.  It should be noted that the Navy conscripted men during World War II.

The Commission's vote on Issue M is therefore inconsistent with its vote on Issue Q, which supported continued exemption of women from conscription.  Because womens' exemption from the draft is inextricably tied by legal precedent to their exemption from combat duty, the only way to avoid the risk of losing that exemption from the draft is to embrace a *consistent* policy against assigning women to any combat military occupation specialty. (CF 4.1 through 4.8)

# III.
# COMMISSIONER
# STATEMENTS

A Dissent From the Recommendation on the Exclusion of Women From Combat Aviation

Dissent on Ground Combat

Dissent to Retention of the DoD Risk Rule

Dissent to the Exclusion of Women From Amphibious Vessels and Submarines

Commissioners' Statement on Conscription: National Service

Individual Commissioner Statements

# A DISSENT FROM THE RECOMMENDATION ON THE EXCLUSION OF WOMEN FROM COMBAT AVIATION

We, the seven undersigned Commissioners, oppose the recommendation adopted by a one-vote majority of the Commission with regard to the assignment of women to combat aircraft. That recommendation suggests the enactment into law of current DoD and Service policies that restrict servicewomen from assignment to Army, Air Force and Naval aircraft flying combat missions, despite the fact that Congress repealed such statutory restrictions on the assignment of women aviators in the Air Force, Navy and Marines in 1991 by an overwhelming margin.[1] The majority recommendation is an unjustified step backward, which may detract from the military effectiveness of the U.S. Armed Forces, and is based on patronizing and antiquated views of women, rather than on their proven abilities and performance potential. We support the establishment of gender-neutral standards for assignment to combat aviation which would allow placement of individuals into those positions on a best-qualified basis.

Military effectiveness and readiness are best served by the Armed Forces' ability to put their most qualified servicemembers into any position where their skills can be best utilized. The Commission's recommendation prevents the Services from doing so with respect to combat aircraft without empirical rationale.[2] In the absence of evidence that important governmental interests would be detrimentally affected, we should not deny women the opportunity to serve their country in the field of combat aviation. The proponents of the Commission's recommendation have never provided such evidence.[3]

Presently, women have qualified as pilots in all high-performance aircraft, with the exception of the A-3, F-14 and F-15.[4] For over ten years, the Navy has trained women in combat aircraft, including air combat maneuvering and weapons delivery. These women, in turn, have trained male Navy and Marine Corps pilots in these skills. In Desert Shield and Desert Storm, women aviators flew AWACS, reconnaissance, transport and refueling aircraft, and assault helicopters.

We recognize and have fully explored the physical strength and endurance differences between men and women. However, we found no evidence -- nor were proponents of the aviation exclusion able to produce any evidence -- that these physical differences affect performance in the cockpits of combat aircraft, just as they now do not affect performance in support aircraft.

An aircrew member's physical capability to perform under combat conditions or in combat aircraft has been found to be a function of individual ability. Physical capability is not a gender issue; neither all men nor all women could qualify as combat aircrew members. Empirical data and the overwhelming majority of testimony presented before the Commission support the conclusion that the supposed physical barriers to women's successful performance in combat aviation simply do not exist.[5] No evidence was presented that proved that physiological differences between men and women would prevent women from performing as well as, or better than, men as combat aviators.[6] The Commission found that the potential for fetal damage in the early stages of pregnancy (during the first nine days, before which pregnancy can be confirmed) appears to be the only notable medical concern in allowing women access to all aviation careers.[7] The risk involved due to flying within this period, however, is no greater than can be expected when undergoing a wide range of other occupational and recreational activities.

Further, the Commission found no persuasive arguments to preclude the assignment of women to the B-1, B-52, or the planned B-2 bomber. The bombers, in fact, have flight performance characteristics and combat mission profiles that are quite similar to those aircraft that women aviators in the Air Force currently fly, i.e., tankers and transport aircraft.

With regard to G-force tolerance in high-performance tactical jet aircraft, no convincing evidence was produced to support the contention that women could not adequately tolerate such stresses as well as men across the performance envelopes of these aircraft.[8] According to Dr. Richard Jennings, a shorter aviator with less distance between his/her eye and heart is more likely to have higher G-tolerance.[9] Centrifuge test data shows no significant difference in tolerance between the genders up to 7 Gz.[10] While one 1992 study with a small sample size showed that there is a slight difference in G-tolerance between men and women at 8 Gz, the author of the study attributed the difference in tolerance to improperly fitted G-suits.[11] This 1992 study also found no significant difference in tolerance between men and women at 9 Gz. Both the Air Force and the Navy reported to the Commission that they can easily custom fit existing G-suits for both men and women aviators.[12]

Because women's physical capability to perform in combat aviation is not seriously in dispute, one must explore other reasons to justify the majority's recommendation to statutorily exclude women from combat missions. These other reasons seem to fall into four subject areas: cohesion, cost, conscription and involuntary assignment, and prisoners of war (POWs).

While the impact of placing women in combat aviation on unit cohesion is a concern, cohesion in aviation units is not a gender issue. Cohesion is a function of leadership, shared purposes, and common risks and rewards. A unit is susceptible to cohesion problems when someone "different" is injected into it, when that difference is perceived to be a contributing factor to the deterioration of unit performance.

No research data is available regarding the effect on unit cohesion of placing women in squadrons that have an offensive aviation combat mission. Therefore, there is no evidence that cohesion would be affected.[13] Evidence does exist, however, regarding cohesion in non-combat aviation units with demanding missions that have become integrated. It shows that cohesion either remained at the same level as in the all-male unit or improved after the entry of women into the unit.[14]

The concern for cohesion voiced by fighter pilots who testified before the Commission came overwhelmingly from young, inexperienced pilots and was based on the fear of the unknown of having women in the squadron.[15] The three experienced Navy and Air Force combat Vietnam veterans who appeared before the Commission, and who between them flew over five hundred combat missions, agree that the exclusion should be lifted on combat aviation.[16] The reasoned voices of these distinguished veteran officers call into serious question the dire consequences of integration which are predicted by the younger and far less experienced pilots.[17]

81

Related to cohesion is the issue of military and public opinion -- what does the military community and society-at-large think about women flying in combat aviation? In a survey of the military community conducted on behalf of the Commission, 43 percent of those surveyed stated that women should be able to volunteer for assignment to combat aircraft.[18] Twenty-five percent responded that they should be required to accept such assignments. Thus, a total of 68 percent of those surveyed believe women should be able to compete for assignment to combat aircraft.[19] When asked in a national public survey whether women should be assigned to combat aircraft, 53 percent of those surveyed said they should be able to volunteer for such positions, while 25 percent said women should be required to accept those assignments.[20] Seventy-eight percent of the individuals surveyed, therefore, believe that women should be able to compete for assignment to combat aircraft.

With regard to the cost element, each Service reported that no modifications would need to be made to combat aircraft in its inventory if combat assignments are opened to women.[21] This judgment is reinforced by the fact that women have already qualified in nearly all of these, or very similar, aircraft. As with physical requirements and cohesion, aircrew anthropometric accommodation is not a gender issue. Rather, it is a "small and large" aircrew problem.[22] While modifications may be necessary to accommodate a wider range of aircrews than is currently provided for in certain aircraft, it may not be feasible for the Services to make such modifications if the individuals who would be newly accommodated would not meet current aviation entrance standards set by the Services.[23] Also, the Services would be under no obligation to make any modifications to accommodate an expanded range of aircrews. Concerns about increased cost, therefore, could not reasonably justify excluding women from combat aviation.

Throughout the Commission's existence, a few Commissioners expressed concern about the inevitability of requiring women to register for the draft if any combat positions were opened.[24] Any fear in this regard, however, could not legitimately justify excluding women from combat aviation, given that aviation assignments are voluntary and competitive, and exclusions are expected to continue in the combat arms of direct land combat.

Finally, a large part of the debate surrounding this issue has focused on the increased risk of women becoming POWs as a result of their assignment to combat aviation. The decisive vote was cast in favor of legislating the existing exclusion policies because of the POW factor.[25] The Air Force conducts Survival, Evasion, Resistance, and Escape (SERE) training that is open to all of the Services. In addition, the Navy and the Army also have SERE schools. Most offensive aviation combat aircrews undergo such training. Evidence demonstrates that women perform as well as men in SERE Training.[26] Despite the women's performance, the claim has been made that the presence of women POWs would be detrimental to national security because of the chivalrous and protective instincts of men toward women: men would provide information to an enemy who threatened to torture a woman POW.[27] SERE training addresses this issue in training for both men and women, recognizing that protective tendencies are not limited to one gender.[28]

Current policies do not prevent women from becoming POWs. Two servicewomen, Major Rhonda Cornum and Specialist Melissa Rathbun-Nealy, were taken prisoner of war during

Desert Storm. Major Cornum explained to the Commission that she was subjected to indecent assault while in captivity.[29] America, as well as Major Cornum and Specialist Rathbun-Nealy, survived their ordeal, with no evidence that their capture was a greater threat to national security than the capture of the men who were with them.[30]

While we recognize the horrors that POWs are forced to suffer, we do not believe that women who are willing to accept those risks should be restricted from competing for combat aviation assignments because of the protective tendencies of others.[31] Women will be taken prisoner in future wars, regardless of whether they continue to be excluded from combat aviation. It is time that the American public recognize that women are capable of accepting the risks associated with the opportunity to serve their country. Laws and policies based on paternalistic notions do not demonstrate the value society places in women. More importantly, they preclude the best fighting force. They demean women's intelligence and abilities, deny them the respect that they deserve as equal members of society, and deny the Armed Forces the use of the best qualified individuals.[32]

In 1948, President Truman ordered the racial integration of the Armed Services through the issuance of Executive Order 9981. He stated, in the first sentence of the Order, that "it is essential that there be maintained in the Armed Services of the United States the highest standards of democracy, with equality of treatment and opportunity for all those who serve in our country's defense." Today, our country is again faced with the exclusion of individuals in the military, not for what they have done, but because of who and what they are. Since 1948 "equality of treatment and opportunity" has benefited not only those black Americans who were previously excluded from positions in the Services, but also the country as a whole, which has had the equal opportunity to receive the talent, courage and dedication of these individuals. It is time once again for the country to benefit from the rich contributions that an excluded group, women, has to offer the Armed Forces.

While a belief in equality of opportunity is a cornerstone of the value system of most Americans,[33] it is not the primary consideration at issue here. The primary issue is the ability of the Armed Forces to draw from the most talented and capable pool of individuals when selecting combat aviators. No compelling evidence has been presented during the tenure of this Commission to persuade us that qualified women would not be able to compete on an equal basis with men for assignment to combat aviation positions. They should be able to compete, based on their performance as aviators. The result would be the best qualified force.

Respectfully,

| | | |
|---|---|---|
| Robert T. Herres | Mary E. Clarke | Thomas V. Draude |
| General, USAF (Ret.) | Major General, USA (Ret.) | Brigadier General, USMC |

| | | |
|---|---|---|
| Mary M. Finch | James R. Hogg | Newton N. Minow, Esq. |
| Captain, USA | Admiral, USN (Ret.) | |

Meredith Neizer

83

# ENDNOTES

1.   National Defense Authorization Act for Fiscal Years 1992 and 1993, Sec. 531, P.L. 102-190, December 5, 1991.  The legislation passed unopposed in the House of Representatives and by a vote of 69-30 on the Senate floor.  The Army has never been statutorily restricted from assigning women to combat aircraft.

2.   When testifying before the Commission, Brig Gen Michael Hall, USAF (Ret), stated:  "[A]s a commander charged with implementing this [exclusion] policy, I cannot acceptively explain to myself or to those I lead why job-qualified women are denied opportunity because of their gender...Job skill qualification for assignment consideration is the only full supportable basis to make decisions." Testimony before the Commission, Sept. 11, 1992, p. 238.

Capt Stuart Greenwald, USMC, a CH-53 pilot, testified that he saw no reason why women should be excluded from flying in the Marine Corps.  He felt that if women were allowed into the field the Marine Corps would benefit because the quality of available pilots would improve as a result of an increased candidate pool. Testimony before the Commission, Aug. 28, 1992, p. 440.

3.   Commissioner Robert Herres, General, USAF (Ret), made the following statement during debate: "I must tell you that the case has not been made to continue the exclusion of qualified women who compete on a best qualified basis for assignments from combat aircraft.  That case has just not been made." Commission Hearing, Nov. 3, 1992, p. 277 (Draft Transcript).

4.   The following is a partial list of the aircraft in which women have qualified as pilots and crewmembers:  A-4, A-6, A-7, F-4, F-86, F-16, F/A-18, TA-4, T-2, T-34, T-28, T-38, T-37, C-2, C-1, T-39 (no aircrew positions), KC-10, KC-135, C-27, C-141, C-5, P-3, E3A, EA-6B, S-3, U-2, H-47, H-53, H-60, H-1, H-2, H-3, and H-46.  Additionally, they have qualified as crewmembers in the A-3, F-14, and F-15.

Currently, there are eight countries recruiting female military aircrew, including the United States.  Of these, six countries -- Belgium, Canada, the Netherlands, Norway, Spain and Great Britain -- have legislation which allows women to fly in combat.  Advisory Group for Aerospace Research and Development (AGARD) Conference Proceedings, No. 491, *Recruiting, Selection, Training and Military Operations of Female Aircrew.*  Presented at the Aerospace Medical Panel Symposium, Tours, France, April 4-5, 1990.

5.   Even Navy and Air Force fighter pilots who oppose placing women in combat aircraft stated that women were physically capable of performing.  See Testimony of LT Tom Downing, USN, Top Gun Panel, Aug. 6, 1992, p. 353; Testimony of Capt John Rush, USAF, Air Force Fighter Pilot Panel, Aug. 28, 1992, p. 144.

84

6. To the contrary, in the 1960s, thirteen out of twenty women pilots successfully completed tests used in the initial Mercury Astronaut Candidate Testing Program. "The women took an exhaustive battery of 75 physical, laboratory, x-ray, and physical competence tests, the same designed as qualifying criteria for the Mercury astronauts. Results in many cases determined that the women not only equaled, but in some instances surpassed the results attained by the men who participated in the testing program." *Jerrie Cobb*, **Ninety-Nine News**, Apr. 1991, at 14.

7. Finding 2.3.6.

8. Commissioner Herres stated during the debate that "[t]he G-tolerance case has not been made." Commission Hearing, Nov. 3, 1992, p. 278 (Draft Transcript).

9. Dr. Richard Jennings. Testimony before the Commission, Aug. 28, 1992, pp. 206-07. Mr. Hugh Moreland, General Dynamics, Aug. 26, 1992.

10. Gillingham, 1986.

11. Fischer, Wiegan, 1992.

12. Findings 2.6.1F and 2.6.4F.

13. Statement by Commissioner Darryl Henderson, Commission Hearing, Aug. 6, 1992, p. 316.

14. Cohesion may be negatively impacted at first, but through studies and testimony the Commission learned that cohesion was as good, if not better, after integration of women than in previously all-male units. Pre-integration studies which focused on men's attitudes regarding women being integrated aboard Navy ships reflected much of the same sentiment that Naval aviators now argue. Post-integration studies found that men enjoyed working with women on average, and women tended to feel more performance pressure, and, thus, worked harder to gain approval from their male counterparts. Acceptance was based on ability, which is one of the key ingredients in building cohesion within the unit or squadron. Greebler, et. al., 1982. Greebler and Thomas, 1983. Testimony before the Commission, Aug. 6, 1982, pp. 363-64.

CDR Chuck Deitchman, USN, who commands a HC-11 integrated squadron, reported to the Commission that the men in his unit initially voiced the same arguments expressed by the Top Gun pilots (see Note 15 below). According to CDR Deitchman, they soon discovered, however, that they were operationally better with women than they were prior to integration, and the esprit and camaraderie was as good as when the unit was all-male. Testimony before the Commission, Aug. 6, 1982, pp. 363-64.

Col Jack Holly, USMC, Combat Service Support Operations Officer for all Marine Corps Logistics Support in Southwest Asia, testified: "Esprit and bonding, we've had no problems.

In fact, a good commander is able to capitalize on that. A good commander knows that women want to work harder to be perceived as equals, and that males don't want to be outdone by their female counterparts, and they generate a synergism that gives you quality of excellence within that organization. And I wouldn't give that up for anything." Testimony before the Commission, Aug. 28, 1992, p. 249.

Commissioner Herres, during the debate on opening combat aviation to women, stated: "We've heard testimony about what has happened to cohesion in units when it was expected to deteriorate drastically. Units were integrated. Women performed admirably, and cohesion improved rather than deteriorated." Commission Hearing, Nov. 3, 1992, p. 277 (Draft Transcript).

15. LT Tom Downing, USN: "I believe right now there are women that can do it. . . . That is not the issue that we have to look at. It's how that woman affects the men that are doing that job, and that is -- my personal feeling is that that is what is going to do it, and you can't grasp it, you can't put it on a piece of paper, you can't do a study about it. It's just something in here." Testimony before the Commission, Aug. 6, 1992, p. 353.

Capt Dave Freaney, USAF: "I guess I'm old-fashioned in my values, but I cannot see myself running around with my flight of four, you know, doing the town in Song Tong City with -- if one of them was a girl...I think it would affect, you know, the effectiveness of my flight squadron." Testimony before the Commission, Aug. 28, 1992, p. 157.

16. Brig Gen Fig Newton, USAF, testified: "As professional aviators given the task of going out and supporting one another, I don't think it would change a bit [if women aviators are introduced into the fighter pilot community]. Again, I repeat that the kinds of things, such as that strong cohesiveness that you do, whether it's in peacetime, whether we deploy for an exercise, or what have you, we'll continue to do those things that are important for the mission...I am convinced of it." Testimony before the Commission, Aug. 28, 1992, p. 158.

Maj Gen Bob Dempsey, USAF, Chief of Staff, Air Mobility Command, testified: "I would have to say, if a female is fully qualified -- that's fully qualified -- she should be allowed to do whatever it is that is under consideration...if they (women) have been through the same sorts of experiences and meet the same entrance standards, they can hack it!...Do you trust your wingmen, and you've got to be able to trust your wingmen, and I think that would come naturally. If they have been brought through the same sorts of experiences and met the same entrance standards, they can hack it. I don't see why they couldn't, again, with the fully qualified disclaimer...I think it's got to be a single standard, because I think the double standard would introduce an undermining that would go at the cohesion, morale, and other things." Testimony before the Commission, June 1, 1992, pp. 189, 273. ( Gen Dempsey has been a pilot in the F-4, a B-52 Wing Commander, and a B-1 Wing Commander. He flew 201 combat missions in the Vietnam War.)

86

CAPT Rick Hauck, USN (Ret.), Vietnam veteran and NASA Astronaut, testified: "I would have no problem going into combat with a highly trained, highly motivated woman as my bombardier-navigator, or as my pilot, or as my wing person, or as my flight leader...We in the United States can ill afford to deny ourselves the advantage of allowing the most capable people to fill every job -- each and every job. The key ingredients, as I see them, are: first, the motivation of the individual to accomplish their job; second, the leadership that establishes the environment that encourages or demands teamwork; third, the pursuit of a clearly defined goal; fourth, the training that gives the individual the skills to work toward that goal. A key element in all of this is mutual respect." Testimony before the Commission, November 1, 1992, pp. 72-73. (CAPT Hauck is a Vietnam veteran, and served 28 years in the Navy on destroyers and carriers as an A-6 pilot. He flew 114 combat and combat support missions. He has also flown the A-7, F-14 and F-4. CAPT Hauck has participated in three space shuttle missions and was the Mission Commander of two. He was the Mission Commander of the first flight after the Challenger accident.)

17. CDR Bob McLane, USN, Commanding Officer of Top Gun, testified: "I don't think that women have a problem in flying fighter aircraft...I don't have any heartburn at all with putting a woman out on my wing and flying up to Iraq or anywhere else we happen to go and blowing somebody away." Testimony before the Commission, Aug. 6, 1992, pp. 318-19.

18. Finding 3.14 (military survey conducted by The Roper Organization).

19. It should be noted that individuals are not involuntarily assigned as combat aviators.

20. Finding 3.14 (national public survey conducted by The Roper Organization).

21. Findings 2.6.1B; 2.6.2; 2.6.3; 2.6.3A; 2.6.4A.

22. Commission Panel 2 Report, pp. 103-04.

23. Findings 2.6.1B and 2.6.3A.

24. The Commission, in an eleven to three vote, recommended that women not be required to register for or be subject to conscription. *See* Discussion of Issue Q.

25. See "Panel Seeks to Limit Women in Combat" *Washington Post,* Nov. 4, 1992, at A3. "The prisoner-of-war issue, however, was the deciding factor for Thurman, the swing vote against opening air combat slots. 'The idea that we would position women in the arena of being subjected to violence, death, depravity as prisoners is one I won't sign up to,' he said afterward."

26. Col John Graham, USAF, Director, Joint Services SERE Agency, testified: "The key point I think that I would like to make, as the executive agent for overseeing captivity training, is that women can adapt and survive captivity. In some cases, they have shown to do this better than men. These same studies show that in many cases it is the cultural background of the woman or the person that is in as a POW that is more important than biological factors such as age or sex." Testimony before the Commission, June 8, 1992, p. 204.

27. Mr. Robert Dussault, Deputy Director, Joint Services SERE Agency Training Division, testified: "Well, I think it [mens overprotectiveness of women] comes out. What I mean, I think it gets eliminated with training. I'm not identifying it as a problem. I think we are really saying, all up here, the same thing, that we feel we can train women and men for a captivity environment where that no longer will be a problem." Testimony before the Commission, June 8, 1992, pp. 230-31.

28.   According to SERE instructors, resistance to this tactic, i.e., showing the captor that it is ineffective, is the only way to minimize the enemy's use of it.

Maj John Bruce Jessen, USAF, Psychologist, Joint Services SERE Agency, testified: "Females were rather neutral in their response to how they would react if another female were exploited. Females were rather neutral in their response if another -- if a male were exploited." Testimony before the Commission, June 8, 1992, p. 228.

29.   Testimony of Former Prisoners of War before the Commission, June 8, 1992, p. 60.

30.   During Operation Desert Shield/Desert Storm, U.S. Aircrews downed and prisoners captured by Service (Information provided by DoD):

    A. USMC:

| | |
|---|---|
| Total number of aircrew | 2588 |
| Total number of captured aircrew | 5 (5 returned) |
| Total percent captured | **0.19%** |

    B. THE NAVY

| | |
|---|---|
| Total number of aircrew | 37,086 |
| Total number captured | 3 |
| Total number KIA | 6 |
| Total percent captured and KIA | **0.024%** |

    C. THE AIR FORCE

| | |
|---|---|
| Total number of aircrew | 5754 |
| Total number captured | 8 |
| Total number MIA | 17 (declared KIA) |
| Total percent captured and MIA | **0.43%** |

31. MAJ Rhonda Cornum, USA, testified regarding society's concern about female POWs being subject to rape and abuse by their captors. She stated, in part, that "[b]eing raped in downtown D.C. or Peoria, Illinois, or somewhere like that is very different than getting raped in a military -- you know, as a POW, just like getting shot. You know, you don't expect that to happen when you walk down the streets of your home town, but it is an occupational hazard of going to war, and you make the decision whether or not you are going to take that risk when you join the military. And so I really think that it is a phenomenon of our society that we worry about it much more than the people who undergo it." Testimony of Former Prisoners of War before the Commission, June 8, 1992, p. 14.

VADM William Lawrence, USN (Ret.), Vietnam POW, when asked how women would handle a POW situation, testified: "Women are tough as hell. And they can handle the POW environment just as good as any man." Testimony before the Commission, June 25, 1992, p. 114.

32. With regard to the POW issue, Commissioner Draude made the following statement during the combat aviation debate:

> [T]his issue [of women being taken POW] is an extremely emotional one. We've spent a great deal of time on it. Although the numbers are relatively small, and we've attempted to get that information -- both percentages and numbers -- it's still people we're talking about. So let's go beyond the numbers and, as Commissioner Minow would indicate, let's put some faces on this and let's talk about people. And when I talk about women aviators, the face that I see is of my daughter Loree. As you know, she's a Navy jet pilot in training in the FA-18 in LeMoore right now. I am proud beyond words of her achievements and the fact that she has chosen a profession to serve her country and to make use of her talents the way that she has and, regardless of what she chose, she would continue, along with her brothers, to be the lights of my life.
>
> But now it's call for question, Draude. Put up or shut up. How do you come down on it? Would you let your daughter fly in combat with the possibility of her becoming a prisoner of war? And my answer is yes, because I believe that we have to send in our best to support our best, and if that means my daughter and my son, and they're the best, and they're the ones who have to, then take up the gauntlet, take up the cudgel, and do what has to be done. So they should go.

Commission Hearing, Nov. 3, 1992, pp. 250-52 (Draft Transcript).

33. Finding 3A10.

# DISSENT ON GROUND COMBAT

We, the undersigned Commissioners, do not concur with the Commission recommendation to retain and codify existing Army policies as they relate to the assignment of servicewomen to Army Aviation, Field Artillery, Air Defense Artillery and Combat Engineers.

Combat power is a function of fire and maneuver, time and position, judgement and luck, and the leader: a whole that is greater than the sum of its parts. These are factors that transcend gender, Service and branch.

A military organization that puts any factor at higher value than the national defense is derelict in its duty. A military organization that allows its combat power to erode or denies itself combat power multipliers does its duty incompletely.

There are four factors that must be addressed regarding the exclusion of women from Army Aviation, Field Artillery, Air Defense Artillery and Combat Engineers. These factors are cohesion, living conditions, fighting as infantry in case of emergency, and the possibility for a combatant becoming a prisoner of war (POW).

### Aviation

Women pilots are now in combat. They fly in the same airspace and are shot at with the same anti-aircraft weapons the same as combat helicopter pilots. The only difference is that they can't shoot back. Women should be allowed to fly attack helicopters. Aviation should be open to the best soldiers available, regardless of gender. Women military aviators have been trained according to male standards. They have measured up in every respect. Why hold women aviators back and keep them from operationally flying all aircraft? It is not a matter of capability but it is a matter of male attitude.

### Field Artillery

Few women currently serve in the Field Artillery as most positions and all weapons systems previously opened to women have been phased out in recent years. Women served effectively in some specialties of the Field Artillery, but the very restrictive assignment policies which they were subjected to have made a viable career path impossible; many were removed and retrained into other occupational specialties. There was no evidence that the women were not contributing, but rather that the convoluted and arbitrary nature of the Army's assignment policy prevented their effective utilization. The Field Artillery branch should be reopened to women and there should be no restrictions on their assignment within the branch. Gender neutral, performance-based physical strength and endurance standards for Army specialties should be adopted as recommended in the full Commission report.

90

### Air Defense Artillery

Women currently play a limited role in the Air Defense Artillery. They attend the same initial training as their male counterparts, but then are restricted to rocket units. These rocket units are located further to the rear areas than the Short Range Air Defense Systems from which woman are restricted. This rear area would have the supposed effect of limiting the risk of death to women. In reality, the long range weapons systems to which women are assigned are a high priority target for the enemy aircraft and Air Defense Systems and are less mobile; therefore, they are more susceptible to enemy attack. These assignment restrictions limit women's professional development within their branch and hence, their ability to contribute, while not giving them any greater protection from risk. The Air Defense Artillery should be totally open to women. Gender neutral strength/endurance and performance-based standards should be adopted as recommended in the full Commission report.

### Combat Engineers

Women currently serve in 24 of 29 enlisted Military Occupational Specialties and all of the officer and warrant officer specialties. They undergo the same training and can demonstrate the same skills as their male counterparts, but are restricted from serving in certain units. Although Combat Engineers have a secondary mission of infantry support, testimony highlighted that combat engineers only receive weapons firing training once a year. This, of course, places a tremendous artificial burden on the personnel system. Despite a demonstrated ability to carry out the tasks expected of them in their specialty, they are not allowed to be assigned to many positions in that specialty.

All engineer positions at brigade level and above should be open to women. By doing so, positions at battalion level and below, which would require women engineers to collocate with the infantry and armor units, should remain closed, but all other positions should be opened. As Major General Christman, Commanding General of the U.S. Army Engineer Center, said: "Female soldiers are already versed in each of these areas and have clearly demonstrated their tactical and professional competence in engineer positions currently open to both sexes. Why ignore this tremendous resource?"

### Relevant Issues

#### Cohesion

Cohesion is a function of individual and group confidence, self confidence, confidence in peers, and confidence in leaders. Individual and group confidence is engendered in military organizations by team building, close association, mutual experience and, ultimately, proven success. The large number of mixed gender organizations that habitually associate, undergo stressful mutual experience, and are proven successes is a matter of public record in every police force, hospital, and mixed-gender military organization in the United States. Cohesion is not a single gender experience, it is a function of good leadership, trust, competence and shared experience.

91

### Prisoners of War

Since U.S. military women have already been POWs, this issue is a question of degree. Undeniably, there will be more women POWs if the exclusion policy is lifted; however, the treatment of POWs is the real issue, not the marginal percentage increase in women POWs. As with our current national policy, we hold our enemies responsible for the treatment of our imprisoned servicemen and women. We will continue to do so. Recent events have reiterated that American memories are long regarding POWs. They are slow to forgive mistreatment, and they never forget. In the Gulf War, two American servicewomen were taken prisoner by the enemy. They have both experienced the risks all servicewomen take by membership in the military. Although neither of these women were in combat specialties, they were still not protected from the risk of becoming a prisoner. Servicewomen understand and accept such risks.

Additionally, U.S. military personnel are protected under the Geneva Convention relative to the treatment of Prisoners of War (August 12, 1949). History is full of the abuse and atrocities visited on non-combatants, in uniform and out. If we do not treat our military women as combatants, we can not expect our enemies to do so.

### Living Conditions

War is brutalizing, and one of the most brutalizing aspects are the living conditions. The lack of privacy, cleanliness, and fresh clothing are inconveniences compared to the loss of respect for humanity and the discounted value of human life that is the result of grinding exposure to prolonged combat.

Women currently train and fight under these conditions. Dropping combat exclusion policies for Army Aviation, Field Artillery, Air Defense Artillery, and Combat Engineers would not change this situation.

### Acting as Infantry in Case of Emergency

One of the arguments used to maintain the combat exclusion policies in Army Aviation, Field Artillery, Air Defense Artillery and Combat Engineers is that if these positions were to fall under attack, all personnel would have to fight as infantry soldiers. This is already true for both men and women, and is not made less true by combat exclusion policies. If anything, it creates a false expectancy in women soldiers that, as non-combatants, they can neglect basic soldier skills. Such false expectations increase the degree of risk to themselves and others, while making our forces less capable.

Mary E. Clarke
Major General, USA (Ret.)

Mary M. Finch
Captain, USA

Meredith Neizer

92

# DISSENT TO THE RETENTION OF THE DOD RISK RULE

We, the undersigned Commissioners, do not agree with the Commission's recommendation to retain the DoD Risk Rule. The Risk Rule has been the unrealistic, inappropriate and subjective standard by which women are restricted from roles in which they could make a valuable contribution, thus limiting the full utilization of all personnel in the Armed Forces. It is now time for this outdated rule to be eliminated.

The DoD Risk Rule was developed in 1988 to help standardize the Services' assignment of women deploying to a hostile area. However, each Service interprets the DoD Risk Rule to reflect its own land, air and sea operational theater environments. The DoD Risk Rule states:

*Risks of direct combat, exposure to hostile fire, or capture are proper criteria for closing noncombat positions or units to women, when the type, degree, and duration of such risks are equal to or greater than the combat units with which they are normally associated within a given theater of operations. If the risk of noncombat units or positions is less than comparable to land, air or sea combat units with which they are associated, then they should be open to women. Noncombat land units should be compared to combat land units, air to air and so forth.*

The DoD Risk Rule was never designed to prevent women from being placed in harm's way. The chaotic environment of war precludes this from occurring. While the DoD Risk Rule has been used to guide planning in the past, the reality of combat, the fluidity of the modern battlefields, and the warfighting doctrine of the U.S. Armed Forces bring into question the validity of such a rule. Lethal and sophisticated weapons have greatly expanded the size of the battlefield to "over the horizon" fighting. Front lines are losing their meaning in an age of fluid battles and highly mobile forces. Military combat support and combat service support personnel, such as logistical, technical and administrative services, are increasingly at risk of injury, capture or death regardless of their location.

Thus, the dynamics of modern combat have irretrievably altered the assumptions behind the Risk Rule. These dynamics are reflected in current military warfighting doctrine. At the highest level, Joint Publication 1, <u>Joint Warfare of the U.S. Armed Forces</u>, (promulgated by the Chairman of the Joint Chiefs of Staff in full coordination with the Service Chiefs and warfighting CINCs) recognizes the changed nature of battle:

- *Warfighting environment.* Joint Publication 1 recognizes the impact of technology on expanding the breadth, depth, scope, and impact of war to unprecedented ranges, due to the impact of precision munitions, information processing, and lethal striking power.

- *Operational conditions.* In discussing the synergy of today's joint force, the publication says:

*Synergy is reinforced when operations are integrated and extended throughout the theater **including rear** areas [emphasis added]. The full dimensional joint campaign is "nonlinear." That is, the dominant effects of air, sea, space, and special operations may be felt more or less independently of the front line of ground troops. The impact of these operations on land battles, interacting with the modern dynamics of land combat itself, helps obtain the required fluidity, breadth, and depth of operations.*

Joint Publication 1 was foreshadowed by similar shifts in Service doctrine. The U.S. Army's Air-Land Battle doctrine (FR 100-5) and the U.S. Marine Corps' renewed emphasis on maneuver warfare (FMFM 1) both stress the fluid nature of combat and the need (in the Army's terminology) to fight the deep, close, and rear battles simultaneously and with equal emphasis.

As concrete reflection of these doctrines, during Commission hearings, service members made frequent references to the fact that some members of combat support units were "ahead" of ground combat units in Desert Storm. For example, Captain Becky Jones commanded the 418th Transportation Company that moved into Iraq ahead of many combat units. In an area with land mines, Jones' troops set up a fueling station. Additionally, the Marines Direct Support Command (with over two hundred women) occupied positions forward of the 1st and 2nd Marine Divisions before the ground war began.

Moreover, many military women believe that they were "in combat" (Moskos and Miller Survey 1992), even though the Department of Defense reported to Congress and the Commission that "current laws and policies were followed" during the deployment to the Persian Gulf (in other words, the DoD Risk Rule was observed). In yet another case, the Marine Corps awarded twenty-three women the Combat Action Ribbon because they were engaged by, or came under enemy fire with Iraqi troops. Additionally, two Army women in combat support and combat service support units were captured and taken prisoner.

Women and men alike were exposed to the risks of Scud attack, chemical warfare and the possibility of an Iraqi counterattack. In other testimony, Major Robert McElroy noted that female technicians who accompanied Multiple Launch Rocket System (MLRS) crews into Iraq, "were as close to the front as anybody." (MLRS's are deployed with infantry units.) In fact, there were instances when the repair technicians got ahead of the vehicles they supported.

Women and men were also exposed to the risks of capture during Desert Storm, regardless of specialty. The two women POWs were in noncombatant specialties. Not allowing servicewomen to accept the same risks as men, due to possible capture and mistreatment as POWs, equates to treating them as children who are incapable of making important decisions and who need to be told what risks they should or should not accept. Servicewomen understand and accept the inherent risks of being in the military regardless of assignment or specialty. All servicewomen are at risk; they accept that risk and they do not want to be protected from positions of risk or held back from positions of responsibility due to the misdirected concerns of senior military leaders and decision makers.

These examples serve to illustrate the difficulty of segregating combat, combat support, and combat service support units in a highly mobile combat environment. In fact, trying to distinguish between combatant and noncombatant has become an increasingly specious, irrelevant, hair-splitting debate, and the effectiveness of the Risk Rule has been reduced to evaluating who is allowed to shoot back. The Risk Rule is demeaning to the service of men and women alike, since those not designated as in "combat positions" are made to feel like second-class citizens.

The DoD Risk Rule is an unrealistic standard upon which to base assignment policies. It limits the full utilization of the U.S. Armed Forces by not allowing women the opportunity to serve in those areas where they could contribute. The Risk Rule does not keep women from being under hostile fire, captured or killed. We deem the Risk Rule an inappropriate, subjective and unenforceable standard which should be eliminated.


Mary E. Clarke
Major General, USA (Ret.)

Thomas V. Draude
Brigadier General, USMC

James R. Hogg
Admiral, USN (Ret.)

Mary M. Finch
Captain, USA

Newton N. Minow

Meredith Neizer

## DISSENT TO THE EXCLUSION OF WOMEN FROM
## AMPHIBIOUS VESSELS AND SUBMARINES

We, the undersigned Commissioners, fully concur with the Commission's recommendation to repeal the current law, which prohibits the assignment of women to vessels with a combat mission. However, we are concerned that the recommendation to exclude by policy certain classes of ships from the assignment of women would be perceived as directive in nature and would unnecessarily restrict the flexibility of the Secretary of the Navy. Maintaining the readiness of naval forces requires that the Secretary have the authority to utilize fully all resources, to include both personnel and ships, in an optimal manner. Inherent in this authority is the determination of those ships, by class or type, which for reasons of extensive habitability modifications, or early decommissioning schedule would make the assignment of women impractical. The Secretary of the Navy is in the best position to make these determinations, and thus ensure the efficient use of all personnel resources, Navy and Marine Corps. Therefore, the current law should be repealed without qualification. The Secretary of the Navy should be given maximum flexibility to meet the requirements of the Naval Services by utilizing their best qualified personnel.

Mary E. Clarke
Major General, USA (Ret.)

Thomas V. Draude
Brigadier General, USMC

James R. Hogg
Admiral, USN (Ret.)

Meredith Neizer

Mary M. Finch
Captain, USA

Newton N. Minow, Esq.

Robert T. Herres
General, USAF (Ret.)

# COMMISSIONERS' STATEMENT ON CONSCRIPTION:

## NATIONAL SERVICE

The Selective Service System brought together millions of American men from all walks of life in the service of their country. Conscription also fostered an ethos of civic responsibility now severely eroded. In addition, G.I. Bill benefits made available job training and higher education to millions of young people. The time is ripe to consider a new version of public service.

Young women and men should be required to participate in a universal national service program with civilian and military options. The military option will be consistent with the recommendations of this Commission and not contravene the effectiveness of the All-Volunteer Force.

Mary E. Clarke
Major General, USA (Ret.)

Thomas V. Draude
Brigadier General, USMC

William Darryl Henderson, PhD
Colonel, USA (Ret.)

James R. Hogg
Admiral, USN (Ret.)

Newton N. Minow

Charles C. Moskos, PhD

97

# MARY E. CLARKE
## Major General, USA (Ret.)

I accepted the appointment to the Presidential Commission on the Assignment of Women in the Armed Forces because I believed my experiences serving in the United States Army from WWII until 1981 would enable me to assess objectively the proper roles for women in the Armed Forces today.

Early on in the deliberations, it became clear that a number of the Commissioners had come with a set agenda and no amount of facts or testimony would change their minds for expanding opportunities for women in the military. This was evident in their questioning techniques of those whose testimony they thought might support women in combat, absenting themselves when they knew testimony would not support their views, and their insistence upon using equal opportunity as a red herring rather than recognizing women's capabilities and contributions to the military services.

In their comments, they constantly used the words "degradation of the mission" when discussing women in the military, even though testimony from commanders of mixed-gender units in all of the services disputed their assumptions.

They refused to acknowledge that Desert Shield and Desert Storm was the type of action that would make a case for expanded roles of women in combat. It would be interesting to interview the families of those who lost their loved ones in this intense conflict as to whether it was combat or not.

One of the most disturbing aspects of their assertions was that many of the active duty military personnel who testified in support of women in combat were unduly influenced by internal and external forces and therefore were not speaking their own minds out of fear of the impact on their careers. I find this insulting to our professional officers and noncommissioned officers.

The Commission was thorough in following the guidance provided in our charter. I participated in several fact finding trips, attended every meeting of the commission, interviewed military men and women and listened to testimony for and against women in combat. My assessment: There is absolutely no reason to keep women out of combat aircraft or combatant ships.

Finally, I would comment on those Commissioners, presumably professional adults, who walked out on the rest of the Commission because they were out-voted on their proposal to amend the agenda. This resulted in their refusal to participate in the process of all of the issues, returning only to vote on those that interested them and that were the critical combat-related ones. I believe this action, on their part, impacts on their credibility, objectivity, and fairness and gives credence to the belief that their minds were made up from the first.

Service on the Commission was a privilege and an experience I will never forget. It is my belief that the results of our findings and recommendations will be of assistance to the President and the Congress in determining an increased role for our military women to enhance the readiness of our country's defense.


Mary E. Clarke
Mary E. Clarke
Commissioner

## SAMUEL G. COCKERHAM
### Brigadier General, USA (Ret.)

*Current Army policy (AR 600-13) closes all specialties with a mission of direct combat i.e., infantry, special forces, armor, cannon artillery, short range air defense, combat engineer and combat aviation. It also closes positions whose routine mission includes collocation with a direct combat unit (i.e., a mechanic or medic position in an infantry unit is closed).*

Military necessity, encompassing national security, combat readiness, combat effectiveness and mission accomplishment was the primary consideration governing my actions as a Commissioner. I gave top consideration to the security and safety of young soldiers, sailors, marines and airmen serving in combat units. We depend on these young men to defend our vital interest and national sovereignty.

The introduction of female personnel into the direct combat environment, which includes combat aviation consisting of APACHE, COBRA and KIOWA Scout helicopters, is a giant distraction that would reduce the effectiveness of combat units across the board. I believe an all-male combat force is the most effective one, and that the current policy of excluding women from "closed" positions be retained.

I fully support Army policy (AR 600-13) and recommend that the Secretary of the Army be given authority to re-examine specialties in combat support and combat service support units to preclude the unnecessary training of female soldiers in specialties that are closed. For instance, I do not believe female soldiers should be trained as heavy track vehicle mechanics, for the ultimate goal of heavy track mechanics is to keep the tanks, and other armored vehicles running in combat.

In the assignment and utilization of women in the Armed Forces, I gave consideration to two approaches: equal opportunity for all members of the Armed Forces and military necessity. I asked myself if the Commission would make a politically correct statement or if it would make its decision on the premise that we must do all we can to protect our nation's vital interests? The politically correct decision would fully support equal opportunity, primarily, and would support secondarily, the goal of military necessity and combat readiness. I chose military necessity as my primary consideration in evaluating the facts gathered by the Commission on whether or not women should be assigned to combat units of all Services. In the words of John Dickinson, a delegate from Delaware to the 1787 Constitutional Convention, "Experience must be our only guide, reason may mislead us."

I believe the current exclusion policies and the DoD Risk Rule provide our nation with its greatest combat capability, especially during the current unstable nature of world conditions, and the drastic force structure reductions all Services are now experiencing. The world has changed, but the nature of combat has not. **Combat always was, is now, and always will be hell!**

*Samuel G. Cockerham*

# ELAINE DONNELLY

During the past eight months, Commissioners visited a number of military bases as part of the fact-finding process. During the many visits I made to bases all over the country, I gained valuable insight from the men and women in uniform who spoke with us and shared their opinions on the subject of women in combat. The following are personal observations and excerpts from the trip reports on file at the Commission:

## Marine Corps - Parris Island/Twenty-Nine Palms/Quantico

In June, women Marines at Parris Island said they preferred to train hard on a single-sex basis, as opposed to training in mixed-gender units. The women performed very well on the "fast rope" and other confidence-building exercises, but the men's training exercises are much more violent and include boxing and pugil stick fighting at Leatherneck Square.

At the Marine Corps Air-Ground Combat Center at Twenty-Nine Palms in California which we visited in July, women Marines expressed little interest in integrated training, co-ed quarters, or combat assignments on the same basis as men.

At Quantico's Officer Candidate School (OCS), the toughest officer training programs remain single-sex and are scored differently to compensate for physical differences. Contrary to recent news reports, we learned that few changes have been made that would suggest women are being trained for combat exactly like men. Although Marines of both sexes throw one grenade from behind a protective wall while attending The Basic School (TBS), the Marines have found that many women cannot throw a grenade beyond the bursting radius.

## Army - Fort Bragg

The highlight of the trip to Fort Bragg was a live-fire field exercise of an assault on an entrenched bunker. We saw several infantrymen carrying heavily-laden fellow soldiers off the battlefield. Some witnesses before the Commission expressed their belief that two or more soldiers, including women, could successfully evacuate a soldier off a battlefield. The infantrymen responded, however, that when under fire the burden must be borne by one soldier because others are needed to continue the attack or to provide defensive cover. In Commission briefings about cohesion, witnesses said a soldier's greatest fear is being left behind when wounded in battle. The ability to rescue a wounded soldier -- and confidence of being rescued -- is an essential element in the trust that must exist in a cohesive ground combat unit.

## Air Force and Naval Aviation - Nellis AFB/NAS Miramar "Top Gun"

Trips to Nellis AFB and the Naval Air Station at Miramar focused on the many issues surrounding combat aviation; i.e., the multi-million dollar cost of training pilots, physical demands related to G-forces, alternative ground assignments, unit cohesion, the prisoner of war question, aeromedical concerns, and problems related to pregnancy and lost time. With some exceptions, most combat aviators were opposed to the assignment of women to air combat units, primarily because of their concerns about the potential effects on unit cohesion which might decrease mission effectiveness and risk lives.

Two Navy and Air Force pilots talked of their experience with double standards in some areas of aviation training, in which some women were not allowed to fail. A follow-up inquiry regarding the Navy showed higher

101

attrition rates for women at most levels of training, but virtually no attrition compared to men in the training for some specific aircraft. (See CF 19 plus accompanying table, OSD Question #3)

## Navy - Special Warfare Command (SEALs)

The trip to Naval Amphibious Base Coronado for a meeting with Navy SEALs confirmed that the physical strength and unit cohesion required to assemble a successful team makes the assignment of women to SEAL teams virtually impossible for women and for most men as well. The success of a SEAL mission depends on heavy survival gear and weapons which the men must carry on their backs. We were also told that forced physical intimacy between the SEALs is frequently necessary on covert land and sea missions. At this base and elsewhere, I noted that support for women in combat seemed to be in inverse proportion to the proximity of actual combat responsibilities and experience.

## USS John F. Kennedy and Other Navy Ships

Visits in July to a tender, an Aegis cruiser and an amphibious ship at the 32nd Street Naval Station in San Diego, the aircraft carrier *USS John F. Kennedy*, plus two attack submarines at Norfolk in October, highlighted the many military and social issues involved with the question of women on combat ships.

Our visit to the carrier *USS Kennedy*, which included a "trap" landing, catapult launch, and the opportunity to witness dozens of take-offs and night landings, was an unforgettable experience. The men aboard the *Kennedy* had been encouraged to speak their minds. Many expressed opposition to the assignment of women to the *Kennedy* or any other combat ship, listing such reasons as physical strength and lost time due to pregnancy, privacy/habitability, and interpersonal relationship issues. Aboard this ship and others, many expressed concern about inevitable romantic involvements and the risk of false charges of sexual harassment. "Leadership" alone, they said, is not the answer. (The average age of sailors aboard the ship is 19.) A number of sailors and officers expressed disappointment -- and even feelings of betrayal -- that Navy leaders have allowed the Tailhook sexual assault scandal to tarnish the entire Navy, giving impetus to an unjustified push for women in combat.

We learned from this trip and others that although Navy officials have a policy of "zero tolerance" regarding sexual harassment, interpersonal relationships on the romantic side are considered acceptable, provided that they do not occur on board ship, between persons in the same unit, or between persons of different ranks. It is reasonable to expect that this policy will lead to foreseeable problems if women are assigned to combatant ships.

## Air Force - F-15 Eagle Flight

At Nellis Air Force Base, I asked so many questions about G-force that the Commanding General invited me to come back for a ride in an F-15 Eagle. On August 5, I returned to experience the ride of a lifetime, starting with a climb to 14,000 feet, streaking straight up. The pilot took me through loops, rolls and other acrobatics, and it was easy for me to understand why combat aviation has such a strong appeal for many men and some women. The first hard turn -- registering 7.8 Gz -- pinned me to the canopy without the strength to move. I gained a healthy respect for anyone who can experience that force and maintain the situational awareness necessary to fight an enemy at the same time.

Having experienced the exhilaration of the "Eagle" flight, it made sense to find out in my next trip what happens when the pilot must eject, when he leaves the relative safety of his cockpit and hits the ground to become a prisoner of war.

## Air Force - Survival, Evasion, Resistance and Escape (SERE) Training

During my August 9-11 visit to the Survival, Evasion, Resistance and Escape (SERE) Training facility at Fairchild Air Force Base, I experienced a small part of the training that prepares both men and women aircrew members for life as a POW. Without knowing what to expect, I found myself locked in a cramped black box that was both physically and psychologically uncomfortable. I also participated in and witnessed interrogation exercises designed to suggest but not duplicate the physical and emotional stress of being a POW.

As the night wore on, a sense of cultural dissonance began to overcome the camp's logic of equality in the simulation of brutality. A woman I watched being interrogated was very capable, but she was totally in the power of a man much stronger than she. What I saw was an unmistakable element of *inequality* which -- in the opinion of many Commission witnesses -- cannot be overcome by peacetime training programs or psychological techniques. As the interrogation continued, it was easy to visualize the possibility of sexual abuse as well as physical harm at the hands of a menacing enemy.

For reasons of survival, SERE training for aircrew members makes sense, and the camp does a good job in this specialized area of military training. However, the politically-correct unisex nature of the resistance training is very seductive; it's easy to become "desensitized," meaning accustomed, to the idea that men and women are interchangeable equals in a world of torture and abuse. The SERE trainers asserted that the entire nation must prepare itself for this very real possibility if women are assigned to combat positions.

The SERE program crystallizes the cultural debate over women in combat. If it is necessary to desensitize the nation to the grim possibility of women being brutalized on an equal basis with men, is that a step forward for civilization, or a step backward? And if the military is being asked to lead the way for social change, where will it lead us?

Whatever the answers to those questions, the purpose in highlighting these thoughts about Commission trips is to give a voice to those members of the service who did not have an opportunity to appear before the Commission but whose views are important nonetheless. They, after all, are the ones who will live and possibly die because of policies that may be implemented in response to this Commission's report. The American military is the finest in the world, and we have an obligation to keep it that way.

*Elaine Donnelly*
Elaine Donnelly
Commissioner

# THOMAS V. DRAUDE
## Brigadier General, USMC

I reported to the Commission with an open mind regarding the question of the proper role of women in combat specialties, despite combat experience virtually devoid of the presence of women. I also made it known that my daughter was in the U.S. Navy and undergoing jet pilot training and my son is a Navy Intelligence Officer.

I took my oath eagerly and listened carefully to the charge of our Chairman: to evaluate objectively the evidence we would receive regarding this critical issue. I believe, however, that objectivity was not the goal of every Commissioner. Some arrived with a pre-determined agenda and sought to sway the Commission in their direction. They displayed their bias in their questions, their comments, and their absences during testimony with which they disagreed.

After evaluating the information gathered through testimony, public and military polls, fact-finding trips, and intense research, I concluded that the issue of women in combat -- ground, sea and air -- comes down to two questions: "can they?" and "should they?"

Without question, they can serve in combat aviation and aboard combatant vessels, to include submarines and amphibious ships. Moreover, I believe they should serve in these specialties and would succeed. The noncombat sectors of these specialties already experience gender integration. The empirical data proves that women are valued members of the aviation communities of the Army, Navy and Air Force, and the shipboard environments of the Navy and the U.S. Coast Guard. Despite the obligatory "machoism" of junior fighter pilots who want the ready room to remain their last bastion, I am convinced from the evidence presented that women can compete and win. (I found it disturbing that the Commission voted down a proposal to merely assign women to combat aviation on a test basis. What have we to fear - success?)

I view ground combat differently. Women cannot, for the most part, serve in the physically demanding environment of ground combat. For those who are physically able to handle the rigors of ground combat, the next question, "should they?" is relevant.

As I stated during the debate on ground combat, I do not believe women should serve in the infantry. My experience in infantry combat leads me to conclude that their presence, regardless of their performance, would be disruptive. This is simply because the fabric of unqualified love necessary to hold men together in infantry combat would be torn by the sexual tension caused by the presence of women. It's not anyone's fault, it's just the way men are. That women are forced to pay the price for this reality is unfortunate to say the least. However, military effectiveness could be threatened as a result of the almost assuredly negative effect that would result from the integration of women into the infantry.

104

Throughout the tenure of the Commission two contentions caused me to object each time they were raised in the hearings: the credibility of Washington-based military witnesses who supported the expansion of roles for women in the Armed Forces and the importance of the Gulf War.

First, questioning the integrity of the Washington-based witnesses was raised six times, by my count, and was patently a case of doubting the testimony of military personnel -- doubting their moral courage. The contention was that they were supportive because they were swayed by political pressure and were not speaking their real beliefs. These aspersions were beneath contempt.

Second, some Commissioners consistently denigrated the performance of women in Desert Shield/Desert Storm by denigrating the war. It was, in the view of these Commissioners, not really combat and not really a war. This notion is an insult to every Gulf War veteran, man or woman.

In closing, I wish to quote, "It is essential that there be maintained in the Armed Services of the United States the highest standards of democracy, with equality of treatment and opportunity for all those who serve in our country's defense." These are not my words and they are not about women in combat. This Presidential quote opens the 1948 Executive Order regarding racial integration of the military. However, there are interesting parallels which I invite to your attention: The President was talking about racially integrating the Armed Forces, which had been closed to black Americans, not for what they had done but because of who and what they were. Similarly, women are currently being denied the opportunity to fully serve their country solely because of their gender. The President used the words "equality of treatment and opportunity" not "military necessity" because the impetus of military necessity would not come until two years later with the Korean War. Military effectiveness was significantly improved by racial integration when the talents, courage and dedication of black Americans were finally used without restrictions. I have every confidence that the same enhanced effectiveness would result from gender integration of combat aviation and all combatant vessels. To best ensure our national security, we must give women the same chance to prove to our great Nation their talents, their courage and their dedication.

I view this opportunity to have served on this Commission as a true highlight of my thirty-four years of service to my country. My support of an expanded role for women in the Armed Forces is my final contribution. I believe we must fill our ranks with our best, regardless of gender, and God forbid send our best to fight and win our wars. In doing so I will proudly risk far more than other Commissioners -- I risk my son and my daughter.

Thomas V. Draude
Brigadier General, USMC

105

# MARY M. FINCH
## Captain, USA

I believe this Commission was established by Congress to make a completely objective assessment of the present and future assignment of women in the Armed Forces. Regrettably, the conservative make up of the Commission did not allow for objective assessment. Those members with current or previous ties to conservative groups had the effect of tipping the results of Commission work against any progress for servicewomen.

Women have proven their value to the Armed Forces and their positive effect on military readiness. Most recently, their exceptional performance in the Gulf War led to the repeal of exclusion laws regarding aircraft and the establishment of this Commission. Unfortunately, it took great effort and much persuasion to get a majority of Commissioners to even acknowledge that any lessons could be learned from Desert Shield and Storm regarding the performance of women.

I do believe, however, that the Commission did uncover a great deal of information and opinion through testimony and research. All of this work should not be ignored. In fact, much important data has been left out of the formal report due to the Commission's conservative bias. Others should read the testimony to separate fact from opinion and emotional argument. The views and opinions of Commissioners who were unencumbered by political agendas should be carefully reviewed and more weight given to fact than emotion.

As a Commission member and active-duty Army officer, I believe that the work of this Commission has been an insult to all servicewomen. From the start, a minority of conservative Commission members attempted to demean and degrade servicewomen and their accomplishments at every turn. Through supposed expert testimony to outright distortion of facts, some Commission members attacked the abilities of women in jobs to which they are already assigned, and disparaged those senior military officials who spoke out in favor of women; all in the name of preserving the supposed high status of women in American society and American family values. These Commissioners would have liked us to believe that were the roles of women in the Armed Forces to expand, American society would be led down the path of moral corruption from which it would never return. Although such emotional arguments have little appeal to me, apparently they had some following amongst the most conservative Commission members. These arguments do a great disservice not only to servicewomen but to all Americans who work to better themselves, their families and in turn American society.

I urge those who review this report and the work of the Commission to do greater justice to our servicewomen, servicemen, and Armed Forces. Military readiness is best accomplished by selecting the best American for the job, not just the best "man" for the job. Military readiness is everyone's primary concern.

Mary M. Finch
Captain, USA

106

# WM. DARRYL HENDERSON, PhD
## Colonel, USA (Ret.)


Cohesion research to date has been useful in considering the problems associated with integrating women into ground combat units. These concerns are reflected in the Commission's report. However, research on cohesion conducted to date has not been very useful in attempts to examine the effects of integrating women into support units, fighter aircraft, and combatant ships. The technological nature of these positions indicates to some that cohesion in these types of units should be considered a more individual, non-gender based phenomenon. While technology is a significant factor, it remains just one of many factors operative on cohesion in these units.

Cohesion research must be accomplished that examines these units under conditions that bring factors of stress, survival, and accomplishment of mission to the fore, as well as technology. When this research has been accomplished, then we will be able to assess the impact of integrating women into these units with more certainty.

## JAMES R. HOGG
## Admiral, USN (Ret.)

### Parental and Family Policies

As a Commissioner who contributed significantly to the debate on the issue "Parental and Family Policies," and one who remains sensitive to the needs of military single parents and their children, I believe it is important to introduce a note of special caution for those who might develop constraining personnel policies on the basis of the Commission's recommended alternatives in this area.

One theme expressed by Commissioners who feel that single parents should be discharged or constrained from deployment is that childcare planning by deploying parents will be inadequate. This fails to recognize the adequacy of the vast majority of childcare plans now in effect, or that military single parents are responsible adults who should be permitted the freedom of choice in such matters -- until such time as military readiness may be impacted. If military readiness is not impacted, these constraining policies are clearly discriminatory.

"Corrective" personnel policies, at times, bring unintended negative results. This is especially so when societal judgements are involved. Such would be the case here, which underscores my note of caution. For example, transferring a servicemember from an operational/deployable unit to a nondeployable position prevents service in the types of assignments essential for qualification in operational specialties; so, the individual is automatically made less competitive for professionally challenging assignments in the future, for promotion, and thus for continued service. In the military vernacular, this is called "second-teaming."

Viewing this issue from another perspective, these constraining policies could generate major personal problems for both parents and children. I say this because, under a policy that "single parents with custodial care of children be discharged," there are only three courses of action available for a career motivated servicewoman.

- *Discharge* (involuntarily) once the child is born. This would, in effect, return the military to the unsatisfactory "forced discharge due to pregnancy" policy of the recent past.

- *Marriage.* This could result in a quick marriage of convenience that may not necessarily be in the best interests of either individual and could eventually adversely impact the child. Additionally, if the marriage were to another servicemember, then difficult career decisions would have to be made by the dual-service couple which could cause further internal strife in the marriage.

- *Abortion,* which is obviously objectional to many individuals.

108

The case I have outlined presents only one of a number of realistic scenarios that single parents -- women <u>and</u> men -- would be forced into by constraining policies derived from alternatives such as those recommended by the Commission. It is my considered professional opinion that the impacts in all scenarios would be highly undesirable, both for the military Services and for individual servicemembers.


James R. Hogg
Admiral, USN (Ret.)

## NEWTON N. MINOW

I blew out the candles on my 18th, 19th and 20th birthday cakes in Army Mess Halls during World War II. I was a sergeant in the China-Burma-India Theater where our battalion built the first telephone line along the Burma Road to connect China with India. I never fired a gun at the enemy, but I was close enough to understand the ghastly horror of war, and I never forgot it.

The only American women we saw were Army nurses and Red Cross workers. At that time, it was unthinkable that women could or should be in military combat. Our whole idea of military service was that it was men protecting women and children safe at home.

I could not have imagined that in my lifetime approximately 40,000 women would be among the Armed Services blowing out birthday candles in the Persian Gulf. Of the women sent to fight that war, thirteen were killed and two were taken prisoner. According to the Department of Defense, none of the women killed or captured were engaged in "combat" -- as "combat" is now defined by our Armed Services. But of course that is clearly wrong. And so a Presidential Commission was created by Congress to assess the role of women in the Armed Forces.

In today's technological fighting, with laser guided bombs, heatseeking missiles, Tomahawks, satellites, AWACS, Hellfires, SLAMS, and Patriots, the traditional military definition of "combat" is hopelessly artificial and obsolete. As military technology continues to advance and the size of our active-duty force is reduced, the need for more brains and less brawn in our Armed Forces will accelerate. We have already seen in the Persian Gulf that, although current laws and regulations officially exclude women from combat, they do not stop women from being killed or captured by the enemy.

The issue was more than just defining "combat." It was also answering the argument that we had to make a choice between equal opportunity for women and national security. To me, there was only one issue--national security. And only one answer: our national security would be diminished by excluding half the brains, talent and courage from the defense of our country.

But what of physical strength, a major issue in the assignment of combat duty? Even in the 21st Century, some combat will include hand-to-hand fighting. Some members of the panel advocated separate physical tests for men and women. Until we can persuade our military adversaries to do the same, that's just unworkable. Each assignment should have tests of bona fide qualifications that should be gender-neutral.

A number of witnesses testified that the presence of women in combat assignments would destroy the cohesion, morale and mutual trust needed for teamwork in the Armed Forces. These are the same arguments advanced in the past against the integration of racial minorities into the military. In 1948, President Truman integrated the services. The disproportionate number of minorities who now serve in the military make it clear that the effectiveness of our Army, Navy, Air Forces, Marines and Coast Guard would be severely impaired if they were excluded from service. General Colin Powell is outstanding proof of that success.

Congress also asked the Commission to consider the legal and policy implications of conscripting women on either the same or a different basis than men. My own view is that Congress should enact a universal one-year public service requirement that applies to both men and women at age 18. This requirement could be fulfilled through many choices in the type of service, including military, educational, environmental, public safety and law enforcement, and public health.

For me, the toughest issue is the effect on the family lives of the men and women who serve in our Armed Forces. A major issue is the effect on children. Today's American military force on active duty includes 76,238 single parents and 46,704 dual-military parents. During Desert Storm, 32,048 children were separated from a single parent who was deployed to the Gulf; 4,656 were separated from both parents. This is wrong, and the question needs far more serious attention than it has received so far. In the case of a dual-military parent family, I believe that a couple should decide in advance which one will be subject to deployment. The other should be assigned in advance to stateside duty only. In the case of single parents up for deployment, the single parent and the Department of Defense must get much more assurance in advance that the children will be well cared for, both while the parent is deployed and in the event the parent is killed. As our military force becomes smaller with the end of the Cold War, we can develop a much more sensitive balance between family and military obligations.

The most unforgettable witness I heard was Major Rhonda Cornum, an army flight surgeon and mother who was shot down during a helicopter rescue mission behind enemy lines. Eight people were in the helicopter, seven men and Major Cornum. When the helicopter was shot down, five of the men were instantly killed; Major Cornum and two men were injured and taken prisoner. Major Cornum suffered a bullet wound in her right shoulder. Her leg and both her arms were seriously injured. The Iraqi soldiers transported Major Cornum in a pick-up truck to a small prison. Major Cornum was sexually molested by one of the Iraqi captors in the pick-up truck. A fellow male prisoner helplessly watched. When she was liberated, she was greeted by General Schwarzkopf. Major Cornum smiled over her two broken arms and said, "I normally salute Four Star Generals."

When asked for her opinion about women in combat, Major Cornum replied: "A soldier needs physical and moral courage, ingenuity and integrity, determination and loyalty, a sense of humor, and of course luck, to be successful in combat. I do not believe and did not see any evidence that these qualities are distributed on the basis of gender or race."

My wife and I have three daughters and three grandchildren (two are granddaughters). We do not want any of them in military combat. But what if the United States was at war and our children and grandchildren were mentally and physically able to serve? All six are eligible someday to become President of the United States and thus Commander in Chief. Why should our country be deprived of the talent and commitment all six could contribute to keeping our nation safe and free?

Newton N. Minow, Esq.

# MEREDITH A. NEIZER

I accepted an appointment to this Commission because I was truly interested in assignment policies for women in the military after Desert Shield and Desert Storm. As a civilian, I relied on the media for updates on our military efforts during the Gulf War. It was clear to me during the deployment and the war that military women were essential and contributed greatly to the war effort. In my opinion, military women were in combat and will continue to serve in combat areas in future conflicts. Therefore, I was not surprised about the next evolution of broadening assignment policies soon after Desert Storm.

The seventeen recommendations contained in the Commission Report synthesize what I believe are the critical issues that need to be addressed by the Department of Defense. Assignment of women to combatant vessels is long overdue. I hope the President and Congress repeal the combat vessel exclusion legislation quickly, and the Navy proceeds with assignment of women to these vessels as soon as possible. Although I do not agree with one particular recommendation, combat aviation, I believe the recommendations are factually based and substantiated by our research.

Regarding combat aviation, I believe the recommendation reflects a vote of emotion and conscience of women as POWs, as opposed to performance and ability. In my opinion, current assignment policies will not protect women aviators and crewmembers from being taken prisoners of war. A rollback of policy is needed to insure such protection, yet that was not the Commission's recommendation. Testimony before the Commission by female aviators clarified their acceptance of this risk, and I believe they should be able to serve our Nation as they choose.

It was a rare opportunity for me to work with many of my fellow Commissioners. They were objective thinkers who were well versed in current military doctrine and personnel policies. They were dedicated to our mission and a pleasure to work with. I was intellectually challenged because of them, and I walk away professionally stronger. The dedication of the Commission staff was also critical to successful completion of our work.

Regarding the "traditional" advocates amongst my fellow Commissioners, I can only say they were a complexity that aggravated the Commission's work. Although they were given a voice and many accommodations were made for them, I believe any recommendation contrary to their viewpoint would never have satisfied them. Their actions say more than I ever could in writing.

Finally, I would like to thank Sea-Land Service, Inc. for allowing me the time to participate in this important military work.

Meredith A. Neizer
Commissioner

113

# RONALD D. RAY

Combat is the most competitive, challenging and physically demanding of human endeavors. Battles and wars for thousands of years have involved armies of men engaged against each other often fighting for national survival. No military in history has willingly chosen to send women as combatants to fight another nation's male soldiers simply because men are inherently better designed for such savage activity.

Often during the Commission's proceedings, testimony was heard which strongly advocated the assignment of women to the combat arms. Though often emotionally compelling, the best such testimony, upon reflection, was really nothing more than sophistry which Plato defines as, "making the worst appear the better cause": that is, using language as a tool of persuasion rather than a means of stating the truth. There was passionate testimony given but little truth was offered or found to support such a drastic change in 375 years of American history and the tradition of exempting women from combat.

The Commissioners who have prepared and signed the Alternative View Report have been accused of demeaning and degrading servicewomen and, somehow, their military service; of having a conflict of interest; and of advancing some unnamed "conservative" cause ahead of the national interest; in short; of misrepresentation and telling lies. This could not be farther from the truth. We do, however, represent the large majority of the American people who remain unconvinced that any possible "equality" gains supposedly to be made from assigning women to combat can outweigh the serious and very likely losses. It was apparent early on that during the hearings that there was no military reason for assigning women to combat given there are unquestionably sufficient numbers of able-bodied men to meet the nation's combat manpower requirements, especially with the significant reductions scheduled for the military. One then concludes that there is another force which is at work. David Horowitz's testimony, as a former 60's anti-war protester and communist sympathizer, offered his insight into this other force behind the "movement" to see women in the combat arms:

> *Gender feminism holds that women are not women by nature, but that the patriarchal society has "constructed" or created them female so that men could oppress them. The system that created them females is called "gender-patriarchy." As the source of their oppression, it must be destroyed. Radical feminists are social engineers in the same way that Communists are social engineers. They deny that there is a human nature, and they deny that there is a female nature, that biology in anyway fundamentally influences who or what we are. The solution to all social problems, conflicts and disappointments in life is to manipulate law and institutions so as to create liberated human beings -- beings who will not hate, have prejudices, exhibit bad sexual manners, get into conflicts, or go to war. By changing institutions especially powerful institutions like the military, and using their administrative powers to brainwash people into adopting attitudes that are politically correct, these radicals believe that the problems that have plagued mankind since the dawn of creation will be miraculously cured. Of course, the gender feminists are not so naive as to admit their radical agendas...they will say that placing women in combat positions is merely an extension of women working outside the home, and of expanding equal opportunity.*

114

The truth is best gained from asking those with actual experience, the ones with the most information on the subject. The Commission inquired, by letter and questionnaire, America's largest living resource on military service and combat, the retired flag and general officers. This extraordinary universe of people was uniquely qualified and offered a research opportunity which is rare indeed. Each possible respondent, on average, had more than 30 years of actual wartime and operating force experience. Therefore, the survey was very reliable, comprehensive and complete, not a mere poll or a random sample.

The 6,109 flag and general officers were queried and approximately 3,500 responded immediately. About one thousand sent letters to give the Commission further benefit of their experience. At the end of the process over 60 percent had responded. **Their responses spoke strongly of their admiration for military women's contribution and service: 63 percent responded that women serving in the military was a success story.** General Joseph J. Went, former Assistant Commandant of Marine Corps, expressed the retired officers sentiments very well:

*My own experience with servicewomen in peacetime is that well qualified, motivated women perform just as well as well qualified, motivated men, and on occasion, better. Simply said, my experience with women in uniform has been very positive. But combat is another matter.*

Even with their positive experience with servicewomen, the majority of retired flag officers adamantly opposed assigning women to combat specialties: 90 percent said NO to women in the infantry; 76 percent said NO to the assignment of women on combat vessels; and 71 percent opposed assignment of women to fighter/bomber aircraft. The primary reason given for their opposition appeared to be the negative impact on military unit cohesion. General Robert Barrow, former Commandant of the Marine Corps and a highly decorated combat veteran of three wars, summed up this issue as he testified, on June 18, 1991, before the U.S. Senate Armed Services Committee on assigning women to combat:

*Those who advocate change have some strange arguments, one of which is that there is a de facto women in combat situations already. That women have been shot at, that they've heard gunfire, that they're close to danger is not combat. Combat is a lot more than that...combat is finding, and closing with, and killing or capturing the enemy...it's killing, that is what it is. And it is done in an environment that is often as difficult as can possibly be imagined. Extremes of climate, brutality, death, dying, it's uncivilized...The requirements for strength and endurance render them [women] unable to do it. And who would be called upon to pick up the rifle and do these things in the ground combat area. The one's who don't want to do it, as well as the ones that are not qualified...I know the female Marines; they're terrific, know them well. They serve with great skill, they have a spirit about them; they're creme de la creme and most of them -- I've never met one -- who wanted to be an infantryman. Who wants them to be an infantryman? The hard line feminists do, they have an agenda, and it doesn't have anything to do with national security. The feminists want to put our daughters at risk, and the other attendant problems that result from such situation...sexual harassment, fraternization, favoritism, resentment, male backlash, all of these things would be an insurmountable problem to deal with. Who deals with that? Not some faceless bureaucrat or political appointee over at the Pentagon, but the corporals and the sergeants, second lieutenants and the captains who have to maintain good order and discipline and also fight the war. IT DOES NOT WORK.*

In conclusion, it may be informative to know more about what has prepared me for service on the Commission: I am a Christian, a husband and the father of three daughters and one son. My work is as an attorney and I am a Marine Reserve Colonel. I served during Vietnam, saw combat and was awarded two silver stars and a purple heart. I have also served in the Pentagon as Deputy Assistant Secretary of Defense.

As a military historian, and as a Christian, I sought direction from the Bible. Earlier in this writing, a feminist view on this issue was presented. I am keenly aware that these two world views, Feminism and Christianity, are in opposition. Christianity is like the military and calls for the subjugation of self to a higher authority. Many feminists find great fault with the Scriptures because of this and believe the Bible to be limiting and the ultimate "patriarchal" document. However, I hasten to add here that General George Washington, our first Commander and Chief, said "it was impossible to rightly govern without God and the Bible," [David Barton, The Myth of Separation (1991)]. For those of us who concur with President Washington and look to the Bible for guidance, it offers the following as Stephen Schlissel, a minister who testified before the Commission, advises:

> In God's law, there is priority given to family over warfare. The military laws of the Old Testament specified the age and gender of combat soldiers: "All able-bodied men twenty years old and up were eligible for military service (Numbers 1:2,3,18,20,45; 26:2,3) This single standard long prevailed and was, for example, the basis of operation in the American War of Independence. We also find in the Bible bulwarks of protection provided to classes of people in accordance with their vulnerability. Acknowledgement of and regard for the vulnerability of a given class results in societal peace. God's declared concern for the "widow and the orphan" is a familiar refrain in Holy Writ. Of all the laws in the Bible, the only accidental act which calls for the death penalty is the destruction of embryonic life (Exodus 21:22-25), because that is the life in need of the most protection. Thus, God's law calls for graded deference. This principle of **deference** is based upon **difference**. In human societies, the treatment accorded women is directly related to the accurate understanding and frank acknowledgement of the real differences between women and men. "Likewise, you husbands, dwell with them with understanding, giving honor to the wife, as to the weaker vessel..." (1 Peter 3:7) Peter, in calling women "the weaker vessel," does not berate or demean her, but simply acknowledges biology and self-evident realty. This "weakness" is the occasion for the injunction to accord women special honor and consideration.

The Supreme Court understood this concept of differences and concurred in Jenness v. Fortson, 403 U.S. 431, 442, (1971):

> Sometimes the grossest discrimination can lie in treating things that are different as though they were actually alike...

_R. D. Ray_

Ronald D. Ray, Esq.

116

# MAXWELL R. THURMAN
## General, USA (Ret.)

The Commission has ratified the current direct combat exclusion of women from air and land assignments in our Armed Services. My reasons for keeping direct combat land units as an all-male force are outlined below. My rationale for retaining the exclusion of women from combat aviation rests in the risks to which combat aircrews are subject, risks which are similar to those faced by direct combat ground troops. I am convinced by the polling data, however, that the American public doesn't fully appreciate the similarity between direct combat land forces and combat air crews and pilots. Direct land combat with the enemy, and air combat over hostile territory with the inherent risks of shoot-down, casualty rates, and the probability of capture, are much more alike for soldiers and airmen than the dissimilar experience of serving aboard most surface combatant vessels. These differences are detailed below where I discuss aircrews, surface vessels and the impact of our recommendations on the draft.

### Assignment To Direct Combat, Land Forces
#### The Central Issue

Central to this issue is the fact that the bulk of American casualties -- wounded, dead, captured -- suffered in American wars in this century have been in units that are engaged in close combat on land.

The leadership tasks, the most dangerous and the most difficult leadership tasks, fall to captains, lieutenants, and noncommissioned officers of land combat units engaged in direct combat with the enemy. The leadership challenge at this level stems from the brutal impact of casualties on unit cohesion, and the need for tactical teamwork in foul weather under hostile fire in appalling living conditions, with the constant threat of disease, wounds, mental stress, death and capture. The challenge to young leaders is to overcome all human disinclination to advance under fire, under risk of death, or to hold ground under desperate conditions.

The sexual activity experienced during Desert Shield and Desert Storm, as reported in the Commission's Roper military poll, shows that 64 percent of the military personnel who served in Desert Shield and Desert Storm in mixed-gender units reported incidents of sexual activity between men and women in their units. In the Army and the Marine Corps, 74 percent and 73 percent, respectively, reported sexual activity between men and women in their units. Mixed-gender units in the Persian Gulf were combat support and combat service support units, not combat units. However, the inference can be clearly drawn: where young men and women are in continuous close proximity of each other, away from their families and under months long stress of imminent combat, human sexuality will manifest itself. It seems to me to be dysfunctional to seriously encumber small unit direct combat leaders, noncommissioned officers, and lieutenants and captains with the enormous burden of relations between the sexes during the prosecution of the harshest tasks of the battlefield -- closing with and defeating an armed enemy, with the inherent risks of death and capture. Sexuality in small units in a combat situation can create catastrophic problems for already severely burdened units and their leaders.

### Commission Polling

What do serving military personnel think about women serving in land combat units? The Roper poll reports that 74 percent of the military personnel polled say no to women in the infantry, 72 percent say no to women in Marine infantry, 66 percent say no to women in Special Operations Forces, 59 percent oppose women in tank crews, and 54 percent say no to women in the artillery. When one asks the same question of military personnel who actually serve in the combat arms, the numbers jump to 83 percent against women in the Army infantry, 83 percent against women serving in Marine infantry, 82 percent against women serving in Special Operations Forces, 71 percent against women serving in tanks, and 64 percent against women serving in artillery. Those that serve in the combat arms know the arduousness of service in those branches.

117

When surveyed by The Roper Organization, 52 percent of the American public questioned said women should not be assigned to the Marine infantry, and 57 percent said women should not be assigned to Army infantry units. Forty-seven percent of the American public said that the current exclusion laws should be changed, while 44 percent approved the current exclusion laws. With a plus-or-minus 3 percent polling error, the combat exclusion issue is a draw with the American people.

### Who Will Serve

And finally, who will serve in the land direct combat forces? The 1992 Miller-Moskos survey of more than 800 Army servicewomen reports that only 12 percent of the enlisted Army women and only 10 percent of the female noncommissioned officers would consider service in direct combat units. Currently serving Army enlisted women will not flock to combat arms units.

I believe the current policies with respect to land combat units should be retained.

### Assignment To Combat, Aircrews

The question of whether combat aircraft assignments should be open to women is not answered by the question, "can women fly combat aircraft?", for it is incontrovertible that women test pilots, pilots, and aircrew members prove their worth every day that they fly the nation's military aircraft. Instead, the question is "should women be assigned to combat aircrews?" Aerospace doctrine envisions carrying the fight to the enemy, to destroy not only his aircraft but to destroy his nation's will to fight. Assigning women to combat aircraft would subject them to routine penetration of enemy airspace, enemy air and ground fire over hostile territory, possible shoot-down, escape and evasion, and the probability of capture with the resulting consequences borne by prisoners of war. Testimony from Vietnam-era POWs substantiated the brutality endured by U.S. servicemen -- ground troops and, Navy, Army, Marine Corps, and Air Force pilots -- at the hands of their Vietnamese captors. One of two U.S. female captives of the Iraq conflict attested to indecent assault at the hands of Iraqi captors. Air Force, Navy, Marine Corps, and Army combat pilots are required to routinely penetrate hostile air space to destroy the enemy, with the inherent prospect of becoming casualties or downed airmen. Escape, evasion, capture, and the eventual molestation and brutalization of U.S. women aviators, when a plentiful supply of males is available to run those risks, is contrary to the American value system as I know it. Therefore, after serious deliberation, I conclude that placing women in combatant aircrews, where they may be subjected to capture by nations which do not share Western values and have shown disregard for the Geneva Conventions, is wrong national policy.

### Assignment To Combatant Surface Vessels

One need only look at the probability of aircraft losses, proximity to hostile fire in enemy territory and POW statistics from World War II, Korea, Vietnam and the Persian Gulf conflict to see the different risks confronted by direct combat soldiers and airmen, as opposed to those faced by their surface ship contemporaries. The testimony received by this Commission and the reality of naval warfare, paint a very different picture of the risks that women would face being assigned to surface combatant vessels. Combat soldiers, combat aircrews, some submariners and some amphibious ship crews routinely move into hostile territory to seek out and destroy the enemy. They operate under enemy fire in, over, or in close proximity to, enemy territory. I believe that a case has been made that surface combatant ships do not routinely serve where their crews are subject to the risk of capture that confronts downed flyers and ground direct combat troops. Because the risks associated with surface combatant vessels are so different than their land and air counterparts, it makes sense to treat them differently. Furthermore, it is our duty to recommend policies and laws that take these differences into account.

A blanket "all or nothing" assignment policy would be symmetrical, but would also ignore our obligation to recognize that the surface sailor, whether male or female, is <u>not similarly situated</u> to combat aircrew members or direct ground combat troops with regard to proximity to enemy troops and risk of capture. The prospect of the enemy capturing women sailors on surface vessels and abusing them, or using the women sailors for propaganda to undermine the national will is remote. Whereas, with land and air assignments, the empirical evidence is clear that these scenarios should be anticipated and expected if women were so assigned.

The Commission's recommendation to open combat assignments aboard surface ships is historic for this country. However, it should not be viewed as unexpected. Over the last 14 years, women have been serving successfully on Navy noncombatant surface vessels. Current law and policy allow women to serve at sea in dangerous environments where mines and other hazards do not differentiate between adjacent combatant and noncombatant vessels. America can open assignments to women on surface combatants with confidence, and look to the successes of the past 14 years for assurance. Officers and enlisted men who testified before the Commission spoke of the transition that confronted them and their families when noncombatant vessels were integrated in the late 1970s. The problems they encountered, and the myths that instilled reluctance and fear then, are similar to concerns articulated by opponents in late 1992. I believe the lessons learned by the Navy when integrating non-combatant ships in the fleet 14 years ago will result in an efficient transition to integrated combatant surface ships.

## *Commission's Recommendations, Impact On Draft Registration*

Will opening combatant ships serve to undermine the premise supporting the all-male draft registration system? I believe not. There is an <u>important governmental interest</u> in ensuring that public support for the military is not undermined by the incursion of large numbers of women casualties during the prosecution of a conflict. Additionally, the government's interest is served by reducing the likelihood that American women would become prisoners of war and be subjected to abuse and exploitation by captors. These interests are substantially related to the continued exclusion of women from assignment to combat aircraft and direct combat ground troops. These interests are not served, however, by retaining the exclusions related to assignment of women to combatant surface vessels. Reducing the above mentioned risks is both legal and an appropriate course for the Congress to pursue under its constitutional authority to raise and support Armies, and is an important interest the President can administer under his authority as Commander in Chief. Furthermore, the Congress has determined that draft registration and the Selective Service System is for the primary purpose of obtaining troops for ground combat.

## *Conclusion*

Opening up surface combatant ship billets to qualified women will not increase the likelihood of women regularly serving on or over hostile foreign soil, will not create a higher risk of capture, nor will it likely result in Congress or the courts subjecting women to conscription obligations. The policy recommendations restricting direct air and land combat assignments are sound and take into account the very real differences vis-a-vis the realities of service aboard combatant surface vessels.

MAXWELL R. THURMAN
General, U.S. Army
(Retired)

## SARAH F. WHITE

It has been a special honor and privilege to serve as a member of the Presidential Commission on the Assignment of Women in the Armed Forces. My focus during our eight months of studying the issues of women in the Armed Services has been first and foremost the impact of any policy changes on national security; secondly, the effects those changes would have on servicemen and women, particularly the enlisted force; and finally, the effect any change would have on society as a whole.

Given my personal experience as an active member of the United States Air Force Reserve for nearly eighteen years and the information and experiences gleaned from my tenure as a Commissioner, I am convinced that the standard of military necessity is the only sound consideration to use when evaluating this issue. It is irresponsible to use the concepts of "equal opportunity" or "full citizenship" as the measures for personnel assignments in the Armed Forces. Military necessity is the only logical choice if we take our national security seriously -- if we are sincere in putting survival and victory first.

The alternative is to structure our military on the civilian equal opportunity basis, and there is no credible comparison between the mission of the Armed Forces and the private civilian sector. In fact, it is the demanding, often discriminatory nature of the Armed Forces which permits the citizens of the United States the luxury of having greater freedom and more abundant opportunities than any other nation in the world.

As a responsible citizen, I, without reservation, assert that there is no military necessity to drop the statutory and policy exemptions which have kept women from combat. In fact, the President and Congress should closely examine and seriously reconsider policies which put women in very physically demanding jobs and into areas of hostile action.

If a crisis develops in which our national security is at risk and there is no alternative, I would be the first to volunteer my services in a combatant position. Other than the gravest of situations, there is no military need to assign women to combat. Compelling evidence (as stated in Section II of this report and in Appendix C: Findings) presents the case that it would not be sound policy to unnecessarily train women as warriors or deploy them into combat.

There is no historical precedent of a nation routinely committing its women to combat. Doing so runs counter to the collective wisdom of all civilizations throughout the history of mankind. If committing women to combat roles was militarily sound and in the best interests of society, it would have been done countless times before now. In fact, it was so repugnant to those few nations who have had to resort to women as combatants in time of war that training women as combatants was immediately halted soon after the crisis ended (Findings 1.111 to 1.123, 1.98, 1.99).

Combat arms specialties in the military are not a "closed club" to keep women out purposely, in a selfish manner. Policy is based on the reality of the militarily significant physical differences between men and women, unit cohesion factors, and because responsible adults recognize where they can best contribute to one another's welfare. Military service is indeed <u>service</u> to one's country. For years women have voluntarily partaken of the privilege of honorably contributing to the Armed Forces where their abilities are best suited -- areas where they still primarily choose to serve. They have not done so with an eye toward earning the "right" to fight, but as an act of service which greatly enhanced our military capability and national defense.

I also believe an element of why men assume the combatant role is that, contrary to the opinions of some women, men take on that brutal responsibility out of self-sacrifice; it is because they do respect, and truly care for women. It is the ultimate act of love and respect to lay down one's life for another. Along with millions of other women, I am grateful for the roles men selflessly assume. In no way do we consider ourselves second class citizens, or of less value to society, just because we do not participate as combatants in our Nation's wars.

It is a minority of women, both in and outside the military, promoting the idea of women in combat. In the military, it is mainly female officers. Many of them are sincere in their goals, and very capable. I truly admire and respect them in many ways. But their goals of achieving high rank based on combat duty and being recognized for valor may well result in excluding many women who would have liked to contribute to their country's defense in noncombatant positions. I believe the number of talented women willing to join the military would decrease significantly if they felt vulnerable to being assigned to combatant positions.

Approximately 88 percent of the women in the Armed Forces are enlisted, and while I would not presume to speak for all enlisted women, my experiences as a Commissioner, reinforced by survey results, show that only a fraction think they would volunteer for combat duty. Their reaction to being subject to the draft is even less favorable. It is true that some women feel they should have the right to serve in combat if they meet the same standards as men, but even fewer feel that it should be compulsory, as it is for men in times of crisis. And the few women who think serving in combat would enhance women's lives do not have direct combat experience.

I urge the President and Congress not to disrupt our historically able and victorious Armed Forces to satisfy ambitious career goals of the few (no matter how courageous and skilled the individuals) over the legitimate concerns and beliefs of the many.

Sarah F. White
Commissioner

121

# IV.
# APPENDICES

# APPENDIX A

## PUBLIC LAW 102-190--Dec. 5, 1991

### SEC. 541. ESTABLISHMENT OF COMMISSION.

(a) ESTABLISHMENT.--There is established a commission to be known as the Commission on the Assignment of Women in the Armed Forces (hereinafter in this subpart referred to as the "Commission").

(b) COMPOSITION.--(1) The Commission shall be composed of 15 members appointed by the President. The Commission membership shall be diverse with respect to race, ethnicity, gender, and age. The President shall designate one of the members as Chairman of the Commission.

(2) The President shall appoint the members of the Commission from among persons who have distinguished themselves in the public or private sector and who have had significant experience (as determined by the President) with one or more of the following matters:

(A) Social and cultural matters affecting the military and civilian workplace gained through recognized research and policymaking, as demonstrated by retired military personnel, representatives from educational organizations, and leaders from civilian industry and non-Department of Defense governmental agencies.

(B) The law.

(C) Factors used to define appropriate combat job qualifications, including physical, mental, educational, and other factors.

(D) Service in the Armed Forces in a combat environment.

(E) Military personnel management.

(F) Experiences of women in the military gained through service as--

(i) a female service member (current or former);

(ii) a manager of an organization with a representative presence of women; or

(iii) a member of an organization with responsibility for policy review, advice, or oversight of the status of women in the military.

(G) Women's issues in American society.

(3) In making appointments to the Commission, the President shall consult with the chairmen and ranking minority members of the Committees on Armed Services of the Senate and the House of Representatives.

(c) PERIOD OF APPOINTMENT; VACANCIES.--Members shall be appointed for the life of the Commission. Any vacancy in the Commission shall not affect its powers, but shall be filled in the same manner as the original appointment.

(d) INITIAL ORGANIZATIONAL REQUIREMENTS.--(1) The President shall make all appointments under subsection (b) within 60 days after the date of the enactment of this Act.

(2) The Commission shall convene its first meeting within 15 days after the first date on which all members of the Commission have been appointed. At that meeting, the Commission shall develop an agenda and a schedule for carrying out its duties.

SEC. 542. DUTIES.

(a) IN GENERAL.--The Commission shall assess the laws and policies restricting the assignment of female service members and shall make findings on such matters.

(b) STUDIES.--In carrying out such assessment, the Commission shall--

(1) conduct a thorough study of duty assignments available for female service members;

(2) examine studies already completed concerning duty assignments for female service members; and

(3) conduct such additional studies as may be required.

(c) MATTERS TO BE CONSIDERED.--Matters to be considered by the Commission shall include the following:

(1) The implications, if any, for the combat readiness of the Armed Forces of permitting female service members to qualify for assignment to positions in some or all categories of combat positions and to be assigned to such positions, including the implications with respect to--

(A) the physical readiness of the Armed Forces and the process for establishing minimum physical and other qualifications;

(B) the effects, if any, of pregnancy and other factors resulting in time lost for male and female service members; in evaluating lost time, comparisons must be made between like mental categories and military occupational specialties rather than simple gender comparisons; and

(C) the effects, if any, of such assignments on unit morale and cohesion.

(2) The public attitudes in the United States on the use of women in the military.

(3) The legal and policy implications (A) of permitting only voluntary assignments of female service members to combat positions, and (B) of permitting involuntary assignments of female service members to some or all combat positions.

(4) The legal and policy implications--

(A) of requiring females to register for and to be subject to conscription under the Military Selective Service Act on the same basis as males if females were provided the same opportunity as males for assignment to any position in the Armed Forces;

(B) of requiring females to register for and to be subject to conscription under the Military Selective Service Act on the same basis as males if females in the Armed Forces were assigned to combat position only as volunteers; and

(C) of requiring females to register for and to be subject to conscription under the Military Selective Service Act on a different basis than males if females in the Armed Forces were not assigned to combat positions on the same basis as males.

(5) The extent of the need to modify facilities and vessels, aircraft, vehicles, and other equipment of the Armed Forces to accommodate the assignment of female service members to combat positions or to provide training in combat skills to female service members, including any need to modify quarters, weapons, and training facilities and equipment.

(6) The costs of meeting the needs identified pursuant to paragraph (5).

(7) The implications of restrictions on the assignment of women on the recruitment, retention, use, and promotion of qualified personnel in the Armed Forces.

SEC. 543. REPORT.

(a) IN GENERAL.--(1) Not later than November 15, 1992, the Commission shall transmit to the President a final report on the results of the study conducted by the Commission.

(2) The Commission may transmit to the President and to Congress such interim reports as the Commission considers appropriate.

(b) CONTENT OF FINAL REPORT.--(1) The final report shall contain a detailed statement of the findings and conclusions of the Commission, together with such recommendations for further legislation and administrative action as the Commission considers appropriate.

(2) The report shall include recommendations on the following matters:

(A) Whether existing law and policies restricting the assignment of female service members should be retained, modified, or repealed.

(B) What roles female service members should have in combat.

(C) What transition process is appropriate if female service members are to be given the opportunity to be assigned to combat positions in the Armed Forces.

(D) Whether special conditions and different standards should apply to females than apply to males performing similar roles in the Armed

Forces.

(c) SUBMISSION OF FINAL REPORT TO CONGRESS.--Not later than December 15, 1992, the President shall transmit to the Congress the report of the Commission, together with the President's comments and recommendations regarding such report.

SEC. 544. POWERS.

(a) HEARINGS.--The Commission or, at its direction, any panel or member of the Commission, may, for the purpose of carrying out the provisions of this subpart, hold hearings, sit and act at times and places, take testimony, receive evidence, and administer oaths to the extent that the Commission or any panel or member considers advisable.

(b) INFORMATION.--The Commission may secure directly from the Department of Defense and any other Federal department or agency any information that the Commission considers necessary to enable the Commission to carry out its responsibilities under this subpart. Upon request of the Chairman of the Commission, the head of such department or agency shall furnish such information to the Commission.

SEC. 545. COMMISSION PROCEDURES.

(a) MEETINGS.--The Commission shall meet at the call of the Chairman.

(b) QUORUM.--(1) Five members of the Commission shall constitute a quorum, but a lesser number of members may hold hearings.

(2) The Commission shall act by resolution agreed to by a majority of the members of the Commission present at a properly called meeting.

(c) PANELS.--The Commission may establish panels composed of less than the full membership of the Commission for the purpose of carrying out the Commission's duties. The actions of each such panel shall be subject to the review and control of the Commission. Any findings and determinations made by such a panel shall not be considered the findings and determinations of the Commission unless approved by the Commission.

(d) AUTHORITY OF INDIVIDUALS TO ACT FOR COMMISSION.--Any member or agent of the Commission may, if authorized by the Commission, take any action which the Commission is authorized to take under this subpart.

SEC. 546. PERSONNEL MATTERS.

(a) PAY OF MEMBERS.--Each member of the Commission who is not an officer or employee of the Federal Government shall be paid at a rate equal to the daily equivalent of the annual rate of basic pay payable for level V of the Executive Schedule under section 5316 of title 5, United States Code, for each day (including travel time) during which the member is engaged in the performance of the duties of the Commission. All members of the Commission who are officers or employees of the United States shall serve without pay in addition to that received for their services as officers or employees of the United States.

(b) TRAVEL EXPENSES.--The members of the Commission shall be allowed travel expenses, including per diem in lieu of subsistence, at rates authorized for employees of agencies under subchapter I of chapter 57 of title 5, United States Code, while away from their homes or regular places of business in the performance of services for the Commission.

(c) STAFF.--(1) The Chairman of the Commission may, without regard to the provisions of title 5, United States Code, governing appointments in the competitive service, appoint a staff director and such additional personnel as may be necessary to enable the Commission to perform its duties. The appointment of a staff director shall be subject to the approval of the Commission.

(2) The Chairman of the Commission may fix the pay of the staff director and other personnel without regard to the provisions of chapter 51 and subchapter III of chapter 53 of title 5, United States Code, relating to classification of positions and General Schedule pay rates, except that no rate of pay fixed under this paragraph may exceed the rate payable for level V of the Executive Schedule under section 5316 of such title.

(d) DETAIL OF GOVERNMENT EMPLOYEES.--Upon request of the Chairman of the Commission, the head of any Federal department or agency may detail, on a nonreimbursable basis, any personnel of that department or agency to the Commission to assist it in carrying out its duties.

(e) PROCUREMENT OF TEMPORARY AND INTERMITTENT SERVICES.--The Chairman of the Commission may procure temporary and intermittent services under section 3109(b) of title 5, United States Code, at rates for individuals which do not exceed the daily equivalent of the annual rate of basic pay payable for level V of the Executive Schedule under section 5316 of such title.

SEC. 547. MISCELLANEOUS ADMINISTRATIVE PROVISIONS.

(a) POSTAL AND PRINTING SERVICES.--The Commission may use the United States mails and obtain printing and binding services in the same manner and under the same conditions as other departments and agencies of the Federal Government.

(b) MISCELLANEOUS ADMINISTRATIVE AND SUPPORT SERVICES.-- The Administrator of General Services shall furnish the Commission, on a reimbursable basis, any administrative and support services requested by the Commission.

(c) GIFTS.--The Commission may accept, use, and dispose of gifts or donations of services or property.

(d) PROCUREMENT AUTHORITY.--The Commission may procure supplies, services, and property and make contracts, in any fiscal year, in order to carry out its duties, but (except in the case of temporary or intermittent services procured under section 546(e)) only to such extent or in such amounts as are provided in appropriation Acts or are donated pursuant to subsection (c). Contracts and other procurement arrangements may be entered into without regard to section 3709 of the Revised Statutes (41 U.S.C. 5) or any similar provision of Federal law.

(e) APPLICABILITY OF FEDERAL ADVISORY COMMITTEE ACT.-- The provisions of the Federal Advisory Committee Act shall not apply to the Commission.

(f) TRAVEL.--To the maximum extent practicable, the members and employees of the Commission shall travel on military aircraft, military ships, military vehicles, or other military conveyances when travel is necessary in the performance of a responsibility of the Commission, except that no such aircraft, ship, vehicle, or other conveyance may be scheduled primarily for the transportation of any such member or employee when the cost of commercial transportation is less expensive.

SEC. 548. PAYMENT OF COMMISSION EXPENSES.

The compensation, travel expenses, and per diem allowances of members and employees of the Commission shall be paid out of funds available to the Department of Defense for the payment of compensation, travel allowances, and per diem allowances, respectively, of civilian employees of the Department of Defense.  The other expenses of the Commission shall be paid out of funds available to the Department of Defense for the payment of similar expenses incurred by that Department.

SEC. 549. TERMINATION OF THE COMMISSION.

The Commission shall terminate 90 days after the date on which Commission submits its final report under section 543(a)(1).

SEC. 550. TEST ASSIGNMENTS OF FEMALE SERVICE MEMBERS TO COMBAT POSITIONS.

(a) TEST ASSIGNMENTS.--In carrying out its duties, the Commission may request the Secretary of Defense to conduct test assignments of female service members to combat positions.  The Secretary shall determine, in consultation with the Commission, the types of tests that are appropriate and shall retain a record of the disposition of each such request.

(b) WAIVER AUTHORITY.--For  the purpose of conducting test assignments of female service members to combat positions pursuant to requests under subsection (a), the Secretary of Defense may waive section 6015 of title 10, United States Code, and any other restriction that applies under Department of Defense regulations or policy to the assignment of female service members to combat positions.

# APPENDIX B

## CURRENT LAWS AND POLICIES REGARDING THE ASSIGNMENT OF WOMEN IN THE ARMED FORCES

In the National Defense Authorization Act for Fiscal Years 1992 and 1993 Public Law 102-190 - December 5, 1991, Congress amended language in 10 U.S.C. 6015 relating to the assignment of women in the Navy and Marine Corps and repealed 10 U.S.C. 8549 which restricted the Air Force's assignment of women. Each Service also has regulations and/or policies governing the assignment of women. (See following pages for service policies.)

### NAVY/MARINE CORPS

The Navy and Marine Corps assignment policies for women are governed by 10 U.S.C. 6015 which reads:

> ...[T]he Secretary of the Navy may prescribe the kind of military duty to which such women members may be assigned and the military authority which they may exercise. However, women may not be assigned to duty on vessels engaged in combat missions *other than as aviation officers as part of an air wing or other air element assigned to such a vessel* nor may they be assigned to other than temporary duty on *other* vessels of the Navy except hospital ships, transports, and vessels of a similar classification not expected to be assigned combat missions.

Italics indicate amendments in P.L. 102-190.

### AIR FORCE

There is no longer a statute restricting assignment of women to combat positions in the Air Force since the repeal of 10 U.S.C. 8549 in Section 531 of P.L. 102-190 - December 5, 1991. There is a regulation, drafted by the Secretary of the Air Force to comply with the former law, that applies to all members of the Regular Air Force, U.S. Air Force Reserve and Air National Guard and has not been amended or repealed by the Air Force since the enactment of P.L. 102-190.

### ARMY

There is no law restricting the Army's assignment of women. The Secretary of the Army, based on the authority granted under 10 U.S.C. 3012, has set policies that exclude women from routine engagement in direct combat.

# DEPARTMENT OF DEFENSE

The Department of Defense (DoD) does not have a directive or regulation that excludes women from combat positions. The Secretary of Defense does, however, issue statements to military departments regarding the assignment of women. For example, Secretary Richard Cheney distributed a memorandum to the Service Secretaries on November 9, 1989 that stated: "...[it is the] policy of the DoD to provide women full and equal opportunity with men," and "women will continue to be eligible to serve in all roles except those prohibited by the combat exclusion laws (10 U.S.C. 6015, 8549) and the policy applicable to the Department of the Army."

The DoD has issued a policy to govern the assignment of women to non-combat positions. In 1988, the Risk Rule was devised to standardize positions closed to women in the Services. The rule is used to evaluate whether a non-combat position should be closed to women. *Each Service interprets the Risk Rule according to its mission.* The rule states:

> Risks of direct combat, exposure to hostile fire, or capture are proper criteria for closing non-combat positions or units to women, when the type, degree and duration of such risks are equal to or greater than the combat units with which they are normally associated within a given theater of operations. If the risk of non-combat units or positions is less than comparable to land, air or sea combat units with which they are associated, then they should be open to women. Non-combat units should be compared to combat land units, air to air and so forth.

DEPARTMENT OF THE NAVY
Office of the Chief of Naval Operations
Washington, DC  20350-2000

OPNAVINST 1300.17
OP-13
5 October 1990

OPNAV INSTRUCTION 1300.17

From:  Chief of Naval Operations
To:      All Ships and Stations

Subj:  ASSIGNMENT OF WOMEN IN THE NAVY

Ref:   (a) SECNAVINST 1300.12A
         (b) OPNAVINST 6000.1A
         (c) Marine Corps Order (MCO)
              1300.8, Marine Corps Personnel
              Assignment Policy (NOTAL)

1.  **Purpose.**  To provide specific guidance for the permanent and temporary assignment of women in ships, squadrons and other units of the Navy.

2.  **Background.**  Reference (a) establishes policy in the Department of the Navy for the assignment of women to ships, aircraft and units of the Navy.

3.  **Policy**

    a.  Officers and enlisted women in the Navy will be assigned to sea and shore duty commensurate with their capabilities and qualifications to the maximum extent practicable under the Combat Exclusion Law (Title 10 USC 6015) and the Department of Defense Risk Rule.

    b.  Women will be assigned duties which they can fulfill in both peacetime and wartime situations.  Women will continue to serve in their assigned billets in the event of mobilization or national emergency, except as directed in paragraph 103j of reference (b).

    c.  All shore and neutral duty activities are available for the permanent assignment of women.

    d.  Permanent assignment of women to non-combat units may be precluded because of inadequate berthing, e.g. ship alterations to berthing compartments not scheduled because of the age of the vessel.

    e.  Women will be fully integrated into the commands to which they are assigned, without a separate chain of command.

    f.  With respect to sea duty in ships, aircraft, and other sea duty units, women members:

        (1)  Will be permanently assigned to duty in tenders, ammunition ships, combat stores ships, fleet oilers, repair ships, salvage ships, submarine rescue ships, hospital ships, cargo ships, an auxiliary aircraft landing training ship, and vessels of a similar classification, including ships of the Military Sealift Command, not expected to be assigned a combat mission.

        (2)  Will be permanently assigned as pilots, naval flight officers, mission specialists, and aircrew in aviation squadrons that do not have combat missions, and as ground support personnel in any land-based squadron.

        (3)  Will be permanently assigned to other non-combat units which qualify as sea duty.  Units which perform their duties aboard combatant vessels on a temporary additional duty (TEMADD) basis, such as mobile training teams and inspection teams, are available for the permanent assignment of women.

    g.  Temporary Additional Duty (TEMADD)

        (1)  Women may be assigned temporary additional duty to any ship, aircraft, or unit in the U.S. Navy not expected to execute a specific combat mission during the period of temporary duty. While ship and squadron deployment mandates higher readiness conditions, deployment in and of itself is not considered expectation to execute a combat mission.

B-3

OPNAVINST 1300.17
5 October 1990

(2) Women assigned TEMADD to a ship or aircraft required to execute a combat mission will be disembarked, if feasible, prior to execution of such mission.

(3) Temporary additional duty assignment of women to ships and squadrons is strongly encouraged for the performance of their military duties (e.g. training and inspection teams) and professional training (e.g. Personal Qualification Standard (PQS), warfare qualification, and rate training).

(4) Periods of temporary additional duty shall not exceed 180 days.

(5) Women will be assigned temporary additional duty without restrictions such as minimum or maximum number, requirement for an officer or petty officer in charge, escorts, or special berthing compartment watches.

(6) Commanding officers will provide temporary berthing accommodations for the women temporarily assigned. The accommodations will be commensurate with rank or rate; exceptions can be made by the commanding officer. Sleeping quarters must be separate from males. Head facilities may be provided on a time sharing basis. Locks will be provided on doors of heads to ensure adequate privacy.

(7) This policy applies to female members of all U.S. military services and the U. S. Coast Guard assigned temporary duty to a U.S. Navy ship or squadron.

h. The assignment and deployment policy for Navy women in support of the Fleet Marine Force is as directed by enclosure (11) of reference (c).

J. M. BOORDA
Deputy Chief of Naval Operations
(Manpower, Personnel and Training)

Distribution:
SNDL Parts 1 and 2
MARCORPS 71000000000
and 71000000100

Chief of Naval Operations
(OP-13C)
Navy Department
Washington, DC 20350-2000 (200 copies)

Chief of Naval Operations
(OP-09B34)
Navy Department
Washington, DC 20350-2000 (220 copies)

Commander,
Naval Data Automation Command
(Code 813)
Washington Navy Yard
Washington, DC 20374-1662 (60 copies)

Stocked:
CO, NAVPUBFORMCEN
5801 Tabor Avenue
Philadelphia, PA 19120-5099 (500 copies)

DEPARTMENT OF THE NAVY
Office of the Secretary
Washington, DC 20350-1000

SECNAVINST 1300.12A
OP-13
20 February 1989

SECNAV INSTRUCTION 1300.12A

From:  Secretary of the Navy
To:    All Ships and Stations

Subj:  ASSIGNMENT OF WOMEN
       MEMBERS IN THE DEPARTMENT
       OF THE NAVY

Ref:   (a) 10 U. S. Code Sec. 6015

1. Purpose. To prescribe the guidelines under which women members, both officer and enlisted, in the Navy and Marine Corps may be assigned to duty on ships, aircraft and units of the Navy and Marine Corps. When the United States Coast Guard is assigned as a service within the Department of the Navy, the policies set out in this instruction will apply to women members of the Coast Guard. This instruction is a complete revision and should be read in its entirety.

2. Cancellation. SECNAVINST 1300.12.

3. Background. Reference (a) authorizes the Secretary of the Navy to prescribe the kind of military duty to which women members may be assigned, but prohibits the assignment of women for duty in vessels or in aircraft that are engaged in combat missions. This law allows women to be permanently assigned to hospital ships, transports, and vessels of a similar classification; furthermore, it allows women to be temporarily assigned to any naval vessel or aircraft squadron for up to 180 days provided the ship or squadron is not expected to be assigned to a combat mission. Navy and Marine Corps women are a valuable personnel resource contributing significantly to the attainment of the Service's mission.

4. Definitions

   a. Combat Mission. A mission of an individual unit, ship or aircraft that individually or collectively as a naval task organization has as one of its primary objectives to seek out,

reconnoiter, and engage an enemy. The normal defensive posture of all operating forces is not included within this definition.

   b. Risk Rule. Risks of direct combat, exposure to hostile fire, or capture are proper criteria for closing noncombat positions or units to women, when the type, degree, and duration of such risks are equal to or greater than the combat units with which they are normally associated within a given theater of operations.

   c. Temporary Duty. Temporary duty (TEMDU) orders are orders which involve detachment from one station and assignment to another station or stations for TEMDU pending further assignment to a new permanent duty station or for return to the old permanent duty station. Members on TEMDU are not attached to any permanent duty station.

   d. Temporary Additional Duty. Temporary additional duty (TEMADD) orders are orders which temporarily assign a member to duty in addition to his or her present duties, and which direct him or her upon completion of this TEMADD to resume regular or temporary duty.

5. Policy. It is Department of the Navy policy that women members, officers and enlisted, will be assigned to billets commensurate with their capabilities to the maximum extent practicable. Accordingly, women members:

   a. May not be assigned to a unit, ship, or aircraft that has a combat mission except as provided below. If assigned on a vessel or aircraft that is required to execute a combat mission, every reasonable effort will be made to disembark women prior to execution of such mission.

   b. May be permanently assigned to duty in hospital ships, oilers, ammunition ships, refrigerated stores ships, transports, training ships, and vessels of a similar classification not expected to be assigned a combat mission.

B-5

SECNAVINST 1300.12A
20 February 1989

c. May be assigned temporary duty (TEMDU or TEMADD) to any ship or aircraft not expected to conduct a combat mission during the period of temporary duty. Such periods of temporary duty may not exceed 180 days. Chief of Naval Operations and Commandant of the Marine Corps may promulgate specific guidelines governing these assignments.

d. Are authorized to participate, including landing on shipboard flight decks under conditions permitting temporary duty on naval vessels, as crew members or passengers in aircraft engaged in training or support not expected to execute a combat mission during the period of the assignment.

e. May be assigned to permanent duty in squadrons where such assignment would not require them to participate as crew members in a combat mission or embark, other than TEMADD, in vessels that may be assigned combat missions. They may be assigned to aircrew and support positions in squadrons that do not have combat missions. Women may be assigned to nonaircrew support positions in land based squadrons with combat missions. The Chief of Naval Operations and the Commandant of the Marine Corps will specify those squadrons in which women may be assigned.

f. Notwithstanding any of the provisions above, the Chief of Naval Operations and the Commandant of the Marine Corps may preclude women from the assignment to a noncombat unit, ship or aircraft when the type, degree, and duration of risk of direct combat, exposure to hostile fire, or capture are equal to or greater than the reasonably anticipated risks for land, air or sea combatant units with which they are normally associated in a theater of operations.

The Chief of Naval Operations and the Commandant of the Marine Corps will determine when the risk equals or exceeds the reasonably anticipated risks for land, air or sea combatant units normally associated in the same theater of operations.

6. Mission. The policy outlined above delineates when women members may serve on board Navy ships, aircraft, and with Marine Corps units, but does not mandate assignment of women members to any particular ship, aircraft, or Marine Corps unit. Specific plans and policy directives for assignment of women members shall be developed by the Chief of Naval Operations and the Commandant of the Marine Corps within the policy contained here. These policies shall be structured to ensure that women members of the Navy and Marine Corps are assigned and utilized to maximize Service benefit and provide for rewarding careers.

H. LAWRENCE GARRETT, III
Acting Secretary of the Navy

Distribution:
SNDL Parts 1 and 2
MARCORPS Codes H and I

Commander
Naval Data Automation Command
(Code 813)
Washington Navy Yard
Washington, DC 20374-1662 (345 copies)

Stocked:
CO, NAVPUBFORMCEN
5801 Tabor Avenue
Philadelphia, PA 19120-5099 (500 copies)

B-6

MCO 1300.8P

WOMEN MARINES CLASSIFICATION, ASSIGNMENT, AND DEPLOYMENT POLICY

1. **General.** The Marine Corps will employ the women of the Corps in all roles except those explicitly prohibited by combat exclusion policies. Women Marines will serve in MOS's and billets commensurate with their individual abilities and in keeping with their potential to contribute to the fulfillment of the Marine Corps' roles and missions. This enclosure sets forth the policy guidance necessary to ensure women are employed in this manner, and are simultaneously assured the opportunity for a full and meaningful career. A full and meaningful career includes the chance to hold billets that ensure development of professional abilities and career opportunities that allow equitable FMF/non-FMF rotation when compared to contemporaries of the same grade and MOS.

2. **Combat Exclusion**

a. Title 10 U.S.C., section 6015 sets forth the legislative basis for the combat exclusion policy. It states that women will not be assigned to duty in vessels or in aircraft that are engaged in combat missions. It allows women to be assigned TAD in vessels of the Navy that are not expected to be assigned combat missions.

b. DoD provides additional guidance to ensure consistent application of legislative intent among the Services. As part of this guidance, DoD established a Risk Rule to evaluate combat-related skills and units for closure to women. That Risk Rule states:

> Risks of direct combat, exposure to hostile fire, or capture are proper criteria for closing noncombat positions or units to women, when the type, degree, and duration of such risks are equal to or greater than the combat units with which they are normally associated within a given theater of operations. If the risk of noncombat units or positions is less than comparable to land, air, or sea combat units with which they are associated, then they should be open to women.

c. The Secretary of the Navy defines a combat mission as a mission of an individual unit, ship or aircraft that individually, or collectively as a naval task organization, has as one of its primary objectives to seek out, reconnoiter, and engage the enemy. The normal defensive posture of all operating units is not included within the definition.

d. For assignment purposes, direct combat action is defined as seeking out, reconnoitering, and engaging hostile forces in offensive action.

e. Based on the above guidance, there are certain MOS's into which women will not be classified, and units or elements of the

B-7

MCO 1300.8P

Marine Air Ground Task Force (MAGTF) into which they will not be assigned regardless of MOS. These restrictions implement the Marine Corps' combat exclusion policy. Subordinate commands will not impose additional restrictions without approval from CMC.

3. Classification

a. Women Marines may be classified within any noncombatant occupational field for which qualified.

b. Women Marines will not be classified within the following combatant occupational fields: 03 (infantry), 08 (artillery), 18 (tank and assault amphibian vehicle), and 75 (pilot/naval flight officer).

c. Women Marines will not be classified within any of the following combat-related/flight-crewmember MOS's:

    0210      (Counterintelligence Officer)
    0211      (Counterintelligence Specialist)
    0250      (Interrogation - Translation Officer)
    0251      (Interrogation - Translation Specialist)
   *0430      (Embarkation Officer)        * Suitable as secondary MOS
    0451      (Air Delivery Specialist)
    0481      (Landing Support Specialist)
    1302      (Engineer Officer)
    1371      (Combat Engineer)
    2110      (Ordnance Vehicle Maintenance Officer)
    2131      (Artillery Weapons/Turret Repairer)
    2141      (Assault Amphibian Vehicle Repairer/Technician)
    2143      (Self-Propelled Artillery Repairer/Technician)
    2145      (Tracked Vehicle Repairer, Tank)
    2147      (LAV Repairer)
    2149      (Ordnance Vehicle Technician)
    2305      (Explosive Ordnance Disposal Officer)
    2336      (Explosive Ordnance Disposal Technician)
    2362      (Ground Nuclear Weapons Assembly Technician)
    2671      (Cryptologic Linguist, Middle East)
    5720      (Ground Nuclear Weapons Assembly Officer)
    5907      (Ground Launched Missile System Maintenance Officer)
    5921-5929 (Improved HAWK Missile Repairers and Technicians)
    5943      (Aviation Fire Control Repairer)
    5947      (Aviation Fire Control Technician)
    6015      (Aircraft Mechanic, AV-8)
    6031-6032 (Aircraft Flight Engineer, KC-130)
    6038      (Maintenance Specialist, AV-8B)
    6112-6115 (Helicopter Mechanic)
    6172-6176 (Helicopter Crew Chief)
    7204      (Antiair Warfare Officer)
    7207      (Forward Air Controller) (Additional MOS only)
    7208      (Air Support Control Officer)
    7212      (LAAD Missile Gunner)
    7222      (HAWK Missile System Operator)

MCO 1300.8P

```
7242   (Air Support Operations Operator)
7371   (Aerial Navigator Trainee)
7372   (First Navigator)
7380   (Aerial Navigation Officer)
7381-7382 (Airborne Radio Operator/Loadmaster)
```

d.  Women Marines will not be given any MOS used to indicate a secondary or billet occupational specialty which is usually assigned only to Marines who have one of the MOS's listed above.

4.  Assignment

    a.  FMF Assignments

        (1) Women Marines may be trained to provide essential support of combat operations; however, they will not be assigned to any unit within which they would likely become engaged in direct combat operations.  Accordingly, women Marines will not be assigned to the following units or any sub-element thereof:

```
Infantry Regiment
Artillery Battalion
Reconnaissance Battalion
Force Reconnaissance Company
Tank Battalion
Assault Amphibian Battalion
LAV Battalion
Communications Company, Marine Division
Firing Batteries, H&S Batteries, LAAM Battalion
LAAD Battalion
Air/Naval Gunfire Liaison Company
Combat Engineer Battalion
Marine Air Support Squadron
Counterintelligence Teams
Interrogation-Translation Teams
Helicopter Squadron (tactical)
AV-8 Squadron (tactical)
Sensor Control and Management Platoons (SCAMP)
```

        (2) Women Marines may be assigned to the command element of the MEF, division, aircraft wing, and force service support group (FSSG).  Additionally, they may be assigned to those FMF units that provide the detachments and units for the command, aviation, ground combat, and combat service support elements of the MEF such that, when the MEF is committed to combat, the women assigned will not likely be engaged in direct combat action.  Women Marines will not be assigned to any of the standing MEB staffs, but may augment that staff if the operational situation permits.

        (3) FMF organizations will be provided at least the number of male Marines needed, by grade and MOS, to deploy two all male MEBs per MEF if sufficient personnel assets exist.  This requirement will be

MCO 1300.8P

based on the deployment of a notional amphibious and prepositioned MEB. In addition to this requirement, the MEF will be provided a sufficient male inventory, by grade and MOS, to establish a 25 percent combat replacement factor, internal to the MEF, for the ground combat and combat service support elements of both MEB's.

(4) Women Marines may be assigned to any fixed-wing squadron or any training (fixed-wing or helicopter) squadron (except as cited in paragraph 4a(1) above) for the purpose of providing the service/ support functions for which they are trained. They may not be assigned as members of the flight crew of any tactical aircraft. In the assignment of women to organizational and intermediate maintenance levels, care must be taken to ensure that MOS compatible males are identified to replace women Marines prior to deployment aboard an aircraft carrier (CV/CVN).

b. Supporting Establishment

(1) Women Marines may be assigned to any supporting establishment unit or duty station for which qualified by grade, MOS, or other special criteria.

(2) Women Marines may be designated as enlisted crewmembers and assigned duties aboard the C-9, C-12, and T-39 operational support airlift (OSA) aircraft.

(3) Women Marines may be assigned to the Marine Support Battalion; however, one·third of that battalion's billets will be designated augmentation ·billets in support of the FMF. Those billets will not be assigned women.

5. Deployment of Women Marines

a. MAGTF Wartime/Combat Contingency Deployment

(1) Marine Expeditionary Force (MEF). Women Marines may be assigned to all elements of the MEF and will deploy with their units subject to the availability of appropriate transportation. Women will not be assigned to support units/elements that would be expected to maneuver with the infantry regiment or its subordinate units, or be collocated with the infantry regiment in a defensive position (e.g., helicopter support teams, FSSG contact teams, counterintelligence teams, interrogator-translator teams, etc.).

(2) Marine Expeditionary Brigade (MEB). Women Marines will not be assigned to the ground combat element of a MEB or combat service support element of a amphibious MEB. Although women Marines will not be assigned to the standing MEB staffs, when augmentation of the staff is required and it is not likely that the MEB command element will be engaged in direct combat action, the MEB commanding general may authorize women Marines to be part of that augmentation. Women Marines may be assigned to the air combat element (ACE) of a MEB and will be deployed with the ACE if appropriate transportation is

available. Women Marines may be assigned to and deploy with the combat service support element of an airlifted (MHP) MEB.

(3) Marine Expeditionary Unit (MEU). Women Marines will not normally be assigned to any of the elements of a MEU.

b. Training Deployments

(1) Women Marines may participate in all MEF and MEB exercises, provided appropriate transportation is available. Their participation in the exercises should be a reflection of their contemplated employment in wartime, and the requirement for all Marines to train in the field to be fully qualified in their MOS.

(2) Women will participate in WestPac unit deployments provided appropriate transportation is available. Women will not participate in MEU deployments either in WestPac or the Mediterranean.

6. Duty Aboard Naval Vessels

a. No billets are currently authorized which would require the permanent assignment of women Marines to a ship.

b. Women may be assigned via temporary duty to a ship that is not expected to have a combat mission during that period of temporary duty. Such an assignment will not exceed 180 days, and is contingent on the availability of adequate accommodations in terms of privacy and security. The assignment of women Marines to temporary duty with units to be deployed in amphibious shipping requires the advance approval of the appropriate fleet commander.

7. Reserves. The assignment of women in Reserve units must be consistent with the assignment criteria established in this Order. This is necessary due to the augmentation and reinforcement roles of the Selected Marine Corps Reserve (SMCR) as well as the 2d MEB/4th Division/Wing team requirements. It may be necessary to administratively assign women Marines to units prohibited by this Order because of demographics; however, these women will be assigned to appropriate mobilization RUC's. Women in the Reserve component will not be classified into restricted MOS's.

8. Overseas Dependents-Restricted Assignments. Women Marines are eligible for assignment to overseas dependents-restricted tours of duty based on grade and MOS requirements.

9. Pregnancy. Marine Corps assignment policy and procedures for pregnant Marines are set forth below: (Marine Corps general policy on pregnant Marines is found in MCO 5000.12.)

a. Pregnant Marines will not be ordered to a dependents-restricted or all others tour.

B-11

MCO 1300.8P

   b.   Pregnant Marines stationed in CONUS and Hawaii will not be detached after their 6th month of pregnancy.  Specific instructions relating to PCSO modifications/cancellation will be obtained from the CMC (MMEA/MMOA as appropriate).

   c.   Pregnant Marines serving overseas in a dependents-restricted tour may be detached at their normal RTD when that date occurs after the 6th month of pregnancy provided medical certification that travel is authorized can be obtained.  In situations wherein it appears that the overseas tour will be involuntarily extended because of the condition (e.g., delivery date approximates RTD), termination of the individual's tour prior to the normal RTD may be authorized by the CMC (MMEA/MMOA as appropriate).  Approval of termination of an overseas restricted tour because of pregnancy will not normally be granted to Marines who have not completed at least 9 months overseas.

   d.   Women Marines on unaccompanied tours overseas who arrive pregnant or who become pregnant during the tour may be reassigned to another overseas location in order to establish a current DAUSDR.  The reassignment will be requested by the command to the CMC (MMEA/MMOA as appropriate) and will state the reasons the reassignment would be in the best interests of the individual and the command.

   e.   Pregnant Marines will not deploy in contingency operations.

   f.   Assignment of a Marine mother to an overseas tour will be deferred for 4 months from the birth of a child when the Marine is directed to a dependent restricted tour or a tour (accompanied) where concurrent travel of the child is denied.  The same deferment also applies to deployment on temporary duty or temporary assignment away from the permanent duty station or homeport, and to the involuntary activation of reservists.  The Marine may waive the deferment if desired.

DEPARTMENT OF THE AIR FORCE
Headquarters US Air Force
Washington DC 20330-5000

AF REGULATION 35-60

18 August 1989

Military Personnel

## COMBAT EXCLUSIONS FOR WOMEN

This regulation outlines combat exclusions affecting the assignment and utilization of Air Force military women; provides a list of aircraft, Air Force specialties and units where the assignment of women is prohibited; and specifies procedures for updating the list of prohibited assignments. It applies to all members of the Regular Air Force, US Air Force Reserve, and Air National Guard.

**1. Combat Exclusions.** The Women's Armed Services Integration Act of 1948, Public Law 625, was the first law to prohibit women from being assigned to aircraft engaged in combat missions. This law later became 10 U.S.C. 8549, which states, "Female members of the Air Force, except those designated under section 8067 of this title, or appointed with a view to designation under that section, may not be assigned to duty in aircraft engaged in combat missions." (Section 8067 pertains to officers appointed as physicians, veterinarians, nurses, dentists, judge advocates, chaplains, biomedical science officers, or medical service officers.) The Secretary of the Air Force is responsible, within the constraints of the law, for establishing and implementing policy for the utilization of women. This regulation is intended to permit commanders to best use all available personnel resources during various wartime scenarios. The objective is to ensure Air Force compliance with the letter and intent of 10 U.S.C. 8549, not to deny equitable assignment opportunities to women.

**2. Assignment and Utilization Limitations:**

a. Combat exclusion policy precludes the assignment of women to the following:

(1) Aircraft, whose principal mission involves aerial combat (figure 1), defined as:

(a) Delivery of munitions or other destructive materials against an enemy.

(b) Aerial activity over hostile territory where enemy fire is expected and where risk of capture is substantial.

(2) Noncombatant positions or units where the type, degree, and duration of risk of direct combat, exposure to hostile fire, or capture is equal to or greater than the air, sea, or land combat units with which they are normally associated in a given theater of operations.

| | |
|---|---|
| A-7 | F-15 |
| A-10 | F-16 |
| AT-38 | F-106 |
| B-1 | F/FB/EF-111 |
| B-52 | CH/HH-3 |
| CV-22 | HH-60 |
| C/HC/MC/AC-130 (note 2) | MH-53 |
| C-141 AIRDROP/SOLL | OV-10 |
| F/RF-4 | OA-37 |
| F-5 | SR-71 |

NOTES:
1. Aircrew and mission crew positions, except for positions such as flight test engineers where the aircraft is not engaged in a combat mission, and where training or experience in combat aircraft is not a prerequisite. Also, this does not preclude women being transported by such an aircraft when not on a combat mission, for example, C-130 aircraft. (Title 10 U.S.C. 8549 precludes line women "from assignment to aircraft engaged in combat missions.")
2. The C-130 mission assigned to the 16TATS and the 189TAG (ANG) Little Rock AFB AR is

Supersedes AFR 35-60, 20 January 1986. (See signature page for summary of changes.)
No. of Printed Pages: 4
OPR: HQ AFMPC/DPMRP (Lt Col Terry Stevens)
Approved by: HQ AFMPC/DPMR (Col Richard A. Hart)
Editor: Dorothy Trevino
Distribution: F

suitable for the assignment of women.

3. The U-2/TR-1 aircraft are under review pending medical/physiological resolution.

**Figure 1. Aircraft With Primary Wartime Missions Not Suitable for the Assignment of Women. (See notes 1 and 3)**

---

(3) Instructor or staff positions where training or experience in combat aircraft is a prerequisite.

b. The exclusions above are based on Air Force plans for employing personnel resources during wartime. Air Force combat exclusion policy does not preclude the assignment of women to a specialty or unit except as indicated in this regulation. Therefore, women assigned to a unit will deploy with that unit. However, on rare occasions, units or unit elements may be tasked to perform certain special missions not normally assigned to the unit or unit element. Where such a special mission meets the criteria outlined in 2a(1) or (2) above, women will be excluded. Attachment 1 provides examples of unusual situations which might occur. Such rare exclusions must be approved at a level no lower than chief of staff of the appropriate major command (MAJCOM), or at the equivalent level in another activity.

c. The basis for evacuation of Air Force military women will be the same as for military men.

---

| 273X0 | Combat Control |
| 275X0 | Tactical Air Command and Control |
| 111X0 | Aerial Gunner |
| 115X0 | Pararescue and Recovery |

NOTES:

1. Special Duty Identifier 99602, Sensor Operator, while not an Air Force specialty, is not open to women.

2. This figure includes only those areas where the entire 5-digit enlisted specialty or the entire officer utilization field is closed to women. (There are no officer utilization fields totally closed to women.) It does not include closed positions within otherwise open specialties or utilization fields; for example, positions which require parachute qualification such as some

enlisted ground radio communicators, some weather personnel, and combat control officers.

**Figure 2. Air Force Specialties Not Open to Women.**

---

Tactical Air Control Parties and Air Support Radar Teams.

Weather elements in direct support of special operations forces or Army combat units.

**Figure 3. Units or Unit Elements Not Open to Women.**

---

3. **Update Procedures.** If the primary wartime mission of an aircraft, skill, or unit changes or when missions for new aircraft, skills, or units are determined, they must be reviewed to see if the exclusion criteria in paragraph 2 apply.

a. MAJCOMs, the functional HQ USAF Deputy Chief of Staff (DCS), or other functional managers through the appropriate HQ USAF DCS, will initiate the regulation change request to Headquarters Air Force Military Personnel Center, Directorate of Assignments, Special Assignments Division (HQ AFMPC/DPMRP) when such a review indicates addition or deletion of information in figures 1, 2 or 3 is necessary. This request must be accompanied by justification that supports the change. Additional information may be requested by the office of primary responsibility.

b. The primary wartime mission of an aircraft, skill, or unit will be compared to the exclusion criteria in this regulation to see if the mission now meets, or still meets, the criteria.

c. Coordination below HQ USAF will be the responsibility of the originator. HQ AFMPC/DPMRP will coordinate the request with Headquarters United States Air Force, Judge Advocate (HQ USAF/JA), other appropriate HQ USAF offices, and Secretary of the Air Force, Deputy Assistant Secretary (Manpower Resources and Military Personnel (SAF/MM)

d. Direct questions concerning whether exclusion criteria affect individual positions to HQ AFMPC/DPMRP

e. HQ AFMPC/DPMRP ensures that an annual review of excluded positions is accomplished.

# DEPARTMENT OF THE ARMY

**1-12. Overall policy for the female soldier**

a. The Army's assignment policy for female soldiers allows women to serve in any officer or enlisted specialty or position except in those specialties, positions, or units (battalion size or smaller) which are assigned a routine mission to engage in direct combat, or which collocate routinely with units assigned a direct combat mission.

b. The DCPC system implements the Army policy for the coding of positions in organization documents and the related assignment of all soldiers to these positions. Once properly assigned, female soldiers are subject to the same utilization policies as their male counterparts. In event of hostilities, female soldiers will remain with their assigned units and continue to perform their assigned duties.

c. Female soldiers will be provided full and equal opportunity to pursue careers in the military and will be assigned to all skills and positions according to the above policy.

d. All commanders and heads of agencies will ensure compliance with the provisions of this regulation and that subordinate commanders and staff are aware of their responsibilities.

**1-13. Policy specific to ARNG**

a. Female soldiers will not be assessed, commissioned, appointed, or later assigned to a closed unit or an open unit which has been identified and confirmed for reorganization or redesignation to a closed unit.

b. When a female soldier's unit is changed from one geographical area to another, reorganized, or disbanded, she may be temporarily assigned to a closed unit for up to 1 year if there is no open coded vacancy in the soldier's residential geographical area per AR 135-91.

c. Female soldiers assigned to closed units and or positions as a result of unit reorganization or redesignation must transition from their closed unit and or position before their expiration term of service (ETS) or 1 year after the reorganization or redesignation, whichever is later.

d. Female Active Guard Reserve (AGR) soldiers who are in closed units and or positions as a result of reorganization or redesignation will have priority consideration for vacant open units and or positions. They may retain their AGR status in their closed unit and or position for 1 year after the reorganization or redesignation or until their ETS, whichever is earlier.

e. Public Law 90-486 requires ARNG military technicians (MTs) to be assigned to compatible military positions or else be separated 30 days after losing their compatible assignments. To comply with the law, female MTs will receive priority consideration for assignment to compatible positions in open units. Every possible effort will be made to effect such assignments as soon as possible. Female MTs may also remain temporarily in closed units up to 1 year provided they remain in a compatible assignment.

f. On mobilization, female soldiers occupying positions in closed units will be reassigned to the State Army Command Headquarters until the unit's departure for its mobilization station.

**1-14. Policy specific to USAR**

a. Female soldiers in USAR troop program units (TPUs) will not be assessed, commissioned, appointed, or later assigned to a closed unit or and or position or an open unit and or position which has been identified and confirmed for reorganization or redesignation to a closed unit in the future.

b. When a female soldier's TPU is changed from one geographical area to another, reorganized, or disbanded, she may be temporarily assigned to a closed unit for up to 1 year, if there is no open coded vacancy in the soldier's residential geographical area per AR 135-91.

c. TPU female soldiers assigned to closed units and or positions as a result of unit reorganization or redesignation must transition from their closed unit and or position within 1 year after the reorganization or redesignation.

d. AGR female soldiers attached to units which become closed as a result of reorganization or redesignation will be given priority placement in another AGR position. They may remain in the current location for up to a year pending ETS or reattachment. If a reattachment offer is turned down, the soldier will be removed from the closed unit and terminated from the AGR program.

e. Female MT personnel assigned to closed units and or positions as a result of reorganization or redesignation, will be reassigned on a case-by-case basis.

f. On call up or mobilization, female soldiers who have not made the transition out of closed units and or positions will be reassigned before the unit's departure for its mobilization station.

## Chapter 2
## Direct Combat Position Coding System

**2-1. Coding process**

a. The DCPC system implements Army policy for assigning women in both the Active Army and Reserve Component.

b. The DCPC system will use the following three dimensions to classify each position within a TOE:

(1) Duties of the position and area of concentration or military occupational specialty.

(2) Unit mission.

(3) Routine collocation.

**2-2. Coding classifications**

a. All TOE positions will be evaluated during the formulation process and be assigned an appropriate DCPC code.

b. The following two codes will be used to classify positions:

(1) P1 will indicate those positions to which women may not be assigned. MTOEs will be coded with the identity code (officer/warrant officer/enlisted) equivalent to the P1 designation per AR 310-49.

(2) P2 (open to women) will be used for all other positions.

**2-3. Coding procedures for closed (P1) and open (P2) positions**

a. Procedures for applying the DCPC codes are found in this regulation and are included in AR 71-31. Establishment and change of identity codes in the MTOE are addressed in AR 310-49 and AR 570-4.

b. Procedures for classifying positions under DCPC will be accomplished as follows.

(1) Positions will be coded closed (P1) (see fig 2-1 below) only if—

(a) The specialty or position requires routine engagement in direct combat.

(b) The position is in a battalion or smaller size unit that has a mission of routine engagement in direct combat.

(c) The position is in a unit that routinely collocates with battalion or smaller size units assigned a mission to engage in direct combat. (See Section II, Terms, Collocation.)

(d) The position is in a portion of a unit that routinely collocates with a battalion or smaller size unit having a direct combat mission.

(2) Positions will be coded open (P2) if they do not meet the criteria of a closed (P1) position as defined above.

**2-4. Coding of tables of distribution and allowance (TDA)**

a. TDA positions will be gender neutral.

b. MACOM must submit requests for exception to policy to HQDA (DAPE-HR-S), WASH DC 20310-0300, before gender coding a TDA position. Requests for exception will be considered

on a case-by-case basis. All requests must clearly justify the rationale and provide a detailed job or duty description. Any civil or military regulations or guidance involving job performance must be included. Sound logic must be evident in the request to justify an exception and permit gender coding. Factors affecting overall combat effectiveness such as readiness, health, welfare, and discipline and order may be justifiable reasons for ODCSPER granting an exception.

c. All such requests will be processed according to AR 570-4, paragraph 9-23. If approved, these positions will be coded in TAADS with standard personnel remark code 80.

# APPENDIX C

## RESULTS OF PANEL FACT FINDING RESEARCH
## COMMISSION APPROVED FINDINGS

### 1: INTRODUCTION

Sec. 543 of Public Law 102-190 provides that the Commission's final report shall contain a detailed statement of the findings and conclusions of the Commission. The enabling legislation was scrutinized to determine the areas of research to be undertaken. The Commission determined that the categories could best be divided among four panels, with each Commissioner assigned to one panel, except the Chairman. The precise focus of each panel is indicated by the panel charter, which precedes related findings. Each panel reported to the full Commission the findings which were determined from its fact-finding efforts.

Through panel reports, Commissioners developed the most significant draft findings for consideration by the full Commission. What follows are those findings derived from panel efforts and individual Commissioners which were approved by the full Commission. A Commission approved finding is defined as "a conclusion relevant to a recommendation, which is based on evidence drawn from testimony, reports, site visits or other avenues of research."

Additional panel findings generated by the research staff but not approved by the full Commission, may be found in finding reports, located in the National Archives, Records Administration, Record Group 220.

Panel One investigated the experiences of foreign militaries that historically or recently assigned women in their military forces. The countries selected for this effort included: Canada, Denmark, Israel, the Netherlands, Germany, Russia and the United Kingdom. Other agencies, including domestic law enforcement as well as the Federal Bureau of Investigation, the Central Intelligence Agency and the U.S. Coast Guard, all of whom have integrated women into their organizations, were studied. Combat and Prisoner of War issues were historically and legally researched, especially as they related to the most recent U.S. combat experience of Desert Shield/Desert Storm. Commissioners who served on Panel One were: MG Mary E. Clarke, USA (Ret.), Dr. William Darryl Henderson, and Ronald D. Ray, Chair.

Panel Two focused on physiological standards as they relate to general fitness or wellness, physiology pertaining to the differences between men and women, physiology of pregnancy and training, as well as specific fitness requirements for MOSs, AFSCs, ratings for job assignments, and the ultimate impact on physical readiness and effectiveness of the military. In addition to the physical aspects of the military environment, the unique factor of cohesion was analyzed. Modifications to equipment, facilities, clothing and training were researched to determine if any cost would be incurred if assignment policies for women were changed. Commissioners who served on Panel Two were: CPT Mary M. Finch, USA, Dr. Charles C. Moskos, and BG Samuel G. Cockerham, USA (Ret.), Chair.

Panel Three researched many of the major social issues and concerns, including the American family, the burdens borne by families of military service members, and current cultural values within American society. Panel Three also reviewed current DoD and individual Service policies concerning pregnancy, deployability, and the issues concerning child care for children of military families. Testimony and literature by recognized experts in fields such as sociology, theology, and psychology were used, as well as a review and analysis of the current DoD regulations and policies for personnel management and assignments. In addition, Panel Three reviewed the U.S. historical legacy of Vietnam, including the Prisoner of War experience. This panel also coordinated the civilian and military surveys conducted by The Roper Organization on behalf of the Commission. Commissioners who served on Panel Three were: Elaine Donnelly, Newton M. Minow, Esq., GEN Maxwell R. Thurman, USA (Ret.), and Meredith A. Neizer, Chair.

Panel Four investigated many of the issues that changes in current policy would have upon the members of the U.S. military. The research focused on personnel management issues in today's military, as well as the relationship between career development and retention to ensure a high standard of a qualified, All-Volunteer Force. The Panel examined the implications of any change in the combat exclusion laws and policies. Many of the core legal issues concerning equal protection, due process, levels of scrutiny as they relate to gender-based discrimination, and the deference which U.S. courts traditionally give to matters concerning national security were reviewed and analyzed. This Panel also researched the recent conflicts of Panama and Grenada to identify any significant lessons learned concerning utilization of women in the military. Commissioners who served on Panel Four were: BGen Thomas V. Draude, USMC, ADM James R. Hogg, USN (Ret.), MSgt Sarah F. White, USAFR, and Kate Walsh O'Beirne, Chair.

# APPENDIX C

## RESULTS OF PANEL FACT-FINDING RESEARCH

## 2: PHYSIOLOGY

The Commission investigated the theory that the physical demands of combat may exceed the physiological capacity of women. The following section contains Commission findings concerning physiological gender differences and their military significance.

### Body Composition

Compared to the average male Army recruit, the average female Army recruit is 4.8 inches shorter, weighs 31.7 pounds less, and has 37.4 pounds less muscle mass and 5.7 pounds more fat mass (Table 1). In general, women are at a distinct disadvantage when performing military tasks requiring muscular strength because of their lower muscle mass. Since fat mass is inversely related to aerobic capacity and heat tolerance, the average woman is also at a disadvantage when performing aerobic activities such as marching with heavy loads and working in the heat.[1] However, women's higher body fat is an advantage in swimming. The higher percentage of body fat allows women to swim higher in the water with less body drag. As a result, gender differences in swimming performance are smaller than other sports such as track and field.[2]

| Table 1. Comparison of Body Composition Measures for Male and Female Army Recruits | | | |
|---|---|---|---|
| | MALE | FEMALE | CHANGE |
| | (N=980) | (N=1003) | |
| MEASURE | MEAN | MEAN | |
| HEIGHT (IN) | 68.9 | 64.1 | -4.8 |
| WEIGHT (LB) | 160.4 | 128.7 | -31.7 |
| LEAN MASS (LB) | 133.5 | 96.1 | -37.4 |
| FAT MASS (LB) | 26.9 | 32.6 | 5.7 |
| % BODY FAT | 16.8 | 25.3 | 8.5 |

Meyers, et al., 1984.

### Muscular Strength

Strength is defined as the maximal force a muscle or muscle group can generate at a specified velocity.[3] Muscle strength is related to the cross sectional area of the muscle. The quality of muscle tissue and quantity of muscle fibers are the same in men and women, but the cross-sectional area of muscle fiber is 30 percent greater in men. This difference in cross-sectional area accounts for much of the difference in performance between genders.[4]

In general, men exhibit higher strength scores than women, but there is a significant degree of overlap between the genders. Women have been reported to have 55 percent of the upper torso, 72 percent of the lower torso and 64 percent of the trunk isometric strength of men.[5] A 1985 U.S. Army investigation found women exhibited 60 to 65 percent of the upper and lower isometric force of men.[6] A U.S. Navy study reported the dynamic upper torso strength of women ranged from 46 percent to 58 percent that of men (Figure 1).[7]

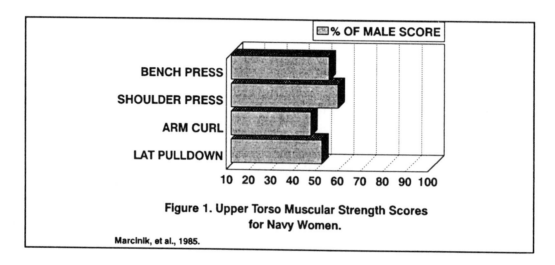

Figure 1. Upper Torso Muscular Strength Scores
for Navy Women.

Marcinik, et al., 1985.

Robertson and Trent reported the overlap in dynamic strength scores between Navy men and women was seven percent (i.e., 17 of 239 women had higher strength scores than the lowest scoring men) (Figure 2).[8]

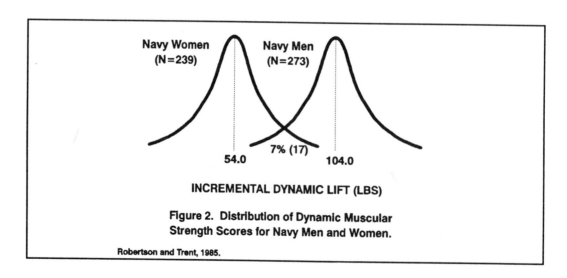

Figure 2. Distribution of Dynamic Muscular
Strength Scores for Navy Men and Women.

Robertson and Trent, 1985.

Higher androgen levels in men account for the large strength differences between the genders. Androgens are potent muscle building hormones that are responsible for much of the muscle enlargement seen in men during the adolescent growth spurt and as a result of strength training. Because women have low levels of androgens, they experience little muscle enlargement from strength training. Women can greatly improve their strength, but they do not develop large muscles.[2] They show an equivalent percentage increase in muscular strength as men who begin at a similar state of training.[3]

## Cardiorespiratory Capacity

Cardiorespiratory capacity is related to the efficiency of the heart, lungs and blood vessels to deliver oxygen to the working muscles. In general, women have a smaller heart mass, heart volume, and cardiac output than men. The amount of blood ejected during each contraction (stroke volume) and blood hemoglobin content of women is lower than that of men. Accordingly, the blood transports less oxygen, which when added to the lower cardiac output, results in a lower female aerobic capacity.[2]

The most widely used laboratory assessment of cardiorespiratory capacity is termed maximal oxygen consumption, or VO2 max. It has been reported that male and female Army recruits, representing a young civilian population, entered the Service with VO2 max scores of 51 and 37 ml/kg/min (women exhibited 73 percent of men's score).[9]

In a field setting, maximal run times have been used by the military Services to assess cardiorespiratory fitness. Research findings indicate that one and two mile run times of Army women were 74 percent and 79 percent those of men, respectively.[9]

The evaluation of cardiorespiratory capacity provides a valuable index of one's ability to sustain submaximal work over a period of time and may be a factor in the success of military operations involving load carrying during extended marches. Figure 3 illustrates the percentage of maximum oxygen consumption required by male and female cadets carrying 44.1 and 70.5 pound military loads at different velocities. It is evident the percentage of maximum oxygen consumption needed by women is significantly greater than men when carrying either load. The military application of this research is significant. During marches carrying the same load at the same velocity, individuals working at a lower percentage of their maximum oxygen consumption will perform more efficiently and will be able to continue marching for a longer period of time.

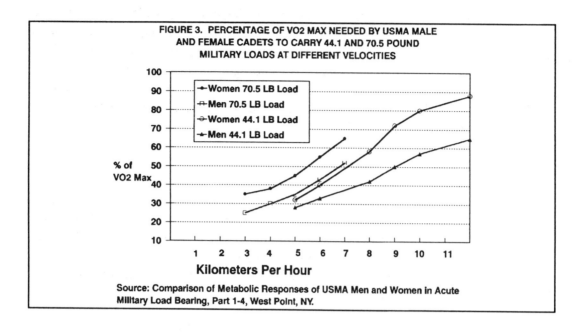

FIGURE 3. PERCENTAGE OF VO2 MAX NEEDED BY USMA MALE AND FEMALE CADETS TO CARRY 44.1 AND 70.5 POUND MILITARY LOADS AT DIFFERENT VELOCITIES

Source: Comparison of Metabolic Responses of USMA Men and Women in Acute Military Load Bearing, Part 1-4, West Point, NY.

## Muscularly Demanding Task Performance

Women in the military Services are currently restricted to non-combat roles. However, many of the occupations women are presently assigned to involve muscularly demanding tasks. During fact finding trips to Nellis AFB, the Marine Corps Air-Ground Combat Center, Naval Air Station Miramar, and Naval Station 32nd St., Commissioners had the opportunity to interview women who fly a wide variety of non-combat aircraft, serve on non-combatant ships and routinely perform physically demanding tasks in combat-support roles. Commissioners also observed women engaging in damage control evolutions aboard the USS Cape Cod (AD-43). This vessel is a destroyer tender with a crew of approximately 1,200 personnel (400 female crew members). Commissioners witnessed a mixed-gender team operating a 1.5 inch fire hose and lifting/carrying an injured individual using a Briggs/Cheney stretcher. It was emphasized that damage control evolutions were team efforts. If individuals had difficulty lifting a pump or stretcher, team members would assist them.

The following research studies were conducted by the Services in order to develop occupationally-based strength standards. Development of strength standards allows the Services to assign personnel to specialties which match their physical capabilities, regardless of their gender.

### Army

An analysis of U.S. Army occupational specialties found the most frequently performed physically demanding tasks involve heavy lifting, carrying, pushing and pulling (Figure 4).[10]

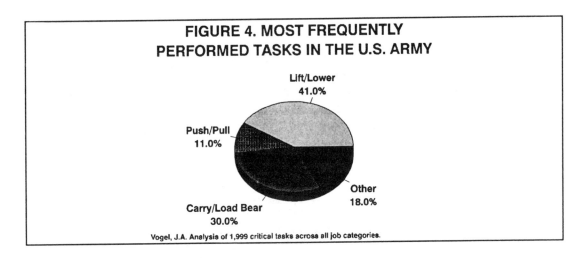

FIGURE 4. MOST FREQUENTLY PERFORMED TASKS IN THE U.S. ARMY

Lift/Lower 41.0%

Push/Pull 11.0%

Carry/Load Bear 30.0%

Other 18.0%

Vogel, J.A. Analysis of 1,999 critical tasks across all job categories.

Based on the data provided by this task analysis, a research study measured specialty-related lifting, carrying, pushing and pulling performance of male and female recruits.[11] The purpose of the lift test was to determine the heaviest weight that a soldier could lift and place on a shelf at chest height. The test simulated a soldier lifting equipment onto the bed of a 2.5 ton vehicle. The carry test measured the distance a soldier could carry the heaviest piece of equipment lifted to chest height. The push test measured the distance a soldier could push a specified weight in 30 seconds. The torque test assessed the maximum amount of torque a soldier could generate by pulling on a stationary bolt. This test simulated such common tasks as engine repair or changing tires. Results of this investigation indicated the performance of women during muscularly demanding lifting, carrying, pushing and pulling tasks ranged from 59.4 percent to 69.6 percent that of men. (Table 2)

| TASK | UNITS | MALE MEAN | FEMALE MEAN | % OF MALE SCORE |
|---|---|---|---|---|
| LIFT | LBS | 111.8 | 66.4 | 59.4 |
| CARRY | KGM | 5447.2 | 3195 | 58.3 |
| PUSH | KGM | 2581.8 | 1638.5 | 63.5 |
| TORQUE | N | 1940.5 | 1351.1 | 69.6 |

TABLE 2. TASK PERFORMANCE TEST SCORES FOR ARMY MEN AND WOMEN

*Navy*

Robertson and Trent have found the majority of physically demanding tasks performed by Navy personnel involve heavy lifting, carrying and pushing efforts.[8]  Figure 5 shows the percent of enlisted Navy men and women meeting performance standards on several muscularly demanding tasks performed within aviation ratings.  The percent of men meeting standards ranged from 100 percent (Drop Tank Carry) to 50 percent (MK-82 Bomb Lift).  The percent of women meeting standards on the same tasks was 68 percent and 0.0 percent, respectively.

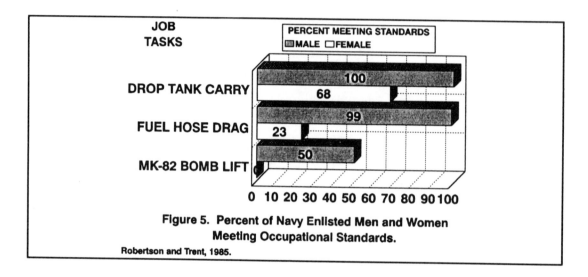

Figure 5.  Percent of Navy Enlisted Men and Women
Meeting Occupational Standards.

Robertson and Trent, 1985.

Figure 6 shows the distribution of scores for Navy enlisted men and women on the MK-82 Bomb Lift.  The overlap in male and female performance was ten percent (26 of 259 women performed better than the lowest performing men).

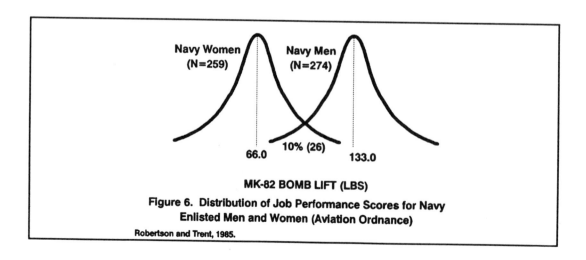

Figure 6.  Distribution of Job Performance Scores for Navy
Enlisted Men and Women (Aviation Ordnance)

Robertson and Trent, 1985.

Robertson and Trent also found significant gender differences in emergency shipboard task performance.[8] The percent of Navy enlisted men and women meeting standards for handling a 2.5 inch fire hose, lifting and carrying a P-250 water pump and extricating an individual via stretcher carry can be found in Figure 7.

The primary muscular demand of handling a fire hose nozzle involves the rapid, continuous sweep (both horizontal and vertical) of the nozzle, while wearing 14 pounds of cumbersome oxygen breathing apparatus.  The emergency P-250 water pump weighs 147 pounds and must be lifted out of a storage case and rapidly carried by two individuals to the scene of a fire or to a flooded compartment.  Two stretcher bearers must carry a victim (the average Navy man weighs 166 pounds) in a Stokes stretcher (25 pounds), up or down very steep ladders and maneuver through very tight spaces.

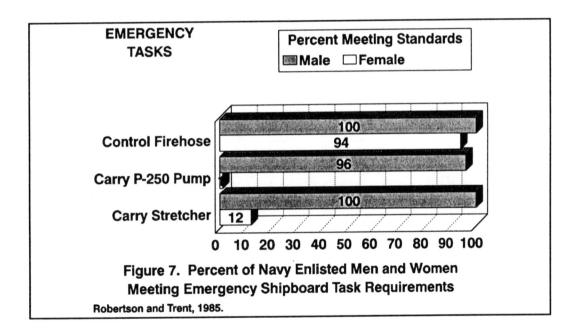

Figure 7.  Percent of Navy Enlisted Men and Women Meeting Emergency Shipboard Task Requirements
Robertson and Trent, 1985.

*Air Force*

Physically demanding tasks within Air Force Specialty Codes (AFSC) were identified to be manual material handling activities requiring lift/lower, push/pull, carry and holding efforts. Women's performance on three specialty-related tasks (holding a box overhead, carrying a tool box and pushing equipment (waist level) ) was found to be 52.8 percent, 55.4 percent, and 70.7 percent that of men, respectively.[12]

*Marine Corps*

Acting on the premise that every Marine is first and foremost a rifleman, it was decided that an analysis of this occupational specialty (MOS 0311) would serve as the foundation for job requirements and fitness standards of the U.S. Marine Corps. Environment and geography are significant factors in the tasks required of Marine riflemen, therefore tasks performed during combat training in desert, high altitude/cold weather, amphibious and jungle environments were described and quantified. This work was conducted by exercise physiologists from the Institute of Human Performance. Since testing involved Marines assigned to combat units, women did not participate as research subjects.

During Combined Arms Exercises in the Mojave Desert, the need for aerobic fitness was determined during repeated assaults on bunker complexes by fire teams from the Battalion Landing Team. An upper body strength requirement was identified as important in the manual handling of supplies.[13]

Observations were also made with the 1st Battalion, 7th Marines at the Marine Corps Mountain Warfare Center, Pickel Meadows, CA in a high-altitude, cold-weather combat environment. A high aerobic and strength requirement was identified during sustained marches on snowshoes. Loads exceeded 100 pounds and marches were accomplished up and down steep inclines, often in the dark and across uneven terrain for periods of several hours.[14]

Several observations of amphibious operations were conducted at Camp Pendleton, CA, Coronado, CA and Hawaii with elements of the 1st Battalion, 3rd Marines. The need for high levels of upper torso strength was most evident during off-loading of a Marine unit. Marines were dressed in full combat gear and were required to climb over the side of a combat cargo ship and onto a landing craft amid 15-20 foot sea swells at night. Clearly one mistake under these conditions would result in a catastrophic injury to either the Marines disembarking or the Navy sailors manning the ladder.[15]

Jungle operations were observed at the U.S. Army's Jungle Operations Training Center in Fort Sherman, Panama. Specific tasks identified as unique to the jungle environment included sustained swimming while towing equipment, rappelling and working with a machete.[16]

*Injury*

Research findings have indicated a high risk for injuries during Army basic combat training.[17] During training 51 percent of women and 27 percent of men were injured. The risk of lower extremity injury for women was 2.13 times that of men and for stress fractures 4.71 times that of men. The higher risk of injury for women was related to a lower level of fitness when compared to men.

It has also been reported that 54 percent of women sustained reportable injuries during Army basic training.[18] These injuries resulted in an average time loss of 13 days. During this study, women participated in an integrated conditioning program and completed extensive road marches wearing combat boots. Incidence of injury was related to greater body weight and body fat and limited leg strength.

*Environmental Stress*

In general, women are more sensitive to the effects of thermal stress due to several factors which include lower cardiorespiratory fitness, higher body fat content, and lower skin surface area. During marches at a set pace, women exercise at a greater percentage of their aerobic capacity than men, resulting in a higher heart rate, oxygen consumption and heat production. Because of this higher metabolic rate, women experience an earlier onset of fatigue and are at greater risk of heat injury than men during forced marches in a hot environment.[19] Studies have not found operationally significant gender differences in heat tolerance among acclimatized men and women of similar fitness.[20][21]

Studies have demonstrated comparable tolerance to acute hypoxia in men and women.[22][23] Women are perhaps more resistant than men to chronic hypoxia or altitude sickness. Women reported less gastrointestinal and cardiovascular symptoms associated with acute mountain sickness.[24] A more recent study has confirmed this reduced female likelihood of acute mountain sickness.[25]

Women have been reported to have an advantage in tolerating cold exposure due to a higher relative body fat content. Not all studies, however, demonstrated this female advantage. When percent body fat is controlled, men at rest in cold water demonstrated less heat loss than women of similar body fat. This may be because thin women have a higher surface to mass ratio than thin men.[26]

G stress is a factor to be considered in certain types of military aviation. A 1986 study compared the +Gz tolerance of 102 women and 139 men and found no significant differences in tolerance of exposures up to +7Gz during gradual onset runs (GOR) and Rapid Onset Runs (ROR) (Figure 8). There was a strong negative correlation between height and G-tolerance, and a weaker positive correlation between weight and G-tolerance. Thus women benefitted by being shorter than men on the average, but were adversely affected by being lighter than men.[27]

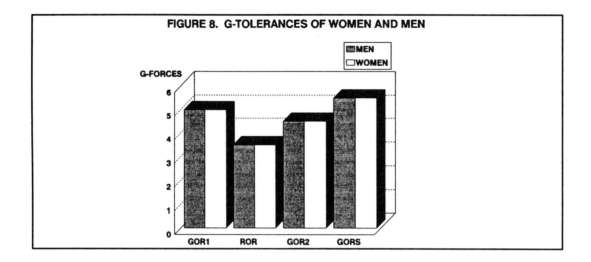

A more recent study conducted by Fischer and Wiegman found that women's G-level tolerance (both relaxed and straining) and G-duration tolerance (at levels above +7Gz) may be less than men's.[28] Results showed that a proportionate number of men and women attempted +8Gz for 15 seconds (55.9 percent and 56.5 percent, respectively) but, of those attempting the run, 63.2 percent of the women, compared to 80.9 percent of the men completed the run. Fewer women than men attempted +9 Gz for 15 seconds (31.4 percent and 42.0 percent, respectively), with 59.4 percent of the women and 72.6 percent of the men completing the run. The authors suggested that some of the difference may be due to the females' poor-fitting anti-G suits.

A Scientific Symposium on Women in Combat Aircraft co-sponsored by the Presidential Commission on the Assignment of Women in the Armed Forces reported there was no evidence in the scientific literature that defined a physiological basis to categorically restrict women from selection opportunity for combat aviation.[29]

A comprehensive review of the literature conducted by Lyons reported that the possibility of fetal damage in the early stages of pregnancy (before the diagnosis of pregnancy) appears to be the single biggest medical concern in allowing women access to all aviation careers.[30]

*Cognitive Factors*

Cognitive differences that exist between the sexes are generally not as clear-cut or consistent as the physical differences. The most well established differences are those in the areas of spatial and verbal abilities. Men have been demonstrated to be quicker than women in forming a mental picture and in distinguishing left from right.[31] Sherman has speculated that spatial ability differences may be the result of differential sex role or sex stereotype experiences.[32] Harris suggests that spatial skills are trainable and that female performance levels might be brought up to male scores with appropriate training.[33]

Female superiority in verbal ability appears to be as well established as male superiority in spatial ability. It has been reported that women score significantly higher in the area of vocabulary and word fluency.[34] Among U.S. Air Force pilot candidates, women performed better on verbal and fine dexterity tests, while men performed better on mechanical tests.[35] A Canadian study reported superior female ability in verbal ability and clerical speed/accuracy, but better male performance on tests of mechanical reasoning, visual/spatial ability, and quantitative ability.[36]

In terms of military significance, empirical data from contemporary research in sensation, perception, and psychomotor skills do not demonstrate meaningful differences in the capabilities and/or limitations of men and women and therefore should not be used as a basis for predicting differences in the abilities of members of either gender to perform effectively in combat aircraft.[37]

*Occupational Standards*

In 1976, the General Accounting Office found that enlisted Army women are in some cases being mis-assigned to MOSs beyond their physical ability. According to the testimony of COL Kowal, this practice still exists and costs about $16,000 for a track vehicle mechanic to be re-assigned to another MOS.[38] Based on these findings, the GAO issued recommendations to the military Services to develop physical and operational fitness standards for specialties which are gender-neutral. The anticipated benefits from using such a system in an operational environment include greater productivity and efficiency, as well as lower injury rates.

*Army*

The Exercise Physiology Division of the U.S. Army Institute of Environmental Medicine (USARIEM), under the direction of Dr. James A. Vogel, was tasked by the Army Deputy Chief of Staff for Personnel in 1977 to develop a fitness test battery to help match soldier capabilities with specific MOS strength requirements. This began a five year effort involving several major on-site field studies prior to the actual implementation of a new screening procedure. A Military Entrance Physical Strength Capacity Test (MEPSCAT) was developed for use at the Military Entrance Processing Station (MEPS) to determine minimum lifting ability and help enlistees select a MOS commensurate with their physical abilities. The MEPSCAT is based on lifting standards developed by the Department of Labor (Figure 9).

Although the Army made a concerted effort to develop this system, the MEPSCAT was never used as intended. It was initially used only as a recruiting guidance tool, and then was eliminated altogether in 1990 for political reasons.[38] The MEPSCAT failed because of disagreement about whether standards should reflect peacetime or wartime requirements.[10]

| JOB TASKS | OCCASIONAL (<20% OF THE TIME) (LBS) | FREQUENT (<20% OF TIME <80%) (LBS) |
|:---:|:---:|:---:|
| **FIGURE 9. ARMY MODIFIED DEPARTMENT OF LABOR PHYSICAL DEMAND CLASSIFICATION SYSTEM** <br> **LIFTING REQUIREMENTS** | | |
| LIGHT | 20 | 10 |
| MEDIUM | 50 | 25 |
| MODERATELY HEAVY | 80 | 40 |
| HEAVY | 100 | 50 |
| VERY HEAVY | 100 | >100 |

Gregor investigated the possibility of developing a gender-neutral standard for evaluating the physical performance of men and women.[39] He found that if current male physical fitness standards were used to evaluate women, then at every stage of an Army career most women would fail, and even superior women would seldom pass the male mean score.

Using data on Army ROTC cadets and published studies, he observed that the physical aptitude of women in the top 20 percent was equal to that of men in the bottom 20 percent. Similarly, despite ROTC training, only three percent of cadet women achieve the male mean score on the Army Physical Aptitude Test and 68 percent would fail under male standards. He compared the physical potential of top cadet men and women and observed a wide gap that no training system could close. In general, cadet women were found to be superior to Army women, but they do not achieve male norms.

Gregor investigated the effects of aging and reported that generally women over the age of 32 failed to meet the minimum male standard for retention. The proportion of mid-career women with permanent orthopedic injuries was also much greater than men.

The wide disparity between the average performance of men and women makes training men and women for direct combat impractical. Doing so would either undermine standards or frustrate women and both results would have harmful consequences on unit performance and morale. Absent a male manpower shortage, LTC Gregor concluded it would be unwise to open assignments in the combat arms to women.

*Navy*

The Navy does not have strength standards for occupational ratings. However, there are four programs which have more stringent fitness standards: (1) Airman, (2) Diver, (3) Explosive Ordnance Disposal, and (4) Sea, Air, and Land (SEAL) teams. All four programs receive their personnel from a variety of ratings and with the exception of the SEAL program are open to women. Only the SEAL Program requires a fitness assessment to maintain qualification in Naval Special Warfare.

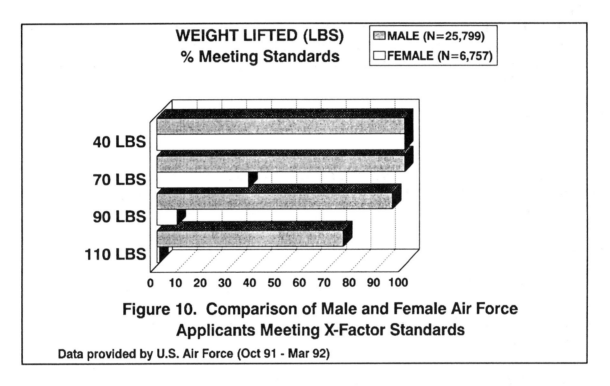

**Figure 10. Comparison of Male and Female Air Force Applicants Meeting X-Factor Standards**

*Air Force*

The Air Force requires strength screening of Air Force applicants for enlistment at the MEPS. Strength standards are based on lifting capacity determined by an incremental lift machine (X-factor). MEPS personnel perform the test as part of the physical exam. The minimum requirement for enlistment in the Air Force is a 40 lb lift. Additionally, some skills require a greater lift requirement. All lift requirements are gender-neutral. All women currently serving in each specialty meet X-factor standards. If an applicant selects a specialty that is above the individual's tested X-factor, the applicant is classified into a different specialty. There have been no approved or documented waiver requests for exceptions to the minimum X-factor. Strength testing can be repeated, if requested by training personnel for cross training purposes after medical personnel clear the individual to repeat the testing. Retesting is conducted by Morale, Welfare and Recreation Personnel.

Figure 10 shows the percentage of male and female Air Force applicants meeting X-factor weight lifting requirements. All of the men and women tested were able to meet the minimum lifting requirement of 40 lbs. However, only 68 percent of men and 0.8 percent of women were able to meet the 110 lb lift requirement.

*Marine Corp*

The Marine Corps does not conduct occupational strength testing at recruit training or at any other level. In addition to the semi-annual PFT, all Marines assigned to Fleet Marine Force units are required to complete a force march, with load carry equipment, two canteens, a helmet, and pack with prescribed load (40 lbs). The Marine also carries an individual or crew-served weapon. The Marine must march 15 miles at a rate of three miles per hour, within a total of five hours.

*Coast Guard*

The Coast Guard does not conduct any entry level physical fitness testing. General fitness, Coast Guard Academy, Officer Candidate School, and recruit training standards are gender-normed. Gender-neutral standards exist for aviators, boat crews, boarding teams, rescue swimmers, and divers.

*References*

[1] Marcinik, E. J., CDR (sel), USN. Testimony before the Commission, 26 June 1992.

[2] Brooks, G.A. and T.D. Fahey. *Exercise Physiology: Human Bioenergetics and Its Applications.* 1984.

[3] Fleck, S.J. *Designing Resistance Training Programs.* Human Kinetics Books, Champaign, IL 1987.

[4] Hosler, W. W. and J.R. Morrow. "Arm and Leg Strength Compared between Young Women and Men After Allowing for Differences in Body Size and Composition." *Ergonomics.* 25(4): 309-31, 1982.

[5] Laubach, L.L. "Comparative Muscular Strength of Men and Women: A Review of the Literature." *Aviation, Space and Environmental Medicine.* 47(5):534-542, 1976.

[6] Wright, J.A., D.S. Sharp, J.A. Vogel, and J.F. Patton. *Assessment of Muscle Strength and Prediction of Lifting in U.S. Army Personnel.* USARIEM Report No. M9/1985.

[7] Marcinik, E. J., J. A. Hodgdon, J.J. O'Brien, and K. Mittleman. *A Comparison of the*

*Effects of Circuit Weight Training on Navy Men and Women.* Naval Health Research Center Report. 1985.

[8] Robertson, D.W. and T.T. Trent. *Documentation of Muscularly Demanding Job Tasks and Validation of an Occupational Strength Test Battery (STB).* Report No. 86-1. Naval Personnel Research and Development Center, San Diego, CA. 1985.

[9] Vogel, J.A., J.F. Patton, R.P. Mello, and W.L. Daniels. *An Analysis of Aerobic Capacity in a Large United States Population.* USARIEM Report No. M28/1985.

[10] Vogel, J.A. Testimony before the Presidential Commission, 7 August 1992.

[11] Myers, D.C. and D. Gephardt. *Validation of the Military Entrance Physical Strength Capacity Test.* USA. 1984.

[12] Ayoub, M.M. *Establishing Physical Criteria for Assigning Personnel to Air Force Jobs.* Institute for Ergonomics Research. Texas Tech University, 1982.

[13] Davis, P.O., A.V. Curtis, and S.A. Bixby. *Physical Performance Tasks Required of U.S. Marines Operating in a Desert Environment.* Fairfax, VA, Institute of Human Performance, 1981.

[14] Davis, P.O., A.V. Curtis, and D. A. Hall. *Physical Performance Requirements of U.S. Marines Operating in a High Altitude Cold Weather Environment.* Fairfax, VA, Institute of Human Performance. 1982.

[15] Davis, P.O., B.J Sharkey, and D.A. Hall. *Physical Performance Requirements of U.S. Marines Operating in Jungle Operations.* Fairfax, VA, Institute of Human Performance. 1983.

[16] Davis, P.O., A. V. Curtis, and D.A. Hall. *Physical Performance Requirements of U.S. Marines during Amphibious Operations.* Fairfax, VA, Institute of Human Performance. 1983.

[17] Jones, B., R. Manikowski, J. Harris, J. Dziados, and J. Vogel. *Incidence of and Risk Factors for Injury and Illness among Male and Female Army Basic Trainees.* USARIEM Report Number T19. 1988.

[18] Kowal, D. *The Nature and Cause of Injuries in Female Recruits Resulting from an 8-Week Physical Training Program.* USARIEM Report No. M. 1979.

[19] Drinkwater, B.L. *Women and Exercise. Physiological Aspects in Exercise and Sport Science Reviews.* R.L. Terjung, Ed. The Collamore Press, Lexington, MA volume 12 pp. 21-51, 1984.

[20] Avellini, B. A., E. Kamon, and J. T. Krajewski. "Physiologic Responses of Physically Fit Men and Women to Acclimation to Humid Heat." *Journal of Applied Physiology.* 49:254- 261, 1980.

[21] Frye, A. J., and E. Kamon. "Responses to Dry and Wet Heat of Men and Women with Similar Aerobic Capacities." *Journal of Applied Physiology.* 50:65-70, 1981.

[22] Drinkwater, B.L., L.J. Folinsbee, J.F. Bedi, , S.A. Plowman, A.B. Loucks, and S.M. Horvath. "Responses of Women Mountaineers to Maximal Exercise during Hypoxia." *Aviation, Space and Environmental Medicine.* 50: 657-662, 1979.

[23] Wagner, J.A., D.S. Miles, S.M. Horvath, and J.A. Reyburn. "Maximal Work Capacity of Women during Acute Hypoxia." *Journal of Applied Physiology.* 47: 1223-1227, 1979.

[24] Harris, C.W., J. L. Shields, and J.P. Hannon. "Acute Mountain Sickness in Females." *Aerospace Medicine.* 37: 1163-1167, 1966.

[25] Kramar, P.O., B.L. Drinkwater, L.J. Folinsbee , and J.F. Bedi. "Ocular Function and Incidence of Acute Mountain Sickness in Women at Altitude." *Aviation, Space and Environmental Medicine.* 54: 116-120, 1983.

[26] McArdle, W.D., J.R. Magel, R.J. Spina, M.M. Toner. "Adjustment to Cold Water Exposure in Exercising Men and Women." *Journal of Applied Physiology.* 56 (6): 1565-1571, 1984.

[27] Gillingham, K.K., C.M. Schade, W.G. Jackson, and L.C. Gilstrap. "Women's G-Tolerance." *Aviation, Space, and Environmental Medicine.* 57:745-53, 1986.

[28] Fischer, M.D. and J.F. Wiegman. "Female Tolerance to Sustained Acceleration - A Retrospective Study." *KRUG Life Science.* San Antonio Division, San Antonio, TX. 1992.

[29] Crisman, Dr. R. Presidential Commission on the Assignment of Women in the Armed Forces. Science Seminar Proceedings. 14-15 September 1992.

[30] Lyons, T.J. "Women in the Fast Jet Cockpit-Aeromedical Considerations." *Aviation, Space, and Environmental Medicine.* 63: 809-18, 1992.

[31] Crowley, J.S. *Cerebral Laterality and Handedness in Aviation: Performance and*

[32] Sherman, J.A. and E. Fennema. "Distribution of Spatial Visualization and Mathematical Problem Solving Scores." *Psychology of Women Quarterly.* 3, 157-167, 1978.

[33] Harris, L. J. *Sex Differences in Spatial Ability: Possible Environmental, Genetic,and Neurological Factors.* In Kinsbourne, M. (Ed.). Asymmetrical Function of the Brain. Cambridge, Cambridge University Press, p. 405-522, 1978.

[34] Hyde, J.S., E.R. Geiringer, and W.M. Yen. "On the Empirical Relation Between Spatial Ability and Sex Differences  in other Aspects of Cognitive Performance." *Multivariate Behavioral Research.* 10, 289-309, 1975.

[35] Kantor, J.E., B.E. Noble, S.A. Leissey, and T. McFarlane. *Air Force Female Pilots Program: Initial Performance and Attitudes.* AFHRL-TR, 1978.

[36] Hicks, R. J. "Female Aircrew: The Canadian Experience." *AGARD Symposium on Recruiting Selection, Training and Military Operations of Female Aircrew.* Tours, France. 4-5 April, 1990.

[37] Boff, K. K.  "Sensory, Perceptual and Psychomotor Performance.  Presidential Commision on the Assignment of Women in the Armed Forces." *Science Seminar Proceedings.*  14-15 September 1992.

[38] Kowal, D.  Testimony before the Commission, 6 April 1992.

[39] Gregor, W. J.  Testimony before the Commission, 12  September 1992.

# TABLES AND FIGURES FOR PHYSIOLOGY

# APPENDIX C

## RESULTS OF PANEL FACT-FINDING RESEARCH

### 3: INTERNATIONAL

The Commission considered the historical context and current policies of foreign militaries in their assignment and utilization of women. Seven countries, Canada, the Netherlands, Denmark, Russia (formerly the Soviet Union), Great Britain, Germany and Israel, were chosen because they either currently utilize or have utilized women in combat or near combat military specialties. As part of this effort, Commissioners made fact-finding trips to Canada, the Netherlands, Denmark, Great Britain and Israel. In addition, Commissioners met with a group of Russian general officers at the John F. Kennedy School of Government at Harvard University.

The international military experience should be considered in the context of each country's cultural and historical background; geographic location and relative size; equal opportunity goals (if any); and importance of military readiness to its national survival.

Although some women presently serve in combat positions in the Netherlands, Denmark, Canada and Great Britain, none have actually served in a direct combat unit under wartime conditions except in the Soviet Army during World War II (WWII).

Comparative analysis has shown that countries which have integrated women into combat positions have made this decision primarily because of equal opportunity (Canada, the Netherlands and Denmark) or demographic considerations (Great Britain). These four countries have pursued a gender-neutral policy in assigning women to military specialties. (See matrix, p. 31.) Although the goal of these countries is a 20 percent "critical mass" for women in the naval, air and ground forces, all are willing to operate at a minimum level of five percent.

The Soviet Union, Germany and Israel have each, to a different degree, utilized women in close combat situations, but did so only when a serious threat to their national survival existed. After the crisis passed, each of the nations adopted policies which excluded women from combat.

## *COUNTRIES THAT UTILIZE WOMEN IN COMBAT POSITIONS*

### *Canada*
The Canadian Forces (CF) established programs in 1990 to ensure that the integration of women into the military forces would cause no threat to national security or discrimination to women who choose to enlist.

A "gender-neutral" career management philosophy guides the CF. It is not an affirmative action program, and there are no quotas or limits. The charter allows "equal opportunities" to exist without institutionalized bias. The CF policy is to identify bias where it does exist and to continually monitor the situation until it is resolved.

Improper relationships between the sexes are a problem in the CF. While this includes "fraternization" and the development of sexual relationships, the most critical one continues to be sexual harassment. In order to better deal with this problem, the Navy has adopted a "zero tolerance" program aimed at controlling behavior. The Canadians stated that these are manageable problems requiring strong leadership.

Task requirements are based on CF needs, meaning neither women nor men have vested rights of service to a particular unit or occupational specialty. This is explained to each new recruit. As a result, each person is required to serve in any capacity the CF determines to be in the best interest of national defense.

### Denmark

The policy of the Ministry of Defence is that women will have the same opportunities as their male colleagues. A stated goal of the Ministry of Defence is that the number of women should rise from its current level of two percent of total force to ten percent by 2005. Based on equal opportunity considerations, women are fully integrated into the Danish Army, Air Force and Navy. They are employed and work together with men in mixed units and are subject to the same chain of command. The Commission was told that combat readiness is not an over-arching concern of the Danish military; Danes believe they will have ample time to prepare their forces as conflicts present themselves.

Physical training requirements are based on a group rather than task specialty requirements, with the physical shortcomings of one servicemember in completing a task being distributed among the others in that unit. Finally, the Danes have tested all-female units and concluded that they were less efficient than units which were mixed-gender.

### The Netherlands

According to the Secretary General of the Dutch Armed Forces, the emphasis on equal opportunity for women in the military is shaped by the country's philosophical approach to equal opportunity. As a result, the Dutch Government is currently trying to increase the percentage of women in the Armed Forces from five to eight percent. The purpose is to have enough women throughout the Armed Forces to ensure a self-supporting "critical mass" of women.

The goal for the Dutch is to increase the number of women in the Army, in spite of difficulties in recruiting them. The Dutch Army now believes that programs initially designed to enhance the integration of women may have in fact produced resentment against women. The male soldiers see "unfair" policies which in turn have resulted in a backlash among men who believe they are at a disadvantage.

## Ground Combat

In the last five to ten years, Canada, Denmark, the Netherlands and Great Britain have opened many, and in some cases, all ground combat occupation specialties to women. (See matrix, p. 31.) It has been difficult, however, for any of these countries to attract and retain women in any significant numbers. In fact, the goal of achieving at least five percent women in ground combat units has not been met by any army integrating women into ground combat forces.

### Canada

A 1989 decision by the Canadian Human Rights Tribunal opened all combat positions in the Canadian Forces (CF) except submarines to women. Based on this decision, the CF invited women from both inside and outside the military to join the infantry; 103 women responded to the offer. Due to limited interest and a need to integrate women quickly, none of the women were prescreened or required to meet any minimum standard before being assigned to a unit. Consequently, attrition was severe, due primarily to physical and endurance considerations, with only one woman able to meet the requirements of the infantry test.

CF personnel staff stated that physical training (PT) standards for infantry specialties were modified to reflect actual requirements, although it appeared that they were relaxed to accommodate the integration of women. For example, the required pack weight for the infantry has been reduced to twenty-four kilos (fifty pounds), and the current test requires that male and female soldiers be able to only carry a soldier of similar weight a set distance.

### Great Britain

In Great Britain, there are currently no women in the ground combat forces (infantry, armor, artillery, combat engineers). The British Army Board, however, is developing tests based on combat standards to determine if women will be permitted to enter these positions.

Within the last year, the Women's Royal Army Corps was dismantled and servicewomen are now formally integrated into the Royal Army. While there are no statutory restrictions prohibiting women from pursuing any job skill in the Army, it is Ministry of Defence policy that women not serve in infantry and armor units until the Army can adequately set standards. Women may be assigned to all positions in the artillery except, due to the weight of the shells, cannon artillery.

### Denmark

Servicewomen must meet the same physical standards as men. In the Army, functions and postings in a unit require different levels of physical strength. Therefore, two physical standards exist, and a unit can be manned with men and women that meet different standards without compromising the total strength necessary for the mission of the unit. The Danish military believes the total strength of the unit is the primary consideration in measuring combat effectiveness and that the stronger would help the weak in completing the task or assignment.

The only physical requirement women must meet to qualify for combat arms positions currently is to run 2100 meters within 12 minutes.

The Danish Army conducted a battery of tests administered to women in combat specialties in the 1980s. The trials included integrating women into infantry companies, two tank companies, a field artillery battery and a short-range air defense battery.

Seventy women, or 20 percent of the unit, participated in the infantry test. Thirty-nine women left after several weeks and the test was discontinued. According to the women, they had difficulty coping with the physical strength requirements, the training program and the military discipline and environment. Since the test was conducted, however, the Danes have integrated women into ground combat arms.

### The Netherlands

The physical standards required for combat arms specialties exclude 20 percent of the men and 80 percent of the women. Currently, there is one woman serving in the infantry, no women assigned to tankers and no women combat engineers. Physical standards are both age-normed and gender-normed.

In the Dutch Army, the overall attrition rate for women in the ground forces is roughly seventy-five percent. A major reason for this, according to the Chairman of the Dutch Parliament's Committee on Defence, is that the physical standards for entrance into the ground combat positions are too difficult for women to attain. The Dutch are re-examining these standards to determine if some can be relaxed without compromising military readiness.

### Combat Aircraft

Currently, Canada, the Netherlands, Great Britain and Norway (see matrix, p. 31) allow women to fly in combat positions. Six women in foreign militaries have been qualified to fly combat aircraft. Two are currently on flight status.

### Canada

Three women have qualified to fly combat aircraft (CF-18) in Canada; one is an active CF-18 pilot, one currently serves in a staff position after a successful tour as a CF-18 pilot (currently on medical profile) and one woman withdrew from the program after a partial tour, based on family considerations and leave incentives.

### The Netherlands

Currently, there is one active F-16 pilot undergoing low-level training and another who failed to complete the training.

### Great Britain

One British servicewoman was in Tornado (British combat fighter) training but she did not complete the program.

### Israel

The Israelis do not allow women to fly combat or support aircraft, although women are allowed to train the men in aircraft simulators. Israeli Air Force (IAF) briefers stated that Israel does not have any women pilots in their Armed Forces. The rationale for this policy is the high cost of training and the potential conflict between a woman's desire to raise a family and the career commitment (length of service) required of pilots by the IAF.

### Denmark

It is the policy of the Danish Armed Forces not to accept female fighter pilots until all of the physical implications of flying high performance aircraft have been evaluated. The Danish Surgeon General and Armed Forces Health Services maintain there are "unknown factors about the female body" (reproductive system) and the long term effects that high performance flying will have on them.

Based on these findings, the Ministry of Defence has kept this restriction on women combat pilots in place. However, according to Danish briefers, there are considerable internal pressures in the Danish Air Force to reevaluate its policy and the possibility exists that this policy may be overturned in 1993.

## Combatant Vessels

Canada, the Netherlands, Denmark and Great Britain allow women to serve on combatant ships. Based on experiences (Canada and Great Britain) and testing (the Netherlands and Denmark), the integration of women into combatant vessels has been considered a success, particularly in occupational areas such as communications.

### Great Britain

In 1990, the British Navy integrated women onto combatant ships, but it will not be until 1994, when the four year enlistments are complete, that the British Navy will be able to fully evaluate the positive and negative impacts women have had on cohesiveness and readiness on combatant vessels.

The goal of 10-15 percent of women crew members on combatant and non-combatant ships has not yet been achieved. To date, only 300 of the 4,000 Navy servicewomen have volunteered for sea duty. It should be noted that the British have had difficulty recruiting men as well as women for sea duty; this is generally attributed to the long hours and difficult work aboard ship. Sailors are on call 24 hours a day and have virtually no privacy while aboard ship. The ship with the largest number of women on board is the HMS Invincible, an aircraft carrier which recently assigned 75 women into a crew of 1,100. This required the reassignment of 75 men to shore duty. Among other duties, women are working on the flight deck, and the British maintain there has been no degradation in combat effectiveness aboard ship, in spite of the difficulties of integrating such a large contingent of sailors aboard ship at one time.

### Denmark

Denmark's Navy, in a series of tests involving women in combat specialties, conducted trials in employing women aboard Danish ships for a four year period between 1981 and 1985. The vessels selected were a seaward defence craft, two minelayers, two fast patrol boats and two fishery protection ships. Attrition rates during the test period were 18 percent for women and 13 percent for men. Men were on sick leave two percent of the time, compared to the women's rate of three percent (not including pregnancy).

While women expressed general satisfaction with their roles on these vessels, men were more inclined to express apprehension toward having women aboard. The tests showed that women were more conscientious in their work and performed well during unfavorable weather and prolonged training periods. The primary weakness in the women's performance was in the heavier deck work and cannon firings. While the women performed well, they generally took longer to accomplish the same work, particularly in strenuous physical tasks.

Female sailors were aboard the Danish naval vessel which was a part of the Maritime Coalition Force during Operation Desert Shield/Desert Storm. At the conclusion of the operation, a report was issued which evaluated the experience. It concluded that women performed admirably, with no degradation in readiness. While the report stated that fraternization and sexual harassment are unavoidable, they can be controlled by having strong leadership and firm guidelines in place. In addition, problems with relationships did develop, and families at home expressed concern about having husbands on cruises with mixed crews.

The Danes maintain, however, that these problems are manageable, that the initial apprehension was understandable, but that they intend to keep women in their naval crews.

### Canada

Although no attempts were made to measure the impact on operational readiness or unit effectiveness at the initial time of integration (1989), it was noted as a general impression by some commanders that higher standards of conduct have been established since women were put aboard ships.

In order to ensure successful integration, the Canadians believe it is necessary to have a minimum number of women, or "critical mass" on each sea vessel. This is done to maintain the well being of the women aboard and provide an adequate social support system. The CF believes that having 25 percent women aboard is the optimum percentage, with five percent being the acceptable minimum.

Berthing women aboard ship has been the most difficult issue for the Canadian Navy.

Before gender integration, berthing was done by rank and functional area to make the shift rotations more efficient. But with women on board, berthing is done by gender. Because there are fewer women than men in the Canadian Navy, berthing in this manner could cause bunks to go unfilled or junior members to be bunked with senior personnel. Without strong leadership, this has the potential to cause morale and cohesion problems.

In terms of the financial costs of integrating women aboard ship, the Commission was told expensive modifications to ships are not necessary to accommodate women, that common sense arrangements are usually as effective as structural modifications to the ship.

### The Netherlands

All combat assignments are open to women in the Royal Dutch Navy, with the exception of submarines and the Marine Corps. The Dutch have nine frigates and five minehunters with mixed crews, with each ship on average having a ten percent female crew.

Women served in combat roles on Dutch ships in the Gulf War. In their work in the operations and communication departments, women served as surface picture operators, air picture operators and communications operators.

## COUNTRIES THAT RESTRICT WOMEN FROM COMBAT POSITIONS

### Israel

The Commission focused on the Israeli military experience more than that of other foreign armies because there has been a misperception that Israel utilizes women in combat positions. In fact, although women are conscripted into the Israeli Defense Forces (IDF), they currently are not allowed to serve in combat units or any position which would place them in "harm's way." This means that they are excluded from, among other specialties, flying combat or support aircraft, serving as drivers, or being involved in any combat support positions which would require direct contact with forward units in time of war.

The National Service Law (1959) defines and regulates military service obligations. The law pertains to all citizens of the State of Israel. Specifically, it obligates all women who are in good health, unmarried, childless, and not prohibited for reason of religion or conscience to serve in the IDF. Approximately 70 percent of the women of conscription age (18 years old) in Israel serve the obligatory term of two years, during which time all serve as enlisted soldiers. Women who wish to become officers are required to serve an additional six months to ensure the IDF makes the most of the skills the women have gained.

The most important role of women in the IDF is that of "combat multiplier." They fill non-combat jobs in order to free men for combat positions. Besides having an adequate number of men to serve in the military, factors which shape the Israeli policy towards the utilization of women are: a traditional Semitic culture, a religious orthodoxy, a constant threat of war, and, perhaps most importantly, a fear of having women captured and exploited by the enemy.

### 1948 Struggle for Independence

In the underground organizations active in Palestine before the Struggle for Independence in 1948, women constituted over 15 percent of total forces. They served as escorts of convoys to besieged areas of the country, took part in operational activities, smuggled explosives and participated in blowing up trains, bridges and buildings.

In the battle for national survival, women were forced into combat-related positions. With a population of only 600,000, there was little choice but to utilize everyone who was available to serve and defend the territory. In spite of this, the use of women in combat-related positions was never recognized formally by the Israelis and was discontinued after 1948.

### Russia

As a result of current demographic conditions, the loss of non-Russian conscripts and the collapse of the Soviet Union, the new Russian government is again considering expanding the role of women in the Russian military. The goal of the Ministry of Defense is to establish a legal basis to define the types of assignments open to women. Russian forces are considering putting women into air defense and ground control units. Despite these new developments, the Commission was told women will not be placed in combat units or in "harms way".

### World War II

In terms of scale and degree of involvement, Soviet women's participation in combat roles during WWII surpassed that of women in all other wars in modern history.

The Commissioners were told by Russian general officers that the heroic involvement of Soviet women in combat was the result of propaganda directed primarily at the Soviet youth movement during WWII. This propaganda was also directed abroad as examples of the success of an egalitarian Soviet society. The officers said the primary purpose of this propaganda was to mobilize the last remaining pool of manpower available to Soviet forces, that much of what has been written historically on the involvement of Soviet women in WWII does not adequately address that point. This is a revisionist view of the role of women in the Soviet forces during WWII and one which needs further review.

The practice of Soviet Armed Forces before WWII was to utilize women in support units only. During the first years of WWII, that policy continued. By 1942, however, the enormous threat to national survival and the great numbers of Soviet men killed by German forces required that the U.S.S.R. mobilize selected women, who constituted the only remaining source of manpower.

By 1943, Soviet women had entered all the Services and assumed roles they would have until the war's end: infantry, anti-aircraft defense, armor, artillery, transportation, communications and nursing.

Soviet women were mobilized on a large-scale, reaching a peak strength during the war, including partisans and irregular forces, of nearly one million troops. Eight hundred thousand women were uniformed troops in the Red Army, and 500,000 of them served either in combat or combat support roles. All served as volunteers, as there was no universal conscription for women. Women constituted roughly eight percent of a total armed force of 12 million in the Soviet Union by the war's end.

Most women served in mixed gender units, and there is little documentation of any problems with integration. However, women did have trouble with tasks involving upper body strength. For example, there were instances of women being killed because they were unable to throw grenades effectively.

The U.S.S.R. activated three female air regiments: the 586th Interceptor regiment which flew Yakovlev fighters; the 587th short-range bomber regiment and the 588th Night (light) Bomber regiment (the Night Witches).

The fighter regiment accompanied Soviet combat units from the Volga River to Vienna, and is reported to have shot down 38 enemy planes. The night bomber regiment flew in light canvas biplanes, and had 4,376 members at its peak. By the end of the war, the regiment was flying up to 300 sorties a night over Poland. The Commission was told that the "Night Witches" flew on dangerous missions with casualty rates of up to 75 percent. The women, considered expendable, were given the worst aircraft to fly. The biplanes could withstand a maximum load of only 600 pounds, and top speed, when armed, was 100 mph.

At the end of WWII, as Stalin and the High Command prepared for what was to become the Cold War, the role of women in the Armed Forces was rapidly diminished to an overall total estimated at roughly 25,000.

*Germany*
The post-war German constitution prohibits the assignment of women in the military, except to medical assignments and the military band.

During WWII, German women served in traditional support roles as well as air defense, anti-aircraft, searchlight, radar and barrage balloon batteries. Women were employed in order to free men for combat duty. By the end of WWII, over 300,000 women had served in all theaters of operation.

A large number of women auxiliaries were captured on the Eastern Front during the latter stages of the war. Reportedly, many were abused and/or executed, while others spent years in Eastern Bloc labor camps. This had a traumatic impact on the psyche of the German people, and has been a consideration in the assignment policies of women in Germany's post-war military.

*Relevant Findings*
*The findings relevant to this section are listed below. These findings may be referenced in Appendix C, part 4. The first number refers to the panel. For example, 1.15 is a Panel 1 finding.*

| | | | | | |
|------|------|-------|-------|-------|-------|
| 1.80 | 1.93 | 1.100 | 1.110 | 1.116 | 1.128 |
| 1.81 | 1.94 | 1.103 | 1.111 | 1.118 | 1.129 |
| 1.82 | 1.95 | 1.104 | 1.112 | 1.122 | 1.130 |
| 1.83 | 1.96 | 1.105 | 1.113 | 1.123 | 1.131 |
| 1.85 | 1.98 | 1.106 | 1.114 | 1.125 | 1.132 |
| 1.92 | 1.99 | 1.109 | 1.115 | 1.126 | 1.135 |

# WOMEN IN FOREIGN MILITARIES

| | United States | Denmark | Canada | Netherlands | Great Britain | Germany | Israel | Russia (CIS) | France | Norway |
|---|---|---|---|---|---|---|---|---|---|---|
| **Total Troop Strength:** | | | | | | | | | | |
| Active: | 1,894,905 | 29,400 | 86,600 | 101,400 | 300,100 | 469,000 | 141,000 | 3,988,000 | 453,100 | 34,100 |
| Reserve: | 1,613,600 | 72,000 | 26,100 | 155,700 | 340,100 | 853,000 | 504,000 | 5,602,000 | 419,000 | 285,000 |
| Paramilitary: | 68,000 | Unknown | 6,600 | 4,700 | Unknown | 21,000 | 6,000 | 530,000 | 91,800 | 700 |
| **Female Troop Strength:** | | | | | | | | | | |
| Active: | 214,899 | 1,000 | 9,400 | 1,750 | 18,100 | 462 | 15,510 | 25,000 | 13,000 | 972 |
| Percent Active Force: | 11.3% | 3.4% | 10.9% | 1.7% | 6.0% | 0.1% | 11% | 0.7% | 2.90% | 2.40% |
| **Women Serve in Combat:** | No | Yes | Yes | Yes | Yes | No | No | No | No | Yes |
| **Combat Exclusion** | | | | | | | | | | |
| Law: | Yes | No | No | No | No | Yes | Yes | Yes | Yes | No |
| Policy: | Yes | No | No | Yes | Yes | Yes | Yes | Yes | Yes | No |
| **Breakdown of Women In Total Force: 1991** | | | | | | | | | | |
| Land | 64,576 | 379 | 1,574 | 1,069 | 5,985 | 0 | Classified | Unknown | 8,608 | 452 |
| Sea | 54,934 | 190 | 746 | 841 | 3,905 | 0 | Classified | Unknown | 2,249 | 315 |
| Air | 58,273 | 379 | Unknown | 109 | 6,827 | 0 | Classified | Unknown | 5,681 | 199 |
| Nursing Corp | 35,270 | Unknown | Unknown | Unknown | 2,380 | 462 | Classified | Unknown | 2,760 | Unknown |
| **Female Roles in the Military:** | | | | | | | | | | |
| **A. Non-Combat** | | | | | | | | | | |
| Administrative: | Yes | Yes | Yes | Yes | Yes | Yes | Yes | Yes | Yes | Yes |
| Medical: | Yes | Yes | Yes | Yes | Yes | Yes | Yes | Yes | Yes | Yes |
| **B. Combat Support:** | Yes | Yes | Yes | Yes | Yes | No | No | No | Yes | Yes |
| **C. Combat** | N/A | | | 134 (Total) | | N/A | N/A | N/A | | |
| Land: | | 7 | 8 | Unknown | No | | | | Limited to | Yes |
| Infantry: | | 3 | 2 | Unknown | No | | | | 3% of total | Yes |
| Artillery: | | 1 | 2 | Unknown | No | | | | land combat | Yes |
| Armored: | | | | | | | | | force. | |
| Sea: | | | | | | | | | | |
| Combat Vessels: | | | 234 | 280 | 500 | | | | No | Yes |
| Submarines: | | 0 | No | No | 0 | | | | No | Yes |
| Air: | | | | | | | | | | |
| Fighter Pilot | | No | 1 | 1 (1 Training) | 0 | | | | No | Yes |
| Helicopter Pilot | | 0 | 8 | 9 | Unknown | | | | No | Yes |

## PANEL ONE CHARTER

Charter approved 1 June 1992

Panel One will conduct a literature and fact finding investigation of American and related foreign military experiences and relevant experience of domestic law enforcement and similar paramilitary agencies on the assignment and utilization of women. The panel will also take the lead in reviewing, in conjunction with other panels, the assignment, utilization and problems encountered by women with U.S. military forces during Operations Desert Shield and Desert Storm. An objective of the panel's investigation, analysis and evaluation is also to develop and ensure a better understanding of the nature of the extraordinary demands of combat, what combat actually involves (land, sea and air), the differences and similarities between military combat and police forces, and the missions they perform. An additional objective is to determine how women have been or may be utilized in the military while achieving and maintaining the highest standards of military and combat readiness. Panel One will investigate the issue of female prisoners of war, testimony of female POWs from Desert Storm as well as other conflicts and historical accounts. In conducting its evaluations, the panel will review the history of the assignment of women in U.S. Armed Forces and related historical examples from other nations, but will concentrate on 20th century combat arms experience and other tests conducted to evaluate the roles, benefits and limits of women in the military and in combat. Specific cases may include, but are not limited to, the combat experience of Israel, Great Britain, Canada, France, Russia, Vietnam and Germany. Countries which do not use women in their armed forces will also be reviewed. The panel will rely on published or otherwise available information, expert testimony, trip reports and new or existing surveys.

## PANEL ONE FINDINGS APPROVED BY THE COMMISSION

1.1        World War I definition of combat: Although the term is not defined, combat is intimately connected with mobile forces, of which the division is the basic organization. There are two general classes of combat, offensive and defensive; decisive results can only be attained through offensive combat.

           a. Panel 1 Report; 23 October 1992, p. 55.
           b. DASD(MM&PP). Response to Question, 10-12 September 1992.

1.2        Post World War II and Korea definition of combat: Throughout the post-World War II period, definition of the term "combat" was absent from both Army and Joint Terminology.

           a. Panel 1 Report; 23 October 1992, p. 58.
           b. DASD(MM&PP). Response to Question, 10-12 September 1992.

1.3        Vietnam definition of combat: "Combat" remained undefined throughout the Vietnam War.

a. Panel 1 Report; 23 October 1992, p. 58.

b. DASD(MM&PP). Response to Question, 10-12 September 1992.

1.4 Historically, the U.S. Army has left the term "combat" undefined. Its definition has been largely determined as a function of specific arms and services. Within the brief compass of this survey, it has not been possible to determine whether this omission stems from a deliberate policy or not. It is possible that Army leaders have sought to avoid the delimitation on Army roles and missions that might have arisen from too strict a definition.

a. Panel 1 Report; 23 October 1992, p. 60.

b. DASD(MM&PP). Response to Question, 10-12 September 1992.

1.5 The Department of Defense currently defines "combat mission" as follows: "A task, together with the purpose, which clearly requires an individual unit, naval vessel or aircraft to individually or collectively seek out, reconnoiter and engage the enemy with the intent to suppress, neutralize, destroy or repel that enemy."

a. Panel 1 Report; 23 October 1992, p. 62.

b. DASD(MM&PP). Response to Question, 10-12 September 1992.

1.6 The Army definition of "direct combat" is: "...engaging an enemy with individual or crew-served weapons while being exposed to direct enemy fire, a high probability of direct physical contact with the enemy, and a substantial risk of capture. Direct combat takes place while closing with the enemy by fire, maneuver, or shock effect in order to destroy or capture, or while repelling assault by fire, close combat, or counterattack."

a. Panel 1 Report; 23 October 1992, p. 61.

b. U.S. AR 600-13.

1.7 The Navy definition of "combat mission" is: "A mission of an individual unit, ship or aircraft that individually, or collectively as a naval task organization, has as one of its primary objectives to seek out, reconnoiter, and engage an enemy. The normal defensive posture of all operating units is not included within this definition."

a. Panel 1 Report; 23 October 1992, p. 61.

b. U.S. SECNAVINST 1300.12A.

1.8 The Air Force defines combat in AFR 35-60 (in reference to the assignment of women) as the following:

(1)     Aircraft, whose principal mission involves aerial combat, defined as:

    (a)     Delivery of munitions or other destructive material against an enemy.

    (b)     Aerial activity over hostile territory where enemy fire is expected and where risk of cature is substantial.

(2)     Noncombatant positions or units where the type, degree, and duration of risk of direct combat, exposure to hostile fire, or capture is equal to or greater than the air, sea or land combat units with which they are normally associated in a given theater of operations.

(3)     Instructor or staff positions where training or experience in combat aircraft is a prerequisite.

    (a)     The exclusions above are based on Air Force plans for employing personnel resources during wartime.

    (b)     The basis for evacuation of Air Force military women will be the same as for the military men.

a.  Panel 1 Report; 23 October 1992, p. 61.
b.  U.S. AFR 35-60.

1.9     The definition of combat by the Marine Corps (in MCO 1300.8P) is:  "For assignment purposes, direct combat action is defined as seeking out, reconnoitering, or engaging in offensive action."

a.  Panel 1 Report; 23 October 1992, p. 62.
b.  U.S. MCO 1300.8P.

1.11    It is key to note in Service definitions of land combat as well as in military history, personal accounts, and testimony before the Commission the repeated emphasis on the extreme physical demand and violent nature of combat. Evidence stress in physically "closing" with the enemy -- this means over difficult ground, under debilitating loads, under the harshest climatic and environmental conditions, and under the duress of mortal danger.  Physical contact with the enemy is a probable condition of combat and risk of capture is inherent at all times when in proximity to the enemy or conducting air or sea operations in contested airspace or waters.

a.  Ray, Ronald.  Personal Statement.  September 1992.

1.12    Technology has made combat more lethal -- it has not altered the fundamentally physical nature of combat and the offensive requirement and prolonged fighting spirit required to "close with" the enemy. Technology has not altered the harshness of the environment on the battlefield nor mitigated the effects of nature which can be more deadly than the enemy. Technology has increased the difficulties which arise from an increased operational tempo and increased requirements for logistical (material) support. Technology, as embodied in increased target acquisition capabilities and increased weapons' ranges, places more people in the area of operations at mortal risk at any given moment in time. Notwithstanding the increased mortal risk to those personnel in combat support and combat service support roles, the units and branches of the Service which by their design and mission are to close with the enemy in close combat and direct fire will remain at far greater risk than those in support roles.

a.  Panel 1 Report; 23 October 1992, pp. 70, 72.
b.  Service Representatives. Testimony before the Commission, 8 June 1992.
c.  Ray, Ronald. Personal Statement. September 1992.

1.13    The Coast Guard places no restrictions upon women regarding the number of women or the occupational specialties in which they can serve.

a.  Panel 1 Report; 23 October 1992, p. 85.
b.  U.S. Department of Transportation, *Women in the Coast Guard Study*, U.S. Coast Guard, 1990, p. I-2.
c.  Kime, J. M., Admiral, USCG. Testimony before the Commission, 1 October 1992, p. 25.

1.14    Joint Pub 1, Joint Warfare of the U.S. Armed Forces, was reviewed in the Commission's work for the definition of combat. JCS Pub 1 describes the nature of modern warfare:

(a)    Environment: "...the ability to project and sustain the entire range of military power over vast distances is a basic requirement for the Armed Forces and contributes, day in and day out, to the maintenance of stability and deterrence worldwide. This projection of power is inherently a joint undertaking because of the inter-Service linkages of modern command, control, and communications, the multi-Service structure of the defense transportation system, and the broad range of forces typically involved."

(b)    Technology: "Forces on land, at sea and in the air now reinforce and complement each other more than ever before: in range of lethal striking power, common logistic and communications capabilities, and many other areas. Overhead, space-based capabilities affect all terrestrial forces, with a potential we have only begun to grasp."

(c)     Speed of Communications and Pace of Events: "...in the modern world have accelerated...joint teams must be trained and ready prior to conflict."

(d)     People: "...([T]he most important and constant elements in warfare) are influenced by the changing environment...all our people must be adept at working with others, both as fellow members of the U.S. Armed Forces and with allies and other foreign partners."

(e)     Friction, Chance, and Uncertainty: "...still characterize battle. Their cumulative effect comprises 'the fog of war.'... Modern technology will not eliminate friction, chance, and uncertainty from military undertakings."

a. Panel 1 Report; 23 October 1992, p. 14.
b. JCS Pub 1, *Joint Warfare of the U.S. Armed Forces*, 11 November 1991, pp. 2-4.

1.15     American women have been historically excluded/exempted from being drafted or serving in combat. This policy is based upon religious principles, military custom, experience and cultural values.

a. Panel 1 Report; 23 October 1992, p. 66.
b. Ray, Ronald. Personal Statement. September 1992.

1.16     The DoD Risk Rule states, "risks of direct combat, exposure to hostile fire, or capture are proper criteria for closing non-combat positions or units to women, when the type, degree, and duration of such risk are equal to or greater than the combat units with which they are normally associated within a given theater of operations."

a. Panel 1 Report; 23 October 1992, p. 67.
b. Ray, Ronald. Personal Statement. September 1992.

1.17     The DoD Risk Rule, developed in 1988 to help standardize assignments of women for non-combat positions in the Armed Forces, is an imperfect standard.

a. Panel 1 Report; 23 October 1992, p. 68.

b. Ray, Ronald. Personal Statement. September, 1992.

1.18    On December 5, 1991, the Air Force restriction (Title 10, U.S.C. 8549) was repealed. The Navy restriction (Title 10, U.S.C. 6015) was amended. The change removed the restriction on female aviation officers and authorized their assignment to combatant ships as part of the air wing or other air element.

a. Panel 1 Report; 23 October 1992, p. 66.
b. 10 U.S.C. 8549.
c. 10 U.S.C. 6015.

1.19    The Army has never had a statute that restricts the assignment of women in the Army, although the Army cites Title 10, U.S.C. 3012 with regard to making assignment policy for soldiers.

a. Panel 1 Report; 23 October 1992, p. 67.
b. Becraft, Carolyn. *Women in the Military*, WREI, 1992.
c. 10 U.S.C. 3012.

1.20    The Army uses a Direct Combat Position Coding (DCPC) System to determine the probability of engaging in direct combat for every position. According to AR 600-13, P1 indicates those positions to which women may not be assigned and P2 is used for all other positions.

a. Panel 1 Report; 23 October 1992, p. 67.
b. U.S. AR 600-13.
c. Hulin, Terry, COL, USA. Personal Statement. 28 October 1992.

1.21    It has become more difficult to separate combat support units from combat units. Over the horizon weapons capability has increased the vulnerability of civilians, as well as personnel in the rear, to injury and death.

a. Panel 1 Report; 23 October 1992, p. 68.
b. Ray, Ronald. Personal Statement. September 1992.

1.22    "...The presence of women aboard Coast Guard vessels involved in Navy operations most likely would be determined by inter-Service or inter-departmental agreement. Under those circumstances, while 10 U.S.C 6015 would not require the Coast Guard to remove female crew members from its vessels, the Navy could, of course, refuse to accept operational control of Coast Guard vessels with women assigned."

According to the 1990 Women in the Coast Guard Study, "...while a Department of the Navy General Counsel opinion has stated that, although Title 14 U.S. Code Section 3 grants the Secretary of the Navy authority to make combat exclusion applicable to the Coast Guard, it was clear that Title 10 U.S. Code Section 6015 contains no statutory requirement for the removal of women from Coast Guard combatants after transfer from the Service to the Department of the Navy (during war)...The issue between the Coast Guard and the Navy remain imperfectly resolved and there is disagreement within each Service as well."

a. Panel 1 Report; 23 October 1992, p. 84.
b. U.S. Department of Transportation, *Women in the Coast Guard Study*, U.S. Coast Guard, 1990, pp. IV-15.
c. Kime, J. M., Admiral, USCG. Testimony before the Commission, 28 October 1992, p. 25.

1.23    Notwithstanding the end of the Cold War, the United States can anticipate a continuation of low and mid intensity conflicts that have been endemic since the onset of the Korean War.

a. Hayden, H. T., *The Shadow War,* Vista, CA: Pacific Aero Press, 1992, pp. 6-16.

1.24    In the modern era, combat frequently occurs without a formal declaration of war. Combat operations without a declaration of war are sometimes referred to as, "low-intensity conflict" or "police actions", a term that lacks legal definition but nevertheless is used to describe the United States' reaction to what it considers a threat to American lives and property, or to a vital national interest, or a gross violation of international law.

a. Panel 1 Report; 23 October 1992, p. 64.
b. Bishop, J. *Encyclopedia of the American Constitution*, Vol. 3., 1986, p. 1399.

1.25    In "operations short of war," combat support and service support units are at increased risk of hostile action by the enemy. The fact that warfare in forms other than direct combat operations has become more dangerous does not mean that direct, offensive, close combat is any less difficult or dangerous in any sense. The fact that women serving in support units as currently authorized, are at risk of terrorist or guerilla action in "operations short of war" or low intensity conflict does not mean that an entirely different set of conditions does not exist in combat units, which by design and mission actively seek to close with and engage the enemy in these scenarios.

a. Panel 1 Report; 23 October 1992, pp. 64, 65, 68.
b. Ray, Ronald. Personal Statement. September, 1992.

1.28    Women serving in positions currently authorized by statute regulation and policy are at risk of death, injury, and capture on the modern battlefield and the high seas. This risk will increase if an expansion of womens' roles is mandated. The evidence regarding womens' performance and the risks they have endured is not drawn from combat as combat is presently defined by the Services. That women have performed adequately in support roles and suffered hardships and risks as entailed in those roles does not necessarily equate to performance in closing with and engaging the enemy in close combat and direct fire.

a. Panel 1 Report; 23 October 1992, pp. 68, 69.
b. Ray, Ronald. Personal Statement. September, 1992.

1.29    Labels such as "low-intensity conflict" and "peacekeeping operations" have no relevance or meaning at the level of the rifleman, the rifle squad, the tank crew, etc...To these individuals and groups every assault is a frontal assault; every battle, every skirmish, is a high-intensity conflict. Further distinctions are meaningless at the small unit and individual level in combat units.

a. Ray, Ronald. Personal Statement. September, 1992.

1.30    The future battlefield will reflect the Military Technical Revolution (MTR), which simply stated is, "...a major change in the nature of warfare brought about by the innovative application of new technologies which, combined with dramatic changes in military doctrine, employment concepts, and force structure, fundamentally alter the character and conduct of military operations."

a. Panel 1 Report; 23 October 1992, p. 75.
b. Office of Secretary of Defense. "Net Assessment, Working Paper," August 1992.

1.31    Civilian law enforcement and paramilitary unit operations cannot be compared to the physically demanding level of intensity, enormity of tasking, and deployability requirements placed upon the U.S. military. They can however attest to womens' individual capacity to handle short-term stress and react to emergency situations.

a. Panel 1 Report; 23 October 1992, p. 77.
b. Ray, Ronald. Personal Statement. September 1992.

1.32    Title VII of the Civil Rights Act of 1964 does not apply to uniformed military personnel. Title VII has not been legally applied to the military in recognition of the fact that its provisions could impose constraints on the United States by which potential military opponents, not operating under the same constraints, might derive an advantage. Warfare is a supranational survival contest in which opposing sides vie for any advantage; unilateral policies adopted to promote principles other than military necessity may place the adopting party at increased risk of defeat.

    a. Panel 1 Report; 23 October 1992, p. 80.
    b. Ray, Ronald. Personal Statement. September, 1992.

1.33    Racial integration of the military Services ordered in 1948 by President Truman was carried to fruition during the Korean War based upon existing manpower needs.

    a. Panel 1 Report; 23 October 1992, p. 81.
    b. Ray, Ronald. Personal Statement. September, 1992.

1.33A   President Truman stated, in signing Executive Order 9981, which ordered the integration of the Armed Forces, "... it is essential that there be maintained in the Armed Services of the United States the highest standards of democracy, with equality of treatment and opportunity for all those who serve in our country's defense."

    a. Executive Order 9981. Issued by President Harry S. Truman. 1948.

1.34    The unprecedented numbers of women who deployed to a combat environment and served in non-traditional roles in Desert Shield/Storm provide some basis for evaluating the assignment of women to combat positions.

    a. Testimony before the Commission, 1 November 1992.

1.35    Because women did not serve in direct combatant positions in the Gulf War no conclusions have been drawn by the Services on the basis of that war regarding the assignment of women to combat positions in land, sea or air forces.

    a. Henderson, Wm. Darryl. Personal Statement. September, 1992.

1.36    Although most women did not have direct combat experience as defined by the Armed Services and DoD, some women did experience combat in Operation Desert Storm.

a. Testimony before the Commission, 1 November 1992.

1.37    Ample scientific evidence exists to definitively establish that although there is an overlap in the physical capabilities of males as a group and females as a group, males on average are larger and physically stronger and faster, and possess higher levels of endurance than females. These differences are significant and of the highest relevance to many combat duties. Wartime physical demands and requirements establish the standards for military selection and training.

a. Gregor, William, LTC, USA. Testimony before the Commission, 12 September 1992.
b. Ray, Ronald. Personal Statement. September 1992.

1.38    There is no current short-fall in military manpower.

a. Ray, Ronald. Personal Statement. September, 1992.

1.39    Lieutenant Colonel Gregor testified before the Commission regarding a survey he conducted at an Army ROTC Advanced Summer Camp last summer on 623 females and 3,540 males. The study focused on whether women meet the same physical fitness standards as men. His conclusion, broadly stated, is that they do not. Evidence Gregor presented to the Commission include:

(a)    Using the standard Army Physical Fitness Test, he found that the upper quintile of women at West Point achieved scores on the test equivalent of the bottom quintile of men.

(b)    From these data he concluded that if the Army selected those who met a nominal standard on the test, 80 percent of the women who applied could not get an Army commission.

(c)    Only 21 women out of the initial 623 (3.4 percent) achieved a score equal to the male mean score of 260.

(d)    On the push-up test, only seven percent of women can meet a score of 60, while 78 percent of men exceed it.

(e)    Adopting a male standard of fitness at West Point would mean 70 percent of the women he studied would be separated as failures at the end of their junior year, only three percent would be eligible for the Recondo badge, and not one would receive the Army Physical Fitness

Badge, because not a single woman achieved a score equal to what men must meet to get the badge.

(f)    Few women can meet the male mean standard.  Men below the standard can improve their scores, whereas the women who have met the standard have already achieved a maximum level beyond which they cannot improve.

(g)    "Given the gap between male and female potential, if you put a women and a man in a small squad, and the woman is achieving a level of fitness that is equivalent to your male population, she is at the upper end, as Gregor pointed out, of her potential and he is at the bottom end of his potential."

(h)    According to Gregor, age also makes a difference:

(i)  "A 20 to 30 year old woman has about the same aerobic capacity as a 50 year old man."

(ii)  Women begin losing bone mass at an earlier age than men, meaning they are more susceptible to orthopedic injuries, which "leads to the conclusion that women initially selected for the combat arms would not survive to career-end."

(iii)  Adopting a single standard for fitness at mid-career in the Army would eliminate most women for failure to meet the standard.

(j)    One of Gregor's questions, given the adoption of one standard, is how the Armed Forces can select for combat from the top quintile of their women for physical fitness, but exclude men from the bottom two quintiles, knowing the bottom two quintiles of men mostly exceed the top quintile of women.  Gregor stated there are women who could meet and even exceed a single objective standard challenging enough for men, but finding the one woman out of 100 who can do so, as opposed to the 60 percent of men who can, would mean "I have just traded off 60 soldiers for the prospect of getting one.  The cost considerations are prohibitive".

a.  Panel 1 Report; 23 October 1992, p. 72.
b.  Gregor, William, LTC, USA.  Testimony before the Commission, 12 September 1992.

1.41 The Geneva Convention applies to all cases of declared war and any other conflict which may arise and may be invoked broadly upon the advent of hostilities. Despite 168 signatory nations (approximate number due to forming of new nations), adherence to the Geneva Convention Relative to the Treatment of Prisoners of War of August 12, 1949 is dependent upon the culture of the captor, the cultural friction between the warring nations, and national leadership.

 a. Panel 1 Report; 23 October 1992, p. 89.
 b. Parks, Hays. Testimony before the Commission, 8 June 1992.
 c. Parks, Hays. Personal Statement. 29 October 1992.

1.42 Desert Shield and Desert Storm U.S. aircrews downed and prisoners captured by Service:

  A. USMC:

| | |
|---|---|
| Total number of aircrew | 2588 |
| Total number of captured aircrew | 5 (5 returned) |
| Total percent captured | 0.19% |

  B. THE NAVY

| | |
|---|---|
| Total number of aircrew | 37,086 |
| Total number captured | 3 (3 returned) |
| Total number KIA | 6 |
| Total percent captured and KIA | 0.024% |

  C. THE AIR FORCE

| | |
|---|---|
| Total number of aircrew | 5754 |
| Total number captured | 8 (8 returned) |
| Total number MIA | 17 (declared KIA) |
| Total percent captured and MIA | 0.43% |

  D. THE ARMY      Not Available

 a. Panel 1 Report; 23 October 1992, pp. 101-102.
 b. DASD(MM&PP). Response to Question 14, 8-9 June 1992.

1.43 During World War II, five U.S. Navy nurses were captured when Guam fell and 85 other U.S. Nurses were captured on Corregidor. Since these women were treated as internees rather than treated as POWs no general observations or conclusions can be readily drawn from their experience as detainees.

 a. Panel 1 Report; 23 October 1992, p. 95.

b. Parks, Hays.  Testimony before the Commission, 8 June 1992.
c. Parks, Hays.  Personal Statement.  29 October 1992.

1.44     Unlike the experience of U.S. female personnel detained during World War II, female soldiers captured today (except for chaplains and medical personnel) will be treated as combatants.  According to the Law of War, a combatant is anyone who is not a chaplain or medical personnel.  In addition, the DoD definition (Joint Pub 1-02) states the definition of detainee "is a term used to refer to any persons captured or interred or detained by an Armed Forces such as a prisoner of war, retained personnel (chaplain and medical personnel) or civilian internees."

a. Panel 1 Report; 23 October 1992, pp. 95- 96.
b. Parks, Hays.  Testimony before the Commission, 8 June 1992.

1.45     Elimination of the threat of sexual abuse of captured female U.S. personnel is impossible.  There are numerous accounts which document signatory nations violating provisions of the Geneva and Hague Conventions.  There is simply no means by which the U.S. can be reasonably assured that if female personnel were captured that they would not be sexually molested.

a. Panel 1 Report; 23 October 1992, p. 96.
b. Ray, Ronald.  Personal Statement.  September 1992.

1.46     Two U.S. female POWs were captured during the war in the Persian Gulf.  A representative from the Army in testimony before the Commission, stated that each was the victim of an indecent assault.  One of the women has denied that any such assault took place.  Indecent assault was described as "touching of private parts without consent."

a. Panel 1 Report; 23 October 1992, p. 96.
b. Testimony before the Commission, 8 June 1992.

1.47     There is no data on the impact of U.S. female POWs upon POW unit cohesion, other U.S. male POWs, and the United States as a nation, because of the scarcity of information and experience available.  However, German experience in World War II with female POWs influenced current German policy regarding not allowing women in the military except in medical units and the military band.

a. Panel 1 Report; 23 October 1992, pp. 52, 98-101.
b. "Federal Republic of Germany", *Women in the NATO Forces*, Brussels, 1991.

1.48    Code of Conduct/Survival, Evasion, Resistance and Escape (SERE) training which lasts 17 days (Fairchild AFB), attempts to simulate the prisoner of war experience. Trainees learn field techniques for creating shelter, finding food and water, and evading detection in a hostile environment.

   a.  Joint SERE Agency. Testimony before the Commission, 8 June 1992.
   b.  U.S. DoD Directive 1300.7.
   c.  Donnelly, Elaine. Personal Statement. 2 November 1992.

1.49    Code of Conduct/SERE training addresses the issue of sexual assault/exploitation by training both men and women how to cope. The providers of training think that resistance of the technique, i.e., showing the captor this approach is ineffective, is the only way to minimize its use by an enemy.

   a.  Panel 1 Report; 23 October 1992, p. 99.
   b.  Joint SERE Agency. Testimony before the Commission, 8 June 1992.

1.50    The Joint Services SERE Agency (JSSA) representatives commented on SERE training as follows:

   A.  In the SERE training course, there are no gender differences in performance between men and women. Colonel Graham stated, "Some of the key findings of that survey [Joint Services SERE Agency Survey], across the board, male, female, students and instructors, they saw no gender differences in the performance of females in the SERE Training Program...we have no evidence to suggest that one sex is more capable than another in enduring captivity."

      1.  Colonel Graham: "These same studies show that in many cases it is the cultural background of the woman or the person that is in as a POW that is more important than biological factors such as age or sex...[W]ell, the cultural background of the individual is the thing that seems to be that aspect which makes the biggest difference, as opposed to whether or not that person is male or female, or what her age is, or what her race is."

      2.  Men react differently when a fellow female SERE trainee is threatened with abuse as opposed to a similar threat to a fellow male SERE trainee. Major Jessen: "...It appears that the concern stems from this need to be responsible, the male perceives, as a result of our culture, and what the students report as we talk to them about the survey is that they feel a

C-45

need to do something, feel a need to stop it, or they feel the need to protect."

3.      Mistreatment of female POWs will have a negative impact on male captives (particularly if the female captive becomes pregnant). Colonel Graham stated, "Females will have a harmful effect on the males. This was not held by the students. In what was probably what they thought was politically correct, neither males nor females thought that females would have any impact on the males in captivity, but the instructors who observed the training -- and some of this training goes on without females in classes; other classes have females -- the instructors, both males and female, noticed a marked difference in the impact that the females had on men in this training. Pregnancy was noted by all involved as a negative impact on morale and discipline in the camp."

4.      According to the JSSA Survey, women are less concerned with themselves being sexually exploited than are their male counterparts. Colonel Graham: "Females are less concerned with sexual exploitation than the men, and this goes back to what I was talking about before, the men are very concerned with what happens to the females in camp."

5.      Three thousand, eight hundred and fifty-five women have graduated Level C SERE training, including aviators, aircrews, SERE instructors, military police and flight surgeons.

a.  Panel 1 Report; 23 October 1992, pp. 99, 100.
b.  Joint SERE Agency. Testimony before the Commission, 8 June 1992.

1.51     There was no sexual abuse substantiated of male U.S. POWs from the Vietnam conflict to present.

a.  DASD(MM&PP). Response to Question 2, 31 July/3 August 1992.

1.52     The training of certain female personnel in SERE is prudent preparation for the contingency that they may be captured.

a.  Joint SERE Agency. Testimony before the Commission, June 8, 1992.

1.53    The physical demands upon downed aviators escaping or evading capture or resisting torture are well exemplified by the American experience during the Vietnam War and to a lesser extent the Gulf conflict.

    a. Panel 1 Report; 23 October 1992, pp. 103, 104.
    b. Ray, Ronald. Personal Statement. September, 1992.

1.54    Desert Storm was an historic military mobilization, not only because of the total number of forces deployed over a short period of time, but also because the Armed Forces deployed up to 40,000 women overseas for the first time in a major American military operation.

    a. Panel 1 Report; 23 October 1992, p. 107.
    b. Becraft, Carolyn. "Women in the U.S. Armed Services: The War in the Persian Gulf," *WREI*, March 1992.
    c. U.S. DoD, "Utilization of American Military Women in Operation Desert Shield and Desert Storm," August 2, 1990 - April 11, 1991.

1.55    Women in the U.S. military comprised approximately 6.8 percent of U.S. forces deployed to the Persian Gulf. By Service, there were approximately 26,000 Army, 3,700 Navy, 2,200 Marine and 5,300 Air Force women deployed.

    a. Panel 1 Report; 23 October 1992, pp. 107, 108.
    b. U.S. DoD, "Conduct of the Persian Gulf War, Final Report to Congress," Appendix R, April 1992.

1.56    Twenty-three Marine women qualified for and received the Combat Action Ribbon, having been engaged by, "or action during which she was under enemy fire" with Iraqi troops.

    a. Panel 1 Report; 23 October 1992, p. 106.
    b. Draude, Thomas V. BGen, USMC. Personal Statement before the Commission. 2 November 1992

1.57    Duties of women during Desert Shield/Desert Storm: Among other specialties, women flew reconnaissance aircraft and helicopters, drove supplies and equipment into Kuwait, brought enemy prisoners of war back into holding facilities, and commanded brigade, battalion, company, and platoon size units in the combat support and combat service support areas.

    a. Panel 1 Report; 23 October 1992, pp. 107, 108.

    b.  U.S. DoD, "Conduct of the Persian Gulf War, Final Report to Congress," Appendix R, April 1992.

    c.  U.S. DoD, "Utilization of American Military Women in Operation Desert Shield and Desert Storm," August 2, 1990-April 11, 1991.

    d.  Beck, M. "Our Women in the Desert," *Newsweek*, 10 September 1990.

1.59        Deployabilty figures for Operation Desert Shield/Desert Storm:

(a)    DoD stated detailed deployability rates by Service, component, or unit are not comparable and therefore must be restricted to overall rates of non-deployability for men and women within the Department of Defense as a whole. Service briefings indicate that women were roughly three times more non-deployable then men. All Services have indicated that military readiness was not affected, however.

(b)    While reported deployability rates differed for each Service, in all cases data indicated non-deployability rates for women in each Service were at least 1-1/2 to approximately 3-1/2 times higher than for men.

(c)    The most prevalent cause of non-deployability, for both men and women, was medical. Reported information indicates over two percent of men and nine percent of women considered for deployment were classified as non-deployable for medical reasons.

(d)    The Army, Navy and Marine Corps all specifically investigated pregnancy in the medical category. Pregnancy accounted for approximately half of the medically non-deployable women. This equated to roughly 4.5 percent for all women considered for deployment from these three Services.

(e)    While DoD stated that detailed results are not meaningful, reported information indicated that overall early return rates were approximately two percent for men and two and one half percent for women.

    a.  Panel 1 Report; 23 October 1992, pp. 109-112.

    b.  DoD, "Utilization of American Military Women in Operation Desert Shield and Desert Storm," August 2, 1990-April 11, 1991.

    c.  DoD, "Conduct of the Persan Gulf War, Final Report to Congress," Appendix R, April 1992.

    d.  Scarborough, Rowan. "Women Fall Short on Battle Readiness," *Washington Times*, 28 July 1992.

    e.  Willis, Grant. "Report Less Deployable than Men During Gulf War," *Air Force Times*, 10 August 1992.

1.60  Some reported in testimony before the U. S. Senate that U.S. Army servicewomen were raped or sexually assaulted while serving in the Persian Gulf region while serving in Desert Shield/Desert Storm.  In several cases, women waited several weeks or months to report the assaults.

a.  Panel 1 Report; 23 October 1992, pp. 114, 115.
b.  Lancaster, John.  "Twenty Four Women Assaulted on Gulf Duty," *Washington Post*, 21 July 1992.

1.62  Thirteen women were killed and two were taken prisoner of war during Operation Desert Shield/Desert Storm.

a.  Panel 1 Report; 23 October 1992, p. 106.
b.  U.S. DoD,  "Utilization of American Military Women in Operation Desert Shield and Desert Storm," August 2, 1990-April 11, 1991.

1.63  Conclusions from Appendix R, a three page section of the "Final Report to Congress, Conduct of the Persian Gulf War" stated:

(a)  Women were fully integrated into their assigned units.
(b)  Women performed vital roles, under stress, and performed well.
(c)  Current laws and policies were followed.

It should be noted that DoD stated there was no department or service mechanism to collect and report gender-specific information to higher headquarters on the deployment of women in the Gulf.  Information provided was only available at the unit level.

However, testimony to the Commission revealed that some combat support or combat service support units in fact got ahead of combat units.   In OSD's view, women were not in combat in the Gulf War.

a.  Panel 1 Report; 23 October 1992, p. 113.
b.  U.S. DoD, "Conduct of the Persian Gulf War, DoD Final Report to Congress," Appendix R, April 1992.
c.  U.S. DoD,  "Utilization of American Military Women in Operation Desert Shield and Desert Storm," August 2, 1990-April 11, 1991.

1.64  The GAO Report, "Operation Desert Storm, War Highlights Need to Address Problem of Nondeployable Personnel" stated, "Data was insufficient to determine the extent of non-deployables."

(a) In a report released on August 31, 1992, the General Accounting Office (GAO) reported that "The Department of Defense said nondeployables were not considered a problem because the Services were able to replace them with other personnel. Nevertheless, available data indicates that the number of nondeployables was sizeable." The causes of nondeployability ranged from incomplete training to varying medical conditions or personal problems.

(b) The GAO also found that soldiers who did not have updated family care and support programs experienced enormous difficulties during deployment, which added stress, morale problems, and affected readiness. Although overall nondeployment rates among women were far lower, in some (Army) units 18 to 20 percent of their female soldiers were nondeployable. The primary reasons for nondeployability among female solders were disqualifying physical profile and pregnancy.

(c) According to the GAO, the prescreening of reservists to avoid calling up those who could not deploy helped to minimize and mask the potential for nondeployability problems.

a. Panel 1 Report; 23 October 1992, p. 110.
b. U.S. GAO. "Nondeployable Personnel in the Persian Gulf," GAO/NSIAD-92-208, 31 August 1992.

1.65 The large deployment of women in the Gulf, and the resulting media coverage that in many cases may have led a number of Americans to believe women served in combat military occupation specialties. They did however serve in a combat area and supported the combat arms.

a. Panel 1 Report; 23 October 1992, p. 114.
b. U.S. DoD, "Conduct of the Persian Gulf War, DoD Final Report to Congress," Appendix R, April 1992.

1.66 The Miller/Moskos survey reveals that of those surveyed, 22 percent of the women soldiers deployed to the Gulf believe they were "in combat roles". Seventy one percent of those surveyed did not believe they were; nine percent were not sure. It should be noted that men did not participate in the survey.

a. Panel 1 Report; 23 October 1992, p. 114.
b. Moskos, Dr. Charles C. and Miller, Laura. "1992 Survey on Gender in the Military [Army]," 28 August 1992.

1.67    Women have moved into such a great variety of non-traditional military occupation specialties that not deploying them would have impaired the ability of the units to which they were assigned to do their job.

    a.  Panel 1 Report; 23 October 1992, p. 114.
    b.  U.S. DoD, "Utilization of American Military Women in Operation Desert Shield and Desert Storm," August 2, 1990-April 11, 1991.
    c.  U.S. DoD, "Conduct of the Persian Gulf War, DoD Final Report to Congress," Appendix R, April 1992.

1.68    Some witnesses have argued that opening combat positions now excluded would increase the pool of candidates, thereby increasing unit effectiveness. However, most testimony has focused on the issue of equal opportunity.

    a.  Panel 1 Report; 23 October 1992, p. 105.
    b.  Ray, Ronald. Personal Statement. September 1992.

1.69    The Roper Organization report, "Attitudes Regarding the Assignment of Women in the Armed Forces: The Military Perspective," September, 1992 discovered the following:

The Roper Poll defined combat as, "...Direct engagement of our military with a foreign enemy, operating deadly weapons with the intent to kill and the risk of being killed. Of all assignments, direct combat exposes members of the military to the highest risk of injury, capture and death."

    (a)    Of the personnel deployed to the Persian Gulf, the performance of men in their unit was rated as excellent or good by 98 percent of the military who served in Desert Shield/Desert Storm. Sixty-one percent of the women who served in Desert Shield/Desert Storm were rated excellent or good. Units as a whole were rated excellent or good by 96 percent of those who served.

        (i)    Of the personnel deployed to the Persian Gulf, the performance of men and women by service were rated as: 52 percent of Army personnel rated womens' performance as only fair or poor (48 percent excellent or good), 56 percent of Marine personnel rated womens' performance as fair or poor (44 percent excellent or good). Sixty-three percent of Navy personnel rated women as excellent or good (37 percent rated them fair or poor), and 83 percent of Air Force personnel rated womens' performance as excellent or good (17 percent fair or poor).

(b)     Fifty-six percent of those who were deployed in Desert Shield/Desert storm with mixed gender units reported that women in their unit became pregnant just prior to, or while deployed in the Gulf. Forty-one percent reported no women became pregnant.

   (i)     Readiness: Of the 56 percent in mixed gender units who reported that women in their unit got pregnant just prior to or while deployed to the Gulf, 46 percent said it had very much or some negative impact on their units readiness. (52 percent said it had little or no impact).

   (ii)    Morale: Of the 56 percent in mixed gender units who reported women in their unit became pregnant just prior to, or while deployed in the Gulf, 59 percent reported that it very much or to some extent impacted negatively on unit morale, (39 percent said it had little or no impact.)

(c)     Sixty-four percent of military personnel deployed to the Gulf who served in mixed-gender units reported that there had been incidents of sexual activity between men and women in their unit. (By Service: 74 percent of the Army, 73 percent of Marines, 64 percent of the Air Force and 41 percent of the Navy).

   (i)     Readiness: 36 percent (64 percent said it had little or no effect) reported that sexual activity within their unit had very much or some negative impact on their units readiness.

   (ii)    Morale: 55 percent reported that the sexual activity within their unit had very much or some negative impact on their units morale.

(d)     Sixty-one percent of the military personnel deployed to the Persian Gulf reported incidents of sexual activity between men and women in their unit and members of other units, (79 percent of the Army, 34 percent of the Navy, 67 percent of Marines and 73 percent of the Air Force.)

   (i)     Readiness: 23 percent said (77 percent said it had little or no impact on readiness) sexual activity between members of their units with members of other units affected the unit's readiness very much or to some extent.

   (ii)    Morale: 36 percent (64 percent said it had little or no impact) reported that the sexual activity negatively impacted very much or to some extent on unit morale.

(e)     Members of the combat specialties in all three Services (Army, Navy and Air Force) said, by the percentages indicated, women should not be assigned to the following combat specialties:

| | |
|---|---|
| Artillery Gunner | 64% |
| Tank Crew Member | 71% |
| Special Forces | 82% |
| Marine Assault Force | 83% |
| Infantry | 83% |
| Pilot/Crew Member | 44% |
| Combatant Ships | 38% |

a.  Panel 1 Report; 23 October 1992, pp. 115-118.
b.  "Attitudes Regarding the Assignment of Women in the Forces:  The Military Perspectve," The Roper Organization, Inc., September 1992.

1.71     Of those countries that have decided to integrate women into combat positions in the ground, naval and air forces, three countries have made this decision primarily because of equal opportunity reasons, and one country because of demographic consideration.  No nation the Commission visited has either for cultural reason or to improve combat effectiveness has yet to put women into combat roles.

a.  Presidential Commission International Trip Report,
        14-27 September 1992.
b.  Presidential Commission Canadian Trip Report, 29-30 July 1992.

1.72     Historically, those nations that have experienced or placed women in close combat situations (Soviet Union, Germany and Israel) have done so due to grave threats to their national survival.  After the crisis passed, each nation adopted policies which excluded the employment of women in combat.

a.  Presidential Commission International Trip Report,
        14-27 September 1992.

1.73     Six women in foreign militaries have been qualified to fly combat aircraft. Two are currently on flight status.

(a)     Canada:  Three pilots:  One active CF-18 pilot, one currently serving in a staff position after a successful tour as a CF-18 pilot (currently on medical profile) and one withdrew due to family considerations and leave incentives.

(b)     The Netherlands:  One active F-16 pilot currently undergoing low-level flight training and one pilot withdrew after citing stress from media coverage.

(c)     Great Britain:  One pilot (29 years old) was not able to qualify after being subjected to extensive media coverage.

a.  Panel 1 Report; 23 October 1992, pp. 18, 28.
b.  Presidential Commission International Trip Report, 14-27 September 1992.
c.  Presidential Commission Canadian Trip Report, 29-30 July 1992.

1.74     No nation, with the exception of Norway, permits women to serve aboard submarines.  This is due to the lack of suitable berthing, head facilities, and a working environment which severely limits privacy.  Norwegian submarines are small with crews of approximately 20 to 30 sailors and perform coastal missions usually lasting one to two weeks.

a.  Henderson, Wm. Darryl, Personal Statement.  13 September 1992.

1.75     On the basis of experiences (Canada and Great Britain) and testing (Denmark), the integrating of women into combatant vessels has been considered a success, especially in some occupational areas.

a.  Panel 1 Report; 23 October 1992, pp. 27, 37.
b.  Presidential Commission International Trip Report, 14-27 September 1992.

1.76     Canada and Denmark have conducted extensive research to determine the effectiveness of women in combat and found little evidence to support the integration of women into ground combat forces.

(a)     The Canadians invited women from both inside and outside the military to join the infantry.  Although 103 women who were interested in joining the infantry, none of them were prescreened or required to meet any minimum standard.  Consequently, attrition was severe due primarily to physical and endurance factors with only one women graduating.  Shortly after graduating, she was reassigned to another unit.  It is important to note that physical attributes and failure to achieve critical mass appeared to be operative in the elimination of all 103 women soldiers interested in the infantry.

(b) Denmark conducted trials with women integrated into mechanized infantry companies, two tank companies, a field artillery battery and a short range air defense battery. Seventy women, comprising between 20-25 percent of the test units, were tested. Of these, 39 women left the test early causing the premature termination of the test. The difficult training program and women's physical capabilities were cited as the primary reasons for attrition. Denmark has since lowered its physical standard and required only that men and women run 2,100 meters in 12 minutes for admission to ground combat units.

a. Panel 1 Report; 23 October 1992, p. 25.
b. Presidential Commission International Trip Report, 14-27 September 1992.
c. Presidential Commission Canadian Trip Report, 29-30 July 1992.

1.77 Canada, Israel, Denmark, the Netherlands and Great Britain all reported to the Commission, that to various degrees, problems with sexual harassment or fraternization exist, but said they were manageable.

a. Presidential Commission International Trip Report, 14-27 September 1992.

1.78 Of those countries that have integrated women into their combat forces, all are willing to operate at a critical mass for women of five percent. However, none has reached its goal of 20 percent critical mass for women in the naval, air or ground forces.

a. Panel 1 Report; 23 October 1992, pp. 19, 26.
b. Presidential Commission International Trip Report, 14-27 September 1992.
c. Presidential Commission Canadian Trip Report, 29-30 July 1992.

1.79 The goal of achieving a critical mass of at least five percent women in ground combat units has not been met by any army that has integrated women into ground combat forces.

a. Panel 1 Report; 23 October 1992, p. 26.
b. Presidential Commission International Trip Report, 14-27 September 1992.
c. Presidential Commission Canadian Trip Report, 29-30 July 1992.

1.80    Women in the Israeli military are not allowed to serve in combat units or positions that would allow then to come into "harm's way" in the IDF.  This includes, among other specialties, flying aircraft, even for support functions, becoming drivers, or being involved in any combat support positions which would require direct contact with forward units in time of war.

   a.  Panel 1 Report; 23 October 1992, pp. 10-11.
   b.  Presidential Commission International Trip Report,
         14-27 September 1992.

1.81    Factors which shape Israeli policy are cultural factors, constant threat of war, fear of having women captured by the enemy and lack of demographic pressures which would necessitate putting women into combat positions according to Israeli sources.

   a.  Panel 1 Report; 23 October 1992, p. 12.
   b.  Presidential Commission International Trip Report, 14-27
         September 1992.

1.82    The primary purpose of conscripting women for military service in Israel is to free the men for operational or combat duties.

   a.  Panel 1 Report; 23 October 1992, p. 12.
   b.  Israeli Defense Force. "The Women's Corp's," IDF Spokesman,
         24 August 1992.

1.83    Israel is one of only two countries in the world which requires compulsory military service from women.  Women are conscripted for two years (2 1/2 for officer candidates) versus three years for the men.  Seventy percent of the women in Israeli society serve in the military.  The remaining 30 percent are exempt from military service based on religious convictions (20 percent), pregnancy, marriage, or criminal records.

   a.  Panel 1 Report; 23 October 1992, p. 11.
   b.  Israeli Defense Force.  "CHEN Translates Charm," IDF Spokesman,
         27 February 1992.  p. 2
   c.  McKenzie, D.  "Use of Women in the Israeli Military," Memorandum,
         29 December 1983.

1.85    Israeli Air Force briefers stated that they do not have any female pilots in their Air Force because it is not cost effective to train them.   Based on this, they believe that they have a sufficient number of men to do the job.

    a.  Panel 1 Report; 23 October 1992, pp. 13, 14.
    b.  Presidential Commission International Trip Report,
        14-27 September 1992.

1.86    IDF officials stated women in the Israeli Defense Forces undergo three weeks of basic training versus six months of training for the men.  The women's training is cursory and inadequate for the requirements of combat.  Women instructors are assigned to combat arms but do not take the same training or meet the same standards as their male counterparts.

    a.  Panel 1 Report; 23 October 1992, p. 13.
    b.  Zilversmit, Ephraim.  "Department of the Army Bi-monthly Liaison
        Activities Repot on a Visit to the IDF Womens' Corp Training Camp,"
        TRADOC LO to the IDF, 3 September 1992.

1.87    Israeli Ministry of Defense officials stated women in the "Palmach," one of the three underground organizations active in Palestine before 1948, constituted 15 percent of its membership at its peak.  The women served as escorts of convoys to besieged parts of the country (such as Jerusalem) and took part in operational activities (blowing up of railway bridges).

    a.  Panel 1 Report; 23 October 1992, p. 9.
    b.  "Women in the Israel Defense Forces," GE 3-257-92, August 1992.

1.88    On the face of it, the choice of tasks in the underground was open equally to both sexes, but in fact the women were sent to a limited number of duties - either by their own choice, or as decided by their command according to practical considerations and social convention.  These included physical limitations and concern over their being taken prisoners by the Arab enemy in Palestine and abroad.

    a.  Panel 1 Report; 23 October 1992, p. 9.
    b.  "Women in the Israel Defense Forces," GE 3-257-92, August 1992, p. 3.

1.89 A precipitating incident regarding the Israeli policy to exclude women from combat:  In December 1947, a woman was killed in action.  She had joined a patrol of men in the Negev Desert, where they were ambushed.  The squad was killed and the murderers mutilated the soldiers' bodies.  Concerns of women being captured, the policy of allowing women to serve in combat units was changed and their operational activity was restricted.  The revised policy stipulated that women would serve in the Armed Forces, but not as combatants.

  a. Panel 1 Report; 23 October 1992, p. 10.
  b. "Women in the Israel Defense Forces," GE 3-257-92, August 1992, pp. 8, 11-12.

1.90 The original intent, after the 1948 war, was to exclude women entirely from combat units.  This situation was reversed in 1953, when a small number of women were allowed to serve in traditional roles to preserve the social and human atmosphere of the line battalions and fill manpower loopholes.  However, upon the start of war, these women were immediately evacuated.

  a. Panel 1 Report; 23 October 1992, p. 10.
  b. "Women in the Israel Defense Forces," GE 3-257-92, August 1992.

1.91 Women are allowed to serve in combat support roles in Israel.

  a. Panel 1 Report; 23 October 1992, p. 10.
  b. Presidential Commission International Trip Report, 14-27 September 1992.

1.92 The British have just begun their integration process, which was motivated by anticipated manpower shortages, for women in their Armed Forces.  Because of this, the results are difficult to evaluate.  More data is expected when the enlistment of the first recruits have an opportunity to re-enlist.

  a. Panel 1 Report; 23 October 1992, p. 18.
  b. Presidential Commission International Trip Report, 14-27 September 1992.

1.93      British Ministry of Defence officials stated that since 1990, women have been allowed to serve on combatant vessels. Due to the relatively small number of women going to sea duty, there has been some resentment from the men because they have to go to sea more frequently. To date, 300 of the 4,000 women in the British Royal Navy have volunteered for sea duty. This should increase as new recruits take advantage of this additional duty option. Women who were in the Navy before the policy change will be allowed to remain in the Service without involuntary assignment to a combatant vessel until retirement

     a. Panel 1 Report; 23 October 1992, pp. 19-20.
     b. Marshall, J. A. "WRNS Sea Service-Situation Report," Ministry of Defence, 13 December 1990.
     c. Presidential Commission International Trip Report, 14-27 September 1992.

1.94      The British have had difficulty recruiting men and women for sea duty. Reasons for this include lack of privacy, difficulty of shipboard work and long hours.

     a. Panel 1 Report; 23 October 1992, p. 20.
     b. Presidential Commission International Trip Report, 14-27 September 1992.
     c. "Report of a Study into the Employment of Women's Royal Naval Service (WRNS) Personnel in the Royal Navy," D/DNMP/18/9/6, March 1990.

1.95      Seventy-five women of a total crew of 1,100 served aboard the aircraft carrier HMS Invincible. There was no degradation in combat effectiveness in spite of the inherent difficulties of unilaterally integrating such a large contingent of sailors at one time. Women worked on the flight deck of the Invincible and performed as efficiently as the men.

     a. Panel 1 Report; 23 October 1992, p. 20.
     b. Marshall, J. A. "WRNS Sea Service-Situation Report," Ministry of Defence, 13 December 1990.
     c. Presidential Commission International Trip Report, 14-27 September 1992.

1.96 Within the last year, the Women's Royal Army Corps was disestablished; women are now formally integrated into the Royal Army. While legally women can go into any job skill in the Army, it is Ministry of Defence policy that women not be allowed to serve in infantry and armor units until the Army can adequately set standards. They are assigned in the artillery except for cannon artillery because of the weight of the shells.

 a. Panel 1 Report; 23 October 1992, p. 18.
 b. Presidential Commission International Trip Report,
   14-27 September 1992.

1.97 During WWII, British women served in military related functions as couriers and spies. Fifty-three women were captured by the Germans and twelve were executed. In British World War II archives, there is no evidence that the capture of women had a negative impact on their fellow male prisoners.

 a. Panel 1 Report; 23 October 1992, pp. 18, 19.
 b. Presidential Commission International Trip Report,
   14-27 September 1992.

1.98 There is a limited role for women in the German military. The German constitution specifically states that women are not eligible to be drafted for military service.

 a. Panel 1 Report; 23 October 1992, p. 50.
 b. "Federal Republic of Germany", *Women in the NATO Forces*, Brussels, 1991.

1.99 Women can serve in only two capacities in the German military: in military hospitals and in the military band. Women are under no requirements to bear arms, even if under attack. Female medical military personnel are sent into the field, but without any weapons training.

 a. Panel 1 Report; 23 October 1992, p. 52.
 b. "Federal Republic of Germany", *Women in the NATO Forces*, Brussels, 1991.

1.100 Women contributed much to German military operations in WWII. They served with distinction as uniformed auxiliaries from 1940 until the end of the war, both within Germany and in all theaters where German forces were engaged. By the end of the war, their numbers had risen to over 300,000.

a. Panel 1 Report; 23 October 1992, p. 49.

b. German Embassy. Response to Commission Questions, September 1992.

1.101 The women in the German forces actual duties and responsibilities were much the same as those of the female soldiers in the military services of the United States and Great Britain. For example, German women's auxiliaries were employed in searchlight, radar, and barrage balloon batteries.

a. Panel 1 Report; 23 October 1992, p. 49.

b. Tuten, Jeff. "Germany and the World Wars." *Female Soldiers-Combatants or Noncombatants*, edited by L. Goldman. Westport: Greenwood Press, 1982.

1.102 German female soldiers were in uniform and subject to military discipline and to the military justice system.

a. Panel 1 Report; 23 October 1992, p. 49.

b. Tuten, Jeff. "Germany and the World Wars."*Female Soldiers-Combatants or Noncombatants*, edited by L. Goldman. Westport: Greenwood Press, 1982.

1.103 Inevitably, large numbers of women's auxiliaries were captured at the end of the war. Fate was not kind to those captured on the Eastern Front. Many reportedly were abused and/or executed. Many others spent years in Eastern bloc labor camps. The horror stories told of them still circulate in Germany today. They no doubt influenced current German views on women in the military.

a. Panel 1 Report; 23 October 1992, p. 49.

b. Tuten, Jeff. "Germany and the World Wars." *Female Soldiers - Combatants or Noncombatants*, edited by L. Goldman. Westport: Greenwood Press, 1982.

1.104A The Danish military briefer stated during the Commission's briefing that combat readiness is not an over-arching concern of the Danish military. They believe they will have ample time to prepare their forces as conflicts present themselves.

a. Panel 1 Report; 23 October 1992, p. 41.

b. Presidential Commission International Trip Report, 14-27 September 1992.

1.105    The policy of the Danish Ministry of Defence is that women will have the same opportunities as their male counterparts. Based on equal opportunity, women are fully integrated in the Danish Army, Air Force and Navy. They are employed and work together with men in mixed-gender units and are subject to the same chain of command.

a.  Panel 1 Report; 23 October 1992, p. 35.
b.  Presidential Commission International Trip Report,
        14-27 September 1992.

1.106    The Danes are not overly concerned if there are disparities in the relative physical capabilities of individual soldiers in a combat unit. They stated any individual shortcomings will be distributed among the others.

a.  Panel 1 Report; 23 October 1992, p. 35.
b.  Presidential Commission International Trip Report,
        14-27 September 1992.

1.107    The Danes tested all-female units and concluded that they were less efficient than mixed-gender units.

a.  Panel 1 Report; 23 October 1992, p. 41.
b.  Presidential Commission International Trip Report, 14-27 September 1992.

1.108    The assignment of women in the Danish military is too limited (1,000) to draw any operational conclusions for the utilization of women in combat.

a.  Panel 1 Report; 23 October 1992, pp. 33, 34.
b.  Presidential Commission International Trip Report, 14-27 September 1992.

1.109    The total cost to modify the Danish fleet (11 ships) to berth both men and women was less than $200,000 to insert bulkheads and separation curtains.

a.  Panel 1 Report; 23 October 1992, p. 38.
b.  Presidential Commission International Trip Report,
        14-27 September 1992.

1.110    The Danes conducted mixed-gender tests for combat arms and combatant vessels. Based on the results of these tests, combat positions were opened up to women. However, the PT standards were lowered. For example, the only test currently used for combat arms requires a soldier to run 2,100 meters in twelve minutes.

    a. Panel 1 Report; 23 October 1992, pp. 37, 40, 41.
    b. Danish Embassy. "Selection, Training and Assignment of Female
        Personnel in the Danish Armed Forces", Memorandum, 18 September
        1992.

1.111    As a result of current demographic conditions and the loss of non-Russian conscripts with the collapse of the Soviet Union, the Russian government is once again considering the role of women in its military. However, the Commission was told this will probably not include putting women into combat units or in harm's way.

    a. Panel 1 Report; 23 October 1992, p. 28.
    b. Presidential Commission International Trip Report,
        14-27 September 1992.
    c. Russian Embassy Response. "Memorandum an Interview with
        Directorate of Personnel," Russian Ministry of Defense, 1992.

1.112    At present, women constitute a negligible portion of the Russian military establishment, perhaps totaling roughly 10,000-25,000 out of an overall force of over four million.

    a. Panel 1 Report; 23 October 1992, p. 31.
    b. Russian Embassy Response. "Memorandum and Interview with
        Direcorate of Personnel," Russian Ministry of Defense, 1992.
    c. U.S. DIA, "Women in the Soviet Armed Forces," DDI-110-109-76,
        1976.

1.113    In World War II, the enormous threat to national survival and the great losses to German forces required that the U.S.S.R. mobilize women. Women saw extensive service in the Soviet Armed Forces in World War II, reaching a peak strength of roughly one million.

    a. Panel 1 Report; 23 October 1992, p. 29.
    b. Greisse, A. and Stites, R. "Russian and Soviet Women in War and
        Peace." Inter-University Seminar on Armed Forces and Society
        National Conference, University of Chicago, 23-25 October 1980.

1.114    Soviet women's participation in all phases of war during WWII surpassed that of all other wars in modern history in terms of scale and degree of female involvement.

    a.  Panel 1 Report; 23 October 1992, p. 29.

    b.  Greisse, A. and Stites, R. "Russian and Soviet Women in War and Peace." Inter-University Seminar on Armed Forces and Society National Conference, University of Chicago, 23-25 October 1980.

1.115      Of the one million women who served in the Soviet forces during WWII, 800,000 were uniformed troops in the Red Army, and 500,000 of those actually served either in combat or support roles.

    a.  Panel 1 Report; 23 October 1992, p. 29.

    b.  Greisse, A. and Stites, R. "Russian and Soviet Women in War and Peace." Inter-University Seminar on Armed Forces and Society National Conference, University of Chicago, 23-25 October 1980.

    c.  Russian Embassy Response. "Memorandum and Interview with Directorate of Personnel," Russian Ministry of Defense, 1992.

1.116      Women constituted roughly eight percent of a total armed force of 12 million in the Soviet Union at the end of the war.

    a.  Panel 1 Report; 23 October 1992, pp. 29, 30.

    b.  U.S. DIA, "Women in the Soviet Armed Forces," DDI-110-109-76, 1976.

1.117      In 1942, the Komsomol (Communist Youth Group) established a sniper school which graduated more than 1,000 women and trained 250,000 women in the use of mortars, heavy and light machine guns and automatic rifles. During the latter stages of the war, graduates of the sniper school were credited with killing approximately 12,000 enemy troops.

    a.  Panel 1 Report; 23 October 1992, p. 30.

    b.  Greisse, A. and Stites, R. "Russian and Soviet Women in War and Peace." Inter-University Seminar on Armed Forces and Society National Conference, University of Chicago, 23-25 October 1980.

    c.  U.S. DIA, "Women in the Soviet Armed Forces," DDI-110-109-76, 1976.

1.118      By 1943 Soviet women had entered all the Services and assumed all the roles they would play until the war's end, including infantry, anti-aircraft defense, armor (all jobs in tank commands), artillery, transportation, communications, aviation and nursing (naval participation was light and almost undocumented).

    a.  Panel 1 Report; 23 October 1992, p. 30.

    b.  Greisse, A. and Stites, R. "Russian and Soviet Women in War and Peace." Inter-University Seminar on Armed Forces and Society National Conference, University of Chicago, 23-25 October 1980.

1.119    Women also participated in intelligence work and partisan warfare behind the German lines.  According to Soviet statistics, almost 27,000 were officially engaged in partisan operations between June 1941 and February 1944.

a.  Panel 1 Report; 23 October 1992, p. 31.
b.  Greisse, A. and Stites, R.  "Russian and Soviet Women in War and Peace."  Inter-University Seminar on Armed Forces and Society National Conference, University of Chicago, 23-25 October 1980.

1.120    Early in WWII, the Germans had captured well over 100,000 Russian female soldiers who held full combatant status.

a.  Panel 1 Report; 23 October 1992, p. 29.
b.  Tuten, Jeff.  "Germany and the World Wars.  *Female Soldiers - Combatants or Noncombatants*," edited by L. Goldman.  Westport: Greenwood Press,  1982.

1.121    The Soviet Union awarded the title of Hero of the Soviet Union to 91 women (35 officers and 56 enlisted) for their feats in battles.  These included a sniper, a Komsomol organizer of a rifle battalion, a driver of a T-34 tank, a commander of an air squadron, and a medical assistant in a rifle regiment.

a.  Panel 1 Report; 23 October 1992, p. 31.
b.  Greisse, A. and Stites, R.  "Russian and Soviet Women in War and Peace."  Inter-University Seminar on Armed Forces and Society National Conference, University of Chicago, 23-25 October 1980.

1.122    According to information given to the Commission by Russian general officers, there were three female air regiments, the most famous being the "Night Witches".  Casualty rates in this unit approached 75 percent by the end of the war.  They were given the worst aircraft to fly and were considered expendable.

a.  Panel 1 Report; 23 October 1992, pp. 31, 33.
b.  Greisse, A. and Stites, R.  "Russian and Soviet Women in War and Peace."  Inter-University Seminar on Armed Forces and Society National Conference, University of Chicago, 23-25 October 1980.

1.123    According to information given the Commission by Russian general officers, the utilization of Soviet women during World War II was accomplished by a propaganda campaign directed at the DOSAF (the Soviet Youth Movement).  The purpose of this propaganda was to mobilize women to supplement the requirements of the Soviet Armed Forces.  This new view was presented by

Russian general officers in September 1992 and contradicts prior findings regarding the service of Soviet women in WWII.

a. Panel 1 Report; 23 October 1992, pp. 32, 33.
b. Presidential Commission International Trip Report, 14-27 September 1992.

1.124   The assignment of limited numbers of women in the Dutch military so far, is too limited to draw operational conclusions for the United States for the utilization of women in combat.

a. Panel 1 Report; 23 October 1992, p. 42.

b. Royal Netherlands Navy. "Lecture and Appendices on the Functioning of Women in Combat Roles in the Royal Netherlands Navy," Directorate of Personnel, 18 September 1992.

1.125   According to the Secretary General of the Dutch Armed Forces, the emphasis on equal opportunity for women in the military is a primary consideration.

a. Panel 1 Report; 23 October 1992, p. 42.
b. Keijsers, E. "Facts and Figures on the Integration of Women in the Royal Air Force," 18 September 1992.
c. Presidential Commission International Trip Report, 14-27 September 1992.

1.126   Standards are gender-neutral in the Netherlands for all combat positions.

a. Panel 1 Report; 23 October 1992, pp. 46, 47.
b. Royal Netherlands Army. "Women in the RNLA," 18 September 1992.

1.127   The Dutch have not been able to attract large numbers of women to the combat arms units.

a. Panel 1 Report; 23 October 1992, pp. 43-45.
b. Royal Netherlands Navy. "Lecture and Appendices on the Functioning of Women in Combat Roles in the Royal Netherlands Navy," 18 September 1992.
c. Royal Netherlands Army. "Women in the RNLA," 18 September 1992.

1.128   Ten percent of the Royal Dutch Navy's personnel on combatant ships are women.

a. Panel 1 Report; 23 October 1992, p. 48.
b. Presidential Commission International Trip Report,
14-27 September 1992.

1.129   In a 1989 decision by the Canadian Human Rights Tribunal, all combat positions in the Canadian Forces (CF) except submarines, were opened to women. The primary consideration was equal opportunity. No attempts were made to consider the impact on operational readiness or unit effectiveness. No credence was given to a military study (SWINTER), ongoing during the time of the decision, which indicated difficulties would be anticipated.

a. Panel 1 Report; 23 October 1992, pp. 22, 23.
b. The Canadian Human Rights Act, In the Matter of, S.C. 1976-1977,
20 February 1989.
c. Pinch, Franklin. *Social and Behavioral Science Considerations Regarding Women's Employment in the Canadian Forces*, National Defence Headquarters, Ottawa, February 1987.
d. Canadian Forces Personnel Applied Research Unit. *Overview of the Social/Behavioral Science Evaluation of the SWINTER Land Trial*, Report Number 85-1, 1989.
e. Presidential Commission Canadian Trip Report, 29-30 July 1992.

1.130   Canadian personnel staff informed us that infantry MOS PT standards were modified to reflect actual requirements, although it appeared that they were relaxed to accommodate women. The current test requires only that male and female soldiers be able to carry a soldier of similar weight, and the required pack weight is limited to fifty pounds.

a. Panel 1 Report; 23 October 1992, p. 25.
b. Presidential Commission Canadian Trip Report, 29-30 July, 1992.
c. Lee, S. "Update 1992, CF Physical Fitness Programs Standards and Evaluation," 15 June 1992.
d. Chahal, S. "Physical Fitness and Performance Standards for the Canadian Army," *Canadian Defence Quarterly*, April 1990, pp. 31-37.

1.131   Currently, there are no women serving in the Artillery and only five who are in the Armor Corps. Women serve in wheeled Armored Personnel Carriers with a 76mm gun-the Cougar. The woman tanker interviewed was hesitant to transfer to larger guns (105, 120mm) on tanks because of serious doubts about her ability to meet the strength requirements.

a. Panel 1 Report; 23 October 1992, p.26.
b. Presidential Commission Canadian Trip Report, 29-30 July, 1992.

1.132      Improper relationships based on sex are a problem in the CF. While this included "fraternization" and the development of "couples," the biggest issue for them continues to be sexual harassment. To combat widespread harassment, the Navy has adopted a zero tolerance type of program aimed at controlling behavior. The Canadians stated that these are manageable problems that require strong leadership.

     a. Panel 1 Report; 23 October 1992, pp. 27, 28.
     b. Presidential Commission Canadian Trip Report, 29-30 July 1992.
     c. Canadian Armed Forces. "Mixed Gender Relationships," CFAO 19-38, 19 February 1988.
     d. Canadian Armed Forces. "Personal Harassment," CFAO 19-39, 19 December 1988.

1.134      Canadian briefers identified as obstacles to the successful integration of women:

     (a)      Quantity and quality of women in combat roles (low number of women with qualities necessary for combat).

     (b)      Training requirements, especially in combat arms (the necessity of not lowering performance standards).

     (c)      Unit norms which allow for total integration (even if standards are met, acceptance can be a problem).

     (d)      Sexual harassment problems (the primary ongoing problem for gender integration in the Canadian Armed Forces).

     (e)      "Inter-Personal" problems (e.g. scheduling for pregnancies).

     (f)      Leadership education (need to ensure leaders are "sensitive" to problems of gender integration).

     (g)      Internal monitoring (e.g. need to improve reporting of harassment which is currently under-reported).

     (h)      Family support roles (e.g. single parents are a readiness problem).

     a. Panel 1 Report; 23 October 1992, pp. 23, 24.
     b. Presidential Commission Canadian Trip Report, 29-30 July 1992.

1.135    The Canadians have a 270 billet ship (HMCS Nipigon), which has at any one time between 50-70 women as crew. The Captain of the ship said women served admirably and that he would welcome an even higher percentage of women under his command.

    a. Panel 1 Report; 23 October 1992, p. 23.
    b. Presidential Commission Canadian Trip Report, 29-30 July 1992.

1.136    Twenty four Canadian women are qualified to fly non-combatant aircraft and Canada has 48 women who are currently in the training pipeline. There are no women currently in the pipeline to fly combat aircraft.

    a. Panel 1 Report; 23 October 1992, p. 28.
    b. Presidential Commission Canadian Trip Report, 29-30 July, 1992.
    c. Tuten, Jeff. "Germany and the World Wars." *Female Soldiers - Combatants or Noncombatants*, edited by L. Goldman. Westport: Greenwood Press, 1982.

PANEL TWO CHARTER

Charter approved 1 June 1992

Panel 2 will investigate the requirements and costs to modify or replace garrison, tactical, training and combat facilities, including personal and unit equipment, to accommodate female service members. The physiological characteristics of men and women, including the physiological aspects of pregnancy, will be examined to determine their effect on training, physical readiness, and deployability. Additionally, the panel will review the process and rationale for establishing physical standards and qualifications for general fitness as well as for specific military specialties and ratings. Physical standards and qualifications for entry, basic, specialty, and unit training will also be examined. In conducting its investigation, the panel will consider the effects of all current or proposed physical qualifications and standards on the morale, cohesion, and combat readiness of the Armed Forces.

PANEL TWO FINDINGS BY THE COMMISSION

2.1.1    In general, women are shorter, weigh less and have less muscle mass and have a greater relative fat content than men. In terms of military significance, due to a lower muscle mass and greater relative fat mass, women are at a distinct disadvantage when performing job tasks requiring a high level of muscular strength and aerobic capacity.

a. Panel 2 Report; 20 October 1992, p. 27.
b. Marcinik, Edward J. CDR (sel), USN. Testimony before the Commission, 26 June 1992.

2.1.2    Female dynamic upper torso muscular strength is approximately 50-60 percent that of males.

a. Panel 2 Report; 20 October 1992, p. 29.
b. U.S. Naval Health Research Center. *A Comparison of the Effects of Circuit Weight Training on Navy Men and Women.* Report 85-13.

2.1.3    Female aerobic capacity is approximately 70-75 percent that of males. In terms of military significance, at the same marching velocity and carrying the same load, the average woman works at a higher percentage of her aerobic capacity and is more susceptible to fatigue than the average man.

a. Panel 2 Report; 20 October 1992, p. 31.
b. U.S. Military Academy Exercise Science Laboratory, 1992.

2.1.4    Women are currently assigned to a wide variety of physically demanding jobs.

a. Panel 2 Report; 20 October 1992, p. 34.

b. Summary Report on Fact-Finding Trip to Nellis AFB, 5-7 July 1992.

2.1.4A    In general, men perform better than women on military tasks requiring heavy lifting, carrying, pushing and pulling efforts. However, there is a significant overlap in task performance between the genders. For aviation related tasks, the overlap in performance ranged between 10 percent (Fuel Hose Drag, and MK-82 Bomb Lift) to 27 percent, (Drop Tank Carry) (i.e., 10 percent - 27 percent of women perform better than the lowest scoring men.)

a. Panel 2 Report; 20 October 1992, pp. 36-41.
b. U.S. Naval Personnel Research and Development Center. *Documentation of Muscularly Demanding Job Tasks and Validation of an Occupational Strength Test Battery.* San Diego, CA, 1985.

2.1.4B    Research studies have identified the need for a high level of aerobic capacity and muscular strength for a variety of Marine Corps combat tasks performed in desert, high altitude/cold weather, amphibious and jungle environments.

a. Panel 2 Report; 20 October 1992, p. 41.
b. Institute of Human Performance. *Physical Performance Tasks Required of U.S. Marines Operating in a Desert Environment.* Fairfax, VA. 1981.
c. Institute of Human Performance. *Physical Performance Requirements of U.S. Marines Operating in a High Altitude Cold Weather Environment.* Fairfax, VA. 1982.
d. Institute of Human Performance. *Physical Performance Requirements of U.S. Marines Operating in Jungle Operations.* Fairfax, VA. 1983.
e. Institute of Human Performance. *Physical Performance Requirements of U.S. Marines during Amphibious Operations.* Fairfax, VA. 1983.

2.1.5    Studies involving Army recruits indicate women are at a higher risk for exercise-induced injuries than men. For example, a study of 124 men and 186 women found that 27 percent of men and 51 percent of women were injured during Army basic combat training (Jones, et al., 1988). Compared to men, women had a 2.13 times greater risk for lower extremity injuries and a 4.71 times greater risk for stress fractures. Men sustained 99 days of limited duty due to injury while women incurred 481 days of limited duty.

a. Panel 2 Report; 20 October 1992, p. 42.
b. U.S. Army Research Institute for Environmental Medicine. *Incidence of Risk Factors for Injury and Illness among Male and Female Army Basic Trainees.* 1988.

2.1.6    In general, women are less tolerant to heat but adapt as well as, or better than males to cold and high altitude environments.

   a.  Panel 2 Report; 20 October 1992, p. 43.

   b.  Avellini, B. A., E. Kamon, and J. T. Krajewski. "Physiologic Responses of Physically Fit Men and Women to Acclimation to Humid Heat." *Journal of Applied Physiology.* 49(1980): pp. 254- 26.

   c.  Drinkwater, B.L. "Women and Exercise." *Physiological Aspects in Exercise and Sport Science Reviews.* 12 (1984): pp. 21-51.

   d.  Drinkwater, B.L., L.J. Folinsbee, J.F. Bedi, S.A. Plowman, A.B. Loucks, and S.M. Horvath. "Responses of Women Mountaineers to Maximal Exercise during Hypoxia." *Aviation Space and Environmental Medicine.* 50(1979): pp. 657-662.

   e.  Frye, A. J., and E. Kamon. "Responses to Dry and Wet Heat of Men and Women with Similar Aerobic Capacities." *Journal of Applied Physiology.* 50(1981): pp. 65-70.

   f.  Harris, C.W., J.L. Shields, and J.P. Hannon. "Acute Mountain Sickness in Females." *Aerospace Medicine.* 37 (1996): pp. 1163-1167.

   g.  Kramar, P.O., B.L. Drinkwater, J.L. Folinsbee, and J.F. Bedi. "Ocular Function and Incidence of Acute Mountain Sickness in Women at Altitude." *Aviation Space Environmental Medicine* 54 (1983): pp. 116-120.

   h.  McArdle, W.D., J.R. Magel, R.J. Spina, M.M. Toner. "Adjustment to Cold Water Exposure in Exercising Men and Women." *Journal of Applied Physiology.* 56, No. 6 (1984): pp. 1565-1571.

   i.  Wagner, J.A., D.S. Miles, S.M. Horvath, and J.A. Reyburn. "Maximal Work Capacity of Women during Acute Hypoxia." *Journal of Applied Physiology.* 47 (1979): pp. 1223-1227.

2.1.6A    Data from a 1986 centrifuge study suggest there is no significant difference between the genders in tolerance up to +7 Gz. A 1992 study reported a statistically significant gender difference in tolerance at +8 Gz but not at +9Gz. The authors suggested this difference may have been due to poor fitting female anti-G suits.

   a.  Panel 2 Report; 20 October 1992, pp. 43-44.

   b.  Gillingham, K.K., C.M. Schade, W.G. Jackson, and L.C. Gilstrap. "Women's G-Tolerance." *Aviation, Space, and Environmental Medicine.* 57 (1986): pp. 745-53.

   c.  KRUG Life Sciences. *Female Tolerance to Sustained Acceleration - A Retrospective Study.* San Antonio, TX, 1992.

2.1.6B    There is no evidence in the scientific literature that defines a physiological basis to categorically restrict women from selection opportunity for combat aviation.

a. Panel 2 Report; 20 October 1992, p. 6.
b. Crisman, R.  Testimony before the Commission, 14-15 September 1992.

2.1.7    Cognitive differences between the sexes are minimal.

a. Panel 2 Report; 20 October 1992, p. 45.
b. Harris, L. J.  "Sex Differences in Spatial Ability: Possible Environmental, Genetic, and Neurological Factors."  In Kinsbourne, M. (Ed.).  *Asymmetrical Function of the Brain.*  Cambridge, Cambridge University Press, 1978.
c. Hyde, J.S., E.R. Geiringer, and W.M. Yen.  "On the Empirical Relation Between Spatial Ability and Sex Differences in other Aspects of Cognitive Performance."  *Multivariate Behavioral Research.*  10 (1975): pp. 289-309.
d. Lyons, T.J.  "Women in the Fast Jet Cockpit-Aeromedical Considerations."  *Aviation Space and Environmental Medicine.*  63 (1992): pp. 809-18, 1992.
e. Sherman, J. A. and E. Fennema.  "Distribution of Spatial Visualization and Mathematical Problem Solving Scores."  *Psychology of Women Quarterly* 3 (1978): pp. 157-167.
f. U.S. Army Research Institute for Environmental Medicine.  *Cerebral Laterality and Handedness in Aviation: Performance and Selection Implications.* 1988.

2.2.1    Wellness can be defined as the capacity to achieve optimal quality of life.  Wellness includes positive mental, social, and physical behaviors which result in optimal health.

a. Panel 2 Report; 20 October 1992, p. 49.
b. Vogel, J. A.  Testimony before the Commission, 7 August 1992.

2.2.1A    Physical fitness can be defined as having a sufficient level of muscular strength, muscular endurance, cardiorespiratory capacity, and flexibility to accomplish a day's work without undue fatigue, and the ability to perform desired physical activities at desired levels.

a. Panel 2 Report; 20 October 1992, p. 49.
b. Marcinik, Edward J., CDR (sel), USN.  Testimony before the Commission, 26 June 1992.

2.2.1B        Wellness, health, physical fitness and job performance are interrelated and not mutually exclusive.

        a. Panel 2 Report; 20 October 1992, p. 49.
        b. Davis, P. Testimony before the Commission, 7 August 1992.
        c. Marcinik, Edward J., CDR (sel), USN Testimony before the Commission, 26 June 1992.

2.2.2        General fitness tests are used by the Services to provide a baseline measure of health and physical capacity. General fitness standards are age and gender-normed, except the Navy's sit-reach test which is age and gender-neutral. All of the Services measure the cardiorespiratory fitness of members on a periodic basis. None of the Services assess muscular strength as a part of general fitness testing.

        a. Panel 2 Report; 20 October 1992, pp. 50-52.
        b. Maurman, Steve, Maj, USAF. Testimony before the Commission, 7 April 1992.

2.2.2A        A snapshot of male and female Army ROTC cadet performance on the Army Physical Fitness Test (APFT) during Advanced Summer Camp revealed the following: 202 of 623 (32 percent) of women met or exceeded the male minimum passing score. Seven percent of women and 78 percent of men could perform 60 push-ups. Six percent of the women and 78 percent of the men could run two miles in under 14 minutes. The APFT forms a portion of cadets' military science grade and determines who receives the Army Physical Fitness Badge and the Cadet Recondo Badge (Gregor,1992).

        a. Panel 2 Report; 20 October 1992, p. 32.
        b. Gregor, William, LTC, USA. Testimony before the Commission, 12 September 1992.

2.2.3        Only the Air Force has occupational strength standards in place. These standards are gender-neutral. Strength test data from over 32,000 Air Force candidates indicate that all men and women were able to meet the minimum lifting requirement of 40 lbs. Sixty eight percent of men and .8 percent of women were able to meet the 110 lb lift requirement.

        a. Panel 2 Report; 20 October 1992, pp. 53-56.
        b. DASD(MM&PP). Air Force Response to Question 9 from 4-6 May 1992.

2.2.3A      According to Roper Poll findings, 70 percent of military respondents stated they strongly agree that physical standards for each direct combat position should reflect the demands of that assignment, whether a man or woman fills it.

        a. Panel 2 Report; 20 October 1992, p. 7.
        b. "Attitudes Regarding the Assignment of Women in the Armed Forces: The Military Perspective," The Roper Organization Inc., New York, 1992.

2.2.3B      Results of a survey on gender in the military indicate that 15 percent of women and 52 percent of men believed Army Physical Fitness Test standards should be gender-neutral. Eighty-one percent of women and 42 percent of men thought standards should be different for men and women.

        a. Panel 2 Report; 20 October 1992, p. 7.
        b. Miller, Laura and Dr. Charles C. Moskos. Testimony before the Commission, 10 September 1992.

2.2.4      Based on a comparison of male and female performance on the Army Physical Fitness Test, adoption of age and gender-neutral fitness standards may adversely affect male and female retention, especially older servicemen and servicewomen.

        a. Panel 2 Report; 20 October 1992, p. 7.
        b. Gregor, William, LTC, USAF. Testimony before the Commission, 12 September 1992.

2.3.1      The Army allows pregnant soldiers to continue to perform duties during the prenatal period, limited by a temporary physical profile, when required, as determined by their attending physicians in the medical treatment facility. Pregnant soldiers may separate voluntarily or may be separated involuntarily whenever a pregnancy or parenthood interferes with military responsibilities.

        a. Panel 2 Report; 20 October 1992, p. 57.
        b. DASD(MM&PP). Army Response to Question 8 from 4-6 April 1992.

2.3.1A      Once an Army aviator is confirmed pregnant, she is grounded for the length of the pregnancy plus six weeks after delivery. The Army has no procedure for an appeal to regain flight status.

        a. Panel 2 Report; 20 October 1992, p. 57.
        b. DASD(MM&PP). Army Response to Question 8 from 4-6 April 1992.

2.3.1B    Pregnant soldiers are ineligible for deployment overseas (Army).

a. Panel 2 Report; 20 October 1992, p. 57.
b. DASD(MM&PP). Army Response to Question 8 from 4-6 April 1992.

2.3.2    The Navy allows women to serve aboard ship through the 20th week of pregnancy until they deploy, unless they can be evacuated to a medical treatment facility within six hours.

a. Panel 2 Report; 20 October 1992, p. 58.
b. DASD(MM&PP). Navy Response to Question 8 from 4-6 April 1992.

2.3.2A    A pregnant Navy aviator is grounded unless she requests a waiver from the Chief of Naval Personnel (OP-59). The waiver, once granted, would extend flight status until the third trimester. For safety of the mother and fetus, the following restrictions are on the type of aircraft flown and are non-waiverable:

a. No single piloted aircraft.
b. No ejection seat aircraft.
c. No high performance aircraft that will operate in excess of +2 Gz.
d. No aircraft involved in shipboard operations.
e. Aircraft must have a cabin pressure altitude of less than 10,000 feet. For sustained operations above that level, supplemental oxygen would be required for both pregnant and non-pregnant personnel.

a. Panel 2 Report; 20 October 1992, p. 58.
b. DASD(MM&PP). Navy Response to Question 19 from 24-27 June 1992.

2.3.2B    Navy women are not permitted to be transferred to deploying units during the period from the 20th week of pregnancy through four months after the expected date of delivery.

a. Panel 2 Report; 20 October 1992, p. 59.
b. DASD(MM&PP). Navy Response to Question 8 from 4-6 April 1992.

2.3.3    Job restrictions for pregnant Air Force personnel are based on occupational and environmental exposure as well as limitations due to problematic pregnancies.

a. Panel 2 Report; 20 October 1992, p. 59.
b. DASD(MM&PP). Air Force Response to Question 8 from 4-6 April 1992.

2.3.3A    Pregnant Air Force aviators are grounded during the first trimester.  A waiver may be granted if the Commanding Officer, Flight Surgeon, and Obstetrician agree on flight status for the second but not the third trimester.  Pregnant aviators are prohibited from flying ejection seat aircraft.

    a.  Panel 2 Report; 20 October 1992, p. 59.
    b.  DASD(MM&PP).  Air Force Response to Question 8 from 4-6 April 1992.

2.3.3B    The pregnancy policy of the Air Force is to restrict assignment action and deployment status during the course of the pregnancy plus an additional six weeks after child birth.  DoD policy defers military mothers from duty away from home for four months after childbirth.

    a.  Panel 2 Report; 20 October 1992, p. 59.
    b.  DASD(MM&PP).  Air Force Response to Question 8 from 4-6 April 1992.

2.3.4    For pregnant Marines, medical officers may recommend job related restrictions to the Commanding Officer, if they relate directly to the health and welfare of mother and child.

    a.  Panel 2 Report; 20 October 1992, p. 59.
    b.  DASD(MM&PP).  Marine Response to Question 8 from 4-6 April 1992.

2.3.4A    Female Marines are restricted from deploying OCONUS or being assigned to a dependents-restricted tour overseas during pregnancy.  DoD policy restricts the TAD assignment or the separation of a military mother from her newborn or the separation of one military parent from their recently adopted child for four months following childbirth/adoption.

    a.  Panel 2 Report; 20 October 1992, p. 60.
    b.  Draude, Thomas V., BGen, USMC.  Personal Statement 2 October 1992.

2.3.5    Pregnant Coast Guard women are not authorized aboard ship if the time for the medical evacuation of the member to a treatment facility capable of evaluating and stabilizing obstetric emergencies is greater than three hours.

    a.  Panel 2 Report; 20 October 1992, p. 60.
    b.  U.S. Coast Guard Response to Question 10 from 27-29 August 1992.

2.3.5A    Coast Guard women are not authorized to remain aboard ship beyond the 20th week of pregnancy.

    a.  Panel 2 Report; 20 October 1992, p. 60.

        b. U.S. Coast Guard Response to Question 10 from 27-29 August 1992.

2.3.6        The possibility of fetal damage in the early stages of pregnancy (before the diagnosis of pregnancy) appears to be the single biggest medical concern in allowing women access to all aviation careers.

        a. Panel 2 Report; 20 October 1992, p. 9.
        b. Lyons, T.J. "Women in the Fast Jet Cockpit - Aeromedical Considerations." *Aviation, Space and Environmental Medicine* 63(1992): pp. 809-18, 1992.

2.3.6A        Research is currently being conducted to determine whether the exposure of Navy members, including pregnant women, to toxic substances aboard ship could have harmful health effects.

        a. Panel 2 Report; 20 October 1992, p. 9.

2.4.1        Each Service has responded that basic training and advanced individual training syllabi will not have to be modified to integrate women into combat if standards are not changed.

        a. Panel 2 Report; 20 October 1992, pp. 64-66.
        b. DASD(MM&PP). Services Response to Question 6 and 7 from 27-29 August 1992.

2.4.1A        In October 1977, the Army began integrated Basic Combat Training (BCT). In May 1982, the Army announced it would discontinue integrated BCT because men were not being challenged enough physically and not attaining their full potential. The exceptions to this policy are the Military Police (MP), and Chemical (CH) One Station Unit Training (OSUT) Programs. OSUT programs are combined programs that include both BCT and Advanced Individual Training for a specific MOS. MP, CH and OSUT are integrated at company level (males and females in separate platoons). The BCT Program of Instruction (POI) is the same for both sexes.

        a. Panel 2 Report; 20 October 1992, p. 9.
        b. DASD(MM&PP). Army Response to Question 136 from 10-12 September 1992.

2.4.1B        The United States Military Academy conducts a co-educational hand-to-hand combat training program as a part of close quarters combat training at two points in the cadet training cycle. Cadets are paired according to size and weight variables with consideration that this is a learning environment.

a. Panel 2 Report; 20 October 1992, p. 64.

b. DASD(MM&PP). U.S. Military Academy Response to Question 135 from 10-12 September 1992.

2.4.1C    Integrated training for Navy male and female recruits is being conducted on an experimental basis at Recruit Training Command, Orlando. The Commander of the Recruit Training Command and the Commander of the Naval Recruit Training Center have recommended the program become permanent.

a. Panel 2 Report; 20 October 1992, p. 65.

b. Summary Report on Fact-Finding Trip to NSB Kings Bay and NTC Orlando, 15 October 1992.

2.4.1D    The Air Force has no training in which men and women participate in hand-to-hand physical contact against one another. However, the security police and Office of Special Investigation (OSI) sometimes place women against men (equal weight) in arrest/restraint scenarios to teach technique/defensive tactics vice hand-to-hand combat.

a. Panel 2 Report; 20 October 1992, pp. 65, 67-68.

b. DASD(MM&PP). Air Force Response to Question 135 from 10-12 September 1992.

2.4.1D    DoD General Code of Conduct training is provided to all male and female service members upon entry. Men and women aviators receive the same POW/SERE training in the Army, Navy, and Air Force. To date, no Marine Corps women have attended SERE training due to the fact that there are no female pilots in the Marine Corps.

a. Panel 2 Report; 20 October 1992, p. 65.

b. DASD(MM&PP). Air Force Response to Question 5 from 4-6 May 1992.

2.4.2    Male enlisted Marines receive both offensive and defensive combat training while female enlisted Marines receive defensive combat training only.

a. Panel 2 Report; 20 October 1992, p. 66.

b. DASD(MM&PP). Marine Response to Question 7 from 27-29 August 1992.

2.4.2A    Marine restrictions preventing women officer students from participating in combat training have now been lifted. Women basic officer students now participate in all aspects of squad and platoon live fire and maneuver, hand-to-hand combat with pugil sticks against other women, practice live firing of M-16 rifles and are trained with hand grenades.

a. Panel 2 Report; 20 October 1992, p. 66.
b. DASD(MM&PP). Marine Response to Question 138 from 10-12 September 1992.

2.4.2B    Close combat/line training is the only training in which there exists a possibility of men and women participating in hand-to-hand combat training against one another. Line training uses an instructional technique that is very controlled thus reducing the chance of injury to students. The decision to allow men and women to participate against one another during close combat/line training is left up to the Commanding Officer/Director of each school. There is no Marine Corps Order prohibiting or mandating that women and men be paired up against each other in line training. Due to the short duration of the enlisted schools, the school directors periodically allow male/female participation if it expedites the evolution.

a. Panel 2 Report; 20 October 1992, pp. 66-67.
b. DASD(MM&PP). Marine Response to Question 135 from 10-12 September 1992.

2.4.4    All of the Services have sexual harassment prevention programs in place to define policy and specify each member's role in preventing, reporting and reducing sexual harassment.

a. Panel 2 Report; 20 October 1992, pp. 70-71.
b. DASD(MM&PP). Services Response to Question 25 from 27-29 August 1992.

Cohesion

2.5.1    Characteristics of Cohesion

Cohesion is the relationship that develops in a unit or group where (1) members share common values and experiences; (2) individuals in the group conform to group norms and behavior in order to ensure group survival and goals; (3) members lose their personal identity in favor of a group identity; (4) members focus on group activities and goals; (5) unit members become totally dependent on each other for the completion of their mission or survival; and (6) group members must meet all standards of performance and behavior in order not to threaten group survival.

a. Panel 2 Report; 20 October 1992, p. 75.
b. Marshall, S. L. A. *Men Against Fire*. New York: William Morrow, 1947.
c. Henderson, Dr. Wm. Darryl. *Cohesion: The Human Element*. National Defense University Press, 1985.
d. Johns, Dr. John. *Cohesion in the U.S. Military*. National Defense University Press. Washington, DC, 1984.

Cohesion can be negatively affected by the introduction of any element that detracts from the need for such key ingredients as mutual confidence, commonality of experience, and equitable treatment.

a. Panel 2 Report; 20 October 1992, p. 75.
b. Henderson, Dr. Wm. Darryl. *Cohesion: The Human Element*. National Defense University Press, 1985.
c. Johns, Dr. John. *Cohesion in the U.S. Military*. National Defense University Press. Washington, DC, 1984.

Cohesion can affect individual as well as unit-oriented motivation (Bird, 1980).

a. Panel 2 Report; 20 October 1992, p. 79.
b. Bird, Anne Marie. "Convergent and Incremental Effects of Cohesion on Attributions for Self and Team." *Journal of Sport Psychology*, 2 (1980): pp. 181-193.
c. Henderson, Dr. Wm. Darryl. *Cohesion: The Human Element*. National Defense University Press, 1985.

2.5.3    Difference Between Male and Female Bonding

The vast majority of research conducted on bonding involved all male groups. There were several studies conducted on mixed-gender groups, however, most were psychological studies and none involved the rigors of a combat environment. A few military studies documented the integration of women into various non-combat units but did not focus on cohesion or bonding.

a. Panel 2 Report; 20 October 1992, p. 79.
b. Marshall, Joan E. and Richard Heslin. "Boys and Girls Together: Sexual Composition and the Effect of Density and Group Size on Cohesion." *Journal of Personality and Social Psychology*, 31, No. 5. (1975): pp. 952-961.

    c. Taylor, John and Donald S. Strassberg. "The Effects of Sex Composition and Interpersonal Learning in Short-Term Personal Growth Groups." *Journal of the Division of Psychotherapy,* 23 (1986): pp. 267-273.

    d. U.S. Navy Personnel Research and Development Center. *Men and Women in Ships: Attitudes of Crew after One to Two Years Of Integration.* November, 1983.

A review of the psychological literature and post-integration studies and testimony before the Commission indicates situations have existed in which women were able to bond with men in various non-combat environments. Also, non-combat mixed-gender units seemed to communicate and work better than single gender units performing similar tasks.

    a. Panel 2 Report; 20 October 1992, p. 85.

    b. Marshall, Joan E. and Richard Heslin. "Boys and Girls Together: Sexual Composition and the Effect of Density and Group Size on Cohesion." *Journal of Personality and Social Psychology,* 31, No. 5. (1975): pp. 952-961.

    c. Taylor, John and Donald S. Strassberg. "The Effects of Sex Composition and Interpersonal Learning in Short-Term Personal Growth Groups." *Journal of the Division of Psychotherapy,* 23 (1986): pp. 267-273.

    d. U.S. Navy Personnel Research and Development Center. *Men and Women in Ships: Attitudes of Crew after One to Two Years Of Integration.* November, 1983.

2.5.3A    Royal Netherlands Navy

The Royal Netherlands Navy (1985) conducted a one-year experimental assignment of women to a combat support ship. The experiment had the following results:

1.    Men accepted women as equal crew members, except where heavy physical work was involved.

2.    Women generally felt accepted as equals by the men, but felt that they were under excessive scrutiny and were subjected to sexual harassment.

3.    The operational readiness of the ship was maintained to required standards during the year. However, extra effort was required to compensate for inadequate training of some of the women and lack of sufficient strength for certain tasks.

4.    The mixed-gender crew was regarded as a positive contribution to the government's policy of equal rights for women.

    a. Panel 2 Report; 20 October 1992, p. 83.

      b. Deutermann, S. W. "A Feasibility Study of the Assignment of Women to DD-963 (Spruance) Class Destroyers," Ph.D. diss., Naval Postgraduate School, Monterey, CA. 1984.

      c. Royal Netherlands Navy Department of Social Research, *Sailing with Women.* 1985.

2.5.3B      Coast Guard

A Coast Guard study of the first women officers and enlisted personnel aboard two combatant "high endurance cutters" (Sinclair, 1977) found that:

1.     Most women felt their ability was not a problem.
2.     Acceptance of non-rated enlisted women as working equals by co-workers was not considered a problem at air stations or training commands. (A minority of those at other operational units did express concern over their acceptance.)
3.     Subordinates' acceptance of women as their supervisors was considered a minor problem that would resolve itself over time.
4.     Of all the women as a group, 63 percent said they "get along fine," and one-quarter of the women said they thought men felt that women should not be in the Coast Guard.

      a. Panel 2 Report; 20 October 1992, p. 83.
      b. Deutermann, S. W. "A Feasibility Study of the Assignment of Women to DD-963 (Spruance) Class Destroyers," Ph.D. diss., Naval Postgraduate School, Monterey, CA. 1984.
      c. Sinclair, T. W. "Perceptions of U.S. Coast Guard Women Concerning Their Integration into Active Service," Ph.D. diss. Naval Postgraduate School, Monterey, CA. 1977.

2.5.3C      U.S. Navy

A male squadron Commanding Officer in a mixed-gender unit believed that women were physically capable of performing a strike fighter mission. However, he thought that bringing women into combat squadrons would reduce cohesion and bonding.

      a. Panel 2 Report; 20 October 1992, p. 80.
      b. Driscoll, D., LtCol, USMC. Testimony before the Commission, 6 August 1992.

A female F-18 pilot testified that cohesion, not ability, was the major issue concerning integrating women into combat aircraft. She stated that a qualified aviator will be able to work well in a unit regardless of gender (8/6/92). She talked about working with men on a daily basis and having men come up to her and say, "I would fly with you off the carrier on my wing any day, but I don't think I like the idea about women coming aboard ship." She stated that there was no problem with unit cohesion in her squadron.

a. Panel 2 Report; 20 October 1992, p. 80.
b. Sheufele, B., LT, USN. Testimony before the Commission, 6 August 1992.

Top Gun pilots were against integrating women into combat squadrons. They indicated in testimony that they had taken a straw poll before their appearance and their colleagues agreed with their opinion. They thought elements like esprit de corps and bonding were difficult to define but were critical to a good fighting unit. The pilots felt that cohesion and the bonding in a squadron would be reduced if women were integrated. However, the Commander of Top Gun stated that he would fly to Iraq with a woman on his wing.

a. Panel 2 Report; 20 October 1992, p. 81.
b. McLane, B., CDR, USN. Testimony before the Commission, 6 August 1992.

2.5.4    Factors Impacting Mixed-Gender Cohesion

There are no military studies concerning mixed-gender combat unit cohesion. However, the issues raised by the Commission were hypothesized as having an impact on cohesion were training and unit leadership.

a. Panel 2 Report; 20 October 1992, p. 87.
b. Henderson, Dr. Wm. Darryl. Personal Statement, 2 October 1992.
c. Moskos, Dr. Charles C. Personal Statement, 2 October 1992.

Some research indicates unit cohesion could be affected by the assignment of women to combat units. The following are several areas where cohesion problems might develop:

1.    Ability of women to carry their weight without male assistance. This entails that ability to meet physical standards of endurance and stamina.
2.    Privacy on the battlefield (i.e., washing, bathing, latrine, etc.).
3.    Men wanting to protect women.
4.    Dysfunctional male/female relationships (i.e., sexual misconduct).

5. Pregnancy-particularly the perceived ability to escape from combat duty.

6. Cultural values.

7. Male bonding.

a. Panel 2 Report; 20 October 1992, p. 86.
b. Binkin, Marty. Testimony before the Commission, 4 May 1992.
c. Devilbiss, Dr. M.C. Testimony before the Commission, 9 June 1992.
d. Henderson, Dr. Wm. Darryl. Testimony before the Commission, 26 June 1992.
e. Jacobs, Dr. Owen. Testimony before the Commission, 5 May 1992.
f. Marlowe, Dr. David. Testimony before the Commission, 5 May 1992.
g. U.S. Army War College. *The Role of Women in the Army and Their Impact on Military Operations and Organizations: A Group Research Project.* May 1975.
h. U.S. Navy Personnel Research and Development Center. *Men and Women in Ships: Attitudes of Crew after One to Two Years Of Integration.* November 1983.

2.5.4B    Physiology

A great concern exists that women will not be able to perform physically demanding tasks in a combat environment. Any differences in physical performance standards between men and women could possibly cause cohesion problems.

a. Panel 2 Report; 20 October 1992, p. 87.
b. Binkin, Marty. Testimony before the Commission, 4 May 1992.
c. Jacobs, Dr. Owen. Testimony before the Commission, 5 May 1992.
d. Marlowe, Dr. David. Testimony before the Commission, 5 May 1992.

Anyone in a key leadership position who is non-deployable could cause cohesion problems at a time of mobilization.

a. Panel 2 Report; 20 October 1992, p. 88.
b. Henderson, Dr. Wm. Darryl. Testimony before the Commission, 26 June 1992.
c. Maier, Mary, LTC, USA. Testimony before the Commission, 5 May 1992.
d. Stegemeyer, Terry, SGM, USA. Testimony before the Commission, 5 May 1992.

The Canadian experience in attempting to integrate women into ground combat units found more than one cohesion factor limiting their success. Of the 103 women recruited, only one succeeded in meeting the physical, endurance and other requirements necessary to complete the training. Lack of pre-screening may have contributed to the failure of this experience. After only a short time in the unit, she was reassigned because she did not bond with the unit. In her words she said the male soldiers were too immature for her. It should be noted that only two factors, physical fitness and bonding, eliminated all 103 women interested in joining a combat unit.

a. Panel 2 Report; 20 October 1992, p. 92.
b. Summary Report on Fact-Finding Trip to Canada, 26 August 1992.

2.5.5          Survey Instruments

Results of a study by The Roper Organization on the attitudes of the public and military suggest that many people feel that the assignment of women to combat positions will have a negative effect on cohesion. Most military personnel (55 percent) believed that male bonding is essential for developing a cohesive unit capable of meeting the stress of combat and assigning women would erode this bonding. Forty one percent of the military felt that there would be a negative affect on cohesion if women were assigned to combat positions. Sixty three percent of military personnel felt that assigning women to combat would lead enemy countries to view our Armed Forces as vulnerable. Further, most military personnel (66 percent) believed that if women were fighting side by side with men in direct combat, men would be less effective and at greater risk of being killed because they would feel they must protect women.

a. Panel 2 Report; 20 October 1992, p. 94.
b. "Attitudes Regarding the Assignment of Women in the Armed Forces:
      The Military Perspective." The Roper Organization Inc., September
      1992: pp. 35, 39, 59, 63.

Forty-one percent of the public believed that male bonding is essential for developing a cohesive unit capable of meeting the stress of combat, while 50 percent disagreed with that statement. Thirty-nine percent of the public believed that assigning women to combat positions would have neither a positive nor a negative effect on cohesion; followed by a negative effect (27 percent); and a positive effect (22 percent). Forty-eight percent of the public believed that if women were fighting side by side with men in direct combat, men would be less effective and at greater risk of being killed because they would feel they must protect the women.

a. "Attitudes Regarding the Assignment of Women in the Armed Forces: The Public Perspective." The Roper Organization Inc., September 1992: pp. 10, 15-19.

In a survey of retired flag and general officers, majorities (71 percent to 90 percent) indicated they are opposed to women in combat positions depending on the combat specialty (i.e., 71 percent for fighter/bomber aircraft, 90 percent for infantry). Fifty-six percent of letters received from retired flag and general officers indicated a negative impact on unit cohesion if the current combat exclusion policy was changed.

a. Johnson, C.B., Maj, USMC. *1992 Survey of Retired Flag and General Officers*. Washington, DC, (1992): pp. 6-10.

2.5.5     Effects of Assigning Women to Combat Positions

The weight of cohesion research as discussed in expert testimony (Marlowe and Jacobs) has focused on all-male Army ground combat units. It indicates that in ground Army combat units the presence of women would be negative. Marlowe and Jacobs agreed that women should still be excluded from Infantry and Armor.

a. Panel 2 Report; 20 October 1992, p. 94.
b. Binkin, Marty. Testimony before the Commission, 4 May 1992, p. 143.
c. Jacobs, Dr. Owen. Testimony before the Commission, 5 May 1992, p. 35.
d. Marlowe, Dr. David. Testimony before the Commission, 5 May 1992, pp. 20, 65.

Binkin stated that "the restrictions on combat aircraft have already been lifted, and I don't see any convincing rationale for reversing that action ... On naval ships, my feeling is that the restriction on naval ships should also be removed. Why? Because I can't find any convincing reasons for not removing them."

a. Binkin, Marty. Testimony before the Commission, 4 May 1992.

Dr. Marlowe stated "Support organizations tend to bond in terms of technical skill to do the job...I can envisage women fulfilling combat roles in everything but Infantry and Armor, and my reasons for it are in part backed by an evolutionary percept, but in other part relate to the nature of the task and the nature of the bonding...I have no problem, by the way, with women flying combat aircraft, helicopters, fixed wing. I have no problem with the development in that context, the wing man kind of teamwork. I think a lot of

C-87

this, again, gets to levels of technical expertise. One of the problems with technical expertise in Infantry and Armor, however, is that a lot of it depends upon sheer strength and the ability of one primate to kill another, when push comes to shove, and I think, from my own personal point of view, the stand I have taken and would take is that I would continue to exclude Infantry and Armor...So, at present, what I would simply say is that for those very fundamental, physical reasons, I would exclude women from infantry and armor, from the places where you have to go and carry the battle to the enemy physically."

a. Marlowe, Dr. David. Testimony before the Commission, 5 May 1992.

Further, the experts believed that dual standards would harm cohesion since other unit members will see the person meeting the lower standard as a weak link that will collapse under stress.

a. Panel 2 Report; 20 October 1992, p. 94.
b. Binkin, Marty. Testimony before the Commission, 4 May 1992, p. 143.
c. Jacobs, Dr. Owen. Testimony before the Commission, 5 May 1992, p. 35.
d. Marlowe, Dr. David. Testimony before the Commission, 5 May 1992, pp. 20, 65.

With regard to mixed-gender units in ground support roles the evidence is inconclusive. On the positive side, cohesion and respect between the sexes improves over time. Men and women increasingly are defined as individuals rather than as sex categories (Devilbiss, Moskos). On the negative side, unit cohesion is affected by lower deployment rates of women, male perception of women not pulling their share of heavy physical labor, and sexual activity between men and women.

a. Panel 2 Report; 20 October 1992, p. 94.
b. Deutermann, S. W. "A Feasibility Study of the Assignment of Women to DD-963 (Spruance) Class Destroyers." PhD diss., Naval Postgraduate School, Monterey, CA. 1984.
c. Devilbiss, Dr. M.C. Testimony before the Commission, 9 June 1992.
d. Moskos, Dr. Charles C. Personal Statement, 2 October 1992.
e. Sinclair, T. W. "Perceptions of U.S. Coast Guard Women Concerning Their Integration into Active Service," PhD diss. Naval Postgraduate School, Monterey, CA. 1977.

The 1992 Roper Poll of military attitudes revealed that most combat pilots indicated women should not be assigned as pilots or other crew-members on bombers or fighter aircraft fighting the enemy from the air. Results indicate the strongest opposition by Marine pilots (75 percent), followed by Air Force pilots (72 percent) and Navy pilots (57 percent). A 1992 opinion survey by the Air Force Personnel Survey Branch revealed the a majority of combat (fighter/bomber/special operations) aviators were opposed to women in air combat (61 percent), followed by agreement (27 percent) and no opinion (12 percent).

a. "Attitudes Regarding the Assignment of Women in the Armed Forces: The Military Perspective." The Roper Organization Inc., September 1992: pp. 90-93.
b. U.S. Air Force Personnel Survey Branch. *Opinion on Women in Combat.* 1992.

There is not much of a data base on the effects of mixed-gender units in combat aircraft.

a. Panel 2 Report; 20 October 1992, p. 94.
b. Henderson, Dr. Wm. Darryl. Testimony before the Commission, 26 June 1992.
c. Moskos, Dr. Charles C. Personal Statement, 2 October 1992.

By most accounts women have performed satisfactorily on non-combatant ships, ground combat support units, aircraft squadrons and missile crews. It must be noted that after a review of all the testimony, men in combat units, across all Services, were more likely to be against women entering combat positions than those in non-combat units of mixed-gender. Of those men that had worked with women, Naval aviators and Navy enlisted personnel, Army combat support units, and USAF missile crews, many responded positively about working with women and others still felt that women should not be in combat positions.

a. Panel 2 Report; 20 October 1992, p. 95.
b. Holly, John, Col, USMC. Testimony before the Commission, 28 August 1992, p. 249.
c. Lawrence, William, VADM, USN. Testimony before the Commission, 25 June 1992, pp. 106-110.
d. U.S. Army Combat Support. Testimony before the Commission, 28 August 1992, p. 322.
e. U.S. Naval Aviators. Testimony before the Commission, 6 August 1992, p. 360.

  f.  U.S. Navy Enlisted.  Testimony before the Commission, 6 August 1992, p. 127.

  g.  U.S. Air Force Missile Crew.  Testimony before the Commission, 14 July 1992, p. 146.

  h.  Royal Netherlands Navy Department of Social Research, *Sailing with Women.* 1985.

## COST AND MODIFICATIONS

Air Force

2.6.1B  If it is recommended that women be assigned to combat aircraft; no aircraft in the current inventory need to be modified to accommodate female pilots if current entrance standards are maintained.  If no modifications are needed, there are minimal, if any, costs to opening combat aviation to women.  The 5th percentile male equates to approximately the 50th percentile female.

  a.  Panel 2 Report; 20 October 1992, pp. 100-101.
  b.  Lynch, M. LtCol, USAF.  Testimony before the Commission, 5 May 1992.
  c.  DASD(MM&PP).  Air Force Response to Question 23 from 24-27 June 1992.
  d.  Zehner, G., R. Mankin, J. Parker, and L.M. Tanner.  Testimony before the Commission, 29 August 1992.

2.6.1B  The cockpit design would need modification to accommodate the 5th percentile female to the 95th percentile male.  It would require a study and analysis initiative from DoD or the USAF to the primary contractors to determine areas of modifications required, if any, and the cost.  The 5th percentile female does not meet aviation entrance standards set by the USAF Surgeon General.

  a.  Panel 2 Report; 20 October 1992, p. 102.
  b.  Lynch, M. LtCol, USAF.  Testimony before the Commission, 5 May 1992.
  c.  DASD(MM&PP).  Air Force Response to Question 7 from 13-17 June 1992.

2.6.1B  The anthropometric design requirements for the C-17 are for the 5th to 95th percentile aviator, per MIL-STD-1472B.  They are the same as the standards for entrance into UPT.  Thus all pilots (male and female) graduating from UPT are eligible to fly the C-17.

  a.  Panel 2 Report; 20 October 1992, p. 102.

b. DASD(MM&PP). Air Force Response to Question 131 from 10-12 September 1992.

2.6.1B The maximum number of Gz an aircraft in the USAF inventory can perform is +9Gz.

a. Panel 2 Report; 20 October 1992, p. 102.
b. General Dynamics. Testimony before the Commission, 26 August 1992.
c. Lyons, T.J. "Women in the Fast Jet Cockpit - Aeromedical Considerations," *Aviation Space and Environmental Medicine,* September 1992.
d. DASD(MM&PP). Air Force Response to Question 3 from 13-15 July 1992.
e. U.S. Air Force Systems Command. *Cockpit Accommodation,* October 1991.
f. Zehner, G., R. Mankin, J. Parker, and L.M. Tanner. Testimony before the Commission, 29 August 1992.

2.6.1C The F-22, the new advanced fighter, is being designed for the .5 to 99.5 percentile anthropometric range for all aviators. The aircraft will accommodate all pilots (male and female) eligible for the aviation field.

a. Panel 2 Report; 20 October 1992, p. 103.
b. DASD(MM&PP). Air Force Response to Question 15 from 27-29 August 1992.
c. U.S. Air Force Systems Command. *Cockpit Accommodation,* October 1991.
d. Zehner, G., R. Mankin, J. Parker, and L.M. Tanner. Testimony before the Commission, 29 August 1992.

2.6.1D Contractors prefer to design cockpits for the smaller pilot. An increase to the upper limits decreases aerodynamic efficiency, decreases the number of weapon systems in the cockpit, increases pressurization requirements in the cockpit, and increases cost. The larger the range of anthropometric specifications, the higher the cost.

a. Panel 2 Report; 20 October 1992, pp. 103-104.
b. DASD(MM&PP). Air Force Response to Question 6 from 13-15 July 1992.
c. U.S. Air Force Systems Command. *Cockpit Accommodation,* October, 1991.
d. Zehner, G., R. Mankin, J. Parker, and L.M. Tanner. Testimony before the Commission, 29 August 1992.

2.6.1E    The Air Force does not anticipate making any changes to facilities to accommodate women in combat specialties.

a.  Panel 2 Report; 20 October 1992, p. 104.
b.  Lynch, M., Lt Col, USAF.  Testimony before the Commission, 5 May 1992.

2.6.1F    Size ranges for personal aviation equipment accommodate all male and female aviators.  Established procedures are set if the equipment does not proportionally fit the aviator.

a.  Panel 2 Report; 20 October 1992, p. 105.
b.  Lynch, M., Lt Col, USAF.  Testimony before the Commission, 5 May 1992.
c.  DASD(MM&PP).  Air Force Response to Question 6 from 13-15 July 1992.

2.6.1F    The Combat Edge G-suit is designed to fit the 5th to 95th percentile male.  Female aviators can be custom-fitted for a smaller female aviator.

a.  Panel 2 Report; 20 October 1992, pp. 105-106.
b.  DASD(MM&PP).  Air Force Response to Question 10 from 6-7 July 1992.
c.  DASD(MM&PP).  Air Force Response to Question 6 from 13-15 July 1992.

2.6.1F    The Disposable Absorption Collection Tank (an urinary relief device for women in a pressure suit) costs $505.  This is a one-time use device.  This device has currently been provided to two female aviators, and as the number of women utilizing this device increases, the cost will decrease.  The cost of an urinary relief device for men in a pressure suit is $100.

a.  Panel 2 Report; 20 October 1992, p. 105.
b.  Devine, Troy, Capt, USAF.  Testimony before the Commission, 12 September 1992.
c.  DASD(MM&PP).  Air Force Response to Question 10 from 27-29 August 1992.

2.6.1F    The cost for an urinary device for men not in a pressure suit is $7.07.

a.  Panel 2 Report; 20 October 1992, p. 105.
b.  DASD(MM&PP).  Air Force Response to Question 4 from 6-7 July 1992.
c.  DASD(MM&PP).  Air Force Response to Question 10 from 27-29 August 1992.

2.6.1F   The USAF is developing the Hollister device for urinary relief for women. The cost is approximately $20 per item and it can be used for an estimated 2 years.

    a. Panel 2 Report; 20 October 1992, p. 105.
    b. Devine, Troy, Capt, USAF. Testimony before the Commission, 12 September 1992.
    c. DASD(MM&PP). Air Force Response to Question 10 from 27-29 August 1992.

2.6.1GH   The average cost to train a pilot for the USAF is $2.5 million. The average cost to train pilots for fighters and bombers is $3.1 million. The cost to retrain aviators when they have been off flight status ranges from "4 to 6 digit figures."

    a. Panel 2 Report; 20 October 1992, pp. 106-107.
    b. DASD(MM&PP). Air Force Response to Question 8 from 4-6 April 1992.
    c. DASD(MM&PP). Air Force Response to Question 20 from 24-27 June 1992.
    d. DASD(MM&PP). Air Force Response to Question 3 from 6-7 July 1992.

2.6.1I   If entrance standards remain the same, the Air Force anticipates negligible costs to admit women into all skills.

    a. Panel 2 Report; 20 October 1992, p. 107.
    b. DASD(MM&PP). Air Force Response to Question 8 from 13-15 July 1992.
    c. DASD(MM&PP). Air Force Response to Question 29 from 31 July/3 August 1992.

2.6.1J   If the number of women in units or squadrons increases, manhours may need to increase because women, on average, are available one hour less per month at the work center due to maternity leave. There is a greater impact on flying units because flying restrictions during pregnancy cause a greater loss of duty time plus time for recertification.

    a. Panel 2 Report; 20 October 1992, p. 107.
    b. DASD(MM&PP). Air Force Response to Questions 132 and 134 from 10-12 September 1992.

2.6.1J      The Air Force has not historically had to adjust unit manning because of gender differences. The assignment process is gender-neutral and based on the requirements of the mission. The burden falls to the unit to absorb any shortfalls in manning requirements.

      a.   Panel 2 Report; 20 October 1992, p. 107.
      b.   DASD(MM&PP). Air Force Response to Question 133 from 10-12 September 1992 .
      c.   DASD(MM&PP). Air Force Response to Question 12 from 4-6 April 1992.

Marine Corps

2.6.2      The Marine Corps does not anticipate the need to modify any equipment or facilities to accommodate women if they are assigned to combat MOSs.

      a.   Panel 2 Report; 20 October 1992, p. 108.
      b.   Brindle, Eugene, LtCol, USMC, LtCol J.D. Engstrom, USMC, LtCol J.W. Hodges, USMC, and Kim Weirick. Testimony before the Commission, 24 June 1992.
      c.   DASD(MM&PP). Marine Corps Response to Question 29 from 31 July/3 August1992.

2.6.2B      Offensive combat training for female enlisted Marines would cost the Marine Corps $1.5 million for 1,700 women Marines per year (number of women recruited FY91). This would bring women's training on line with the men's.

      a.   Panel 2 Report; 20 October 1992, p. 108.
      b.   Brindle, Eugene, LtCol, USMC, LtCol J.D. Engstrom, USMC, LtCol J.W. Hodges, USMC, and Kim Weirick. Testimony before the Commission, 24 June 1992.
      c.   DASD(MM&PP). Marine Corps Response to Question 11 from 24-27 June 1992.
      d.   DASD(MM&PP). Marine Corps Response to Question 29 from 31 July/3 August 1992.

2.6.2D      Women presently do not fly USMC aircraft. The Navy provides all flight training and aircrew equipment for USMC aviators. If the standard gear does not proportionally fit an aviator, procedures provide for custom fitted equipment.

      a.   Panel 2 Report; 20 October 1992, p. 109.

b. Brindle, Eugene, LtCol, USMC, LtCol J.D. Engstrom, USMC, LtCol J.W. Hodges, USMC, and Kim Weirick. Testimony before the Commission, 24 June 1992.

c. DASD(MM&PP). Marine Corps Response to Question 6 from 13-15 July 1992.

2.6.2.F    The Marine Corps does not anticipate the need to increase manhours or personnel assigned to a unit if the numbers of women increase in that unit.

a. Panel 2 Report; 20 October 1992, p. 109.

b. DASD(MM&PP). Marine Corps Response to Question 12 from 4-6 April 1992.

c. DASD(MM&PP). Marine Corps Response to Questions 132, 133 and 134 from 10-12 September 1992.

Army

2.6.3    No significant changes or modifications are anticipated by the Army for equipment, platforms, clothing, facilities, etc. if women are assigned to currently closed MOSs.

a. Panel 2 Report; 20 October 1992, p. 110.

b. Hulin, Terry, COL, USA, COL M. McKean, USA. Testimony before the Commission, 24 June 1992.

2.6.3    If women are assigned to currently closed MOSs, the Army anticipates ARI researching the implementation process at a cost of $1.5 million per year for five years.

a. Panel 2 Report; 20 October 1992, p. 110.

b. DASD(MM&PP). Army Response to Question 29 from 31 July/3 August 1992.

2.6.3A    Fixed wing aircraft would require few, if any, modifications to accommodate the 5th percentile female.

a. Panel 2 Report; 20 October 1992, p. 110.

b. DASD(MM&PP). Army Response to Question 7 from 13-15 July 1992.

2.6.3A    If the recommendation is made to accommodate to the 5th percentile female, rotary wing aircraft would need to be modified for the 5th to 19th percentile female. The estimated cost for the prime contractors to study the modifications necessary is approximately $750,000.

a. Panel 2 Report; 20 October 1992, p. 110.
b. DASD(MM&PP). Army Response to Question 7 from 13-15 July 1992.

2.6.3B     Pilots are only required to go through retraining courses if they have been off flight status for over two years. If retraining is necessary for those aviators off flight status for under two years, it is the unit's responsibility to retrain and use its resources.

a. Panel 2 Report; 20 October 1992, pp. 110-111.
b. DASD(MM&PP). Army Response to Question 8 from 4-6 April 1992.

2.6.3C     Preliminary findings of a study underway by the Army Recruiting Command indicate that it costs approximately 50 percent more to recruit a female candidate. The primary reasons for the expense are increased manhours for recruiting, medical costs, and women tend to attrite at a higher rate in the Delayed Entry Program (DEP).

a. Panel 2 Report; 20 October 1992, p. 111.
b. DASD(MM&PP). Army Response to Question 29 from 31 July/3 August 1992.

2.6.3.D    If the number of women increases in the Army, they will not deviate from their present manning policy. The present policy ensures that all authorized spaces have personnel to fill that position. Only two units in the Army are manned in excess of 100 percent because they have a high priority mission.

a. Panel 2 Report; 20 October 1992, p. 111.
b. DASD(MM&PP). Army Response to Question 12 from 4-6 April 1992.
c. DASD(MM&PP). Army Response to Questions 132, 133, 134 from 10-12 September 1992.

Navy

2.6.4A     Women have flown in all platforms in the inventory. No modifications are necessary to assign women to combat aircraft as long as current standards remain. Minimal, if any, cost is anticipated if combat aviation is opened to women.

a. Panel 2 Report; 20 October 1992, p. 112.
b. McDermaid, S., CAPT, USN, CAPT B. D. Cole, USN. Testimony before the Commission, 5 May 1992.
c. DASD(MM&PP). Navy Response to Question 29 from 31 July/3 August 1992.

2.6.4A      The maximum Gz an aircraft in the Naval inventory performs is +7.5Gz.

         a. Panel 2 Report; 20 October 1992, p. 114.
         b. DASD(MM&PP). Navy Response to Question 3 from 13-15 July 1992.

2.6.4A      The Navy no longer utilizes male percentiles for anthropometric ranges. Instead they use multi-variate anthropometric ranges for all cockpits by assigning personal codes for anthropometric increments. The initial anthropometric ranges were based on 1964 Caucasian males and did not take into consideration ethnic and gender variables which are important in 1992.

         a. Panel 2 Report; 20 October 1992, p. 112.
         b. DASD(MM&PP). Navy Response to Question 7 from 13-15 July 1992.
         c. DASD(MM&PP). Navy Response to Question 7 from 4-6 May 1992.

2.6.4A      Sitting height (buttocks to crown of the head) is the key anthropometric dimension used in assigning aircraft. Presently 95 percent of white females and 73 percent of black females meet the minimum measurement for sitting height.

         a. Panel 2 Report; 20 October 1992, p. 113.
         b. Lyons, T.J. "Women in the Fast Jet Cockpit - Aeromedical Considerations." *Aviation Space and Environmental Medicine*, September, 1992.
         c. DASD(MM&PP). Navy Response to Question 7 from 4-6 May 1992.
         d. DASD(MM&PP). Navy Response to Question 23 from 24-27 June 1992.
         e. DASD(MM&PP). Navy Response to Question 20 from 31 July/3 August 1992.

2.6.4B      The Combat Logistics Force was opened to women in 1987. Approximately $17 million will be spent by FY96 for 23 ships to accommodate women aboard. By FY96, six of these ships will be transferred to the Military Sealift Command (MSC).

         a. Panel 2 Report; 20 October 1992, p. 114.
         b. McDermaid, S., CAPT, USN, CAPT B. D. Cole, USN. Testimony before the Commission, 5 May 1992.
         c. DASD(MM&PP). Navy Response to Question 31 from 4-6, April 1992.
         d. DASD(MM&PP). Navy Response to Question 8 from 4-6 May 1992.
         e. DASD(MM&PP). Navy Response to Question 23 from 24-27 June 1992.

f. DASD(MM&PP). Navy Response to Question 4 from 31 July/3 August 1992.

2.6.4B    All ships do not need to be modified to accommodate women. Enlisted berthing is the primary cause for SHIPALTs to be necessary. Officer berthing is not a concern.

a. Panel 2 Report; 20 October 1992, pp. 114, 116.
b. McDermaid, S., CAPT, USN, CAPT B. D. Cole, USN. Testimony before the Commission, 5 May 1992.

2.6.4B    The cost to modify combatant vessels for the accommodation of women ranges from approximately $66,000 to $305,000 per ship (i.e., frigates, destroyers, mine-countermeasures). The average cost for amphibious ships is approximately $138,171 per ship. Modifications to aircraft carriers would cost approximately $2-4 million per ship.

a. Panel 2 Report; 20 October 1992, pp. 114-116.
b. DASD(MM&PP). Navy Response to Question 21 from 24-27 June 1992.
c. DASD(MM&PP). Navy Response to Question 25 from 31 July/3 August 1992.
d. DASD(MM&PP). Navy Response to Staff Memo from 19 August 1992.

2.6.4B    FFTs, the new training frigates, will accommodate the assignment of women. Cost for modifications is approximately $500,000 per ship.

a. Panel 2 Report; 20 October 1992, p. 115.
b. DASD(MM&PP). Navy Response to Question 8 from 4-6 May 1992.
c. DASD(MM&PP). Navy Response to Question 13 from 31 July/3 August 1992.

2.6.4B    No modifications have been necessary to accommodate women aboard combatant vessels TAD (Temporary Additional Duty).

a. Panel 2 Report; 20 October 1992, p. 116.
b. DASD(MM&PP). Navy Response to Question 37 from 4-6 April 1992.
c. DASD(MM&PP). Navy Response to Questions 17 and 24 from 31 July/3 August 1992.

2.6.4C    Costs to assign women to SSBN and SSN-688 submarines range from no or minimal cost to approximately $1 million per ship depending on the number of women assigned. It is not necessary to completely overhaul the submarine to place women aboard. The SSBN would more easily accommodate women aboard.

    a.  Panel 2 Report; 20 October 1992, p. 117.
    b.  Summary Report on Fact-Finding Trip to NSB Kings Bay and NTC Orlando, 15 October 1992.
    c.  DASD(MM&PP). Navy Response to Question 13 from 4-6 May 1992.

2.6.4D      No additional costs were experienced to integrate the recruit training program at RTC Orlando.

    a.  Panel 2 Report; 20 October 1992, p. 117.
    b.  Summary Report on Fact-Finding Trip to NSB Kings Bay and NTC Orlando, 15 October 1992.

2.6.4E      A woman returning to full flight status following a pregnancy does not usually require FRS (Fleet Replacement Squadron). If she has been absent for an extraordinary period of time, she would go through a partial syllabus of FRS and the cost would depend on the type of aircraft flown. All policies for retraining are the same for men and women and depend on how long the aviator has been off flight status.

    a.  Panel 2 Report; 20 October 1992, pp. 117-118.
    b.  DASD(MM&PP). Navy Response to Question 8 from 4-6 April 1992.
    c.  DASD(MM&PP). Navy Response to Question 20 from 24-27 June 1992.

2.6.4F      Personal equipment for aviators currently accommodates all female aviators. If custom-fitting for males or females is necessary, there are procedures in place. Custom-fitted torso harnesses cost approximately $1,200 for either men or women.

    a.  Panel 2 Report; 20 October 1992, p. 113.
    b.  DASD(MM&PP). Navy Response to Question 6 from 13-15 July 1992.

2.6.4F      Urinary relief devices for men and women cost $7.61 each.

    a.  Panel 2 Report; 20 October 1992, p. 113.
    b.  DASD(MM&PP). Navy Response to Question 10 from 27-29 August 1992.

2.6.4FG        The Navy does not anticipate any modification to equipment, facilities (except ships) or clothing as a result of women being assigned to units with a combat mission.

        a. Panel 2 Report; 20 October 1992, p. 118.
        b. DASD(MM&PP). Navy Response to Question 5 from 24-27 June 1992.
        c. DASD(MM&PP). Navy Response to Question 13 from 27-29 August 1992.

2.6.4H        Monetary costs are not separated by gender for recruiting. If gender-neutral recruiting resulted in a higher number of women being contracted, costs would increase to cover DEP replacement of females if they attrite at a higher rate. The Navy does not anticipate a larger number of women being contracted if combat positions are opened to women.

        a. Panel 2 Report; 20 October 1992, p. 119.
        b. DASD(MM&PP). Navy Response to Question 8 from 13-15 July 1992.
        c. DASD(MM&PP). Navy Response to Question 29 from 31 July/3 August 1992.

2.6.4I        The Navy does not anticipate additional costs for retraining or retaining if women are assigned to combat missions.

        a. Panel 2 Report; 20 October 1992, p. 119.
        b. DASD(MM&PP). Navy Response to Question 29 from 31 July/3 August 1992.

2.6.4J        No personnel overages would result from an increase in the number of women assigned to units, squadrons, and ships. The Command's Manning Document outlines the number of personnel to fill all billets. This is done on a gender-neutral basis.

        a. Panel 2 Report; 20 October 1992, p. 119.
        b. DASD(MM&PP). Navy Response to Questions 132 and 134 from 10-12 September 1992.

2.6.4J        Combatant ships have a greater OPTEMPO (i.e., ships with more underway time) and would rarely be able to keep pregnant sailors aboard until the 20th week of gestation. Sailors removed from the ship may not immediately be replaced. An increased number of women aboard ships with a high OPTEMPO could create a potential manning shortage problem. Consequently, although there is no personnel overage in ships with increased numbers of women, the potential overhead cost resulting from pregnancy needs to be considered with the assignment of women to ships with a greater OPTEMPO.

    a.  Panel 2 Report; 20 October 1992, p. 119.
    b.  DASD(MM&PP).  Navy Response to Questions 132, 133 and 134 from 10-12 September 1992.

## Coast Guard

2.6.5        The U.S. Coast Guard modified ships for the assignment of women during the normal course of maintenance availabilities.  Costs were not broken down to specifically include how much was spent to accommodate women.

    a.  Panel 2 Report; 20 October 1992, p. 120.
    b.  U.S. Coast Guard Response to Question 6 from 15 September.

2.6.5        All facilities are gender-neutral, therefore no costs were incurred when all specialties and billets were opened to women.

    a.  Panel 2 Report; 20 October 1992, p. 120.
    b.  U.S. Coast Guard Response to Question 6 from 15 September.

# PANEL THREE CHARTER

Charter approved 1 June 1992

Panel Three will conduct fact finding research in four major areas with a focus on women in the Armed Services. The first area will assess public attitudes on the utilization of women in the Armed Services. The Panel will seek the opinions of both the military community and the American public. The research will include existing surveys and media reports, and an independent survey will be conducted to assess Commission and panel objectives. The second area will focus on social and family issues related to women in the military. The Panel will examine issues which have a particular impact on deployability. Specific deployability issues identified are pregnancy, child care, and single parent/dual career military. The Panel will also conduct research on family/spouse related issues on fraternization, and the possible familial effects of sexual harassment. The third area will be a comprehensive review of past and current conscription policies and practices of the U.S. The final area will explore lessons learned about women in the military during the Vietnam War.

## PANEL THREE FINDINGS APPROVED BY THE COMMISSION

3.1      In a national survey of the American public in 1992, those surveyed were asked whether, all things considered, they think there are too many women in the Armed Forces, about the right number, or too few. Thirty-nine percent of those surveyed said there were too few women in the military, while 32 percent thought the number was about right. Eleven percent felt that there were too many women in the military, while 17 percent didn't know. (Questions 2-3, Roper public poll)

     a. Panel 3 Report; 23 October 1992, pp. 3-4.
     b. "Attitudes Regarding the Assignment of Women in the Armed Forces: The Public Perspective," The Roper Organization Inc., September 1992, p. 9.

3.2      In a national public survey, 52 percent of Americans believed both men and women should be drafted in the event of a national emergency, even if an ample pool of young men exists. Thirty-nine percent felt that only young men should be drafted. Nine percent of those polled did not know. (Question 6)

     a. Panel 3 Report; 23 October 1992, p. 4.
     b. "Attitudes Regarding the Assignment of Women in the Armed Forces: The Public Perspective," The Roper Organization Inc., September 1992, p. 13.

3.3      In a national survey of the American public, 52 percent of Americans believed special exemptions should apply for women. Forty percent believed women should be drafted on the same basis as men. Eight percent of those polled did not know. (Question 8)

    a. Panel 3 Report; 23 October 1992, pp. 3-4.
    b. "Attitudes Regarding the Assignment of Women in the Armed Forces: The Public Perspective," The Roper Organization Inc., September 1992, p. 16.

3.4       From WWII to 1992, public opinion polls indicate that the public attitude regarding the drafting of women has been evenly divided.

    a. Panel 3 Report; 23 October 1992, p. 9.
    b. Verdugo, Naomi, "Public Opinion on Women in the Military and in Combat," review of civilian surveys conducted by the Plans and Analysis Division, Human Resources Directorate, Office of the Deputy Chief of Staff for Personnel, Headquarters, Department of the Army, 8 May 1992, page 9.

3.5       In a national survey of the American public, 44 percent favored and 47 percent opposed the current military policy not to assign women to any direct combat positions. Factoring in the survey's sampling error of +/- three percent we see the American public is evenly split on this issue. (Question 20, Roper)

    a. Panel 3 Report; 23 October 1992, p. 5.
    b. "Attitudes Regarding the Assignment of Women in the Armed Forces: The Public Perspective," The Roper Organization Inc., September 1992, p. 31.

3.6       In a national survey of the American public, 93 percent believed that a woman who is expecting a baby should not serve in a direct combat position. Forty-four percent felt that a man whose wife is expecting a child should not serve in a direct combat position.(Question 12, Roper )

    a. Panel 3 Report; 23 October 1992, p. 7.
    b. "Attitudes Regarding the Assignment of Women in the Armed Forces: The Public Perspective," The Roper Organization Inc., September 1992, p. 61.

3.7        In a national survey of the American public, 69 percent believed that a single woman with young child(ren) should not serve in a direct combat position,while 48 percent of those surveyed felt a man so situated should not serve in combat positions. (Question 12, Roper)

a.  Panel 3 Report; 23 October 1992, p. 7.
b.  "Attitudes Regarding the Assignment of Women in the Armed Forces: The Public Perspective," The Roper Organization Inc., September 1992, p. 61.

3.8        In a national survey of the American public, 55 percent of respondents stated that in the case of dual military parents, the wife should be exempt from direct combat.  Two percent said the husband should be exempt, and 14 percent believed both members should be exempt from direct combat. (Question 13, Roper)

a.  Panel 3 Report; 23 October 1992, pp. 3-4.
b.  "Attitudes Regarding the Assignment of Women in the Armed Forces: The Public Perspective," The Roper Organization Inc., September 1992, p. 62.

3.9        When asked in a national public survey whether women should be assigned to combat aircraft, 53 percent of those polled said only if they volunteer, 25 percent said women should be required to take the assignment, 18 percent said women should not be assigned, and three percent did not know. Among those polled who had prior military experience, 42 percent supported women volunteering for combat aircraft, 26 percent supported requiring women to serve in combat aircraft, and 28 percent believed women should not be assigned to combat aircraft. (Question 16, Roper)

a.  Panel 3 Report; 23 October 1992, p. 6.
b.  "Attitudes Regarding the Assignment of Women in the Armed Forces: The Public Perspective," The Roper Organization Inc., September 1992, p. 25.

3.10    When asked in a national public survey whether women should be assigned to combat ships, 51 percent of those polled said only if they volunteer, 29 percent said women should be required to take the assignment, 17 percent said women should not be assigned, and three percent did not know.  Among those polled who had prior military experience, 38 percent supported women volunteering for combat ships, 31 percent supported requiring women to serve in these roles, and 28 percent felt that women should not be assigned to combat ships. (Question 17, Roper)

a.  Panel 3 Report; 23 October 1992, pp.6-7.
b.  "Attitudes Regarding the Assignment of Women in the Armed Forces: The Public Perspective," The Roper Organization Inc., September 1992, p. 27.

3.11    When asked in a national public survey whether women should be assigned to ground combat, 45 percent of those polled said only if they volunteer, 25 percent said women should be required to take the assignment, 27 percent said women should not be assigned, and three percent did not know. (Question 18, Roper)

a.  Panel 3 Report; 23 October 1992, p. 7.
b.  "Attitudes Regarding the Assignment of Women in the Armed Forces: The Public Perspective," The Roper Organization Inc., September 1992, p. 27.

3.12    The difference in views concerning women in ground combat among those polled who had some military experience is substantial.  Here, for the first time we find that the plurality of those who had prior military experience believe women should not be assigned to this particular combat role.  Thirty-four percent felt women should be able to volunteer for ground combat.  Twenty-five percent of this group felt that women should be required to serve in ground combat roles. (Question 18)

a.  Panel 3 Report; 23 October 1992, p. 7.
b.  "Attitudes Regarding the Assignment of Women in the Armed Forces: The Public Perspective," The Roper Organization Inc., Cross Tabulations, September 1992.

3A1      Among those in a national public survey who favored the current policy of not assigning women to combat, 51 percent felt that women should be given combat aircraft assignments if they volunteer and another 15 percent felt they should be required to take combat aircraft assignments. One in three (33 percent) of them say women should not be assigned to combat aircraft. (Questions 16-18)

      a.  "Attitudes Regarding the Assignment of Women in the Armed Forces: The Public Perspective," The Roper Organization Inc., September 1992, p. 35.

3A2      Among those in a national public survey who favored the current policy of not assigning women to combat, 49 percent felt that women should be given combat ship assignments if they volunteer and another 16 percent felt they should be required to take combat ship assignments. One in three (32 percent) said women should not be assigned to combat ships. (Questions 16-18)

      a.  "Attitudes Regarding the Assignment of Women in the Armed Forces: The Public Perspective," The Roper Organization Inc., September 1992, p. 35.

3A3      Among those in a national public survey who favored the current policy of not assigning women to combat, 39 percent felt that women should be given ground combat assignments if they volunteer and another 12 percent felt they should be required to take ground combat assignments. Nearly one-half (48 percent) said women should not be assigned to ground combat. (Questions 16-18)

      a.  "Attitudes Regarding the Assignment of Women in the Armed Forces: The Public Perspective," The Roper Organization Inc., September 1992, p. 35.

3A4      Among those in a national public survey who favored the current policy of not assigning women to combat, 66 percent felt if women were fighting side by side with men in direct combat, men would be less effective and at greater risk of being killed because they would feel they must protect the women. (Question 11)

      a.  "Attitudes Regarding the Assignment of Women in the Armed Forces: The Public Perspective," The Roper Organization Inc., September 1992, p. 41.

3A5 In a national public survey, 68 percent of those polled disagreed with the statement "women are not aggressive enough to serve in direct combat." (Question 11a)

  a. Panel 3 Report; 23 October 1992, p. 5.
  b. "Attitudes Regarding the Assignment of Women in the Armed Forces: The Public Perspective," The Roper Organization Inc., September 1992, p. 41.

3A6 In a national public survey, 75 percent of those polled agreed with the statement "if a woman meets the qualifications required by a direct combat assignment, the military should be able to assign her there." (Question 11b)

  a. Panel 3 Report; 23 October 1992, p. 4.
  b. "Attitudes Regarding the Assignment of Women in the Armed Forces: The Public Perspective," The Roper Organization Inc., September 1992, p. 40.

3A7 In a national public survey 59 percent of those polled felt women should be assigned as members of the Special Forces operating behind enemy lines. (Question 9c)

  a. "Attitudes Regarding the Assignment of Women in the Armed Forces: The Public Perspective," The Roper Organization Inc., September 1992, p. 55.

3A8 The Commission uncovered no all-encompassing statement or concept which completely conveys the American approach to women's roles in the military.

  a. Panel 3 Report; 23 October 1992, p. 11.

3A9 The concept of individual choice and freedom is often at the root of American attitudes. "We do see a tendency on the part of the American public in a variety of surveys to express fairness. There tends to be a desire to allow choice. This survey [The Roper Public Survey] is consistent with a whole body of survey data that says that the American public, where offered an option that implies fairness, comes out in that direction."

  a. Setlow, Carolyn. Roper Public Survey Results, Testimony before the Commission, 11 September 1992.

3A10    The belief in equality of opportunity, of selecting the best person for a position, regardless of gender, nationality, or social status is an American tenet.

    a.  Kennedy, Edward M., U.S. Senator (D-MA).  Testimony before the Commission, 25 June 1992.

3A13    None of the major religious establishments in the United States has proposed a concrete position either for or against the question of women being assigned to combat on the basis of theology.

    a.  Panel 3 Report; 23 October 1992, pp. 16-17.

3A14    The Catholic Church takes a view that the state has a duty to protect innocent human life from conception until natural death, and this would preclude a pregnant woman serving in combat.  American Catholic bishops recognize a woman's right to seek her fulfillment educationally and professionally, as well as her right to choose to stay with her children.  Catholic theologians state that U.S. Catholic bishops would likely say that a woman should be protected from conscription.

    a.  Panel 3 Report; 23 October 1992, p. 17.
    b.  *Pastoral Letter of the National Conference of Catholic Bishops on War and Peace*, May 1983.
    c.  Roach, Father Richard.  Testimony before the Commission, 13 July 1992.

3A15    The Lutheran Church recognizes gender differences as part of the Divine Designer's plan, which is related to "respect for one another's uniqueness and our God-given responsibility to the family."  In addition, the Lutheran concept of servanthood holds that personal rights or ambitions "should never take the priority position over the moral good of the family, the church, the community or the nation."

    a.  Panel 3 Report; 23 October 1992, pp. 17-18.
    b.  Beyer, Rev. Arthur.  Testimony before the Commission, 13 July 1992.

3A16    The pastor of the Church of the Advocate feels that the basic American values would not be undone if women were allowed to voluntarily participate in combat [emphasis added].  However, reinstating the draft, even for men only, would be devastating.  A Baptist theologian also stated that "both men and women should be able to choose whether or not they want to be in combat."

    a.  Panel 3 Report; 23 October 1992, p. 19.

   b. Miller, Rev. Isaac. Testimony before the Commission, 10 September 1992.

   c. Campolo, Anthony. Testimony before the Commission, 10 September 1992.

3A17  The Jewish position holds that while men and women are morally equal, there are gender differences. People who believe men and women are fundamentally the same, stated the Director of the Center for Ethical Monotheism, are mistaken.

   a. Panel 3 Report; 23 October 1992, p. 19.

   b. Prager, Dennis. Testimony before the Commission, 6 August 1992.

3.13  Fifty-seven percent of the military personnel polled favor the current military policy of not assigning women to direct combat, while 42 percent oppose the policy. Men tended to favor this policy to a greater degree than women (57 percent v. 42 percent, respectively), while those in combat specialties tended to favor the policy to an even greater degree (72 percent) than the military as a whole (57 percent). The Marine Corps and Army most strongly favored the current policy: 63 percent and 78 percent, respectively. Only the Navy had a majority (53 percent) opposed to the policy. (Question 18, Roper military poll)

   a. Panel 3 Report; 23 October 1992, p. 23.

   b. "Attitudes Regarding the Assignment of Women in the Armed Forces: The Military Perspective," The Roper Organization Inc., September 1992, p. 54.

3.14  Regarding the assignment of women to combat aircraft, 43 percent of the military respondents favor a policy of allowing women to serve in this role only if they volunteer. Twenty-three percent feel women should be required to serve in combat aircraft, and 30 percent feel women should not be assigned to combat aircraft. Among military subgroups, combat pilots from the Air Force, Navy and Marine Corps are much more negative on this question: only 16 percent of this group favored a volunteer option, 14 percent felt women should be required to serve in combat positions, and fully 69 percent felt women should not be assigned to combat aircraft. (Question 15)

   a. Panel 3 Report; 23 October 1992, pp. 24-25.

   b. "Attitudes Regarding the Assignment of Women in the Armed Forces: The Military Perspective," The Roper Organization Inc., September 1992, p. 41.

3.15    The largest proportion of the military respondents also supports allowing women to serve on combat ships only if they volunteer. Thirty-nine percent said women should be allowed to serve on combat ships on a voluntary basis only, 30 percent felt women should be required to serve in that role, and 29 percent felt women should not be assigned to combat ships. One half of Navy respondents felt that women should be required to serve on combat ships. (Question 15a)

   a. Panel 3 Report; 23 October 1992, p. 25.
   b. "Attitudes Regarding the Assignment of Women in the Armed Forces: The Military Perspective," The Roper Organization Inc., September 1992, p. 46.

3.16    Military attitudes toward women serving in ground combat depart substantially from those demonstrated with combat ships and combat aircraft. Nearly half (49 percent) of the respondents in this case stated that women should not be assigned to ground combat positions. Thirty percent said women should be able to serve in ground combat positions only if they volunteer, and 19 percent said women should be required to serve in ground combat. (Question 16)

   a. Panel 3 Report; 23 October 1992, p. 25.
   b. "Attitudes Regarding the Assignment of Women in the Armed Forces: The Military Perspective," The Roper Organization Inc., September 1992, p. 50.

3.17    Among the military subgroups, we find the Marines most strongly opposed to assigning women in ground combat (75 percent); in the Army, 56 percent were opposed. In the subgroup comprised of combat specialties from all services, 67 percent believe women should not be assigned to ground combat. (Question 16)

   a. Panel 3 Report; 23 October 1992, p. 25.
   b. "Attitudes Regarding the Assignment of Women in the Armed Forces: The Military Perspective," The Roper Organization Inc., September 1992, p. 53.

3.18    Respondents in the military poll were evenly split on the question of drafting women during a national emergency in the event there are enough men available to serve (52 percent in favor, 48 percent opposed).  Fifty-three percent of military respondents initially opposed to drafting women favored such a draft during a national emergency if an ample pool of young men did not exist.  Forty-six percent were opposed even under this circumstance. (Questions 4 and 5)

    a.  Panel 3 Report; 23 October 1992, pp. 23-4.
    b.  "Attitudes Regarding the Assignment of Women in the Armed Forces: The Military Perspective," The Roper Organization Inc., September 1992, pp. 24, 26.

3.19    On the question of special exemptions for women in the event they are drafted, 49 percent of the military respondents felt that women should be drafted on the same basis as men, while 46 percent felt that special exemptions for women should apply.  Military women tended to favor the exemptions to a greater degree than military men (55 percent v. 44 percent, respectively). (Question 6)

    a.  Panel 3 Report; 23 October 1992, p. 24.
    b.  "Attitudes Regarding the Assignment of Women in the Armed Forces: The Military Perspective," The Roper Organization Inc., September 1992, p. 29.

3.20    On the question of whether physical standards for each combat assignment should reflect the demands of that assignment on a gender-neutral basis, fully 70 percent of the military strongly agreed, and another 17 percent mostly agreed.  Only 12 percent of military respondents disagreed with this statement to any degree. (Question 19)

    a.  Panel 3 Report; 23 October 1992, p. 26.
    b.  "Attitudes Regarding the Assignment of Women in the Armed Forces: The Military Perspective," The Roper Organization Inc., September 1992, p. 82.

3.21      Military respondents who served in mixed gender units in Desert Shield/Desert Storm rated the performance of men and women. Ninety-seven percent of Army and 98 percent of Marine Corps men were rated Excellent/Good, contrasted with 48 percent of Army women and 44 percent of Marine Corps women in mixed gender units who received the same rating. Three percent of Army men and one percent of Marine Corps men were rated Fair/Poor, contrasted with 52 percent of Army women and 56 percent of Marine Corps women in mixed gender units who received the same rating. Performance differences between the sexes in the Navy and Air Force were less marked. Overall, 96 percent of the military respondents in Desert Shield/Desert Storm rated their unit's performance as Excellent/Good. (Question 24)

     a. Panel 3 Report; 23 October 1992, p. 28.
     b. "Attitudes Regarding the Assignment of Women in the Armed Forces: The Military Perspective," The Roper Organization Inc., September 1992, pp. 116- 117.

3.22      On family issues relating to military assignments, 93 percent of the military polled felt that a woman who is expecting a baby should not be assigned to a combat position, while only 26 percent felt that a man whose wife is expecting a baby should not be so assigned. (Question 10)

     a. Panel 3 Report; 23 October 1992, p. 30.
     b. "Attitudes Regarding the Assignment of Women in the Armed Forces: The Military Perspective," The Roper Organization Inc., September 1992, p. 107.

3.23      Seventy-two percent of the military believed a single woman with children should not be assigned to combat, while 48 percent believed a single man with children should not be so assigned. (Question 10)

     a. Panel 3 Report; 23 October 1992, p. 30.
     b. "Attitudes Regarding the Assignment of Women in the Armed Forces: The Military Perspective," The Roper Organization Inc., September 1992, p. 107.

3.24      Fifty-four percent of military respondents did not believe a married woman with children should be assigned to combat, while only 14 percent felt that a married man with children should not be so assigned. (Question 10)

     a. Panel 3 Report; 23 October 1992, p. 30.

b. "Attitudes Regarding the Assignment of Women in the Armed Forces: The Military Perspective," The Roper Organization Inc., September 1992, p. 107.

3.25    Regarding dual military parents with young children, 65 percent of military respondents felt that the wife in such a couple should be exempt from direct combat; 27 percent felt that neither should be exempt from direct combat. (Question 11)

a. Panel 3 Report; 23 October 1992, p. 30.
b. "Attitudes Regarding the Assignment of Women in the Armed Forces: The Military Perspective," The Roper Organization Inc., September 1992, p. 109.

3.26    Forty-one percent of the military polled felt that women being assigned to direct combat would have a negative effect on the ability of the military to win a war. Thirty-eight percent said it would not have an effect, and 19 percent said it would have a positive effect. (Question 13)

a. Panel 3 Report; 23 October 1992, pp. 25-26.
b. "Attitudes Regarding the Assignment of Women in the Armed Forces: The Military Perspective," The Roper Organization Inc., September 1992, p. 33.

3.27    Majorities of all military subgroups say that the assignment of women to combat would not have much of an effect on their likelihood of re-enlisting or remaining in the military. Thirty-nine percent of the Marine Corps, and 25 percent of the Army said it would decrease their likelihood of re-enlistment. (Question 14)

a. "Attitudes Regarding the Assignment of Women in the Armed Forces: The Military Perspective," The Roper Organization Inc., September 1992, p. 77.

3.28    Due to sampling size, the military women respondents in the Roper military poll cannot be broken down by service, by officer/enlisted, nor by military specialty. Therefore, it is not possible to determine in a statistically reliable fashion the attitudes of these subgroups or combinations of subgroups (for example, women Army officers). Only military women as a whole can be legitimately reported as findings, although with a much higher degree of uncertainty.

a. Panel 3 Report; 23 October 1992, p. 22.

3.29    In general, the Roper poll revealed that members of the military with direct experience in the demands of combat are most opposed to eliminating the combat exclusion policy.

    a.  "Attitudes Regarding the Assignment of Women in the Armed Forces: The Military Perspective," The Roper Organization Inc., September 1992.

3.31    In a 1992 Survey on Gender in the Military, 12 percent of Army enlisted women, ten percent of Army women non-commissioned officers, and 14 percent of Army women officers surveyed stated they would volunteer for the combat arms if it were possible. Seventy percent, 79 percent and 71 percent, respectively, stated they would not, and 18 percent, 11 percent and 15 percent, respectively said they were not sure. (Table 5)

    a.  Panel 3 Report; 23 October 1992, p. 32.
    b.  Moskos, Dr. Charles C. and Laura Miller. "1992 Survey on Gender in the Military," 28 August 1992.

3.32    In a 1992 Survey on Gender in the military, 18 percent of women Army officers, 20 percent of women Army non-commissioned officers, and 21 percent of Army enlisted women surveyed stated they are satisfied with the present Army regulations that exclude women from direct combat roles. Seventy percent of the female officers, 77 percent of the female noncommissioned officers, and 75 percent of female enlisted persons stated that women should be allowed to volunteer for combat roles. Eleven percent, two percent and four percent, respectively, stated that women should be treated exactly like men and serve in the combat arms just like men. (Table 13)

    a.  Panel 3 Report; 23 October 1992, p. 32.
    b.  Moskos, Charles C. and Laura Miller. "1992 Survey on Gender in the Military," 28 August 1992.

3B1    Seventy-four percent of the military polled felt if women were assigned to direct combat positions, time lost for illness, pregnancy, or other health reasons would have a negative effect. (Question 12)

    a.  Panel 3 Report; 23 October 1992, p. 36.
    b.  "Attitudes Regarding the Assignment of Women in the Armed Forces: The Military Perspective," The Roper Organization Inc., September 1992, p. 39.

3B2       Sixty-six percent of the military polled felt women should not be assigned as a member of Special Forces operating behind enemy lines, while 34 percent felt they should be assigned. (Question 7)

       a.  "Attitudes Regarding the Assignment of Women in the Armed Forces: The Military Perspective," The Roper Organization Inc., September 1992, p. 97.

3B3       Sixty-one percent of the military polled disagreed with the statement "women are not aggressive enough to serve in direct combat." (Question 9)

       a.  "Attitudes Regarding the Assignment of Women in the Armed Forces: The Military Perspective," The Roper Organization Inc., September 1992, p. 65.

3.33      Active Duty Strengths as of 31 March 1992:

## BASELINE CHART
*As of: 31 March 1992*

|  | MEN | WOMEN | TOTAL | % WOMEN |
|---|---|---|---|---|
| ARMY | 584,853 | 76,887 | 661,740 | 11.6 |
| NAVY | 493,733 | 54,849 | 548,582 | 10.0 |
| AIR FORCE | 422,848 | 70,917 | 493,765 | 14.4 |
| MARINE CORPS | 182,181 | 8,643 | 190,824 | 4.5 |
| ACTIVE DUTY | 1,683,615 | 211,296 | 1,894,911 | 11.2 |

*  Source: Defense Manpower Data Center, 20 August 1992

a.  Defense Manpower Data Center, "Fact Sheet: Women in the Military," 20 August 1992

3.34    Single and dual military parents comprise over 6.5 percent of the Active Duty Force.

   a. Panel 3 Report; 23 October 1992, p. 46.
   b. DASD(MM&PP). Response to Question 1, 25-26 March 25-26 1992.

3.35    Among the single parents serving on Active Duty, women comprise a disproportionate segment compared to their overall representation. They are 11.2 percent of the total force, yet make up 34.7 percent of service-reported single parents. (Army single parent data does not exclude non-custodial parents.)

   a. Panel 3 Report; 23 October 1992, p. 46.
   b. Defense Manpower Data Center, "Fact Sheet:  Women in the Military," 20 August 1992.

3.36    Within the Active Duty Force, 12.5 percent of women and 2.9 percent of men are single parents. (These figures also include Army non-custodial parents.)

   a. Panel 3 Report; 23 October 1992, p. 46.
   b. Defense Manpower Data Center, "Fact Sheet:  Women in the Military," 20 August 1992.

3.37    During the Gulf War, 36,704 children were separated from their parents due to the deployment of either a single parent or both parents (includes children of active duty and reserve parents so situated).  Over 32,000 of this group were separated from a single parent, while over 4,600 had both parents deployed.

   a. Panel 3 Report; 23 October 1992, p. 47.
   b. Department of Defense, "DoD Report on Title III of the Persian Gulf Conflict and Supplemental Authorization and Personnel Benefits Act of 1991:  Public Law 102-25" (hereafter referred to as "DoD Report on Title III"), pp. 4-5.

3.38    DoD currently does not assess the welfare of children of single parent/dual military families when their parent(s) are deployed.  The Air Force has research underway which takes an historical look at how these children fared during Desert Shield/Storm, but the results will not be available before the conclusion of the Commission.

   a. Department of Defense, Service Representatives.  Testimony before Panel 3, 26 September 1992.

b. DASD(MM&PP).   Response to Question 167, 23 September 1992.

3.39   Military research is underway studying the effects of the Gulf War on children of military parents, to include single/dual military parents.  They have found that many children suffered from the effects of separation:  anxiety, behavior problems, sleeping disorders, and eating disorders.  Full results of the research are not complete at this time.

a. Department of Defense, Service Representatives.  Testimony before the Commission Panel 3, 26 September 1992.
b. DASD(MM&PP).   Response to Question 167, 23 September 1992.

3.40   Commanders and supervisors who testified before the Commission reported that deployments of single/dual military parents in Desert Shield/Storm was not a readiness problem.

a. Active duty service members.  Testimony before the Commission:  9 June, 25 June, 26 June, 15 July, 6 August, 7 August, 28 August, 12 September 1992.

3.41   Results of the Navy's 1992 NPRDC study indicate that some ship commanders felt that pregnancy, single parenthood, and dual military parenthood did constitute a readiness problem.

a. Thomas, Patricia and CAPT Martha L. Whitehead,  USN. "Navy Lost Time Briefing," Testimony before the Commission, 1 October 1992.

3.42   There is no formal outreach program for care-givers of military children to assist them in their specific role.  Thirty-three percent of caregivers of Active duty children during Desert Shield/Desert Storm used some of the Family Support systems on nearby installations.

a. Panel 3 Report; 23 October 1992, p. 48.
b. "DoD Report on Title III," Issue 5, p. 15.

3.43      Child development experts agree that the psychological and emotional effects of parental separation on young children is greatly increased when there is risk of death in war. Their research demonstrated that separation from the primary caregiver (mother or father, mother in particular) greatly reduces a child's feelings of security. An infant/toddler who does not have a secure attachment is less likely to explore his/her surroundings and relate to others. The mother is most often cited by experts as the preferred and most critical parent for childcare. After prolonged and/or repeated separations, attachment theory research showed that children tended to be more depressed and anxious, and less willing to re-attach to the parent upon reunion. Attachment theorists assert that the negative effects of separation on young children can affect them into their later childhood and adult years. The younger the child is at the time of separation, the greater the effects on his/her emotional/psychological makeup.

     a. Panel 3 Report; 23 October 1992, pp. 48-51.
     b. Family Issues and Psychology Panels. Testimony before the Commission, June 1992.

3.44      Testimony by military and civilian experts also establishes that the quality of family life prior to a separation, the long-term emotional and financial security of the family, and the conditions under which reunion takes place are stronger considerations than the physical separation itself.

     a. Panel 3 Report; 23 October 1992, pp. 49-51.
     b. Family Issues and Psychology Panels. Testimony before the Commission, June 1992.

3.45      Child development experts agree that a stable, long-term relationship to a substitute caregiver is needed to adequately provide for a young child's needs when the parent(s) must be absent.

     a. Panel 3 Report; 23 October 1992, pp. 48-51.
     b. Family Issues and Psychology Panels. Testimony before the Commission, June 1992.

3.46      Experts also cite that there are negative effects on parents when they are separated from their young children, which may effect both their commitment to the service and their ability to re-attach to the child(ren).

     a. U.S. Air Force. "A Study of the Effectiveness of Family Assistance Programs in the Air Force During Operation Desert Shield/Storm."

3.47    The military currently subsidizes center-based child care at military child development centers. In addition, allowances are also made for use of appropriated funds "to provide assistance to family home day care providers so that family home day care services can be provided to members of the Armed Forces at a cost comparable to the cost of services provided by military child development centers."

a.  Military Child Care Act of 1989, P.L. 101-189, 29 November, 1989.

3.48    The Department of Defense has recently published new, stricter guidelines for Family Care Plans which require extensive documentation and verification, but they do not include evaluation of a caregiver's relationship with the child. DoD has instituted an annual Inspector General requirement to examine these plans at each installation. Each Service has completed or is completing Service-specific policies which adhere to or exceed the new DoD standards.

a.  Panel 3 Report; 23 October 1992, p. 48.
b.  DoD Instruction 1342.19, "Family Care Plans," 13 July 1992.

3.49    DoD has issued a regulation allowing military members who are new mothers or one member of a dual military family who adopts a child, a 4-month period during which they are exempted from the requirement to deploy. The impact on personnel readiness has not been assessed at this time.

a.  Panel 3 Report; 23 October 1992, p. 52.
b.  Change 1 to DoD Directive 1315.7; implemented August 21, 1991.

3.50    The Coast Guard has established a program of voluntary, 6-month to 2-year periods of leave without pay to parents of young children. A higher proportion of women than men select this program. The program is still in its early stages, so it is not yet possible to determine the rate of its success.

a.  Panel 3 Report; 23 October 1992, p. 52.
b.  U.S. Coast Guard, Commandant Instruction 1040.5, 10 June 1991.

3.51    The system of pay and benefits currently in place for military personnel includes benefits for family members that serve as incentives for the retention of military personnel to remain in the service for a period beyond which they might otherwise not remain. Nevertheless, the effects of this system may serve as an incentive for military personnel to have families.

a.  Panel 3 Report; 23 October 1992, p. 53.

b. Department of Defense, Service Representatives. Testimony before
Panel 3, 26 September 1992.

3.52        Point-in-time pregnancy rates among servicewomen are as follows: Army: 7.9
percent; Navy: 8.9 percent (enlisted only); Air Force: 3.2 percent (officers),
5.4 percent (enlisted); Marine Corps: 2.0 percent (officers), 5.8 percent
(enlisted).

a. Panel 3 Report; 23 October 1992, p. 57.
b. DoD response to Question 4, March 25-6 Hearings.
c. Navy Personnel Survey, (NPS), 1990 Survey Report Volume 2.

3.53        Navy research analysts state that an annual pregnancy rate can be
approximated by multiplying the point-in-time pregnancy rate by a factor of
1.5. Service annual rates based on this calculation are a follows:  Army: 11.9
percent; Navy: 13.4 percent (enlisted only); Air Force: 4.8 percent (officers),
8.1 percent (enlisted); Marine Corps: 3.0 percent (officers), 8.7 percent
(enlisted).

a. Panel 3 Report; 23 October 1992, p. 57.
b. Thomas, Patricia. Telephone Conference Testimony before
Panel 3, 26 September 1992.

3.54        During Operations Desert Shield/Desert Storm, women experienced a rate of
nondeployability of approximately 3:1 in comparison to men in each of the
services, largely due to pregnancy.

a. U.S. Army, Briefing on Non-Deployability, Testimony before the
Commission, 8 August 1992.
b. U.S. Navy, Briefing on Non-Deployability, Testimony before the
Commission, 11 September 1992.
c. U.S. Air Force, Briefing on Non-Deployability, Testimony before the
Commission, 11 September 1992.
d. U.S. Marine Corps, Briefing on Non-Deployability, Testimony before the
Commission, 11 September 1992.

3.55        Due to the percentages of women assigned to units which were designated to
deploy to the combat theater during Desert Shield/Desert Storm, the higher
rate of female nondeployability had minimal impact on the overall
nondeployability of the force.

a. U.S. Army, Briefing on Non-Deployability, Testimony before the
Commission, 8 August 1992.

C-120

        b. U.S. Navy, Briefing on Non-Deployability, Testimony before the
           Commission, 11 September 1992.

        c. U.S. Air Force, Briefing on Non-Deployability, Testimony before the
           Commission, 11 September 1992.

        d. U.S. Marine Corps, Briefing on Non-Deployability, Testimony before the
           Commission, 11 September 1992.

3.56      Army figures on the incidence of voluntary and involuntary separations for enlisted personnel show significant increases in Fiscal Year 1991, compared to previous years, in the categories of parenthood, sole parenthood and pregnancy.

        a. Panel 3 Report; 23 October 1992, pp. 60-61.
        b. Department of the Army, DCSPER 598 Report.
        c. DASD(MM&PP).   Response to Questions 171 and 175.

3.57      DoD policy guidance states that a single/dual military parent who cannot execute a Family Care Plan in the event of deployment may be discharged with impunity.

        a. Moskos, Dr. Charles C.  Q & A during Panel 3 Fact-Finding Brief before
           the Commission, 11 September 1992.

3.58      Some women from each service were evacuated from the combat theater during Desert Shield/Storm prior to the return of their units for reasons of pregnancy.  Precise figures of women returned early for this reason, and comparisons with numbers and reasons for males returning are not available at this time.

        a. DASD(MM&PP).   Response to Question 117.

3D1      In Fiscal Year 1989, 4,992 active duty enlisted women were voluntarily discharged for pregnancy; this constitutes 2.6 percent of the 195,532 enlisted women serving on active duty that fiscal year.  In FY 1990, 5,042 active duty enlisted women were voluntarily discharged for pregnancy; this constitutes 2.7 percent of the 188,913 enlisted women serving on active duty that fiscal year. In FY 1991, 5,201 active duty enlisted women were voluntarily discharged for pregnancy; this constitutes 2.9 percent of the 182,219 enlisted women serving on active duty that fiscal year.

        a. DASD(MM&PP).   Response to Questions 171 and 175.
        b. Defense Manpower Data Center statistics for active duty enlisted
           separations and active duty strengths in FY 1989, 1990, 1991.

3D2      Currently, the Services do not have policies for replacing women in deployable units, including women serving in key positions in deployable units, when those women become pregnant. Rather, pregnant women, including those serving in key positions, are required to be replaced only at the time their unit is actually required to deploy.

           a. DASD(MM&PP). Response to Question 143, 10-12 September 1992.

3.59      Historically, the Selective Service has established several exemptions for dependency reasons and hardship/privation to wife, child, or parent. Agriculture and other vocational exemptions have also applied for those required to register. These exemptions have served society in recognizing individual family and other obligations that may outweigh military obligations.

           a. Panel 3 Report; 23 October 1992, pp. 63-69.
           b. Selective Service Regulations, P.L. 65-12 (May 18, 1917).
           c. Selective Service Regulations, P.L. 82-51 (Jun 19, 1951).
           d. Selective Service Regulations, P.L. 90-40 (Jun 30, 1967).

3.60      The Selective Service's current policy allows registrant deferment because of hardship to dependents, sole survivorship, etc. Any future conscription scenario involving women might incorporate exemptions which would protect society's interest in preserving the integrity of the family. However, such exemptions would be subject to constitutional challenge.

           a. Panel 3 Report; 23 October 1992, pp. 67-68.
           b. Military Selective Service Act, 50 U.S.C. App. 453.

3.61      Over 5,500 American military women served in Vietnam proper. This figure does not include all of Southeast Asia. It is estimated 7,500 women served in all of Southeast Asia.

           a. Panel 3 Report; 23 October 1992, p. 71.
           b. U.S. Army Center of Military History.
           c. U.S. Navy, Director of Naval History.
           d. U.S. Air Force, Center for Air Force History.
           e. U.S. Marine Corps, Marine Corps Historical Center.
           f. DASD(MM&PP). Response to Question 19 from 4-6 May 1992.

3.62      Eight American military women died in Vietnam (one due to hostile fire, seven non-hostile).

           a. Panel 3 Report; 23 October 1992, p. 72.

b. U.S. Army Center of Military History.
c. U.S. Navy, Director of Naval History.
d. U.S. Air Force, Center for Air Force History.
e. U.S. Marine Corps, Marine Corps Historical Center.

3.63    No American military women were captured or missing in Vietnam.

a. Panel 3 Report; 23 October 1992, pp.72-73.
b. U.S. Army Center of Military History.
c. U.S. Navy, Director of Naval History.
d. U.S. Air Force, Center for Air Force History.
e. U.S. Marine Corps, Marine Corps Historical Center.

3.64    Women who served in Vietnam suffered from exposure to fire, emotional trauma, and were required to perform under great stress. An estimated ten percent of U.S. nurses who served in Vietnam have been diagnosed with Post-Traumatic Stress Disorder.

a. Panel 3 Report; 23 October 1992, p. 72.
b. Jacobs, Marianne Scherer. "The Best of Times, The Worst of Times: The Vietnam Experiences of and Post-Traumatic Stress Disorder Among Female Nurse Veterans." Ph.D. dissertation, University of Washington, 1990.

# PANEL FOUR CHARTER

Charter approved 4 May 1992

Panel 4 will investigate the legal and policy implications of changing the Combat Exclusion Restrictions in an All-Volunteer Force or in a Conscription Force. Combat effectiveness, morale and cohesion, personnel effects (fraternization, recruiting, retention, career opportunities), for officer, NCO and enlisted ranks, will be studied in the following categories: All-Volunteer Force - voluntary assignments/combat positions, involuntary assignments/combat positions; Conscription Force - involuntary male and voluntary female assignments/combat positions, both male and female involuntary assignments/combat positions, involuntary male assignments/combat positions and females subject to conscription under the Military Selective Service Act on a different basis than males if females were not assigned to positions on the same basis as males. Panel 4 will examine the role of women in the Panama and Grenada conflicts. Based upon investigation, the Panel will make recommendations to the Commission on the legal and policy implications of changing the Combat Exclusion Restrictions in both the All-Volunteer Force and the Conscription Force environment.

## PANEL FOUR FINDINGS APPROVED BY THE COMMISSION

4.1     The U.S. Supreme Court traditionally reviews sex-based classifications under the equal protection guarantee of the Constitution on an intermediate level of scrutiny.

    a. Panel 4 Report; 23 October 1992, pp. 5-6.
    b. Craig v. Boren, 429 U.S. 190, 197, 97 S.Ct. 451, 457 (1971).
    c. Rostker v. Goldberg, 453 U.S. 57 (1981).
    d. Military Selective Service Act, 50 U.S.C. App. 453.

4.2     When a court reviews a statute or policy relating to the military on equal protection grounds, a review of past court decisions indicates that it will apply the following level of review: Does the statute or policy serve an important government interest and does this statute or policy substantially relate to that government interest? This test will likely be tempered by the courts' longstanding practice of deference to the Congress and the Executive Branch in the area of military affairs.

    a. Panel 4 Report; 23 October 1992, pp. 5-10, 12.
    b. Craig v. Boren, 429 U.S. 190, 197, 97 S.Ct. 451, 457 (1971).
    c. Rostker v. Goldberg, 453 U.S. 57, 70 (1981).
    d. Military Selective Service Act, 50 U.S.C. App. 453.
    e. "Judicial Review and Soldiers' Rights: Is the Principle of Deference a Standard of Review?" 17 Hofstra L. Rev. 465, 475, (1989).
    f. U.S. Constitution, Art. 1, Sec. 8, cl. 12-14.

    g. Chappell v. Wallace, 462 U.S. 296, 301 (1983).
    h. Goldman v. Weinberger, 475 U.S. 503, 507 (1986).
    i. Schlesinger v. Ballard, 419 U.S. 498, 510 (1975).
    j. Gilligan v. Morgan, 413 U.S. 1, 10 (1973).

4.3    Based on the U.S. Supreme Court ruling in Rostker v. Goldberg, where the Court found that male-only draft registration was primarily for a "pool of combat troops," excluding women from ground combat positions by statute or policy may allow the Court to uphold the ruling that women are not required to register or be subject to conscription, even if other combat positions are opened to them.

    a. Panel 4 Report; 23 October 1992, p. 6.
    b. Rostker v. Goldberg, 453 U.S. 57, 70 (1981).
    c. Military Selective Service Act, 50 U.S.C. App. 453.

4.4    Information available from the Selective Service System and the National Archives shows the Army received the majority of draftees during World War II (83 percent), Korea (95 percent), and Vietnam (98 percent).

    a. Panel 4 Report; 23 October 1992, p. 28.
    b. Military Selective Service Act, 50 U.S.C. App. 453.

4.5    When federal courts review a statute or policy that addresses a matter relating to the military, the courts give great deference to the Congress and the Executive Branch when deciding the constitutionality of the statute or policy.

    a. Panel 4 Report; 23 October 1992, pp. 6-10.
    b. Rostker v. Goldberg, 453 U.S. 57, 70 (1981).

4.6    As the courts review the "important" interests put forth by the government in support of its actions, the likelihood of them upholding a statute or policy increases with the amount of empirical evidence which is available linking the discriminatory component of the statute or policy with the important government interest. Government interests accepted as important by the courts have included: the need to raise and support armies, Rostker v. Goldberg; the ability to ensure the general mobility and readiness of military personnel, Crawford v. Cushman, holding unconstitutional a Marine Corps regulation that mandated discharge for pregnancy; and uniformity and discipline, Goldman v. Weinberger.

    a. Panel 4 Report; 23 October 1992, p. 12.
    b. Rostker v. Goldberg, 453 U.S. 57, 70 (1981).

    c. Crawford v. Cushman, 531 F.2d 1114 (2nd Circuit 1976).
    d. Goldman v. Weinberger, 475 U.S. 503, 507 (1976).

4.7        If all combat positions are open to women, different assignment policies for men and women to some/all positions may be subject to legal challenge. Any differential treatment must be justified by the government and meet the legal test of intermediate scrutiny with deference to the military.

        For example, combat positions are open to women and women are assigned on a volunteer basis while men are assigned involuntarily to the same positions.

    a. Panel 4 Report; 23 October 1992, pp. 5-10,13.
    b. Rostker v. Goldberg, 453 U.S. 57, 70 (1981).

4.8        If women were required to register for and be subject to conscription under the Military Selective Service Act (MSSA) on a different basis than men, the government would have the burden of showing why it is treating the sexes differently. The courts would review the differential treatment under equal protection grounds and apply an intermediate level of scrutiny review that includes deference to the military.

        For example, if single mothers are exempted from registration under MSSA yet single fathers are required to register, the burden would be on the government to show why the differential treatment.

    a. Panel 4 Report; 23 October 1992, pp. 4, 25-27.
    b. Military Selective Service Act, 50 U.S.C. App. 453.

4.9        If the MSSA is amended to require registration and conscription of women on the same basis as men, gender specific exemptions or deferments would not be legally permissible.

        For example, requiring registration and conscription on the same basis would mean that gender neutral exemptions are mandated. Gender neutral exemptions include single parents instead of single mother/father.

    a. Panel 4 Report; 23 October 1992, pp. 13, 21.
    b. Military Selective Service Act, 50 U.S.C. App. 453.

4.10      If all combat positions are opened to women and the assignment policies are the same for men and women, there would not be a basis for an equal protection challenge.

For example, combat positions on ships are open to women and women are assigned involuntarily to those positions just like men are assigned.

    a.  Panel 4 Report; 23 October 1992, pp. 18, 23.
    b.  Rostker v. Goldberg, 453 U.S. 57, 70 (1981).

4.11       It may be legally permissible to assign women on a different basis than men if women and men are dissimilarly situated by a law or policy which excludes women from some combat positions that are open to men.

For example, a woman in today's Army can be trained as a communications specialist. The Army's policy would prohibit her assignment to an infantry battalion.

    a.  Panel 4 Report; 23 October 1992, p. 17.
    b.  Rostker v. Goldberg, 453 U.S. 57, 70 (1981).

4.12       A statute requiring females to register for and be subject to MSSA on a different basis than males if females are not assigned to combat positions on a same basis as men could be constitutional if the rationale for registration and assignment meets the judicial test of intermediate scrutiny with deference to the military.

For example, if women are excluded from ground combat positions by statute/policy, and registration and conscription is determined to be primarily for ground combat troops, women may either have different registration requirements and/or gender-specific exemptions.

    a.  Panel 4 Report; 23 October 1992, pp. 25-26.
    b.  Military Selective Service Act, 50 U.S.C. App. 453.

4.13       In an all volunteer force, if combat positions are opened to women and men are involuntarily assigned to those combat positions, then women should also be involuntarily assigned to those same positions. Different assignment policies would have a deleterious effect on morale, as women would have the privilege of volunteering for combat, but not the burden of being involuntarily assigned.

    a.  Panel 4 Report; 23 October 1992, p. 20.
    b.  Rostker v. Goldberg, 453 U.S. 57, 70 (1981).

4.14    If assignment procedures change in an all volunteer force to require women to be involuntarily assigned to combat positions, affected women who joined prior to the change should be given an opportunity to separate from the service or be given an exemption from reassignment effective until their contract period is expired.

    a.  Panel 4 Report; 23 October 1992, p. 18.

4.15    In response to a question from the Commission, the services did not report significant lessons learned about the utilization of women from either the Panama or Grenada conflicts.

The Marine Corps learned in Desert Shield (as the Army learned in Grenada) that women should not be pulled from deploying units based on only gender.

    a.  Panel 4 Report; 23 October 1992, pp. 53-54.
    b.  Bird, Julie.  "AF Women Filled Many Roles in Panama Mission." *Air Force Times,* 29 January 1990.
    c.  Miles, Donna.  "The Women of Just Cause." *Soldiers,* March 1990.
    d.  McClellan News.  "Grenada Mission Provides Female MPs Valuable Combat Experience." *50th WAC Anniversary Report,* 15 May 1992.
    e.  DASD(MM&PP).  Response to Questions 3 and 11 from 25-26 March 1992.
    f.  Wine-Banks, Jill.  Testimony before the Commission, 13 July 1992.
    g.  Steele, William M., BG, USA.  Testimony before the Commission, 7 August 1992.

4.16    There is no single DoD-wide policy definition on fraternization.  Each Service has its own policy and enforces it accordingly.

    a.  Panel 4 Report; 23 October 1992, p. 45-47.
    b.  Maurmann, Steve, Maj, USAF.  "DoD Definition of Fraternization." Testimony before the Commission, 5 May 1992.
    c.  U.S. Department of Defense Directive 1350.2.  "The Department of Defense Equal Opportunity Program." 23 December 1988.
    d.  U.S. Department of Defense Memorandum.  "DoD Definition of Sexual Harassment."  July 1988.
    e.  Martindale, Dr. Melanie.  "Sexual Harassment in the Military." *Defense Manpower Data Center,* September 1990.
    f.  DASD(MM&PP).  Response to Questions 3, 24, 27, and 124, 24 June - 12 September 1992.
    g.  "Attitudes Regarding the Assignment of Women in the Armed Forces:

The Military Perspective." The Roper Organization Inc., September 1992.

h. Beck, Blurton, Bushey, Carey, Hammond, Jacobs, Marlowe, Mattox, Moates and Roggerio. Testimony before the Commission, 25 March and 26 August 1992.

4.17     The four Services do not formally track recruiting costs by gender, but the Army estimates that the cost of recruiting a female is 50 percent higher than the cost for a male. The Air Force estimates there is no cost difference for recruiting women than for recruiting men.

a. Panel 4 Report; 23 October 1992, p. 33.
b. DASD(MM&PP). Response to Question 8, 13-15 July 1992.
c. Deegan, Gene A., MajGen, USMC. Testimony before the Commission, 15-16 June 1992.

4.18     If women were involuntarily assigned to combat positions, then recruitment of women would almost certainly be more difficult, except possibly for the Air Force.

a. Panel 4 Report; 23 October 1992, p. 31.
b. "Attitudes Regarding the Assignment of Women in the Armed Forces: The Public Perspective." The Roper Organization Inc., August 1992.
c. Moskos, Dr. Charles C. and Ms. Laura Miller. "1992 Survey on Gender in the Military [Army]." 28 August 1992.
d. Deegan, Mertz, McShane, Recruiting Panel. Testimony before the Commission, 5 May - 15 July 1992.

4.19     Many non-traditional fields have been opened to women, yet most military women still gravitate toward traditional positions such as health care and administration.

a. Panel 4 Report; 23 October 1992, p. 40.
b. "Attitudes Regarding the Assignment of Women in the Armed Forces: The Military Perspective." The Roper Organization Inc., September 1992.
c. U.S. GAO. "Women in the Military: Serving Her Country." January 1990.
d. Wolffe, Jim. "Men, Women Enlist for Similar Reasons, Study Finds." *Air Force Times,* 19 March 1990.
e. DASD(MM&PP). Response to Question 29, 10-12 September 1992.
f. Lien, Maurice L., Lt Col, USAF (Ret.). "Women and the All-Volunteer Force." *The Retired Officer,* October 1992.

g. Navy: Response to Question 21, 25-26 March 1992.

h. Sellman, Dr. Wayne S. and CAPT Martha L. Whitehead, USN. Testimony before the Commission, 6 April and 25 June 1992.

4.20    The Services screen men and women completing an enlistment to determine how many are eligible to reenlist. Generally, individuals must meet professional growth standards, meet medical and physical standards, and meet standards relating to criminal convictions and incarceration. With the exception of the Army, men had higher eligibility rates than women after the first term enlistment.

a. Panel 4 Report; 23 October 1992, p. 35.

b. U.S. GAO. "Women in the Military: Serving Her Country." January 1990.

c. U.S. GAO. "Women in the Military: Attrition and Retention." July 1990.

d. DASD(MM&PP). Response to Questions 7 and 31, 25-26 March and 13 - 15 July 1992.

4.21    With the exception of the Army, retention rates, which are based on how many eligible persons reenlist, are generally lower for females than males.

a. Panel 4 Report; 23 October 1992, p. 35.

b. U.S. GAO. "Women in the Military: Attrition and Retention." July 1990.

c. Navy Women's Study Group. "Update Report on the Progress of Women in the Navy." 1990.

d. Carey, Dr. Sandra, MajGen Gene A. Deegan, USMC and Paul E. Jones. Testimony before the Commission, 26 March and 15-16 June 1992.

e. Army: Response to Question 7, 25-26 March 1992.

4.22    If all the combat exclusions are eliminated, there will be a negative impact on retention for some of the services.

a. Panel 4 Report; 23 October 1992, p. 32-33.

b. "Attitudes Regarding the Assignment of Women in the Armed Forces: The Military Perspective." The Roper Organization Inc., September 1992.

c. Moskos, Dr. Charles and Ms. Laura Miller. "1992 Survey on Gender in the Military [Army]." 28 August 1992.

d. Recruiting Panel. Testimony before the Commission, 16 July 1992.

4.23    As a fully integrated force, Coast Guard retention for enlisted and officer female personnel for the past five years has been comparable with male counterparts.

    a.  Panel 4 Report; 23 October 1992, p. 35.
    b.  USCG:  Response to Question 3, 15 September 1992.
    c.  Carey, Dr. Sandra.  Testimony before the Commission, 26 March 1992.

4.24        Women's rates for promotion are similar to men's.

    a.  Panel 4 Report; 23 October 1992, p. 41.
    b.  "Attitudes Regarding the Assignment of Women in the Armed Forces: The Military Perspective."  The Roper Organization Inc., September 1992.
    c.  Moskos, Dr. Charles and Ms. Laura Miller.  "1992 Survey on Gender in the Military [Army]."  28 August 1992.
    d.  U.S. GAO.  "Women in the Military: Career Progression Not a Current Problem but Concerns Remain."  September 1989.
    e.  "Years in Service at Promotion."  Times Supplement, *Air Force Times,* 7 September 1992.
    f.  DASD(MM&PP).  Response to Questions 3 and 129, 26 March and 12 September 1992.

4.25        Requiring women to register and be subject to conscription under MSSA on the same basis as males, if females were provided the same opportunity for assignment to any position, would be constitutional because men and women are being treated equally.

    a.  Panel 4 Report; 23 October 1992, p. 18.
    b.  Military Selective Service Act, 50 U.S.C. App. 453.

4.27        Repeal of combat exemptions may have an effect on the willingness of family members to support a young woman's decision to join the military.

    a.  "Attitudes Regarding the Assignment of Women in the Armed Forces: The Public Perspective."  The Roper Organization, August 1992.
    b.  "Attitudes Regarding the Assignment of Women in the Armed Forces: The Military Perspective."  The Roper Organization Inc., September 1992.

4. 28       All but the Air Force has explicit or implicit goals for the recruitment of women or the assignment of women to non-traditional roles.

a. DASD(MM&PP).  Response to Questions 12 and 21, 23, 13-15 July 1992.
b. Hammond, Judith D., CDR, USCG.  Testimony before the Commission, 26 March 1992.

4.29    Majorities of all military subgroups say that the assignment of women to combat would not have much of an effect on their likelihood of reenlisting or remaining.  For the Marine Corps, 39 percent said it would decrease their likelihood of reenlistment; for the Army this figure is 25 percent; the Navy is 16 percent; the Air Force is 9 percent.

A similar study by Dr. Moskos and Ms. Miller indicates that 34 percent of men are likely to leave the Army and 52 percent of women are likely to leave the Army if women are compelled to serve in the combat arms.

a. "Attitudes Regarding the Assignment of Women in the Armed Forces: The Military Perspective."  The Roper Organization Inc., September 1992.
b. Moskos, Dr. Charles and Ms. Laura Miller.  "1992 Survey on Gender in the Military [Army]." 28 August 1992.

4.30    While the topic was not specified in the statute, the Commission heard opinions that incidents of sexual harassment in military units will be reduced or eliminated if combat exclusion policies in the services are repealed.  The Commission has not found evidence one way or the other that sexual harassment will diminish if combat exclusion/exemption laws and policies are repealed and rescinded.

a. Department of Transportation.  "Women in the Coast Guard Study." 10 July 1990.
b. Navy Women's Study Group.  "Update Report on the Progress of Women in the Navy." 1990.
c. Rogers, Robin.  "A Proposal for Combatting Sexual Discrimination in the Military." California Law Review, Fall 1990.

## COMMISSIONER SUBMITTED FINDINGS APPROVED BY THE COMMISSION

1.       In comparison with previous years, the Army reported significant increases in the numbers of voluntary and involuntary discharges during FY 90-91 for reasons of parenthood or pregnancy.

2.       During the time periods of August 1989 and August 1990 to August 1991, voluntary and involuntary discharge figures for the "convenience of the government" (including such categories as hardship/dependency, pregnancy/childbirth, and parenthood) were roughly twice as high among women as among men.

   a.  OSD: Response to question 171, 23 October 1992.

3.       In 1989, Canada's Human Rights Tribunal, acting on several complaints of discrimination, ordered that tests to evaluate combat units in which women would serve with men be stopped, and that women be integrated into all areas of the forces except submarines.

   a.  The Ottawa Citizen, 25 April 1990, p. A3.
   b.  Presidential Commission Canadian Trip Report, 29-30 July 1992.

4.       The Department of Defense has no long-term plans which would have the effect of reducing the numbers of young children who are at risk of being separated for long periods of time from their deployable parents, or orphaned if a single parent or both parents are killed during a future war.

5.       In Fiscal Year 1990, 1145 pregnant women on ships needed to be reassigned, at an average of 95 a month.

   a.  Thomas, Pat. Testimony before the Commission, 1 October 1992, p. 314.

6.       ENLISTED SOLDIER DISCHARGES

| | FY89 | FY90 | FY91 |
|---|---|---|---|
| Chapter 5 Parenthood (Involuntary Separation) | | | |
| Male | 33 | 42 | 152 |
| Female | 87 | 85 | 610 |
| Total | 120 | 127 | 762 |

Chapter 6 Parenthood
(Voluntary Separation)

| | | | |
|---|---|---|---|
| Male | 272 | 338 | 281 |
| Female | 609 | 765 | 982 |
| Total | 881 | 1,103 | 1,263 |
| | | | |
| Chapter 8 Pregnancy | 2,136 | 2,351 | 2,651 |

a. Panel 3 Report; 23 October 1992, pp. 60-61.
b. DCSPER 598 Report. Mr. John Slone, DAPE-MPE, Report pages 60-61.

7.  A Navy study published in 1992 found that less than 50 percent of single and dual service parents had a valid Dependent Care Plan, and in a spot check throughout the Navy, less than 25 percent of Navy personnel were in compliance with Dependent Care Certificate requirements.

   a. Panel 3 Report; 23 October 1992, p. 47
   b. Thomas, Pat. "The Impact on Navy Systems," February 1992.

8.  During the first fifteen months of the Coast Guard's Care for Newborn Children Policy (CNC) nineteen enlisted women and four women officers had their applications approved. In addition eight enlisted men had their CNC requests approved.

   a. Panel 3 Report; 23 October 1992, p. 52.
   b. Commandant Instruction 1040.5, 12 June 1991.

9.  Some civilian and military experts stress that though children have a high rate of resilience in dealing with deployability of their parent(s). Too often the children's vulnerability is not addressed.

   a. Testimony before the Commission, 9 June 1992.

10. Public concern about parents going to war during Desert Shield and Desert Storm led to the introduction of several bills in Congress. These bills, known as the 'Gulf Orphan' bills, would have exempted some parents from deployment under certain circumstances.

11. The Department of Defense advises and requires applicants, who at the time of enlistment have a child(ren) in the custody of another person, to certify their intent not to enter into the Army with the express intention of regaining custody after enlistment. If an applicant regains custody during his/her term of enlistment the applicant will be advised that he/she are in violation of the stated intent of their enlistment contract. Unless the individual can show cause for recustody, they will be processed for separation (involuntary) for fraudulent enlistment.

   a. OSD: Response to Question 145, 12 September 1992.

12. It is important that any changes to the current family policy and childcare system be implemented before the next conflict calling for the prolonged deployment of a substantial number of single/dual parents.

13. Expert's stated that the recent Persian Gulf conflict took a special toll on children for several reasons. First, the conflict included a higher percentage of American military personnel with dependent children being deployed in this century. Second, the Persian Gulf conflict was the first major conflict in which mothers were deployed in such great numbers. Third the remaining parent of those children who had a parent deployed was more likely to be employed, and therefore presumably less accessible to the child(ren) then in previous conflicts.

   a. Panel 3 Report; 23 October 1992, pp. 49-50.
   b. Mattox, William. Testimony before the Commission, 9 June 1992.

14. A majority of the people that indicated support for women in combat positions such as fighter aircraft and aircraft carriers thought that women were already assigned to these positions.

   a. "Attitudes Regarding the Assignment of Women in the Armed Forces: The Public Perspective." The Roper Organization Inc., September 1992.

15.   ENLISTED SEPARATIONS FOR CONVENIENCE OF GOVERNMENT

|  | % Discharged-- 89/08 to 90/08 | | |
| --- | --- | --- | --- |
|  | Total Sex | Female | Male |
| Convenience of Government | 26.75 | 42.75 | 24.63 |
| -Early Release/Demobilization | 12.92 | 11.07 | 13.16 |
| -Entry into Officer Programs | 1.87 | 1.38 | 1.93 |
| -Hardship/Dependency | 1.44 | 2.82 | 1.26 |
| -Pregnancy or Childbirth | 1.61 | 13.72 | 0.01 |
| -Parenthood | 0.45 | 2.60 | 0.17 |
| -Other Reasons | 8.45 | 11.16 | 8.09 |

|  | % Discharged--90/08 to 91/08 | | |
| --- | --- | --- | --- |
|  | Total Sex | Female | Male |
| Convenience of Government | 23.16 | 46.04 | 19.84 |
| -Early Release/Demobilization | 7.33 | 5.08 | 7.65 |
| -Entry into Officer Programs | 1.88 | 1.43 | 1.95 |
| -Hardship/Dependency | 1.79 | 3.56 | 1.53 |
| -Pregnancy or Childbirth | 2.14 | 16.76 | 0.02 |
| -Parenthood | 1.01 | 6.17 | 0.26 |
| -Other Reasons | 9.01 | 13.03 | 8.43 |

a. OSD: Response to Question 171, 23 October 1992.

16.   In a report released on August 31, 1992, the General Accounting Office (GAO) found that a number of active and reserve personnel were unable to deploy for Operations Desert Shield and Storm. The causes of nondeployability ranged from incomplete training to varying medical conditions or personal problems. GAO reported that "The Department of Defense said nondeployables were not considered a serious problem because the Services were able to replace them with other personnel. Nevertheless, available data indicates the number of nondeployables was sizeable."

a. Panel 3 Report, 23 October 1992, p. 61.
b. "Operation Desert Storm, War Highlights Need to Address Problem of Nondeployable Personnel," GAO/NSIAD-92-208, 31 August 1992.

17.   GAO also found that:
o   Data was not available to develop a reliable, composite picture on nondeployables, and that the pre-screening of reservists to avoid calling up those who could not deploy helped to minimize and mask the potential for nondeployability problems. (p.34)

o   "Soldiers that fail to update, in detail, their family care plans and family support programs experienced enormous difficulties during deployment, which added stress, morale problems, and affected readiness." (p. 20)

o   In some (Army) units 18 to 20 percent of their female soldiers were nondeployable. The primary reasons for nondeployability among female soldiers were disqualifying physical profile and pregnancy. (p. 20)

a.  Panel 3 Report; 23 October 1992, pp. 61-62.
b.  "Operation Desert Storm, War Highlights Need to Address Problem of Nondeployable Personnel," GAO/NSIAD-92-208, 31 August 1992.

18.   The Prisoner of War captivity experience encompasses sickness, torture, death as well as mental depression and a sense of hopelessness. During the Vietnam Era, American servicemen were captured and held from less than one year to over eight years. During the Gulf War, American servicemen and servicewomen were held for much shorter periods, up to one and one half month; the war was measured in days versus years.

a.  Donnelly, Elaine. Personal Statement. 2 November 1992.

19.   The testimony of two aviators suggests that in certain areas of pilot training, female trainees have, in effect, not been allowed to fail. Figures from the Chief of Naval Aviation and Training and other aviation commands indicate higher attrition rates for women at most levels of training, but virtually no attrition compared to men in some categories of Naval aviation training.

## SUMMARY

DoD: Pilot
FY 87-92 TOTAL

| | | |
|---|---|---|
| Total Acceded Flight Training | 28,596 | 100.00% |
| Male | 27,636 | 96.64% |
| Female | 960 | 3.36% |
| | | |
| Total Completed Flight Training | 24,632 | 86.14% |
| Male | 23,898 | 86.47% |
| Female | 734 | 76.46% |

| Total Attritted Flight Training | 4,695 | 16.01% |
| Male | 4,530 | 15.93% |
| Female | 165 | 18.35% |

(SEE TABLE ATTACHED)

20. All male Marines, including clerk typists, are trained to meet combat infantry requirements.

21. According to 1976 GAO findings, enlisted women are in some cases being mal-assigned to MOSs beyond their physical ability; testimony suggests that this practice is still allowed because physical standards have not been established. It costs about $16,000 for a track vehicle mechanic to be reassigned to another MOS.

22. Although the Army made a concerted effort in the early 1980's to design a physical testing system which would match individual physical capacities to the demands of each MOS (MEPSCAT), the system was never used as intended. It was first used only as a recruiting guidance tool, and then was eliminated all together for reasons alleged to have been based on political reasons. The MEPSCAT system failed because of disagreement about whether standards should reflect peacetime or wartime requirements.

23. The Martin Baker seat designed for use in the JPATS, the new training aircraft for the Air Force and the Navy, will accommodate approximately the 5th percentile female to the 95th percentile male.

   a. Panel 2 Report; 20 October, 1992, pp. 103, 113.
   b. "JPATS Martin-Baker Ejection Seat Based on Design for EFA, Rafale."
      *Aviation Week and Space Technology*, August 3, 1992.
   c. Gaffney, Timothy R. "New Trainer Plane Put on Hold." *Dayton Daily News*, August 16, 1992.

24. The minimum absolute (nude) weight that can safely eject from a F-15 and F-16 is 103 lbs., 101 lbs. for the T-37, 140 lbs. for the T-38, and 133 lbs. for the F-4 and B-52. This is not an entrance criteria. All individuals below the minimum design weight must utilize additional weight with either their flight gear, or a 25 lbs. seat kit which is placed in the life support equipment. Seat design specifications for the T-38 are for 140 lbs., however, published test results indicate a margin of safety of at least 20 lbs.

   a. Panel 2 Report; 20 October, 1992, p. 102.

    b. U.S. Department of the Air Force (AFMC). Quick Look Egress Matrix. August 14, 1992.

    c. Report of the Study Group on USAF Female Aircrew Requirements for Life Support Equipment and Protective Clothing. Aeronautical Systems Division, U.S. Air Force Systems Command. October, 1977. ASD-TR-77-32.

    d. Calkins, R.B. ACES II Ejection Seat Small Occupant Study. Douglas Aircraft Company, McDonnell Douglas Corporation. October 30, 1992.

25.    Some USCG vessels did not experience any alterations to accommodate a mixed-gender crew. Some vessels underwent dockside availability and rearranged spaces to accommodate for women, this was done at little or no cost.

    a. Panel 2 Report; 20 October, p. 120.

    b. USCG. U.S. Coast Guard Response to Question 6 on 15 September 1992.

    c. USCG. U.S. Coast Guard Headquarters Workforce Diversity Staff Response to Questions 1 and 2 from 1 October Commission Hearing.

# APPENDIX D

## SURVEY RESEARCH

## 1: THE ROPER ORGANIZATION POLL SUMMARIES

### *The Roper Organization Survey of the American Public*

*Introduction*

Using a survey questionnaire of 35 questions developed in coordination with the Presidential Commission, The Roper Organization conducted a random telephone survey of 1,500 adults representative of the American public. Participants were questioned in a 20-minute telephone interview about their attitudes toward the assignment of women in the U.S. military, including the assignment of women to direct combat specialties, which are currently restricted by law or military policy.

*Methodology Limitations*

Telephone surveying has the advantage of reaching a representative random sample of the public at large in a short amount of time. Generally, however, telephone surveys are viewed as a weaker research tool compared to other scientific methods of empirical data collection. Limitations to achieving "sample randomness" through telephone surveys may include the following:

- homes selected for the sample do not have telephones;
- time and date of call determine availability of respondents;
- selected respondents may or may not agree to participate in a lengthy phone interview;
- interviewers' responses to questions may not be consistent, possibly affecting respondents' answers;
- opportunity for respondents to request clarification of questions during interview makes them more apt to answer questions that would receive a "don't know" response in other methods.

*Results*

A) When respondents were presented with three options concerning women in direct combat specialties (one that included the assignment of women to combat, only if they volunteer), about half favored a volunteer-only option for assignment to combat aircraft (53 percent), combat ships (51 percent) and direct ground combat positions (45 percent).

B) Respondents were statistically split (47 percent opposed and 44 percent in favor) when asked whether they support or oppose the current policies restricting women from direct combat assignments.

C) In the event of a draft for a national emergency or threat of war (and assuming an ample pool of young men exists), 52 percent indicated women should be drafted, about 39 percent indicated women should not be drafted, and 10 percent responded they did not know.

D) When asked about current restrictions on the assignment of women to combat positions, civilian respondents demonstrated a significant degree of misunderstanding of the facts. For example, 23 percent thought women were already serving in the infantry, while 26 percent did not know. Forty-five percent thought women were already serving on combat ships, while 27 percent did not know.

E) The poll indicated that the public favored making certain distinctions between assignments for men and women. For example, the survey participants were clearly more likely to advise a young man to join the military than a young woman. In addition, pregnancy and other medical factors unique to women that lead to lost time, were viewed as a significant detraction from combat readiness (43 percent indicated a negative effect on national security, 34 percent neither a positive nor negative effect, 13 percent a positive effect, and 10 percent did not know). Lastly, the participants indicated favoring certain assignment distinctions between men and women in light of their family responsibilities. Of the respondents, 65 percent said married women with children should not be assigned to combat (43 percent say married men with children should not be); 69 percent said single mothers should not be assigned to combat (48 percent said single fathers should not be); 55 percent said that in a dual military service couple with young children, the mother should be exempt from combat (two percent said that the father should be exempt).

### Summary

The public attitude poll produced a mixture of results. When asked if women should fill direct combat roles, the public preferred the "only if they volunteer" option. This is consistent with the tendency polling experts say the American public has to favor "choice" options in surveys. The participants were split as to whether or not they supported current policies restricting women from combat assignments. Furthermore, opinions on women in direct combat differed depending on the type of combat assignment presented. The public poll showed a clear distinction between assignments of men and women to combat positions depending on family responsibilities. Overall, the participants were strongly opposed to assigning mothers to combat.

## The Roper Organization Survey of the U.S. Military

### Introduction

Using a confidential, mailed questionnaire of 45 questions developed in conjunction with the Commission, The Roper Organization surveyed 8,000 military personnel representing a random sample of the four Services, the Reserve, and the National Guard. The subject of the survey was the assignment of women in the military, in particular the assignment of women to combat specialties in the air, on sea, and on the ground.

### Methodology Limitations

The written survey was self-administered and deliberately constructed to ensure strict confidentiality. The overall sample of 8,000 military personnel was conducted randomly to include all Service, Reserve and Guard personnel. However, oversamples in selected combat specialties (fighter pilots and ground combat), combined with the lack of oversample of women, resulted in a low number of women surveyed. This low subsample for women did not permit a statistical elaboration of that group with an acceptable level of confidence.

*Descriptive Statistics*

Of the 8,000 military surveys mailed, the return rate was 62 percent; nine percent of the surveys were undeliverable. The method was to oversample the officer grades, senior enlisted fighter/bomber pilots (Air Force, Navy and Marine Corps), and ground combat military specialties (Army and Marine Corps). The data was weighted to ensure that all subgroups surveyed were in proportion to the military universe.

*Results*

A) <u>Current Laws and Policies</u>. Overall, 57 percent of those surveyed favored current laws and policies restricting women from combat; 72 percent of combat specialty respondents favored present restrictions.

B) <u>National Security</u>. Forty-one percent of all military personnel surveyed, active and reserve, indicated that the assignment of women to combat positions would have a negative impact on the military's ability to defend the nation and win a war (62 percent of the Marine Corps, 53 percent of the Army, 36 percent of the Air Force and 32 percent of the Navy); while 38 percent of military personnel indicated neither a positive nor negative impact, and 19 percent indicated assignment of women to combat would have a positive impact.

C) <u>Volunteer Option</u>. When given three choices (one that included the assignment of women to combat "<u>only if they volunteer</u>"), 43 percent said women should be able to volunteer for combat aircraft, 39 percent said women should be able to volunteer for combat ships, and 30 percent said women should be able to volunteer for ground combat. For the other two options, 25 percent indicated women <u>should be required</u> to take assignments for combat aircraft, 30 percent for combat ships, and 19 percent for ground combat. Finally, 30 percent of those surveyed indicated women <u>should not be assigned</u> to combat aircraft, 29 percent said not to combat ships, and 49 percent said not to ground combat.

D) <u>Retention and Recruitment</u>. Seventeen percent of the active duty personnel surveyed (with 39 percent of the Marine Corps, 25 percent of the Army, 16 percent of the Navy and 9 percent of the Air Force) indicated that allowing women in combat would decrease the likelihood of their remaining in the military. Also, 35 percent of the respondents indicated that altering policy would decrease the likelihood of their encouraging a daughter to join the military; 12 percent said it would increase the likelihood. Under the current policy, 78 percent of the respondents would advise a young man to join the military, while 49 percent would advise a young woman to join.

E) <u>Changing Current Policy</u>. Forty-one percent indicated that changing current policy would have an adverse effect on unit cohesion; 54 percent of the active duty personnel predicted an increase in fraternization between officers and enlisted personnel, and 74 percent indicated adverse impacts of lost time due to pregnancy and other health issues related to women.

F) <u>Family Matters</u>. The military respondents indicated favoring clear distinctions between the assignment of men and women depending on family matters. Seventy-two percent indicated a single mother should not be assigned to combat while 48 percent said a single father should not. For dual service couples with young children, 65 percent said the mother should be exempt from combat, while one percent said the father should be; 27 percent said neither should be exempt.

G) Gulf War Performance Ratings. Over 44 percent of the respondents, active and reserve, had served in or near a combat zone, and 62 percent of this group had served in Desert Shield/Storm. Ninety-eight percent of Gulf War respondents rated the performance of men in their unit as "excellent/good," and 96 percent rated their unit as a whole as "excellent/good." However, 61 percent of the same Gulf War respondents (with 44 percent Marine Corps, 48 percent Army, 63 percent Navy and 83 percent Air Force) rated the performance of women in their unit as "excellent/good" (enlisted personnel rated the performance of women lower than the officers did).

H) Gulf War Mixed-Gender Units. Fifty-six percent of those in mixed-gender units in the Gulf War indicated they knew of women in their unit who got pregnant just prior to, or while in, the Persian Gulf. Forty-six percent of this group said that pregnancy within their units had "some" or "very much" negative impact on unit readiness, and 59 percent said such pregnancies had "some" or "very much" negative impact on unit morale. Sixty-four percent of those in mixed-gender units in the Gulf War indicated there were sexual incidents between men and women within their unit, with 55 percent of this group indicating that this sexual activity had a negative impact on unit morale. Sixty-one percent of the Gulf War respondents from mixed-gender units indicated there were sexual incidents between men and women in their unit and members of other units; 36 percent of this group indicated this sexual activity had a negative impact on unit morale, while 61 percent of the group indicated that the activity had "not that much" or "no" effect.

*Summary*

The responses from the different services were significant. The Marine Corps as a group had the most homogenous response rate and the strongest opposition to changing current policy (78 percent favored current policy). The Army, Air Force and Navy were also supportive of the current policy, but to different degrees. However, a plurality of Navy personnel (50 percent) stated that women should be required to serve on combat ships, and another 23 percent of the Navy felt that women should be able to volunteer for combat ships. In addition, those respondents in specific combat specialties (fighter/bomber pilots and ground combat MOSs) were the most homogeneous subgroup and were consistently opposed to allowing women into any combat specialty.

# APPENDIX D

## SURVEY RESEARCH

## 2: ADDITIONAL SURVEYS AND STUDIES

### *1992 Survey on Gender in the Military*

A 1992 survey concerning gender differences among Army personnel was conducted by Ms. Laura Miller and Dr. Charles Moskos, Professor of Sociology at Northwestern University. A total of 1,651 soldiers in the Army were surveyed, of which 868 were women and 783 were men. The survey instrument consisted of a confidential questionnaire which was administered by the authors at several U.S. Army bases around the country. In addition, the authors conducted informal discussion groups and personal interviews among approximately ten percent of those surveyed. Fifty-one percent of the women surveyed served in Desert Shield/Storm and three percent served in Operation Just Cause (Panama).

The demographics of those surveyed were similar to the overall population of the U.S. Army in terms of race as well as military rank. Sixty-eight percent of the women surveyed were between the grades of E1 and E5. Fifteen percent of the women surveyed were between the grades of E6 and E9, while only 17 percent were women officers. Forty-nine percent of the women surveyed were black, 39 percent were white, and 12 percent were of other races.

One of the significant findings of the survey was that only 12 percent of Army enlisted women, 10 percent of Army women non-commissioned officers, and 14 percent of Army women officers surveyed stated they would volunteer for the combat arms if it were possible. Seventy percent, 79 percent and 71 percent, respectively, stated they would not volunteer, and 18 percent, 11 percent and 15 percent, respectively, said they were not sure if they would volunteer.

Another significant finding was that 18 percent of women Army officers, 20 percent of women Army non-commissioned officers, and 21 percent of Army enlisted women surveyed stated that they were satisfied with the current Army regulations which exclude women from direct combat roles. However, 70 percent of the women officers, 77 percent of the women non-commissioned officers, and 75 percent of enlisted females stated that women should be allowed to volunteer for combat roles. Eleven percent, two percent and four percent, respectively, stated that women should be treated exactly like men and serve in the combat arms just like men.

The survey is estimated to be one of the largest ever conducted concerning women in the Army which took place at the soldiers' place of duty. There have been larger surveys conducted through mail questionnaires, but because of the virtually 100 percent return rate and on site group interviews, this survey provides a valuable perspective of U.S. Army attitudes regarding the role of women in combat.

D-5

# NAVY PERSONNEL RESEARCH AND DEVELOPMENT CENTER

Starting in 1988, the Navy Personnel Research and Development Center (NPRDC) conducted a multi-year study on the issue of lost time. The goal of the study, was to assess five areas: (1) rates of pregnancy and single parenthood; (2) lost time rate due solely to pregnancy; (3) lost time of women as compared to men; (4) impact of pregnancy and single parents on personnel systems; (5) and impact of pregnancy and single parents on mission accomplishment.

To study the first area, NPRDC surveyed representative samples of Navy women and men during the summers of 1988, 1990, and 1992. The second area of the NPRDC project was analyzed through an interviewing process conducted at prenatal clinics and in the workplaces by asking supervisors how much time they thought assigned pregnant women lost in the San Diego and Norfolk areas. To compare lost time of women and men, NPRDC reviewed Bureau of Naval Medicine (BUMED) and Joint Uniform Military Pay System (JUMPS) data tapes, as well as specified work diaries. The fourth area of the NPRDC survey was researched by reviewing policies, data tapes, Bureau of Naval Personnel (BUPERS) records, and detailed surveys of all enlisted personnel for both the fiscal and calendar years of 1990. The fifth area was studied through interviews, and a thorough review of work diaries and data tapes. The survey sample included officers and Command master chiefs at 50 commands, E-1s to E-6s at 50 commands, and other specified enlisted personnel.

The average time lost due to pregnancy as reported by the pregnant women was 7.4 hours per month. The estimated time more than doubled from second to third trimester, from 5.6 hours/month to 12.4 hours/month, due to the need for more frequent routine medical appointments required of women in their third trimester of pregnancy.

The numbers reported by women's supervisors were similar to those reported by the pregnant women themselves. The average lost time per month reported by the supervisors was 7.9 hours. Only pregnant women were included in the survey, and thus figures for hospitalization for labor and delivery and convalescent leave time of those recovering from childbirth are not included.

The Navy compared the lost time of women and men and found that when hospitalization due to pregnancy and convalescent leave after childbirth were excluded, men had more recorded lost time than women. Lost time comparisons of a 1985 cohort with matched samples for the first enlistment period indicated that women lost less than two days per year (excluding pregnancy-related hospital time and convalescent leave due to childbirth) and men lost an average of three days per year. When time lost for pregnancy, childbirth, and convalescent leave for childbirth are factored in, using the current annualized pregnancy rate of 13 percent, Commission researchers calculated that the women lost 12 days per year. In addition, the NPRDC study reported pregnancy accounted for 3.5 percent of all enlisted separations.

In a presentation to the Presidential Commission, NPRDC reported that Navy pregnancy rates are comparable to those in the civilian sector. They found little evidence that the presence of single parents impacts on the mission; however, pregnant women were perceived as impacting the workload of co-workers and thereby reducing readiness on ships.

### 1992 Commission Survey of Retired Flag and General Officers

The Presidential Commission sent 6,109 survey letters to all known retired flag and general officers of the four services, soliciting their views on the assignment of women in the Armed Forces, specifically the assignment of women to direct combat and direct combat specialties. The officers were asked to return an enclosed response card and were given the option to submit a narrative letter with the response card as well. A total of 3,224 officers responded, and 947 also submitted a narrative letter with their response card. Response percentages varied by service. The Marine Corps had the highest return rate, with 70 percent of the retired generals returning a response card and/or letter. The response rates of the other services were: Army, 57 percent; Navy, 41 percent; Air Force, 56 percent.

Systematic methodology was used to analyze the flag and general officer response cards, as indicated in the following charts. Consistent with data collection and research methodology, only verified data points were analyzed. To ensure objectivity, no research interpretation of data collection was developed.

A consistent majority of retired flag and general officers opposed the assignment of women to combat and combat specialties. However, the degree of opposition to altering policy was not consistently proportional for the eight combat specialties listed. For example, 90 percent of the respondents said they opposed the assignment of women to the infantry, while 76 percent were opposed to the assignment to combat vessels and 71 percent were opposed to the assignment of women to fighter/bomber aircraft.

It should be noted that this survey was not a random sample. To the contrary, in this research, "all" known retired flag and general officers were surveyed. This means the entire universe of this particular military population was included. However, it should also be noted that the survey group, with few exceptions, consisted of men. Date of retirement for these officers ranged from a group of 132, who retired prior to 1960, to a group of 213 officers who retired between 1990 and 1992.

Within this flag officer and general officer military community, there was consistent opposition to assigning women to direct combat. The primary reason cited by 56 percent of the officers who responded was a belief that there would be negative impact on unit cohesion. The degree of opposition to women in combat varied in degree between the combat specialties: ground combat drew the strongest opposition, while combat aircraft (fighter/bomber) received the least degree of opposition. The officers most recently retired (1990-1992) indicated a lower degree of opposition to the assignment of women to certain combat specialties than earlier retirement year groups.

## RETIRED FLAG OFFICER SURVEY
## COMBAT ASSIGNMENT RESPONSE RATES BY SERVICE *

| | Return Rate | Fighter/Bomber | | Attack Helicopter | | Combat Ships | | Combat Engineers | | Artillery | | Armor | | Infantry | | Special Operations | |
|---|---|---|---|---|---|---|---|---|---|---|---|---|---|---|---|---|---|
| | | YES | NO | YES | NO | YES | NO | YES | NO | YES | NO | YES | NO | YES | NO | YES | NO |
| ARMY | 57% | 32% | 68% | 26% | 74% | 26% | 74% | 15% | 85% | 23% | 77% | 10% | 90% | 8% | 92% | 16% | 82% |
| (number) | | 423 | 888 | 350 | 1005 | 342 | 963 | 197 | 1157 | 308 | 1045 | 129 | 1216 | 105 | 1258 | 221 | 1123 |
| NAVY | 41% | 29% | 71% | 26% | 74% | 23% | 77% | 22% | 78% | 22% | 78% | 15% | 85% | 12% | 88% | 21% | 79% |
| (number) | | 223 | 513 | 179 | 510 | 167 | 569 | 146 | 527 | 142 | 518 | 100 | 556 | 79 | 580 | 141 | 526 |
| MARINES | 70% | 17% | 83% | 10% | 90% | 10% | 90% | 3% | 97% | 6% | 94% | 1% | 99% | 1% | 99% | 6% | 94% |
| (number) | | 39 | 192 | 23 | 208 | 22 | 206 | 7 | 225 | 15 | 217 | 3 | 228 | 2 | 232 | 13 | 220 |
| AIR FORCE | 56% | 28% | 72% | 25% | 75% | 27% | 73% | 22% | 78% | 26% | 74% | 18% | 82% | 14% | 86% | 19% | 81% |
| (number) | | 221 | 579 | 193 | 578 | 200 | 553 | 170 | 588 | 189 | 549 | 135 | 614 | 107 | 643 | 147 | 613 |
| TOTAL RATE: | 55% | 29% | 71% | 24% | 76% | 24% | 76% | 17% | 83% | 22% | 78% | 12% | 88% | 10% | 90% | 17% | 83% |
| (number) | | 906 | 2172 | 745 | 2301 | 731 | 2301 | 520 | 2497 | 654 | 2329 | 367 | 2614 | 293 | 2713 | 521 | 2482 |

\* Response rates indicate the proportion of actual flag officers responses.

HAS THE INCREASED UTILIZATION OF WOMEN IN THE MILITARY OVER THE PAST TWENTY YEARS BEEN SUCCESSFUL?

YES   63%      NO   24%      UNCERTAIN OR NO ANSWER   12%

# RETIRED FLAG OFFICER SURVEY
## COMBAT ASSIGNMENT RESPONSE RATE BY RETIREMENT YEAR GROUP

| | * Mean Number of Responses | Fighter/ Bomber | | Attack Helicopter | | Combat Ships | | Combat Engineers | | Artillery | | Armor | | Infantry | | Special Operations | |
|---|---|---|---|---|---|---|---|---|---|---|---|---|---|---|---|---|---|
| | | YES | NO | YES | NO | YES | NO | YES | NO | YES | NO | YES | NO | YES | NO | YES | NO |
| Pre-1960 | 132 | 24% | 76% | 21% | 79% | 14% | 86% | 16% | 84% | 17% | 83% | 9% | 91% | 8% | 92% | 31% | 69% |
| 1960-1964 | 115 | 26% | 74% | 20% | 80% | 22% | 78% | 18% | 82% | 20% | 80% | 10% | 90% | 11% | 89% | 30% | 70% |
| 1965-1969 | 260 | 23% | 77% | 17% | 83% | 16% | 84% | 10% | 90% | 16% | 84% | 7% | 93% | 8% | 92% | 17% | 83% |
| 1970-1974 | 580 | 25% | 75% | 21% | 79% | 18% | 82% | 11% | 89% | 15% | 85% | 9% | 91% | 7% | 93% | 13% | 87% |
| 1975-1979 | 560 | 28% | 72% | 24% | 76% | 24% | 76% | 15% | 85% | 21% | 79% | 11% | 89% | 8% | 92% | 13% | 87% |
| 1980-1984 | 570 | 30% | 70% | 24% | 76% | 25% | 75% | 16% | 84% | 21% | 79% | 11% | 89% | 8% | 92% | 13% | 87% |
| 1985-1989 | 642 | 31% | 69% | 29% | 71% | 30% | 70% | 21% | 79% | 27% | 73% | 15% | 85% | 13% | 87% | 19% | 81% |
| 1990-1992 | 213 | 44% | 56% | 39% | 61% | 42% | 58% | 30% | 70% | 37% | 63% | 24% | 76% | 17% | 83% | 23% | 77% |
| TOTAL RATE: | 3224 | 29% | 71% | 24% | 76% | 24% | 76% | 17% | 83% | 22% | 78% | 12% | 88% | 10% | 90% | 17% | 83% |

* Some officers did not indicate answers to all eight specialties. Percentages represent the proportion of YES/NO of those who answered.

SAMPLE

# PRESIDENTIAL COMMISSION ON THE ASSIGNMENT OF WOMEN IN THE ARMED FORCES

September 11, 1992

*Chairman*
Robert T. Herres

*Commissioners*
Mary E. Clarke
Samuel G. Cockerham
Elaine Donnelly
BGen Thomas V. Draude
CPT Mary M. Finch
Wm. Darryl Henderson
James R. Hogg
Newton N. Minow
Charles C. Moskos
Meredith A. Neizer
Kate Walsh O'Beirne
Ronald D. Ray
Maxwell R. Thurman
Sarah F. White

*Staff Director*
W. S. Orr

Dear

The Defense Authorization Act of December 5, 1991 mandated the creation of the Presidential Commission on the Assignment of Women in the Armed Forces. The Commission is tasked with assessing the laws and policies restricting the assignment of female service members. On November 15, 1992 the Commission will submit a final report to the President.

As part of our historical research effort, we are examining and evaluating the issues from a number of perspectives. In view of the historical deference given to the military and its leadership, we are interested in having the benefit of your experience. Additionally, we are seeking insights from all other retired flag rank officers, which we believe will be invaluable to our assessment of the proper role and assignment of women in our military.

To this end, we would like to have your input. We ask that you give us your views, including responding to the questions on the enclosed postage-paid card, as soon as possible so we can tabulate the data and include it in a summary matrix. Additionally, we would appreciate your taking the time to give us your perspective on the questions that follow:

*   Congress has repealed its exclusion for assignment of women to combat aircraft and is considering opening up combatant ships to women. Consideration is also being given to legislation that would require the Army to eliminate its exclusion policy for service by women in the combat arms (Infantry, Armor, Field Artillery and Combat Engineers). Do you favor the assignment of American servicewomen into any of these currently excluded fields? Why or why not?

*   Several witnesses have characterized the policy dispute as a conflict between "equal opportunity" and "national security." Other witnesses characterize the issue as under-utilization of women who are well qualified to

perform duties from which they are now excluded. Still others agree that women should be exempt from direct combat roles. Please describe your position on the issue.

*   Concern has been expressed regarding the capabilities of women to perform various military duties, particularly in combat roles. Strict criteria might be established to assure both men and women are fully qualified, physically and otherwise, for the duties to which they might be assigned. Assuming assignment quotas are not used and such criteria can be met, would any of your answers change?

*   Unit cohesion has been cited as a significant factor in combat effectiveness that might be influenced by the assignment of women to combat positions. What are your views on this question?

*   From the standpoint of national security or combat readiness, what do you see as the primary advantages and disadvantages regarding the broader utilization of women in the armed forces since 1973?

*   With the advent of the all volunteer force, what was your original view, of the then-proposed policy for increasing the number of women in the military, and has your opinion changed over time? (Utilization of women in 1973 was 2% and is currently about 12%) Why or why not?

*   The policy of deploying male and female single-parents and dual-service parents, and of not deploying pregnant servicewomen, stirred controversy during the Gulf War because of the perceived effect on unit readiness and the impact on the children involved. Given that contractual obligations must be fulfilled at a time of mobilization, do you feel that the family and military child care policies as stated above are "about right" at the present time, or should they be revised before the next war begins? Why or why not?

If you have any questions, please contact W. S. Orr, Staff Director. Your response by September 25, 1992 will be helpful to the Commission as we begin our deliberations in October to prepare and present our report to the President.

Sincerely,

Robert T. Herres
Chairman

SAMPLE

# Retired Flag/General Officers

**Service:**

Army        Navy        Marine        Air Force        Retirement Year _____

**Do you favor women being assigned to any or all of the following military specialties?**

| | | | | | |
|---|---|---|---|---|---|
| Artillery | Yes | No | Fighter/Bomber Pilots | Yes | No |
| Armor | Yes | No | Navy Combatant Vessels | Yes | No |
| Infantry | Yes | No | Combat Engineer | Yes | No |
| Attack Helicopters | Yes | No | Special Operations | Yes | No |

**Do you believe that the increased utilization of women in our armed forces over the past twenty years has been successful?**

Yes        No

_____
Signature

SSN: _____

## Additional Studies

The Commission received existing surveys and studies in its research and analysis. These studies are documented in each Commission Panel's Bibliography and include reports by the General Accounting Office (GAO), the Department of Defense (DoD), and the individual Services, as well as the U.S. Coast Guard and foreign militaries. A sample of these studies are summarized below:

*Women in the Military: More Military Jobs Can be Opened Under Current Statutes (GAO/NSAID-88-222, September 1988)*

Senators William Proxmire (D-WI), William Cohen (R-ME), and Dennis DeConcini (D-AZ) requested that GAO review how Service policies which restrict women from combat positions affect women in the military, and whether other Service exclusions that are not combat related limit opportunities for servicewomen. The GAO found that the Services limited the number of jobs that women may hold beyond the requirements of the combat exclusion law. It recommended the Services allow women to compete for all positions not presently closed by statute or program needs.

*Women in the Military: Career Progression Not a Problem But Concerns Remain (GAO/NSAID-89-21BR, September 1989)*

This GAO report was prepared in response to a request from Congresswoman Beverly Byron (D-MD). Her purpose was to determine whether impediments existed to career progression for women in the military. The study included interviews with 181 military personnel representing all Services, who stated that the opportunities for assignments, promotions and education were fair to women. The GAO assessed positions held by both men and women and found women were being promoted at rates similar to men. The study did not determine whether factors such as the combat exclusion laws impeded a woman's chances of being promoted. The women interviewed were split over the question of whether the combat exclusion laws should be repealed.

*Women in the Military: Attrition and Retention (GAO/NSAID-90-87BR, July 1990)*

This GAO report was prepared in response to a request from Congresswoman Beverly Byron (D-MD) who wanted a comparison of the attrition and retention rates for men and women in the Services. The GAO divided its study to include rates for both the officer and enlisted communities. Records were analyzed for each of the four Services for enlisted women. The GAO found that attrition rates were higher for women than men (4.5 percent higher for enlisted women and two percent higher for officers, respectively). Consistent losses for both sexes occurred during the first three months of basic training, and early exits were largely due to individuals pursuing higher education. The most significant differences in attrition and retention rates between men and women occurred in the middle of the enlistment period. The majority of men separated because of drug and alcohol problems, while most women separated at their own request due to pregnancy.

*Utilization of American Military Women in Operations Desert Shield and Desert Storm
(August 1990 - April 1991. U.S. Department of Defense)*

The purpose of this DoD report was to analyze the deployability statistics of military women in the Persian Gulf War and review the utilization issues associated with this deployment. The report reviewed "early returns from deployment," as well as pregnancy and casualty figures.

The report identified two difficulties in collecting the data. First, although the Service definitions of "non-deployable" were very similar, the individual unit commanders had latitude in determining who was classified as "non-deployable." This flexibility allowed those commanders who were tasked to deploy only a portion of their units to be selective in who was deployed. Secondly, personnel from units were frequently cross-assigned to other units. This "cross-leveling" made it virtually impossible to accurately collect information, especially after units returned to their home stations.

The report concluded, based on combining the figures from all four Services, that women were more non-deployable than men. The statistics showed that some two percent of men and nine percent of women considered for deployment were classified as non-deployable for medical reasons. In the Army, Navy and Marine Corps, in which pregnancy was specifically broken out within the medical category, pregnancy accounted for approximately half of the medically non-deployable women. The report also noted that pregnancy rates within the Services remained stable during the war.

*Opinion on Women in Combat
(U.S. Air Force Personnel Survey Branch, 1992)*

The U.S. Air Force Personnel Survey Branch performed a survey in 1992 focusing on how the assignment of women to combat roles would affect morale, cohesion, combat readiness and performance. Two surveys were actually conducted: one of servicemembers and the other of commanders who would be implementing policy changes if combat restrictions were removed. Results revealed a majority of combat aviators (61 percent) were opposed to women in air combat, while 27 percent supported the idea of women in combat aviation and 12 percent had no opinion. Of all servicemembers surveyed, a majority of respondents (56 percent) favored assigning women to air combat, 32 percent opposed such assignments, and 12 percent had no opinion.

*Recommendations Related to the Culture and Climate Assessment of the U.S. Coast Guard
Academy
(Gordon George, Paul Bierly, Laurie Davison, Nancy DiTmaso. Princeton Economic Research,
Princeton NJ, 1992)*

Princeton Economic Research was contracted by the U.S. Coast Guard to perform a survey of U.S. Coast Guard members, as well as cadets and staff of the U.S. Coast Guard Academy. The survey measured the encouragement of initiative, critical thinking, productivity, and appreciation of diversity and enculturation/morale. The survey was initiated because women cadets reported disconcerting information about their treatment at the Academy. The report concluded that women, in many respects, have been successfully integrated into the Coast Guard Academy. However, there was evidence that women experience gender discrimination in their day-to-day environment in the form of occasional incidents of sexual harassment, jokes and/or slurs. Women cadets also thought they lived and worked in an environment where they felt they constantly had to prove themselves.

# APPENDIX E

## FACT FINDING TRIPS

The Presidential Commission on the Assignment of Women in the Armed Forces conducted thirty-two fact finding trips from April through October 1992. The purpose of these trips was to provide Commissioners first-hand knowledge of the United States Armed Forces through visits to facilities and installations. In addition to insight gained from observation of training exercises, equipment and operations, the visits allowed Commissioners to hear a wide range of opinions from American and foreign military experts, government officials, and service members.

Commissioners selected trip locations which would provide data for their particular Panel's research areas. Information obtained from the trips was recorded by Commissioners and staff in comprehensive trip reports which were briefed to the full Commission. Copies of these reports are on file with the Commission's documents in the National Archives and Records Administration, Record Group 220.

----------------------------------------------------------------------------

| DATE (1992) | LOCATION | UNIT/COMMAND |
|---|---|---|
| April 21-22 | Annapolis, MD | U.S. Naval Academy |
| May 11 | Fort Carson, CO | 4th Infantry Division |
| May 15-17 | Fort Riley, KS | 1st Infantry Division |
| May 17-19 | Norfolk, VA | Norfolk Naval Station |
| May 28 | Seymour Johnson AFB, NC | 4th Composite Wing |
| May 29 | Camp Lejeune, NC | II Marine Expeditionary Force |
| June 10-11 | Fort Stewart, GA | 24th Mechanized Infantry Division |
| June 15 | Parris Island, SC | Marine Corps Recruit Depot |
| June 15-16 | Fort Bragg, SC | XVIII Airborne Corps |
| July 6-7 | Nellis AFB, NV | USAF Weapons and Tactics Center |
| July 7-8 | Twentynine Palms, CA | USMC Air-Ground Combat Center |
| July 8 | NAS Miramar, CA | USN Fighter Weapons School |

| DATE (1992) | LOCATION | UNIT/COMMAND |
|---|---|---|
| July 8-9 | Naval Station 32nd Street, CA | Naval Surface Fleet, Pacific |
| July 10 | Naval Amphibious Base, CA | Naval Special Warfare Command |
| July 12 | NAS Glenview, IL | Aircraft Static Display |
| July 20-22 | USS John F. Kennedy | CV-67 / Carrier Air Wing 3 |
| July 28-31 | Ottawa, Canada | Military Representatives |
| August 5 | Nellis AFB, NV | USAF Weapons and Tactics Center |
| August 9-11 | Fairchild AFB, WA | Survival, Evasion, Resistance and Escape School |
| August 10-11 | NSB Kings Bay, GA | Submarine Group Ten |
| August 11-12 | NTC Orlando, FL | Recruit Training Center, Orlando |
| August 17 | West Point, NY | U.S. Army Military Academy |
| August 26 | Fort Worth, TX | General Dynamics |
| September 13 | Naval Station, Norfolk, VA | Commander Submarine Fleet Atlantic |
| September 14-15 | San Antonio, TX | Aeromedical Seminar |
| September 14-16 | Harvard University, MA | Russian Flag Officers |
| September 16-18 | The Netherlands | Military and Civilian Representatives |
| September 19 | Denmark | Military Representatives |
| September 21 | The United Kingdom | Military Representatives |
| September 23-25 | Israel | Military and Civilian Representatives |
| October 6 | Quantico, VA | USMC Officer Candidate & Basic Schoo |
| October 7 | MacDill AFB, FL | HQ, US Central Command, and HQ, US Special Ops Command |

# APPENDIX F

## AGENDA OF MEETINGS AND LIST OF WITNESSES

### March 25, 1992 - Washington, DC

Swearing in of Commissioners
Mr. Kenneth W. Starr
      Solicitor General of the United States

Commission Administrative and Legal Brief
Mr. Robert J. Moore, Esq.
      General Counsel, Commission Staff
Mr. David Anderson
      Director of Administration and Operations, Commission Staff

Review of DoD Policies Concerning Women in the Armed Forces
Mr. Robert L. Gilliat
      Deputy General Counsel, Personnel and Health Policy, DoD Office of the General Counsel
LTG Thomas P. Carney, USA
      Deputy Chief of Staff for Personnel, USA
LtGen Matthew T. Cooper, USMC
      Deputy Chief of Staff for Manpower and Reserve Affairs, Headquarters USMC
VADM Ronald J. Zlatoper, USN
      Chief of Naval Personnel
Lt Gen William J. Boles, USAF
      Deputy Chief of Staff, Personnel, Headquarters USAF

### March 26, 1992 - Washington, DC

Survey of Research Studies
RADM George D. Passmore, USCG
      Chief, Office of Personnel and Training
Mr. Robert Gilliat
      Deputy General Counsel, Personnel and Health Policy, DoD Office of the General Counsel
COL Terry M. Hulin, USA
      Chief Soldier Policy Division, Human Resources Directorate, Office of the Deputy Chief of Staff for
      Personnel, Headquarters USA
COL Anthony Durso, USA
      Chief, Plans, Analysis and Evaluation, Headquarters USA
LTC Marcene Etchieson, USA
      Personnel Staff Officer, Women in the Army Policy, Soldier Policy Division, Human Resource
      Directorate, Headquarters USA
Maj Karen Heck, USMC
      Policy Analyst, Headquarters USMC
CAPT Martha L. Whitehead, USN
      Special Assistant for Women's Policy to the Chief of Naval Personnel
Col Al Schroetel, USAF
      Director of Officer Personnel Plans, Headquarters USAF
CDR Judith Hammond, USCG
      Women's Policy Advisor, Work Force Planning, Office of Personnel and Training, USCG

Dr. Sandra Carey, Ph.D.
>    Human Resource Research Analyst, Work Force Planning, Office of Personnel and Training, USCG

Mr. Paul L. Jones
>    Director, Defense Force Management Issues, National Security and International Affairs Division, General Accounting Office (GAO)

Survey of International Models

Maj Steven F. Maurmann, USAF
>    Deputy Director, Personnel Utilization, Office of the Assistant Secretary of Defense (Force Management and Personnel)

The Honorable Christopher Jehn
>    Assistant Secretary of Defense for Force Management and Personnel

## April 6, 1992 - Washington, DC

DoD Physical Fitness and Physical Strength Standards

Maj Steven F. Maurmann, USAF
>    Deputy Director, Personnel Utilization, Office of the Assistant Secretary of Defense (Force Management and Personnel)

Col Donald L. Mapes, MD, USAF
>    Director of Professional Affairs, Office of the Assistant Secretary of Defense (Health Affairs)

COL Oliver Johnson, USA
>    Chief, Personnel Readiness Division, Human Resource Directorate, Office of the Deputy Chief of Staff for Personnel

Col Richard F. Jones, USAF
>    Chief, Flight Medicine, Headquarters USAF

LTC Marcene Etchieson, USA
>    Personnel Staff Officer, Women in the Army Policy, Soldier Policy Division, Human Resource Directorate, Headquarters USA

LtCol Eugene Brindle, USMC
>    Head, Manpower Policy Section, Headquarters USMC

Lt Col Roger U. Bisson, USAF
>    Research Medical Officer, Armstrong Lab/CFTO

LCDR Doug Forcino, USN
>    Physical Readiness Program Officer, Bureau of Naval Personnel (PERS 6)

Demographics Briefing

Dr. Wayne S. Sellman, Ph.D.
>    Director of Accessions Policy, Office of the Assistant Secretary of Defense (Force Management and Personnel)

Women in the Army Policy Review - 1982

COL Dennis Kowal, USA
>    Command Psychologist, U.S. Army Intelligence Command

COL Terry M. Hulin, USA
>    Chief Soldier Policy Division, Human Resource Directorate, Office of the Deputy Chief of Staff for Personnel, Headquarters USA

"Progress of Women in the Navy" - 1987 plus update

CAPT Martha L. Whitehead, USN
>    Special Assistant on Women's Policy to the Chief of Naval Personnel

"Report on Progress of Women in the Marine Corps" - 1988
Maj Karen Heck, USMC
　　　　Policy Analyst, Headquarters USMC
Col Nicholas Grosz, USMC
　　　　Assistant Vice President, Navy Mutual Aid Association


"Women in the Military Cockpit" - 1991
Col Richard F. Jones, USAF
　　　　Chief, Flight Medicine, Headquarters USAF
Col Donald R. Spoon, USAF
　　　　Deputy Director, Crew Systems, Armstrong Lab/CF
Lt Col Roger U. Bisson, USAF
　　　　Research Medical Officer, Armstrong Lab/CFTO


## April 7, 1992- Washington, DC

Discuss Panel Charters and Procedures


## May 4, 1992 - Washington, DC

Overview of External Resources
Dr. Kathleen Robertson
　　　　Director of Research and Analysis, Commission Staff


External Resources Review by Commission Staff
General Accounting Office (GAO)
　　　　Mr. William Delaney
　　　　Research Analyst, Commission Staff
Media and Public Opinion
　　　　Mr. Richard Goldberg
　　　　Research Analyst, Commission Staff
Think Tanks
　　　　Mr. David Kuo
　　　　Research Analyst, Commission Staff
Congressional Resources
　　　　Ms. Elizabethe Bogart
　　　　Research Analyst, Commission Staff
Legal Resources
　　　　Ms. Mary Ann Hook
　　　　Assistant General Counsel, Commission Staff


External Research Methodology
Ms. Carolyn Becraft
　　　　Former Member of Women's Equity Action League, Women's Research and Education Institute, and
　　　　the International Center for Research on Women
Mr. Brian Mitchell
　　　　Former Research Consultant to the Heritage Foundation, Family Research Council, concerned Women
　　　　for America, and Eagle Forum; Author, Weak Link
Mr. Marty Binkin
　　　　Senior Fellow, Brookings Institution


Polling Organizations
Mr. Gary Ferguson
　　　　Vice President, American Viewpoint

Mr. William McInturff
> Founder and Research Analyst, Public Opinion Strategies

Ms. Carolyn Setlow
> Senior Vice President, The Roper Organization

## May 5, 1992 - Washington, DC

Cohesion Concept and Research Methodologies
Maj Charles B. Johnson, USMC
> Deputy Director of Research and Analysis, Commission Staff

Cohesion Panel
Dr. David Marlowe
> Chief, Department of Military Psychiatry, Walter Reed Army Institute of Research, Washington, DC

Dr. Owen Jacobs
> Chief, Strategic Leadership Technical Area (SLTA) of the Army Research Institute

Legal Briefing and Analysis of Recent Court Decisions
Mr. Robert J. Moore, Esq.
> General Counsel, Commission Staff

Ms. Stephanie Ritter, Esq.
> Professor, The George Washington University National School of Law

Mr. Vincent M. Garvey, Esq.
> Deputy Director of Federal Programs, Civil Division, U.S. Department of Justice

Dr. Henry N. Williams, Esq.
> General Counsel, U.S. Selective Service System

## June 8, 1992 - Washington, DC

Women in Foreign Military, Domestic Law Enforcement and Other Non-Traditional Roles
MG Charles A. Hines, USA
> Commanding General, U.S. Army Chemical and Military Police Centers, Ft. McClellan

Service Specific Definition of Combat
LtGen Matthew T. Cooper, USMC
> Deputy Chief of Staff for Manpower and Reserve Affairs, Headquarters USMC

Lt Gen Buster C. Glosson, USAF
> Deputy Chief of Staff for Operations, Headquarters USAF

LTG J. H. Binford Peay III, USA
> Deputy Chief of Staff for Operations and Plans, Headquaters USA

VADM Leighton W. Smith, Jr., USN
> Deputy Chief Naval Operations for Plans, Policy and Operations, USN

Laws of War and Geneva Convention with Emphasis on Prisoners of War
Mr. Hays Parks, Esq.
> Chief of International Law Branch of the International and Operational Law Division, Office of the Judge Advocate General, USA

Joint Services Survival, Evasion, Resistance and Escape (SERE)
Col John D. Graham, USAF
> Director, Joint Services SERE Agency

Mr. Robert G. Dussault
> Deputy Director, Joint Services SERE Agency, Training Division

Maj John Bruce Jessen, USAF
> Psychologist, Joint Services SERE Agency

Mr. John M. Mitchell
        Chief, Joint Services SERE Agency, Training Division

Testimony by Former Prisoners of War
The Honorable Everett Alvarez, Jr.
        Prisoner of War - Vietnam
Col Fred Cherry, USAF (Ret.)
        Prisoner of War - Vietnam
MAJ Rhonda Cornum, USA
        Prisoner of War - Desert Storm
LT Mary Rose Harrington Nelson, USN (Ret.)
        Prisoner of War - World War II
Col Norman A. McDaniel, USAF (Ret.)
        Prisoner of War - Vietnam


**June 9, 1992 - Washington, DC**

Definition and Applications of Cohesion Panel
Dr. M.C. Devilbiss
        Author, Women and Military Service: A History, Analysis, and Overview of Key Issues
Dr. Paul E. Roush, Col, USMC (Ret.)
        Associate Professor, Department of Leadership and Law, U.S. Naval Academy
Maj Wayne G. Stone, USAF
        Associate Professor of Organizational Science, Air Force Institute of Technology


Damage Control Efforts
CAPT Paul X. Rinn, USN
        Former Commanding Officer, USS Samuel B. Roberts
BMCM (SW) George E. Frost, USN
        Former Command Master Chief, USS Samuel B. Roberts
MSCM Kevin Ford, USN
        Damage Control, USS Samuel B. Roberts
OS2 George Tanner, USN
        Damage Control, USS Samuel B. Roberts


American Cultural Values
Dr. William A. Galston
        Visiting Fellow, Woodrow Wilson Center
Dr. Joyce Ladner
        Vice President of Academic Affairs, Howard University
Mrs. Phyllis Schlafly
        President, Eagle Forum
Mr. Donald Feder
        Nationally Syndicated Columnist
Dr. Sonya Friedman
        Host "Sonya Live," CNN


Family Issues
Dr. Jay Belsky
        Professor of Human Development and Family Studies, Pennsylvania State University
Dr. Brenda Hunter
        Psychologist, Minirth-Meier & Byrd Clinic, P. A.
Mr. William R. Mattox
        Director of Policy Analysis, Family Research Council
Dr. Mady Segal
        Professor of Sociology, University of Maryland

Psychology
CDR Peter C.K. Graham-Mist, MSC, USN
        Head of Outpatient Psychology, National Naval Medical Center
Mrs. Judy Hampton
        Branch Head, Family Programs Branch, Headquarters USMC
COL (Dr.) Richard A. Manning, USA
        Child Psychiatrist, Walter Reed Army Medical Center
Mrs. Gail McGinn
        Director, Office of Family Policies, Support, and Services, Office of the Secretary of Defense
Col (Dr.) Ibis Sigas, USAF
        Child Psychiatrist, Malcolm Grow Medical Center
Dr. Robert Ursano, Col, USAF (Ret.)
        Professor and Chairman of the Department of Psychiatry, Uniformed Services University of Health
        Sciences


**June 25, 1992 - Washington, DC**

Polling Survey Instrument Legal Brief
Mr. Robert J. Moore, Esq.
        General Counsel, Commission Staff


Congressional Testimony and Advocacy Group Testimony
Mr. Robert Morrison
        Policy Analyst and Editor, Washington Watch, Family Research Council
Senator Edward M. Kennedy (D-MA)
        Member of the Senate Armed Services Committee
BG Evelyn Foote, USA (Ret.)
        Military Advisor, Federally Employed Women's Association
Mr. William S. Lind
        Director of the Center of Cultural Conservatism, Free Congress Foundation, Former Defense Advisor
        to a U.S. Senator
Senator John Warner (R-VA)
        Ranking Minority Member of the Senate Armed Services Committee
VADM William Lawrence, USN (Ret.)
        President, Association of Naval Aviation
Congressman Robert K. Dornan (R-CA)
        Member of the House Armed Services Committee
Congresswoman Beverly Byron (D-MD)
        Member of the House Armed Services Committee
CDR Rosemary Mariner, USN
        President, Women's Military Aviation Association
Congressman Tom DeLay (R-TX)
        Member, House Appropriations Committee, Military Construction Subcommittee
Ms. Ellen Smith
        Legal Counsel, Concerned Women for America
Mr. Eldon Yates
        Chairman and Founder, Vietnam Veterans Institute


Personnel Issues and Women in the Military
MajGen Gene A. Deegan, USMC
        Commanding General, Marine Corps Recruiting Depot/Commanding General, Eastern Recruiting
        Region, Parris Island, South Carolina
MajGen Charles Krulak, USMC
        Director, Personnel Procurement Division, Manpower and Reserve Affairs Department, Headquarters
        USMC

## June 26, 1992 - Washington, DC

Cohesion
Dr. William Darryl Henderson
Commissioner

Physiological Gender Differences, Physical Performance, and Occupational Standards
Dr. Edward J. Marcinik, CDR (sel), USN
Physiologist, Commission Staff
Ronald P. Crisman, Ph.D.
Deputy Director, Laboratory for Aerospace Cardiovascular Research; Fellow, American College Sports
Medicine

Service Senior Enlisted Advisors
SMA Richard A. Kidd, USA
Sergeant Major of the Army
MCPO Duane R. Bushey, USN
Master Chief Petty Officer of the Navy
CMSgt Gary R. Pfigston, USAF
Senior Enlisted Advisor, USAF
Sgt Maj Harold G. Overstreet, USMC
Sergeant Major of the Marine Corps

Historical Perspective - Utilization of Women in Israel's War of Independence, 1948
Dr. Martin Van Creveld
Professor, Hebrew University, Jerusalem; Oppenheimer Chair, Marine Corps University, Quantico, VA

Impact of Policy Changes On Enlisted Male Personnel
SGT Kermit L. Smith, USA
Personnel, Old Guard
SGT Bobby G. Stringfellow, USA
Infantry Squad Leader
SSgt Joseph Lloyd, USAF
Combat Control Operator
SSgt Wai M. Li, USAF
Personnel Specialist
SGT Steven Philip, USMC
Field Artillery/Nuclear Technician
SGT James Graffeo, USMC
Heavy Vehicle Operator
OS2 Jeffrey Ackers, USN
Operations Specialist
AK2 Wayne R. Desautels, USN
Aviation Storekeeper

Military Women and Family Issues
RADM Roberta L. Hazard, USN
Assistant Chief of Naval Personnel, Personal Readiness and Community Support; Chairwoman of
Women in NATO Forces

Impact of Policy Changes On Enlisted Female Personnel
SGT Karol J. Dawson, USA
Nuclear/Bio/Chemical Specialist
SGT Janet A. O'Neil, USA
Records Specialist

SSgt Nancy M. Smith, USAF
        A-10 Crew Chief
SSgt Mary Y. MacKenney, USAF
        Electronic and Environmental Systems Specialist
SGT Elizabeth Dobrzanski, USMC
        Military Police
SGT Michelle E. Chapman, USMC
        Motor Vehicle Operator
HM2 Leslie A. Distasio, USN
        Hospital Corpsman
YN2 Denise R. Schultze, USN
        Yeoman

Air/Ground Issues of Combat
RADM Richard C. Allen, USN
        Director, Program Resource Appraisal Division, Office of the Chief of Naval Operations
Col John W. Ripley, USMC
        Commander, Navy-Marine Corps ROTC Unit, Virginia Military Institute

## July 13, 1992 - Chicago, IL

The Midwestern Perspective
Dr. Allan Carlson
        President, The Rockford Institute, Rockford, IL
Dr. Maria Lepowsky
        Professor of Sociology and Anthropology, University of Wisconsin-Madison

Theological Perspectives
Reverend Arthur Beyer
        Director of Divinity, Pastor, Trinity Lutheran Church, Lisle, IL
Father Richard R. Roach, Ph.D.
        Associate Professor of Theology, Theological Department of Marquette University

Advocates from the Midwest
COL James Francis Baker, USA (Ret.)
        Illinois Benedictine College, Member of The Retired Officers Association
Ms. Jill Wine-Banks, Esq.
        Former General Counsel to the Army
Mrs. Elizabeth Clarke
        Daughters of the American Revolution
LCDR Donna Fournier, USNR
        Illinois Council of Women Veterans
Mrs. Mary Lawlor
        Pro America Foundation
Ms. Marian H. Neudel
        Midwest Committee for Military Counseling

Air Force Study, "Women in Combat"
Capt Katherine Simpson, USAF
        Scientific Analyst, Air Force Military Personnel Center

1991 Marine Study of Professional Identity, "Why We Serve"
Maj Charles B. Johnson, USMC
        Deputy Director of Research and Analysis, Commission Staff

## July 14, 1992 - Chicago, IL

<u>USAF Missile Squadron Commanders</u>
Col Michael J. Roggero, USAF
      Commander, 310th Training and Test Wing, Vandenberg AFB, CA
Lt Col William J. Beck, USAF
      Commander, 741st Missile Squadron, Minot AFB, ND
Maj Linda Aldrich, USAF
      Deputy Chief, Personnel Plans, STRATCOM, Offutt AFB, NE

<u>USAF Mixed Gender Missile Crews</u>
Capt Angela Stout, USAF
      Instructor, Missile Crew Commander, Peacekeeper, F.E. Warren AFB, WY
1st Lt Charles Miller, USAF
      Instructor, Deputy Missile Crew Commander, Peacekeeper, F.E. Warren AFB, WY
Capt Mark Gillespie, USAF
      Missile Combat Crew Flight Commander, Minot AFB, ND
1st Lt Leann Derby, USAF
      Deputy Missile Combat Crew Flight Commander, Minot AFB, ND

<u>Air Mobility Command</u>
Maj Gen Robert E. Dempsey, USAF
      Chief of Staff, Air Mobility Command, Scott AFB, IL

<u>USAF Flying Squadron Commanders</u>
Lt Col William K. Osborn, USAF
      Commander, 11th Air Refueling Squadron (KC-135), Altus AFB, OK
Lt Col Peter W. Moates, USAF
      Commander, 15th Airlift Squadron (C-141), Norton AFB, CA

<u>USAF Mixed Gender C-130 Crew</u>
Capt Kevin William Oatley, USAF
      Aircraft Commander
Capt Isabella Schwarz, USAF
      Aircraft Commander
1st Lt Heather Ann Schofield, USAF
      Co-Pilot
1st Lt Michael G. Loncar, USAF
      Navigator
MSgt Richard C. Biggs, USAF
      Flight Engineer
SrA Elizabeth Jane Rogers, USAF
      Loadmaster

<u>Regional Recruiting</u>
MG Jack C. Wheeler, USA
      Commander, Army Recruiting Command
MAJ Marsha M. Takao, USA
      Recruiter
Mrs. Rausta F. Reynolds
      Department of the Army, Civilian Analyst
TSgt Christy Ann Lee, USAF
      Recruiter
SFC Carlos R. DeJesus, USA
      Recruiter

SSG Vera Bella Akomah, USAR
      Recruiter
PO1 Theadius L. Mapp, USN
      Recruiter
PO1 Eva Mae Alegre, USN
      Recruiter
MSGT Ernest E. Lloyd, Jr., USMC
      Recruiter


**July 15, 1992 - Chicago, IL**

Perspectives on Gender Differences
Dr. Steven Goldberg
      Chairman of the Department of Sociology, City College of New York
Dr. Helena Lopata
      Director, Center for the Comparative Study of Social Roles, Loyola University of Chicago


B-1 Crew
Capt Ronald P. Gaulton, USAF
      Aircraft Commander
Capt Matthew R. Bartlett, USAF
      Pilot
Capt Donald M. Schauber, USAF
      Offensive Systems Officer
Capt Scott W. Plumb, USAF
      Defensive Systems Officer
Capt Randel L. Averet, USAF
      Pilot


Army Enlisted Women
SGT Catherine Blurton, USA
      Military Police, Chicago Recruiting Battalion, Libertyville Station, IL
SGT Amy L. Brandt, USAR
      Crane/Forklift Operator, 377th Maintenance Company
SGT Susie M. Chalupsky, USA
      Communications Systems, U.S. Army Information Systems Command, Fort Sheridan, IL
SGT Eula Hartley, USAR
      Chemical Equipment Specialist
SGT Lori L. Mertz, USAR
      Parts Clerk, 395th Ordinance Battalion, Warsaw, WI
SGT Mary E. Rader, USA
      Unit Supply, 213th Supply and Service Battalion, Warsaw, WI


**August 6, 1992 - Los Angeles, CA**

The West Coast Perspective
Mr. David Horowitz
      President, Center for the Study of Popular Culture, Chairman, Committee on Media Integrity

Theological Perspective
Mr. Dennis Prager
      Director, Center for Ethical Monotheism
Rev. John Stewart
      Non-Denominational Protestant Minister

Navy Enlisted Personnel with Integrated Ship Experience
DC2 Ronald Grimes, USN
        Damage Control, USS Jason, San Diego, CA
DC2 Susan Worden, USN
        Damage Control, USS Jason, San Diego, CA
EM2 Eugene Hartman, USN
        Electrician's Mate, USS Jason, San Diego, CA
EM2 Sherri Tarver, USN
        Damage Control, USS Jason, San Diego, CA


Submarine Crew Members
LCDR Eric R. Anderson, USN
        Strategic Weapons Officer, USS Alaska, Bangor, WA
LCDR Steve McShane, USN
        Executive Officer, USS Louisville, San Diego, CA
ETCM Bob Brien, USN
        Chief of the Boat, USS Georgia, Bangor, WA
ETCM(SS) Steve Kyle, USN
        Engineering Department, USS Gurnard, San Diego, CA


Commanding Officers of Ships With Women Assigned
CAPT Gary Bier, USN
        Former Commanding Officer, USS Cape Cod (AD-43), San Diego, CA
CAPT Bill Pickavance, USN
        Former Commanding Officer, USS Mars (AFS-1), Concord, CA


Commanding Officers of Ships Without Women Assigned
CAPT Richard Dean Raaz, USN
        Commanding Officer, USS Georgia, Bangor, WA
CDR William Lilliard, USN
        Commanding Officer, USS Lewis D. Puller, Long Beach, CA


Fighter Weapons School Aviators
CDR Bob McLane, USN
        Commanding Officer, Top Gun F-14, Miramar, CA
Capt Patrick M. Cooke, USMC
        Pilot, F/A-18/IP, Miramar, CA
LT John Clagett, USN
        Pilot, F/A-18/IP, Miramar, CA
LT Tom Downing, USN
        Pilot, F/A-18/IP, Training Command Instructor Pilot, Miramar, CA


Naval Aviators, Mixed Gender, Shipboard Experience
CDR Chuck Deitchman, USN
        Commanding Officer, HSC-11, North Island, CA
LtCol Daniel A. Driscoll, Jr., USMC
        Commanding Officer, VMA-101, Marine Air Group-11, VFA-125, NAS Lemoore, CA
LT Silvia Rivadeneira, USN
        Carrier On-Board Delivery Pilot, San Diego, CA
LT Brenda Sheufele, USN
        F/A-18 Pilot, VAQ-34, Miramar, CA

**August 7, 1992 - Los Angeles, CA**

Occupational Standards and Health/Wellness Issues
Dr. Paul O. Davis
> President, Applied Research Associates Human Services

Dr. James Vogel
> Director, Occupational Health and Performance Directorate, U.S. Army Institute of Environmental Readiness

Dr. John Butterfield
> Executive Director, President's Council on Physical Fitness

Role of the Naval Reserve and the Assignment of Women to Combatant Ships (FFT)
LT Holly Graf, USN
> Weapons Officer, USS Ainsworth (FFt. 1090), Staten Island, NY

LT Walter Towns, USN
> Combat Systems Officer, USS Moinester (FFt. 1097), Norfolk, VA

OSC(SW) Ralph Parker, USN
> LCPO-Operations, USS Donald B. Beary (FFt. 1086), Staten Island, NY

OSCS(SW) Mary E. Prise, USN
> LCPO-Operations, USS Ainsworth (FFT-1090), Staten Island, NY

Doctrinal Overview of Combined Arms Operations
BG(P) William Steele, USA
> Deputy Commandant, CGSC, Ft. Leavenworth, KS

LtCol Roger J. Mauer, USMC
> Doctrine Analyst, Marine Corps Warfighting Center, Quantico, VA

Role of Infantry in Combined Arms Operations
LTC Stephen Scott Smith, USA
> Operation Desert Shield/Storm Mechanized Infantry Battalion Commander, U.S. Army War College

CPT William Don Farris II, USA
> Operation Desert Shield/Storm Company Commander, 82nd Airborne Division

Capt Ailneal Morris, USMC
> Marine Corps Company Commander, Operation Desert Shield/Storm

SSgt Michael T. Wagner, USMC
> Platoon Sergeant, Operation Desert Shield/Storm

Role of Armor in Combined Arms Operations
LTC Douglas Tystad, USA
> M-1 Battalion Commander, Operation Desert Shield/Storm, School of Advanced Military Studies, Ft. Leavenworth, KS

CPT Benjamin Valenzuela, USA
> M-1 Company Commander, Operation Desert Shield/Storm

1stLt James D. Consalves, USMC
> M-1 Company Commander, Operation Desert Shield/Storm

SFC Ronald Bloomfield, USA
> M-1 Platoon Sergeant, Operation Desert Shield/Storm

Role of Field Artillery in Combined Arms Operations
LTC Lawrence R. Adair, USA
> Battalion Commander, Operation Desert Shield/Storm, 155 Direct Support Artillery Battalion with Previous MLRS Command, National War College

CPT Jeffrey Lieb, USA
> Battery Commander MLRS, Operation Desert Shield/Storm

Capt Kevin J. McCarthy, USMC
> Battery Commander, Marine Corps 198/155, Operation Desert Shield/Storm

SFC Michael D. Sarisky, USA
> Platoon Sgt, 82nd Airborne Division 105mm, Operation Desert Shield/Storm

Role of Combat Engineers in Combined Arms Operations

LTC Hans Van Winkle, USA
> Battalion Commander, Engineer Unit Attached to a Mechanized Infantry/Armor Unit, FORSCOM, Ft. Ord, CA, Operation Desert Shield/Storm

Capt Vincent J. Samang, USMC
> Company Commander, Operation Desert Shield/Storm

1SG Rex A. Wertz, Sr., USA
> 1SG of Combat Engineer Unit, FORSCOM, Ft. Leonard Wood, MO, Operation Desert Shield/Storm

SSgt Barry F. Bell, USMC
> Commanding Officer, Combat Engineer, Operation Desert Shield/Storm

Role of Aviation in Combined Arms Operations

COL Robert Seigle, USA
> Operation Desert Shield/Storm and Operation Just Cause (Panama) command experience

LTC William Bryan, USA
> Attack Helicopter Battalion Commander, U.S. Army Aviation Center, Operation Desert Shield/Storm, command experience in both Assault and Attack Aviation Units

MAJ Wendy Mullins, USA
> Commanded Assault Unit in Operation Desert Shield/Storm; Command and General Staff College, Ft. Leavenworth, KS

Capt Michael A. Rocco, USMC
> Cobra Pilot and Commander of Marine Attack Helo Unit in Operation Desert Shield/Storm

## August 8, 1992 - Los Angeles, CA

Military Issues Advocates

Ms. Jane Chastain
> First woman sportscaster; Board Member, Renaissance Women

Ms. Stacy Fletcher
> National President, Alliance of Women Veterans

Army Non-Deployability Briefing

COL Terry Hulin, USA
> Chief Soldier Policy Division, Human Resource Directorate, Office of the Deputy Chief of Staff for Personnel, Headquarters USA

## August 27, 1992 - Dallas, TX

The Southern Perspective

Dr. Mel Bradford
> Endowed Professor of American Literature, University of Dallas

Dr. John Butler
> Chairman, Sociology Department, University of Texas at Austin

Theologians

Rev. Buckner Fanning
> Pastor, Trinity Baptist Church, San Antonio, TX

Dr. Stephen Long
> Professor of Christian Ethics and Director of Continuing Education, Duke University, Divinity School, Durham, NC

General Counsel Brief on Legal Implications of Commission Recommendations
Mr. Robert Moore, Esq.
> General Counsel, Commission Staff

Ms. Mary Ann Hook
> Assistant General Counsel, Commission Staff

Ms. Kelly Carlson
> Assistant General Counsel, Commission Staff


Special Operations Forces Panel
LTG Wayne A. Downing, USA
> Commander, U.S. Army Special Operations Command, Ft. Bragg, NC

RADM Raymond C. Smith, Jr., USN
> Commander, Naval Special Warfare Command, Coronado, CA

COL Bryan D. Brown, USA
> Commander, 1/160th Special Operations Aviation Regiment (Airborne), Ft. Bragg, NC

Col Charles R. Holland, USAF
> Commander, 1st Special Operations Wing, Hurlburt Field, FL


Use of Simulators for Screening, Training and Evaluation
Col Lynn Carroll, USAF
> Chief of the Armstrong Laboratory, Aircrew Training Research Division, Williams AFB, AZ

CDR Dave Dickens, USN
> Tactical Aircraft Simulator Requirements Officer for the Chief of Naval Operations

CDR Dennis McBride, USN
> Program Manager, Warfighting Simulation, Defense Advanced Research Projects Agency, Advanced Systems Technology Office

Mr. Hugh Moreland
> Manager, Pilot Vehicle Integration, General Dynamics, Fort Worth, TX


Trip Reports
Canada
> Briefed by Richard Goldberg, Research Analyst, Commission Staff; Commissioners attended: Clarke and Henderson

USS John F. Kennedy
> Briefed by Mary Ann Hook, Assistant General Counsel, Commission Staff; Commissioners attended: Clarke, Donnelly, Cockerham, and White

Fairchild AFB Survival, Evasion, Resistance and Escape School
> Briefed by David Kuo, Research Analyst, Commission Staff; Commissioner attended: Donnelly

U.S. Naval Academy
> Briefed by David Kuo, Research Analyst, Commission Staff; Commissioners attended: White, Donnelly, Neizer, and Draude


Review Draft Fact Finding Reports
> Panel 2
> Panel 4


**August 28, 1992 - Dallas, TX**


USAF Bomber/Airlift Operations Panel
Col Michael P. Loughran, USAF
> Commander, 416th Bombardment Wing, Griffiss AFB, NY

Capt Thomas R. Tighe, USAF
> B-52 Flight Commander, Carswell AFB, TX

Capt John L. Mitchell, USAF
> B-52 Standard Evaluation Pilot, Wurtsmith AFB, MI

Capt Pollyanna A. Padden, USAF
> C-141 Aircraft Commander, Charleston AFB, SC

Capt Lois Evans, USAF
> C-141 Flight Examiner, McChord AFB, WA

USAF Fighter Pilots

Brig Gen Lloyd W. Newton, USAF
> Commander, 49th Fighter Wing, Holloman AFB, NM

Capt Stephen T. Lambert, USAF
> Pilot, F-16, Hill AFB, UT

Capt David T. Freaney, USAF
> Pilot, F-15, Fighter Weapons School Instructor, Nellis AFB, NV

Capt John H. Rush, USAF
> Flight Commander, F-111, Cannon AFB, NM

NASA Physiological Research

Dr. Victor A. Convertino
> Senior Research Scientist, Kennedy Space Center, FL

Dr. Richard Jennings
> Chief, Flight Medicine Clinic, Johnson Space Center, TX

Overview of Combat Support and Combat Service Support Doctrine

COL Michael E. Hawk, USA
> Director, Concepts and Doctrine Directorate, U.S. Army Command and General Staff College, Ft. Leavenworth, KS

COL Richard E. Cadorette, USA
> Deputy Commander for Training, U.S. Army Combined Arms Support Command, Ft. Lee, VA

Col John J. Holly, USMC
> Assistant Chief of Staff, G-3, 1st Force Service Support Group, Camp Pendleton, CA

Officers in Combat Support/Combat Service Support Roles

LTC Daniel L. Fairchild, USA
> Deputy Chief, Plans and Operations, Division J4, FORSCOM, Ft. McPherson, GA

CPT Rebecca W. Jones, USA
> Former Company Commander, 418th Transportation Company, Operation Desert Shield/Storm

CPT Christina C. Mortel, USA
> Former Company Commander, 183rd Maintenance Company, Operation Desert Shield/Storm

Capt Michael G. Dana, USMC
> 1st Landing Support Battalion, 1st Force Service Support Group, Camp Pendleton, CA

Enlisted in Combat Support/Combat Service Support Roles

SSgt Laura D. Gonzales, USMC
> Motor Transportation Instructor, 8th Engineer Support Battalion, Camp Lejeune, SC

SSG Lonney Smalley, USA
> 54th Maintenance Battalion, Ft. Hood, TX

SGT David Lockett, USA
> Assistant Squad Leader, 365th Transportation Company, Ft. McClellan, AL

SGT Cynthia Pratt, USA
> Mechanic, 169th Maintenance Battalion, Ft. Hood, TX

Officers in Field Artillery

MAJ Albert J. Gomez, Jr., USA
> Secretary to the General Staff, U.S. Army Field Artillery School, Ft. Sill, OK

MAJ Anne F. Jameson, USA
> Executive Officer, Combat Developments Directorate, U.S. Army Field Artillery School, Ft. Sill, OK

MAJ Robert H. McElroy, USA
>    Chief, Rocket and Missile Division, Gunnery Dept, U.S. Army Field Artillery School, Ft. Sill, OK

CPT Ann L. Booth, USA
>    S-3, 1st Battalion, 78th Field Artillery, U.S. Army Field Artillery School, Ft. Sill, OK

Enlisted in Field Artillery

SFC Everett L. Baumgaertel, USA
>    Platoon Sergeant, 6/27 Field Artillery, Multiple Launch Rocket System, Ft. Sill, OK

SFC Patricia L. Caruso, USA
>    Intelligence Sergeant, Headquarters and Headquarters Battery, 75th Field Artillery Training Center, Ft. Sill, OK

SFC Dennis W. Floden, USA
>    Drill Sergeant, B Battery, 2d Battalion, 80th Field Artillery, U.S. Army Field Artillery Training Center, Ft. Sill, OK

SFC Janice F. Murrell, USA
>    Operations Sergeant, Headquarters and Headquarters Battery, Headquarters Command, Ft. Sill, OK

Assault and Transport Helicopter Pilots

LTC Robert L. Johnson, Jr., USA
>    Chief Aviation Proponency Office, Ft. Rucker, AL

CPT Lisa Ann Hudon, USA
>    Assistant Operations Officer, S-3, 9th Battalion, 101st Aviation Regiment, Ft. Campbell, KY

Capt Stuart J. Greenwald, USMC
>    Assistant Operations Officer, HMH-462, CH-53 Pilot

Capt Eric B. Treworgy, USMC
>    Pilot, CH-46

## August 29, 1992 - Dallas, TX

Human Factors/Anthropometrics

Capt Jaquelyn Parker, USAF
>    Test Pilot, Wright-Patterson AFB, OH

Dr. Reed W. Mankin
>    Pilot-Vehicle Interface Team, General Dynamics, Fort Worth Division, TX

LT Lori Melling Tanner, USN
>    Test Pilot, Patuxent River NAS, MD

Mr. Greg Zehner
>    Anthropometric Engineer, Wright-Patterson AFB, OH

Panels Review Draft Fact Finding Reports.
>    Panel 1
>    Panel 3
>    Panel 4

## September 10, 1992 - Washington, DC

1992 Survey of Army Women

Dr. Charles Moskos
>    Professor of Sociology, Northwestern University

Ms. Laura Miller
>    Doctoral Candidate, Department of Sociology, Northwestern University

Cultural Values Panel: Theological Perspectives

Dr. Anthony Campolo
>    Baptist Theologian and Professor of Sociology, Eastern College, St. Davids, PA

Rev. Isaac J. Miller
    Rector, Church of the Advocate (Episcopalian), Philadelphia, PA

Commissioner Generated Testimony
Mr. Eric Orsini
    Deputy Assistant Secretary of the Army for Logistics
Rev. Stephen Schlissel
    Administrative Director of Meantime Ministries, Brooklyn, NY

Defense Advisory Committee on Women in the Services (DACOWITS)
Mrs. Jean Jackson
    Chair, Defense Advisory Committee on Women in the Services

Panel 2 Fact Finding Brief

Panel 4 Fact Finding Brief

## September 11, 1992 - Washington, DC

Service Non-Deployability Briefing
CAPT Martha Whitehead, USN
    Special Assistant for Women's Policy to the Chief of Naval Personnel
Lt Col Mike Lynch, USAF
    Chief Officer, Accessions, Plans and Policy, Headquarters USAF
LtCol Eugene Brindle, USMC
    Head, Manpower Policy Section, Headquarters USMC

Roper Organization Briefing of Initial Public Survey Data
Ms. Carolyn Setlow
    Senior Vice President, The Roper Organization

Life Aboard Amphibious Ships
USN/USMC video presentation

Panel 3 Fact Finding Brief

Commissioner Generated Testimony
Brig Gen Michael G. Hall, USAF
    Commander, New York Air National Guard, Adjutant General of the State of New York
VADM Dudley Carlson, USN (Ret.)
    Former National Security Advisor and Chief of Naval Personnel

Panel 1 Fact Finding Brief

## September 12, 1992 - Washington, DC

Commissioner Generated Testimony
LTC William Gregor, USA
    Department Chair, Department of Military Science, University of Michigan
Capt Troy Devine, USAF
    U-2 Pilot

## Female Army Officers
MAJ Lil Pfluke, USA
> Ordnance Corps, R&D Assignment, Army Space Program Office, Washington, DC

CPT Linda Suttlehan, USA
> Company Commander, 124 Military Intelligence Battalion, 24th Infantry Division, Ft. Stewart, GA

2LT Christina Weber, USA
> Ordnance Corps

## Commissioner Generated Testimony
Dr. Judith Reisman
> Director, Institute for Media Education, Consultant for the U.S. Department of Health and Human Services and U.S. Department of Education

BG Theodore C. Mataxis, USA (Ret.)
> National Security Speakers Bureau of the American Security Council Foundation

Mr. Robert Knight
> Director, Cultural Studies Project, Family Research Council

Mrs. Claude Swafford
> Member of the Defense Advisory Committee on Women in the Services

MAJ Charles Hawkins, USA
> Commander, Rifle Company, Vietnam; Member of the Historical Evaluation & Research Organization (HERO)

LtGen Edward Bronars, USMC (Ret.)
> Chairman, Freedom Alliance Foundation

## Panel Meetings
Panels confirm taxonomy/tasking of staff to produce matrix of alternatives for recommendations

## October 1, 1992 - Washington, DC

## U.S. Coast Guard
Admiral J.M. Kime
> Commandant of the Coast Guard

## Astronaut
CAPT Rick Hauck, USN (Ret.)
> President and Chief Operating Officer, International Technology Underwriters, Bethesda, MD

## GAO Briefing on Women in Desert Storm and the Service Academies
Mr. Paul Jones
> Director, Defense Force Management, National Security and International Affairs Division, GAO

Mr. William Beusse
> Assistant Director, Defense Force Management, National Security and International Affairs Div., GAO

Mr. Foy Wicker
> Assistant Director, Defense Force Management, National Security and International Affairs Div., GAO

Ms. Beverly Bendekgey
> Senior Evaluator, Defense Force Management, National Security and International Affairs Div., GAO

Ms. Marty Dey
> Senior Evaluator, Defense Force Management, National Security and International Affairs Div., GAO

## Navy Lost Time Briefing
CAPT Martha L. Whitehead, USN
> Special Assistant for Woman's Policy to the Chief of Naval Personnel

Ms. Patricia Thomas
> Director, Office of Women and Multicultural Research, Navy Personnel Research and Development Center, San Diego, CA

<u>Roper Briefing</u>
Ms. Carolyn Setlow
   Senior Vice President, The Roper Organization

<u>Report Format Briefing</u>
Ms. Mary Ann Hook
   Assistant General Counsel, Commission Staff

<u>Final Review of Panel Findings</u>
Panel 1

## October 2, 1992 - Washington, DC

<u>Final Review of Panel Findings</u>
Panel 3
Panel 4
Panel 2

## October 3, 1992 - Washington, DC

<u>Initial Definition of the Issues</u>

<u>Proposed Additional Findings</u>

<u>Format Options</u>

<u>Review and Initial Selection of Panel Findings</u>

## October 22, 1992 - Washington, DC

<u>Outstanding Trip Reports</u>
International
   Briefed by Mr. Richard Goldberg, Research Analyst, Commission Staff; Commissioners attended:
   Clarke and Henderson
Kings Bay, GA/NTC Orlando, FL
   Briefed by Elizabethe Bogart, Research Analyst, Commission Staff; Commissioners attended: Clarke,
   Draude and Finch
SUBLANT, Norfolk
   Briefed by Mark Byrd, Research Analyst, Commission Staff; Commissioners attended: Donnelly,
   Henderson and Neizer
CENTCOM/USSOCOM
   Briefed by Maj Chuck Johnson, USMC, Deputy Director of Research, Commission Staff;
   Commissioner attended: Cockerham
USMA, West Point, NY
   Briefed by Dr. Ed Marcinik, Commission Staff Physiologist; Commissioners attended: Finch and
   Draude
MCCDC, Quantico
   Briefed by Dr. Ed Marcinik, Commission Staff Physiologist; Commissioners attended: Donnelly and
   White
DCICEM, Canada
   Briefed by Dr. Ed Marcinik, Commission Staff Physiologist; Commissioners attended: none

<u>Brooks AFB Symposium Brief</u>
Dr. Ronald Crisman, Ph.D.
   Fellow, American College Sports Medicine; Deputy Director, Laboratory for Aerospace Cardiovascular
   Research

<u>Public Opinion and Military Survey Briefing</u>
Mr. David Napior
       Senior Vice President, STARCH (Parent company to The Roper Organization)
Mrs. Kathleen O'Neil
       Senior Project Director, The Roper Organization

<u>Status of Outstanding DOD tasks</u>
Maj Steven F. Maurmann, USAF
       Deputy Director, Personnel Utilization, Office of the Assistant Secretary of Defense (Force Management and Personnel)
Dr. Kathleen Robertson
       Director of Research and Analysis, Commission Staff

**October 22, 1992 - Washington, DC**

<u>Commissioners' Comments</u>
       Ten minutes per Commissioner

<u>Discussion of Issues</u>

<u>Define/Finalize Issues</u>

**October 23, 1992 - Washington, DC**

<u>Approve Issues</u>

<u>Approve Findings</u>

<u>Pregnancy on Admission and Entry</u>
COL Terry M. Hulin, USA
       Chief Soldier Policy Division, Human Resources Directorate, Office of the Deputy Chief of Staff for Personnel, Headquarters USA

<u>Flag and General Officer Survey</u>
Maj Charles B. Johnson, USMC
       Deputy Director of Research and Analysis, Commission Staff

**October 24, 1992 - Washington, DC**

<u>Approval of Findings (continued)</u>

<u>Discuss Sequence of Issues</u>

**November 1-3, 1992 - Washington, DC**

<u>Discuss Report Format</u>

<u>Commission Deliberates and Votes on Decision Options/Recommendations</u>

**November 9-10, 1992 - Washington, DC**

<u>Review and Approve Draft Commission Report</u>

**November 15, 1992 - Washington, DC**

Final Report Transmitted to the President

**December 15, 1992 - Washington, DC**

Final Report with President's Comments and Recommendations Transmitted to Congress

# APPENDIX G

## STATEMENTS FOR THE RECORD

Mr. Gary L. Bauer, President, Family Research Council, "Mothers at War"

Ms. Carolyn Becraft, The Ford Foundation, Statement for the Record

Reverend Arthur Beyer, Director of Divinity, Pastor, Trinity Lutheran Church, Statement for the Record

Mr. Peter B. Booth, "Women in Combat... a Moral Issue"

AVCM (AW) Duane R. Bushey, USN, Master Chief Petty Officer, Statement for the Record

Congresswoman Beverly Byron (D-MD), Member, Committee on the Armed Services, U.S. House of Representatives, Statement for the Record

SSG Joni Carter, USAR, Advisory of the Vietnam Veterans Institute, "Position Paper of the Vietnam Veterans Institute" and Statement for the Record

Ms. Jane Chastain, Radio Commentator, Statement for the Record

MG Daniel W. Christman, USA, Statement for the Record

Mr. E. Edward Chynoweth, "Women in the Military"

Senator William S. Cohen (R-ME), Member, Committee on the Armed Services, United States Senate, Statement for the Record

The Honorable Mary Collins, P.C., M.P., Associate Minister of National Defence, "Full Integration of Women in the Canadian Forces" as presented to the Women's Research and Education Institute

MAJ Rhonda Cornum, USA, Prisoner of War - Desert Storm, Statement for the Record

LTC Roger D. Cunningham, USA, Defense Attache, Statement for the Record

Dr. Paul O. Davis, President, ARA Human Services, Synopsis of Scientific Data on Physical Performance Requirements

MajGen Gene A. Deegan, USMC, Commanding General, Marine Corps Recruiting Depot; Commanding General, Eastern Recruiting Region, Parris Island, SC, Statement for the Record

Congressman Tom DeLay (R-TX), Member, Appropriations Committee, Military Construction Subcommittee, U.S. House of Representatives, Statement for the Record

1st Lt Leann Derby, USAF, Deputy Missile Combat Crew Flight Commander, Minot AFB, ND, Statement for the Record

Congressman Robert K. Dornan (R-CA), Member, Committee on the Armed Services, U.S. House of Representatives, Statement for the Record

BG Evelyn P. Foote, USA (Ret.), Military Advisor, Federally Employed Women's Association, Statement for the Record

LCDR Donna Fournier, USNR, Illinois Council of Women Veterans, Statement for the Record

CAPT Rick Hauck, USN (Ret.), President and Chief Operating Officer, International Technology Underwriters, Bethesda, MD, Statement for the Record

COL Michael E. Hawk, USA, Director, Concepts and Doctrine Directorate, US Army Command and Staff College, Ft. Leavenworth, KS, Statement for the Record

MAJ Glen R. Hawkins, USA, "Report on Training Changes at West Point Since the Admission of Women"

Maj Gen Jeanne M. Holm, USAF (Ret.), "Women in the Military: the Next Phase"

Mr. David Horowitz, President, Center for the Study of Popular Culture, "The Feminist Assault on the Military"

Mr. Douglas A. Johnson, Executive Director, The Center for Victims of Torture, Testimony to the U.S. House of Representatives Subcommittee on Foreign Operations, Export Financing and Related Programs

Senator Edward M. Kennedy (D-MA), Member, Committee on the Armed Services, United States Senate, Statement for the Record

SMA Richard A. Kidd, USA, Statement for the Record

Dr. Kay Krohne, CDR, USN (Ret.), Statement for the Record

MajGen Charles Krulak, USMC, Director, Personnel Procurement Division, Manpower and Reserve Affairs Department, Headquarters USMC, Statement for the Record

VADM William Lawrence, USN (Ret.), President, Association of Naval Aviation, Statement for the Record

Ms. Mary Lawlor, Pro America Foundation, Statement for the Record

CDR Rosemary Mariner, USN, President, Women's Military Aviation Association, Statement for the Record

CAPT Eugene McDaniel, USN (Ret.), President, The American Defense Institute, Statement for the Record

Mr. Brian Mitchell, former research consultant to the Heritage Foundation, Family Research Council, Concerned Women for America, and Eagle Forum, Statement for the Record

Lt Col Peter W. Moates, USAF, Commander, 15th Airlift Squadron (C-141), Norton AFB, CA, Statement for the Record

Mr. Robert Morrison, Policy Analyst and Editor, Washington Watch, Family Research Council, Statement for the Record

MG John E. Murray, USA (Ret.), "Women, War and Failed Remembrance"

Lt Col William K. Osborn, USAF, Commander, 11th Air Refueling Squadron (KC-135), Altus AFB, OK, Statement for the Record

Mr. W. Hays Parks, Chief, International Law Branch, International and Operational Division, Department of the Army, Office of the Judge Advocate General, "The 1949 Geneva Convention and Women Prisoners of War"

LTG J. H. Binford Peay III, USA, Deputy Chief of Staff for Operations and Plans, Statement for the Record

CPT Connie Reeves, USA, Aviation Officer, "Women as Warriors," "Pregnancy and Army Aviators," and "Dual-Service and Single Parents: What about the Kids?"

Sally Ride, PhD, Astronaut, Statement for the Record

Col John W. Ripley, USMC, Commander, Navy-Marine Corps ROTC Unit, Virginia Military Institute, Statement for the Record

Mrs. Phyllis Schlafly, President, Eagle Forum, Statement for the Record

1st Lt Heather Ann Schofield, USAF, Co-Pilot, Statement for the Record

Capt Katherine Simpson, USAF, Scientific Analyst, Air Force Military Personnel Center, Statement for the Record

Ms. Ellen Smith, Legal Counsel, Concerned Women for America, Statement for the Record

VADM Leighton W. Smith, Jr., USN, Deputy Chief Naval Operations for Plans, Policy, and Operations, Statement for the Record

Maj Wayne G. Stone, USAF, Associate Professor of Organizational Science, Air Force Institute of Technology, Statements for the Record

Mr. Claude Swafford, Member of DACOWITS, Statement for the Record

LTC Carter S. Thomas, USA, Statement for the Record

Rear Admiral J. Steven Tichelman, Royal Netherlands Navy, Netherlands Defense and Naval Attache, Statement before the House Armed Services Committee

Senator Strom Thurmond (R-SC), Member, Committee on the Armed Services, United States Senate, Statement for the Record

Ms. Jill Wine-Banks, Former General Counsel to the Army, Statement for the Record

Senator John Warner, (R-VA), Ranking Minority Member, Committee on the Senate Armed Services, United States Senate, Statement for the Record

Mr. Eldon Yates, Chairman and Founder, Vietnam Veterans Institute, Statement for the Record


The Commission received over 10,000 letters from citizens registering their opinions on the assignment of women to combat positions. These letters were submitted for the record and are on file with the other Commission documents in the National Archives, Record Group 220.

# APPENDIX H

## GLOSSARY

ACCESSION To bring personnel into the military service.

APFT Army Physical Fitness Test

ASD(FM&P) Assistant Secretary of Defense (Force Management & Personnel)

BAQ Basic Allowance for Quarters - Supplemental pay for housing costs for military personnel who do not live in government quarters.

BCT Basic Combat Training

CODIFY To enact legislation based on existing policy.

COMBAT SERVICE SUPPORT The essential logistic functions, activities, and tasks necessary to all elements of an operating force in an area of operations. Combat Service Support includes but is not limited to administrative services, chaplain services, civil affairs, finance, legal service, health services, military police, supply, maintenance, transportation, construction, troop construction, acquisition and disposal of real property, facilities engineering, topographic and geodetic engineering functions, food service, graves registration, laundry, dry cleaning, bath, property disposal, and other logistic services.

COMBAT SERVICE Those elements whose primary missions are to provide combat support to the combat forces and which are a part, or prepared to become a part, of a theater, command, or task force formed for combat operations. Combat service includes, but is not limited to combat communications, intelligence, and engineer functions.

CONUS Continental United States

CLF Combat Logistics Force

DASD (MM&PP) Deputy Assistant Secretary of Defense (Military Manpower & Personnel Policy)

DCPC Direct Combat Probability Coding

DMDC Defense Manpower Data Center

| | |
|---|---|
| DoD | Department of Defense |
| DUAL MILITARY COUPLE | Married servicemembers concurrently serving on Active Duty. |
| FAMILY CARE PLAN | Written plan submitted by a single parent or dual military servicemember to provide for care of dependent, custodial children in the event that the servicemember is deployed. |
| FLAG OFFICER | A term applied to an officer holding the rank of general, lieutenant general, major general, or brigadier general in the US Army, Air Force, or Marine Corps or admiral, vice admiral, rear admiral or commodore in the US Navy or Coast Guard. |
| G-FORCE | A unit of force exerted by gravity on a body at rest and used to indicate the force to which a body is subjected when accelerated. |
| MEPS | Military Entrance Processing Center |
| MEPSCAT | Military Entrance Physical Strength Capacity Test |
| MODIFY | To alter, enlarge, extend, amend, limit or reduce a law or policy |
| MOS | Military Occupational Specialty |
| NPRDC | Navy Personnel Research and Development Center |
| OCONUS | Outside Continental United States (overseas) |
| OSD | Office of the Secretary of Defense |
| POW | Prisoner of War |
| PT | Physical Training |
| REPEAL | The abrogation or annulling of a previously existing law by the enactment of a subsequent statute which declares that the former law shall be revoked. |
| ROTC | Reserve Officer Training Corps |
| RESCIND | The abrogation or annulling of a previously existing policy by the enactment of subsequent policy which declares that the former policy shall be revoked. |

RETAIN    To continue to hold, have, use, or recognize a law or policy.

SEAL    Sea-air-land team - A group specially trained and equipped for conducting paramilitary operations and to train personnel of allied nations in such operations including surveillance and reconnaissance in and from restricted waters, rivers, and coastal areas.

SERE    Survival, Evasion, Resistance, and Escape

SSBN    Ballistic Missile Submarine, Nuclear-powered

SSN    Attack Submarine, Nuclear-powered

TDY    Assignment to a location for a period of less than six months away from home station.

# APPENDIX I

## PANEL ONE BIBLIOGRAPHY

Allen, H. "The Matter-of-Fact Major's War Story." *Washington Post*, 8 August 1992.

Alvarez, Everett, Col Fred Cherry, USAF (Ret.), Col Norman McDaniel, USAF (ret.), MAJ Rhonda Cornum, USA. Testimony before the Commission, 8 June 1992.

"Alvarez - POW." *60 Minutes,* CBS, 26 November 1972.

Amnesty International. "Human Rights Violations, Iraq/Occupied Kuwait Since August 2, 1990." December 1990.

Amnesty International. "Rape and Sexual Abuse." 19 January 1992.

Amnesty International. "Women in the Front Line." December 1990.

Andrade, J. *World Police & Paramilitary Forces.* Stockton Press, 1985.

Associated Press. "Lizhen Is Dead at 83; Chinese Army General." *New York Times*, 25 March 1990.

Associated Press. "Marines Make Combat Drills Coed." *Washington Times*, 12 August 1992.

Associated Press. "Indian Air Force to Allow Women." *CNARS News Highlights*, 2 December 1991.

Associated Press. "Women Enter Military Academy." *European Stars & Stripes*, 5 April 1992.

Associated Press. "Women Flunk Combat Drill." *Ottawa Citizen*, 25 April 1992.

Atwood, D. Deputy Secretary of Defense. Personal Statement. 28 April 1992.

Australian Defense Force. *Employment of Women in the Australian Defense Force (ADF)*. Embassy Position Paper, 3 December 1991.

Australian Defense Force. Embassy Position Paper, 5 June 1992.

Auten, J.  "Relative Firearms Performance of Male and Female Police Officers."
*Law and Order*, September 1989.

Bahme, C. *The Fireman's Law Book.*  Los Angeles:  Bahme, 1952.

Balkin, J.  "Why Policemen Don't Like Policewomen."  *Journal of Police Science and
Administration*,  March 1988.

Barker, A.J. *Prisoners of War.*  New York:  Universe Books, 1975.

Beck, M.  "Women in the Armed Forces."  *Newsweek*, 18 February 1980.

Becraft, Carolyn.  "Appendix - Combat Exclusions."  *WREI,* March 1991.

Becraft, Carolyn.  Testimony before the Commission, 4 May 1992.

Becraft, Carolyn.  "Women in the US Armed Services:  The War in the Persian Gulf."
*WREI,* March 1991.

Becraft, Carolyn.  "Women and the Military:  Bureaucratic Policies and Politics."
*Bureaucrat*, Fall 1989.

Berg, B. *Defeminization of Women in Law Enforcement.*  New York:  AMS Press, 1987.

Bird, J. "Breaking the Barrier."  *Air Force Times*, 4 December 1989.

Bird, J. "Results of Mock Combat Show a Woman Can Succeed."  *Air Force Times*,
4 December 1989.

Boulegue, Jean.  "'Feminization' and the French Military:  An Anthropological Approach."
*Armed Forces and Society* 17, no. 3  (1991):  pp. 343-362.

Bray, L. "A Woman in Uniform."  *New York Times*, 7 January 1990.

British Ministry of Defence. *Information Paper*, 17 July 1992.

Broder, J.  "Aid Law Enforcement Agencies; Guard Units on Front Line in Nation's War on
Drugs." *Los Angeles Times*, 28 May 1989.

Brown, R.  "Memorandum."  *Women Marines in Persian Gulf*,  12 November 1991.

Campbell, D'Ann.  "Combatting the Gender Gulf."  Indiana University.  n.d.

Campbell, D'Ann. "Servicewomen of World War II." *Armed Forces and Society* 16, no. 2 Winter 1990.

Campbell, D'Ann. *Women in Combat*. FL: Defense Equal Opportunity Management Institute, 1991.

Campbell, D'Ann. *Women in Combat: The World War Two Experience in the United States, Great Britain, Germany and the Soviet Union.* Indiana University, 1991.

Canadian Defence Force. "Briefing Guide on Peacekeeping Operations." 28 July 1992.

Canadian Defence Force. *Overview of the Social/Behavioral Science Evaluation of the 1979-1985 Canadian Forces Trial Employment of Servicewomen in Non-Traditional Environments and Roles.* Research Report 86-2.

Canadian Defence Force. DGPCOR/DGPCO. "Canadian Forces Career Management and the Employment of Women." Introduction to briefing for the Commission, 29 July 1992.

Canada Defence Force. "Canadian Persfacts." 30 June 1992.

Canadian Defence Institute. *Women in Military Service Around the Globe*, 31 July 1992.

*Canadian Forces Personnel Newsletter.* July 1987.

"The Canadian Human Rights Act, In the Matter of." S.C. 1976-77.

Carlson, Kelly. Legal Memorandum for Commission Staff, Title VII and 42 USC 2000e-1, 30, July 1992.

Chahal, S. "Physical Fitness and Performance Standards for the Canadian Army." *Canadian Defence Quarterly* (April 1990): pp. 127-135.

Chahal, P. et al. "Physical Fitness and Work Performance Standards: A Proposed Approach." *International Journal of Industrial Ergonomics,* September 1992.

Cheney, Richard, Secretary of Defense. Address to the Federal City Council. 21 April 1992.

Cheney, Richard, Secretary of Defense. News briefing. 26 March 1992.

Cheney, Richard, Secretary of Defense. News conference. 9 November 1989.

Cheney, Richard, Secretary of Defense and General Colin Powell. News briefing. 26 March 1992.

Collier, Ellen. *CRS Issue Brief: Women in the Armed Forces.* Washington: Congressional Research Service, 1992.

Conant, J. "Women in Combat?" *Newsweek,* 11 November 1985.

Concannon, J. F. "Defense Office Report re: Hungary." 29 June 1992.

*Congressional Record - Senate.* Washington, D.C. 9 April 1992.

Conway, J. "Title VII and Competitive Testing." 15 *Hofstra L. Rev.* 299 (1987).

Cooper, Matthew T. LtGen, USMC. Testimony before the Commission, 8 June 1992.

Cornum, Rhonda. MAJ, USA. Testimony before the Commission, 8 June 1992.

Cox, F. "Angel of Bataan." *Soldiers Magazine.* September 1989.

Crabtree, J. "Women of Bravo Battery." *ADA Magazine.* September-October 1991.

Danish Armed Forces. *Policy Information on Women in the Danish Armed Forces.* 1991.

Davis, J. "Perspectives of Policewoman in Texas and Oklahoma." *JPSA* 12, no. 4. 1984.

Deegan, Gene A., MajGen, USMC. Testimony before the Commission, 25 June 1992.

Department of the Army. *Army Regulation 600-13, Army Policy for Assignment of Female Soldiers.* March 1992.

Department of the Army. Memorandum re: Female Cadre, 3 June 1992.

Department of the Army. *Public Opinion on Women in the Military and in Combat.* Report by Naomi Verdugo, 8 May 1992.

Department of the Army. *Women in Combat.* Fort Belvoir, VA, n.d.

DePauw, L. "Women in Combat." *Armed Forces and Society* 7, no. 2 (Winter 1981): pp. 209-226.

Diestenfrey, S. "Women Veterans' Exposure to Combat." *Armed Forces and Society* (Summer 1988): pp. 549-588.

Dillingham, W.E. "The Possibility of American Military Women Becoming POWs: Justification for Combat Exclusion Rules?" *Federal Bar News & Journal,* May 1990.

Donnelly, Elaine. Memorandum to the Presidential Commission on the Assignment of Women in the Armed Forces, 18 June 1992.

Donnelly, Elaine. *Politics and the Pentagon, The Role of Women in the Military.* 5 May 1991.

Dorsey, R. "Assessing Gender Differences in Levels of Cynicism Among Police Officers." *American Journal of Police*, Spring 1986.

Dunney, R. "Women in Combat Closer than You Think." *US News and World Report,* 3 March 1980.

Dussault, Robert G. Testimony before the Commission, 8 June 1992.

Elshtain, J. *Women and War.* New York: Basic Books, Inc., 1987.

*Encyclopedia of the American Constitution,* S.v. "State of War," "Police Action," and "Declaration of War," by J. Bishop, and "War Powers," by C. Lofgren, 1986.

Epstein, S. "Women in the Firehouse, Second Circuit Upholds Gender Biased Firefighters Exam." 54 *Brooklyn L. Rev.* 511 (1988).

Federal Bureau of Investigation. *Police Woman.* Rockville, MD: FBI Academy, 1982.

Firestone, J. "Sexist Ideology and the Evaluation Criteria Used to Assess Women's Integration into the Army." *Population and Research Review* 3, 1984.

Firestone, J. "Occupational Segregation: Comparing the Civilian and Military Work Force." *Armed Forces and Society*, Spring 1992.

Firestone, J. "Sex-Appropriate Roles: Comparing the Attitudes of Civilian and Military Youth." *Population and Research Review* 6, 1987.

"Flora Sandes - Military Maid." *History Today,* March 1989.

Foote, Evelyn, BG, USA. Testimony before the Commission, 25 June 1992.

France. Etat-Major des Armees. *Information Paper*, 1989.

Frank, M. *Army and Navy Nurses Held As POWs During WWII.* Office of the Assistant Secretary of Defense, 1985.

Fry, L. "Preliminary Examination of the Factors Related to Turnover of Women in Law Enforcement." *JPSA,* June 1983.

Gal, R. *A Portrait of the Israeli Soldier.* Contributions in Military Studies, No 52. New York: Greenwood Press, n.d.

Garrett, R. . *POW.* London: David & Charles, 1981.

Garrison, C. "Utilization of Police Women." *The Police Chief,* September 1988.

*Geneva Convention Relative to the Treatment of Prisoners of War of August 12, 1949.*

Gilder, G. "The Case Against Women in Combat." *NY Times Magazine*, 28 January 1979.

"Give Message on Behavior to Military." *Morning Call,* Allentown, PA, 30 June 1992.

Glosson, Buster, Lt Gen, USAF. Testimony before the Commission, 8 June 1992.

Goldman, N. *Utilization of Women in Combat: The Case of Israel.* [DAHC19-78-c-0011], Appendix G, n.d.

Gomez, R. V. "American Women's Participation in the Military." 8 July 1992.

Gradstein, L. "In Israel, It's a Man's Army." *Chicago Tribune,* 23 June 1991.

Graham, John D., Col, USAF. Testimony before the Commission, 8 June 1992.

Green, Brian. "Women in Combat." *Air Force Magazine,* June 1990.

Greene, P. "Women in the US Armed Forces." Address to the Women's Research and Education Institute International Conference on Women in the Military, Washington, DC, 30 April 1992.

Greisse, A. and R. Stites. "Russian And Soviet Women in War and Peace." Paper given at Inter-University Seminar on Armed Forces and Society National Conference, 23-25 October 1980.

Gross, J. "Federal War on Drug Trafficking, Women are Playing Greater Role." *New York Times*, 16 February 1986.

"Gulf Crisis: Coalition Forces Order of Battle." *The Military Balance 1991-1992*. Brassey's, 1991.

Heller, C. *Economy of Force.* Strategic Studies Institute, 1992.

H.F.S. "Soviet Women in Uniform." *Air Force Magazine*, March 1976.

H.F.S. "Women in the Soviet Armed Forces." *Air Force Magazine*, March 1988.

Hackworth, David H. "Should Women Fight to Kill?" *Newsweek,* 5 August 1991.

Hale, D. *Women in Policing.* Cincinnati: Anderson, 1992.

Harper, J. "Swiss Conference on Women in Armed Forces." 15-17 October 1990.

Hasenauer, H. "Women at West Point." *Soldiers*, July 1991.

Hawkins, G. MAJ, USA. Report on Training Changes at West Point, 22 September 1992.

Hayden, H. T. *Shadow War.* Vista, CA: Pacific Aero Press, 1992.

Hazard, Roberta L., RADM, USN. Testimony to the Commission, 26 June 1992.

Hazleton, L. *Israeli Women: The Reality Behind the Myths.* New York: Simon and Schuster, 1977.

Hill, J. "The Women and the Military Project in the Federal Republic of Germany." *Minerva* (Fall/Winter 1989): pp. 5-56.

Hines, Charles A., MG, USA. Testimony before the Commission, 8 June 1992.

Holguin, R. "Women Officers Are Still a Rarity." *Los Angeles Times*, 10 May 1987.

Holm, J. *Women in the Military.* Presidio Press, 1982.

Holm, J. "Women in the US Military: The Next Phase." Address to the Women's Research and Education Institute, 30 April 1992.

Hooker, R.  "Affirmative Action and Combat Exclusion:  Gender Roles in the US Army."  *Parameters*, December 1989.

Horowitz, David.  Testimony before the Commission, 6 August 1992.

Hubbell, J.  *POW.*  Reader's Digest Press, 1976.

Hyde, J. C.  "Gender Gap Narrows in Allied Services But Women Still Fight for Combat Roles."  *Armed Forces Journal*, June 1989.

Inman, T.  "Role of Males and Male Myths Win a Round."  *Greenville South Carolina News*, 23 June 1991.

"An Iraqi Prison Diary."  *The Economist*, 4 May 1991.

Isherwood, J.  "Denmark, in Historic First, Opens Combat Jobs to Women."  *Armed Forces Journal International*, (July 1988):  pp. 25.

Israel Defense Force.  *IDF Spokesman:  Chen Translates Charm.*  Publication No. 14/89, 1989.

Israel Defense Force.  *IDF Spokesman:  Chen - Women's Corps*, 27 February 1980.

Israel Defense Force.  *The Israeli Defense Forces:  A People's Army.*  Report by L. William.  Tel Aviv:  Ministry of Defense Publishing House.  n.d.

Jacobs, P.  "How Female Police Officers Cope with Traditionally Male Positions."  *Sociology and Social Research*, October 1987.

Janus, S.  "Women in Police Work."  *Police Studies,* Fall 1988.

"Japanese to Allow Women Officers."  *Jane's Defence Weekly,* 26 October 1991.

Jessen, John B., Maj, USAF.  Testimony before the Commission, June 8, 1992.

Johnson, L.  "Job Strain Among Police Officers."  *Police Studies,* Spring 1991.

Kallsch, B and P. Kallsch.  "Nurses Under Fire:  The World War II Experience of Nurses on Bataan and Corregidor."  *Nursing Research,* November-December 1976.

Kampeas, R.  "Combat Ready."  *The Jerusalem Post,* 4 October 1991.

Keijsers, Elly. *Facts and Figures on the Integration of Women in the Royal Netherlands Air Force*, 1992.

King, Larry. "Does Our POW Training Work?" *Larry King Live*. CNN, 26 January 1991.

King, Larry. "Returned POW Navy LT Robert Wetzel." *Larry King Live*. CNN, 26 April 1991.

Kitfield, J. "Total Force." *Government Executive*, March 1991.

Krulak, Charles, MajGen, USMC. Testimony before the Commission, 25 June 1992.

Laffin, J. *The Anatomy of Captivity*. London: Abelard-Schuman, 1968.

Lamerson, C. D. "Integration of Women in the Canadian Forces." n.d.

Lancaster, J. "24 Women Assaulted on Gulf Duty." *Washington Post*, 21 July 1992.

Landers, R. "Should Women be Allowed Into Combat?" *Congressional Quarterly*, 13 October 1989.

Lawrence, W. Testimony before the Commission, 25 June 1992.

Lazar, N. *Aspects of the Service of Women Soldiers in the Israeli Defense Force*, n.d.

Lee, S. *Update 1992, CF Physical Fitness Programs Standards and Evaluation*, 15 June 1992.

Levie, H. "The Employment of POWs." *American Journal of International Law* 57, n.d.

Levie, H. "International Law Aspects of Repatriation of Prisoners of War During Hostilities: A Reply." *American Journal of International Law* 67, n.d.

Levie, H. "Maltreatment of Prisoners of War in Vietnam." *Boston University Law Review*, 1968.

Levie, H. "Prisoners of War and the Protecting Power." *American Journal of International Law* 55, n.d.

Levie, H. "Penal Sanctions for Maltreatment POWs." *American Journal of International Law* 56, n.d.

Levie, H. Vol. 59 and 60, *Naval War College, International Law Studies.* Newport: Naval War College Press, 1979.

Levin, S. "Women and Violence: Reflections on Ending The Combat Exclusion." *New England Law Review,* Spring 1992.

Levin, Michael. *"Women as Soldiers the Record so Far."* (Summer 1984): pp. 31-44.

Lind, William S. Testimony before the Commission, 25 June 1992.

Lord, L. "Comparison of Male and Female Peace Officers' Stereotypic Perceptions." *Journal of Police Science Administration,* June 1986.

Love, K. "Self-Efficacy." *Police Studies,* Summer 1988.

Luddow, R. "$500,000 Ad Campaign Set to Sell Women on Combat." *Southam News,* 27 October 1987.

Lunneborg, P. *Women Police Officers.* Springfield, IL: Thomas, 1989.

Maginnis, Robert L. "The Future of Women in the Army." *Military Life Supplement,* (10 July 1992): pp. 21-27.

Mann, J. "Who's Not Measuring Up?" *Washington Post,* 29 July 1992.

Manning, M. "Angels of Mercy and Life Amid Scenes of Conflict and Death: The Combat Experience and Imprisonment of American Military Nurses in the Philippines 1941-1945." 1 April 1985.

Mariner, Rosemary Bryant, CDR, USN. "A Soldier is a Soldier." National War College Essay. 1992.

Martin, S. *Female Police Officers on the Move: A Status Report.* Prospect Heights: Waveland Press, 1989.

Martin, D. "Status of Women in Law Enforcement." *Law Enforcement Technology,* February 1991.

Martin, S. *On the Move, Status of Women in Policing.* New York: Ford Foundation, 1990.

Maurmann, Steve, Maj, USAF. Testimony before the Commission, 26 March 1992.

Maze, R. "Combat Jobs for Women Closer." *Air Force Times*, 20 May 1991.

Maze, R. "Women in Combat: Military Witnesses Reflect Split." *Air Force Times*, 1 July 1991.

McCarthy, L. "Gender Double Standards." *Marine Corps Gazette*, October 1991.

McDaniel, Norman A., Col, USAF. Testimony before the Commission, 25 June 1992.

McKenzie, D. "Use of Women in the Israeli Military." 29 December 1983.

"Medical Aspects of Torture." *Danish Medical Bulletin,* January 1990.

Meid, P. "Marine Corps Women's Reserve in World War II." rev. ed., 1968.

"The Military Service of Women in the Kibbutz." In *Women in the Kibbutz.* New York: Harcourt Brace Jovanovich, 1975.

Mishkin, B. "Female Police in the US." *Police Journal,* January-March 1981.

*Mixed-Gender Relationships.* CFAO 19-38, 19 February 1988.

Moore, B. "African-American Women in the U.S. Military." *Armed Forces and Society,* 1991.

Moore, M. "Canada's Leap to Equality in Combat." *Washington Post,* 26 September 1991.

Morden, B. *The Women's Army Corps, 1945-19 78.* Washington, DC: Government Printing Office, 1989.

Nalty, B. *Strength for the Fight.* NY: Freedom Press, 1989.

National Defense Headquarters. *Military Family Support Program,* 1991.

New Zealand Defence Council. *The Employment of Women in the Armed Forces: Implementation Instruction,* 25 November 1981.

Nighswander, M. "Captivity in Iraq: Airmen Faced Beatings, 'Talkman." *Detroit News Wire Services,* 15 March 1991.

North Atlantic Treaty Organization. *1991 Conference of the Committee on Women in the NATO Forces,* Brussels, Memorandum, 1 August 1991.

North Atlantic Treaty Organization. *1991 Conference of the Committee on Women in the NATO Forces,* Brussels, 18-21 June 1991.

North Atlantic Treaty Organization. *1991 Women in NATO Report, "Annex J."* Brussels, 1991.

North Atlantic Treaty Organization. *National Report From Denmark on the Meeting of the Committee on Women in The NATO Forces,* London, 8-22 May 1991.

North Atlantic Treaty Organization. "Policies and Statistics on Women in the NATO Forces, Memorandum." Brussels, 13 May 1992.

North Atlantic Treaty Organization. "Statistics on the Royal Danish Navy and Air Force." *Women in the NATO Forces.* Brussels, 1991.

North Atlantic Treaty Organization. Advisory Group for Aeronautical Research and Development. AGARD Symposium on Recruiting, Selection, Training and Military Operations of Female Aircrew, Tours, France, 4-5 April 90. AGARD-CP-491, AD-A229642. Brussels. n.d.

Norton, D. "It's Time." *Proceedings.* February 1992.

Norway, Royal Ministry of Defence. *Equal Status Between Men and Women in the Armed Forces.* Oslo, 1988.

Norway, Royal Ministry of Defence. *Programme of Action to Promote Equal Status Between the Sexes in the Armed Forces, 1986-1990.* Oslo, 1987.

OD Systems. *The Status of Women in Federal Law Enforcement: Survey Analysis,* 24 July 1989.

Oelke, M. *Women in Combat Roles Past and Future.* Air War College, Report No. AU-AWC-88-188, 1988.

P.L. 102-25, 1991.

P.L. 102-90, 1991.

Palmer, E. "Senate Debates Rights, Role of Women Warriors." *Congressional Quarterly*, 22 June 1991.

Parks, Hays, Esq. Testimony before the Commission, 8 June 1992.

Peay, Binford, LTG, USA. Testimony before the Commission, 8 June 1992.

*Personal Harassment.* CFAO 19-39. 9 December 1988.

Pictet, J. "Commentary, Geneva Convention Relative to the Treatment of POWs." ICRC, 1960.

Pinch, F. "Combat Related Employment of Women." February 1992.

Pinch, F. *Social and Behavioral Science Considerations Regarding Women's Employment in the Canadian Forces.* February 1987.

Poole, E. "Factors Affecting the Decision to Remain in Policing." *J. Police Science and Administration*, March 1988.

Powell, Colin. "The Base Force: A Total Force." 25 September 1991.

Powell, Colin. "Testimony of General Colin L. Powell, Chairman, JCS on the FY93 Defense Budget (Base Force Concept)." *National Military Strategy*. 1992.

Rahe, R. *Good Morning America.* ABC, 12 March 1991.

Rapport, Senat General. *La feminisation dans les armees: des non-dits preoccupants,* 19 November 1991.

Remington, P. *Policing the Occupation and the Introduction of Female Officers.* Lanham, MD: University Press, 1981.

"Reminiscences of a Nurse POW." *Navy Medicine*, May-June 1992.

*Report to Congress on Firefighter Safety and Health.* Federal Emergency Management Agency (FEMA), September 1980.

Reuters. "Sri Lankan Women Fight for Guerillas." *Los Angeles Times*, 10 November 1991.

Ripley, John W., Col, USN. Testimony before the Commission, June 26, 1992.

Roessner, B. "Military Women Under Siege." *Daily Review,* Hayward, CA, 7 July 1992.

Rogers, R. "A Proposal for Combatting Sexual Harrassment in the Military: Amendment of Title VII." 1990.

Royal British Navy. "Briefing Guide: Mixed Gender Service: Commander's Considerations." June 1992.

Royal British Navy. "Mixed Gender Service: Chiefs and Petty Officers." July 1992.

Royal British Navy. "Mixed Gender Service Junior Enlisted." July 1992.

Royal British Navy. "Mixed Gender Service Junior Officers, Lesson Plans." July 1992.

Royal British Navy. *Report of a Study into the Employment of Women's Royal Naval Service (WRNS) Personnel in the Royal Navy.* March 1989.

Royal British Navy. *WRNS Sea Service - Situation Report,* 13 December 1990.

Royal Danish Embassy. Response to Commission Inquiries. 12 June 1992.

Royal Netherlands Army. "Briefing Guide: Women in the RNLA." 18 September 1992.

Royal Netherlands Navy. "Briefing Guide: Lecture and Appendices on the Functioning of Women in Combat Roles in the Royal Netherlands Navy." 18 September 1992.

Scheff, Z. *A History of the Israeli Army (1870-1974).* San Francisco: Straight Arrow Books, 1974.

Segal, D. *The Impact of Gender Integration on the Cohesion, Morale, and Combat Effectiveness of Military Units.* University of MD, 1986.

Segal, D. and H. W. Sinaiko. *Life in the Rank and File.* McLean, VA: Pergamon-Brassey's, 1986.

Segal, M. "The Argument for Female Combatants." In *Female Soldiers: Combatants or Non-Combatants.* Westport, 1982.

Seigle, G. "Some May Never Get the Message." *Navy Times,* 3 August 1992.

Seigle, G. "Women Present Case for Combat." *Army Times,* 6 July 1992.

Seigle, G. "Women-in-Combat Supporters." *Air Force Times*, 16 July 1992.

Shafritz, J. et al. *The Facts on File Dictionary of Military Science.* New York, 1989.

Smith, D. "Introspective Intellectual Freewheeling Woman Police Captain 1 in 64." *Los Angeles Times*, 16 March 1986.

Smith, Jr., Leighton W., VADM, USN. Testimony before the Commission, 8 June 1992.

Smith, Ellen. Testimony before the Commission, 25 June 1992.

Smolowe, J. "The UN Marches In." *Time*, 23 March 1992.

Stanley, S. et al. "Military Women in NATO: An Update." *Armed Forces and Society* 14, no. 4, Summer 1988.

Stevens, P. "At Issue: Women in Combat." *Air Force Times*, 27 November 1974.

Stremlow, M. *A History of the Women Marines.* Washington, DC: History and Museums Division Headquarters, US Marine Corps, 1986.

Summary Report on Fact-Finding Trip to Ottawa, Canada (Canadian Ministry of Defence), 29-30 July 1992.

Summary Report on Fact-Finding Trips to John F. Kennedy School of Goverment, Harvard University (Russian General Officers), The Hague, The Netherlands (Ministry of Defence), Copenhagen, Denmark (U.S. Embassy), London, England (U.S. Embassy), Tel Aviv, Israel (Ministry of Defence and military installations.) 14-27 September 1992.

Thompson, J. "Women in Combat: The Battlefield Experience." *CISS Datalink*, July 1985.

"Those Magnificent Women in their Flying Machines." *Soviet Life,* 5 May 1990.

Timmins, W. "Attracting and Retaining Females in Law Enforcement." *Int. J. Offender Therapy and Comparative Criminology*, December 1989.

Towell, Pat and Elizabeth A. Palmer. "Women of War." *Congressional Quarterly*, 11 May 1991.

Truby, D. *Women At War: A Deadly Species.* Boulder: Paladin Press, 1977.

Tuohy, William. "Role of Women in the Military Being Reviewed." *Los Angeles Times*, 13 August 1991.

United Nations. Memorandum by J. Hutter, 24 August 1992.

United Nations. Security Council. *Prisoners of War in Iran and Iraq*, 22 February 1985.

U.S. Air Force. *Air Force Regulation 35-60, Combat Exclusions for Women*, 18 August 1989.

U.S. Central Intelligence Agency. *CIA Mission Statement*, 1992.

U.S. Coast Guard. *Mission and Purpose*, 1992.

U.S. Code. General Index, T-Z , 1988.

U.S. Defense Attache. *Information on Women in the WRNS*, n.d.

U.S. Department of Defense. *Conduct of the Persian Gulf War: Final Report to Congress. Appendix R.*, April 1992.

U.S. Department of Defense. *Dictionary of Military and Associated Terms.* 1 December 1989.

U.S. Department of Defense. *Directive 1300.7: Training and Education Measures Necessary to Support the Code of Conduct*, 23 December 1988.

U.S. Department of Defense. *Executive Summary, Joint Low-Intensity Conflict Project*, 1 August 1986.

U.S. Department of Defense. *Fact Sheet: Women in the Military Services, WWI to Present.* n.d.

U.S. Department of Defense. "The Forgotten POW: Second LT Reba Z. Whittle, AN." USAWC Military Studies Program Paper, 1 February 1990.

U.S. Department of Defense. Information Memorandum on Visit of Colonel Amiro Dotan, Chief of the Women's Corps, January 1984.

U.S. Department of Defense. Memorandum summary of DIA study on women in the Soviet forces. 2 November 1978.

U.S. Department of Defense. *Military Women in Other Countries*. Report by Steve Maurmann, March 1992.

U.S. Department of Defense. *Public Affairs Guidance in Deployment of Women in Conjunction with Operation Desert Shield*. Memorandum for the Record, 5720, PA. n.d.

U.S. Department of Defense. *Report of Defense Review Committee for the Code of Conduct*, 1976.

U.S. Department of Defense. *Report: Task Force on Women in the Military*, January 1988.

U.S. Department of Defense. Special briefing for the Commission on drug enforcement and FISC. 9 March 1990.

U.S. Department of Defense. *Utilization of American Military Women in Operations Desert Shield and Desert Storm."* 2 August 1990 - 11 April 1991.

U.S. Department of Defense. "Women in the Armed Forces." 26 March 1992.

U.S. Department of Defense. *Women in the Military*. October 1981.

U.S. Department of Defense. Joint SERE Command. "Background Reading List re: POWs." Summer 1992.

U.S. Department of Defense. Slides and testimony before the Commission, 8 June 1992.

U.S. Department of Defense. Maritime Command. Briefing to the Commission, July 1992.

U.S. Department of Transportation. *Women in the Coast Guard Study*. DOT Publications 5312.1 and 5312.17, 1990.

U.S. Federal Bureau of Investigation. Press Office. *FBI Mission Statement,* n.d.

U.S. Joint Chiefs of Staff. *Doctrine for Joint Operations and Low Intensity Conflict,* January 1990.

U.S. Joint Chiefs of Staff. *Doctrine for Joint Special Operations,* January 1990.

U.S. Marine Corps. *Marine Corps Order 1300.8: Marine Corps Assignment Policy*, 12 May 1988.

U.S. Marine Corps. *MCO 1300.8P: Women Marines Classification, Assignment, and Deployment Policy,* 12 August 1988.

U.S. Marine Corps. "Potential Force Reduction Impacts on Women in the Military." February 1992.

U.S. Marine Corps. Division of Public Affairs. *Women Marines in the 1980's.* October 1986.

U.S. Marine Corps. History and Museums Division. *75 Years of Marine Corps Aviation -- A Tribute.* 1986.

U.S. Marine Corps. *Women Marines in World War I.* Washington, D.C., 10 June 1974.

U.S. Naval Academy. Women Midshipmen Study Group. *The Assimilation of Women in the Brigade of Midshipmen.* Report to the Superintendent, 1990.

U.S. Navy. *Executive Summary of the US Navy, WWII to the Present.* OP-01W, 1992.

U.S. Navy. *Highlights of History and Progress of Women in the Navy.* OP-01W, 1992.

U.S. Navy. *SENAV 1300.12A: Assignment of Women Members in the Department of the Navy.* 20 February 1989.

U.S. PAO. *Casualties: Operation Desert Shield/Storm/Provide Comfort.* January 1992.

U.S. Congress. Senate. Committee on Armed Services. Statement of R. Barrow, June 1991.

U.S. Congress. Senate. Committee on Armed Services. Testimony of Becky Constantino, Chair of DACOWITS, 18 June 1991.

U.S. Congress. Senate. Committee on Armed Services. Testimony of B. Holdener, n.d.

U.S. Congress. Senate. Committee on Armed Services. Testimony of Shirley Sagawa from the National Women's Law Center, 18 June 1991.

U.S. Congress. Senate. Subcommittee on Manpower and Personnel. *Hearing on the Utilization of Women in the Military,* 18 June 1991.

U.S. Congress. Senate. Committee on Budget. Testimony of Defense Secretary Richard Cheney, 3 February 1992.

"Utilization of Women in Combat." Technical Report. Alexandria, VA: DTIC, 1982.

Van Creveld, Martin. *Technology and War.* New York: Free Press, 1989.

Van Creveld, Martin. Testimony before the Commission, 26 June 1992.

Vandernuck, G. "Women in Combat: Good Idea, Bad Practice." *Marine Corps Gazette,* October 1991.

Vega, M. "Female Police Officers as Viewed by their Male Counterparts." *Police Studies,* Spring 1982.

Walker, Keith. *A Piece of My Heart,* 1985.

Warner, G. "Rape in Military: Vexing Problem, but Difficult to Measure." *The Orange County Register,* 11 July 1992.

*WAVES Newsletter,* May 1946.

Webb, J. "Women in Combat Information Paper." 13 June 1991.

Webster, A. "Paradigms of the Contemporary American Soldier and Women in the Military." *Strategic Review,* Summer 1991.

Weeisheit, R. "Women in the State Police: Concerns of Male and Female Officers." *Journal of Police Science and Administration,* June 1987.

West, J. "Pfingston: Women Help Readiness." n.d.

Wexler, J. *Role Styles of Women Police Officers.* Sacramento: Western Psychological Association, 1982.

Wexler, J. "Considerations in the Training and Development of Women Sergeants." *JPSA* 13, no. 2, 1985.

Wild, W. R. "Integration of Women in Air Force Operational Occupations and Roles." July 1992.

Williams, D. "To the Angels: US Women in Military Service." n.d.

Witham, D. "Environmental Scanning Pays Off." *Police Chief,* March 1991.

"Women in Combat." *Dallas Morning News,* 3 August 1992.

*Women in the Coast Guard Newsletter.* Fall, 1991; Spring, Winter 1992.

"Women in the Israel Defense Force." GE3-257-1992, August 1992.

"Women in the Soviet Armed Forces." DIA, DDI-110-109-76, 1976.

"Women in Uniform." IDF Journal, Volume 21, n.d.

"Women to be Fighter Pilots." *Jane's Defence Weekly,* 14 December 1991.

"The Women's Army Corps in World War II." *Profile of the New Army,* n.d.

"WRNS Sea Service - Situation Report." British Ministry of Defence, 13 December 1990.

"Xpres Evaluation." Briefing to Commission from Canadian Trip, 29 July 1992.

Zittan, B. "Reports on Women in Combat Positions." 27 July 1992.

Zurcher, Louis, et al. *Supplementary Military Forces.* London: Sage Publications, 1978.

# PANEL TWO BIBLIOGRAPHY

"Attitudes Regarding the Assignment of Women in the Armed Forces: The Public Perspective." The Roper Organization, Inc., August, 1992.

"Attitudes Regarding the Assignment of Women in the Armed Forces: The Military Perspective." The Roper Organization, Inc., September, 1992.

Avellini, B. A., E. Kamon, and J.T. Krajewski. Physiologic Responses of Physically Fit Men and Women to Acclimation to Humid Heat. *Journal of Applied Physiology.* 49 (1980): pp. 254- 26.

Binkin, M. Testimony before the Commission, 4 May 1992.

Bird, Anne Marie. "Convergent and Incremental Effects of Cohesion on Attributions for Self and Team." *Journal of Sport Psychology* 2 (1980): pp. 181-193.

Boff, K. K. Testimony before the Commission, 14-15 September 1992.

Brindle, Eugene, LtCol, USMC, LtCol J.D. Engstrom, USMC, LtCol J.W. Hodges, USMC, Kim Weirick. Testimony before the Commission, 24 June 1992.

Brooks, G.A. and T.D. Fahey. *Exercise Physiology: Human Bioenergetics and Its Applications.* 1984.

California Commission on Peace Officer Standards and Training. *Recruitment and Retention of California's Female Police Officers: A 21st Century Challenge.* Sacramento, CA, 1990.

Calkins, R.B. *ACES II Ejection Seat Small Occupant Study.* McDonnell Douglas Corporation, 1987.

Cordner, Gary W. and Donna C. Hale. *What Works in Policing: Operations and Administration Examined* (1992): pp. 125-142.

Crisman, R. Testimony before the Commission, 14-15 September 1992.

DASD(MM&PP). Air Force Response to Questions 8, 12 from 4-6 April 1992.

DASD(MM&PP). Air Force Response to Question 9 from 4-6 May 1992.

DASD(MM&PP). Air Force Response to Questions 20, 23 from 24-27 June 1992.

DASD(MM&PP). Air Force Response to Question 3, 4, 10 from 6-7 July 1992.

DASD(MM&PP). Air Force Response to Questions 3, 6, 8 from 13-15 July 1992.

DASD(MM&PP). Air Force Response to Question 29 from 31 July 1992.

DASD(MM&PP). Air Force Response to Question 29 from 3 August 1992.

DASD(MM&PP). Air Force Response to Questions 10, 15 from 27-29 August 1992.

DASD(MM&PP). Air Force Response to Questions 131, 132, 133, 134, 135 from 10-12 September 1992.

DASD(MM&PP). Army Response to Questions 8, 12 from 4-6 April 1992.

DASD(MM&PP). Army Response to Question 7 from 13-15 July 1992.

DASD(MM&PP). Army Response to Question 29 from 31 July 1992.

DASD(MM&PP). Army Response to Question 29 from 3 August 1992.

DASD(MM&PP). Army Response to Questions 132, 133, 134, 136 from 10-12 September 1992.

DASD(MM&PP). Coast Guard Response to Question 10 from 27-29 August 1992.

DASD(MM&PP). Navy Response to Questions 7, 8, 37 from 4-6 April 1992.

DASD(MM&PP). Navy Response to Questions 7, 8, 13 from 4-6 May 1992.

DASD(MM&PP). Navy Response to Questions 5, 10, 19, 20, 23 from 24-27 June 1992.

DASD(MM&PP). Navy Response to Questions 3, 6, 7, 8 from 13-15 July 1992.

DASD(MM&PP). Navy Response to Questions 13, 17, 24, 25, 29 from 31 July 1992.

DASD(MM&PP). Navy Response to Questions 13, 17, 24, 25, 29 from 3 August 1992.

DASD(MM&PP). Navy Response to Commission Memo from 19 August 1992.

DASD(MM&PP). Navy Response to Questions 10, 13 from 27-29 August 1992.

DASD(MM&PP). Navy Response to Questions 132, 134 from 10-12 September 1992.

DASD(MM&PP). Marine Corps Response to Questions 8, 12 from 4-6 April 1992.

DASD(MM&PP). Marine Corps Response to Question 11 from 24-27 June 1992.

DASD(MM&PP). Marine Corps Response to Question 6 from 13-15 July 1992.

DASD(MM&PP). Marine Corps Response to Question 29 from 31 July 1992.

DASD(MM&PP). Marine Corps Response to Question 29 from 3 August 1992.

DASD(MM&PP). Marine Response to Question 7 from 27-29 August 1992.

DASD(MM&PP). Marine Response to Questions 132, 133, 134, 135 138 from 10-12 September 1992.

DASD(MM&PP). Military Academy Response to Question 135 from 10-12 September 1992.

DASD(MM&PP). Services Response to Questions 6, 7, 25 from 27-29 August 1992.

Davis, P. Testimony before the Commission, 7 August 1992.

Deutermann, S. W. "A Feasibility Study of the Assignment of Women to DD-963 (Spruance) Class Destroyers." Ph.D, Naval Postgraduate School, Monterey, CA, 1984.

Devilbiss, Dr. M.C. "Gender Integration and Unit Performance: A Study of GI Jo." *Armed Forces & Society* 11, No. 4, Summer 1985.

Devilbiss, Dr. M.C. Testimony before the Commission, 9 June 1992.

Devine, Troy, Capt, USAF. Testimony before the Commission, 12 September 1992.

Donnelly, Elaine. Personal Statement, 2 October 1992.

Dorn, Dr. Edwin. "Who Defends America? Race, Sex, and Class in the Armed Forces." *Joint Center for Political Studies Press,* 1989.

Draude, Thomas V., BGen (USMC). Personal Statement, 2 October 1992.

Drinkwater, B. L., L. J. Folinsbee, J. F. Bedi, S.A. Plowman, A. B. Loucks, and S. M. Horvath. "Responses of Women Mountaineers to Maximal Exercise during Hypoxia." *Aviatiation Space and Environmental Medicine* (1979): pp. 657-662.

Drinkwater, B.L. "Women and Exercise." *Physiological Aspects in Exercise and Sport Science Reviews* (1984): pp. 21-51.

Driscoll, LtCol, USMC. Testimony before the Commission, 6 August 1992.

Etzioni, Amitai. *A Comparative Analysis of Complex Organizations.* New York: Free Press, 1975.

Fleck, S. J. *Designing Resistance Training Programs.* Champaign, IL: Human Kinetics Books, 1987.

Frye, A. J., and E. Kamon. "Responses to Dry and Wet Heat of Men and Women with Similar Aerobic Capacities." *Journal of Applied Physiology* (1981): pp. 65-70.

Gal, Reuven. *A Portrait of the Israeli Soldier.* Westport, CT: Greenwood Press, 1986.

General Dynamics. Testimony before the Commission, 26 August 1992.

Gillingham, K. K., C. M. Schade, W. G. Jackson, and L. C. Gilstrap. "Women's G Tolerance." *Aviation, Space, and Environmental Medicine* (1986): pp. 745-53.

Gordon, George, Paul Bierly, Laurie Davison, Nancy DiTmaso. *Recommendations Related to the Culture and Climate Assessment of the U.S. Coast Guard Academy.* Princeton, NJ: Princeton Economic Research, 1992.

Gregor, W. J. Testimony before the Commission, 12 September 1992.

Gutek, Barbara, and B. Morash. "Sex Ratios, Sex-Role Supervisors and Sexual Harassment of Women at Work." *Journal of Social Issues* 38 (1982): pp. 55-74.

Gutek, Barbara. *Sex and the Workplace.* San Francisco, CA: Jossey-Bass, Inc., 1985.

Harris, C.W., J. L. Shields, and J.P. Hannon. "Acute Mountain Sickness in Females." *Aerospace Medicine.* 37 (1996): pp. 1163-1167.

Harris, L. J. "Sex Differences in Spatial Ability: Possible Environmental, Genetic, and Neurological Factors." In Kinsbourne, M. (Ed.). *Asymmetrical Function of the Brain.* Cambridge: Cambridge University Press, 1978.

I-24

Henderson, Dr. William Darryl. "Can-Do NCOs-With Clout Help Cohesion Problem." *Army*, March 1992.

Henderson, Dr. William Darryl. *The Hollow Army: How the U.S. Army is Oversold and Undermanned.* Greenwood Press, 1990.

Henderson, Dr. William Darryl. Testimony before the Commission, 26 June 1992.

Henderson, Dr. William Darryl. *Cohesion: The Human Element.* National Defense University Press, 1985.

Henderson, Dr. William Darryl. Personal Statement, 2 October 1992.

Hicks, R. J. "Female Aircrew: The Canadian Experience." Paper Presented at AGARD Symposium on Recruiting Selection, Training and Military Operations of Female Aircrew. Tours, France. 4-5 April 1990.

Holly, Col, USMC. Testimony before the Commission, 28 August 1992.

Hosler, W. W. and J. R. Morrow. "Arm and Leg Strength Compared Between Young Women and Men After Allowing for Differences in Body Size and Composition." *Ergonomics* (1982): pp. 309-31.

Hulin, Terry, COL, USA and COL M. McKean, USA. Testimony before the Commission, 24 June 1992.

Hyde, James C. "Gender Gap Narrows in Allied Services, but Women Still Fight for Combat Roles." *Armed Forces Journal International,* June 1989.

Hyde, J.S., E.R. Geiringer, and W.M. Yen. "On the Empirical Relation Between Spatial Ability and Sex Differences in other Aspects of Cognitive Performance." *Multivariate Behavioral Research* (1975): pp. 289-309.

Institute for Ergonomics Research. *Establishing Physical Criteria For Assigning Personnel to Air Force Jobs.* Texas Tech University, 1982.

Institute of Human Performance. *Physical Performance Requirements of U.S. Marines Operating in a High Altitude Cold Weather Environment.* Fairfax, VA, 1982.

Institute of Human Performance. *Physical Performance Requirements of U.S. Marines Operating in Jungle Operations.* Fairfax, VA, 1983.

Institute of Human Performance. *Physical Performance Requirements of U.S. Marines During Amphibious Operations.* Fairfax, VA, 1983.

Institute of Human Performance. *Physical Performance Tasks Required of U.S. Marines Operating in a Desert Environment.* Fairfax, VA, 1981.

Isherwood, Julian. "Denmark, in Historic First, Opens Combat Jobs to Women." *Armed Forces Journal International,* July 1988.

Jacobs, Dr. Owen. Testimony before the Commission, 5 May 1992.

Johns, Dr. John. *Cohesion in the US Military.* Washington, DC: National Defense University Press, 1984.

Johnson, C. B., Maj, USMC. *1992 Survey of Retired Flag and General Officers,* Washington, DC, 1992.

Kanter, Rosabeth Moss. *Men and Women of the Corporation.* New York: Basic Books, 1977.

Kowal, D. Testimony before the Commission, 6 April 1992.

Kramar, P. O., B. L. Drinkwater, L. J. Folinsbee, and J. F. Bedi. "Ocular Function and Incidence of Acute Mountain Sickness in Women at High Altitude." *Aviation Space Environmental Medicine* (1983): pp. 116-120.

KRUG Life Sciences. *Female Tolerance to Sustained Acceleration - A Retrospective Study.* San Antonio, TX, 1992.

Laubach, L. L. "Comparative Muscular Strength of Men and Women: A Review of the Literature." *Aviation, Space and Environmental Medicine* (1976): pp. 534-542.

Lawrence, VADM, USN, Testimony before the Commission, 25 June 1992.

Little, R. W. *The New Military: Changing Patterns of Organization.* New York: Russell Sage Foundation, 1964.

Lynch, M. LtCol, USAF. Testimony before the Commission, 5 May 1992.

Lyons, T. J. "Women in the Fast Jet Cockpit - Aeromedical Considerations." *Aviation Space and Environmental Medicine* 63 (1992): pp. 809-18.

Macdonough, J. "Integration of Women Aboard a U.S. Coast Guard Cutter." *Gender Integration in the Military*, 1982.

Maier, LTC, USA. Testimony before the Commission, 5 May 1992.

Marcinik, E. J., CDR (sel), USN. Testimony before the Commission, 26 June 1992.

Marlowe, Dr. David. Testimony before the Commission, 4 May 1992.

Marshall, Joan E. and Richard Heslin. "Boys and Girls Together: Sexual Composition and the Effect of Density and Group Size on Cohesion." *Journal of Personality and Social Psychology* 31, No. 5 (1975): pp. 952-961.

Marshall, S. L. A. *Men Against Fire.* New York: William Morrow, 1947.

Martin, Dr. Susan. *Breaking and Entering: Police Women on Patrol.* Berkely, CA: University of California Press, 1980.

Martin, Dr. Susan. *The Status of Women and Policing.* Police Foundation, Washington, DC, 1990.

Maypole, Donald E. "Sexual Harassment in the Workplace." *Social Work*, September-October 1983.

McArdle, W. D., J. R. Magel, R. J. Spina, M. M. Toner. "Adjustment to Cold Water Exposure in Exercising Men and Women." *Journal of Applied Physiology* No. 6 (1984): pp. 1565-1571.

McDermaid, S. CAPT, USN and CAPT B. D. Cole, USN. Testimony before the Commission, 5 May 1992.

McLane, CDR, USN. Testimony before the Commission, 6 August 1992.

Miller, Laura and Charles Moskos. Testimony before the Commission, 10 September 1992.

Moskos, Charles C. Personal Statement, 2 October 1992.

Moskos, Charles C. *The American Enlisted Man.* New York: Russell Sage Foundation, 1970.

Rolbant, S. *The Israeli Soldier: Profile of an Army.* Cranbury, NJ: Thomas Yoseloff, 1970.

Roush, Dr. Paul. Testimony before the Commission, 9 June 1992.

Royal British Navy. *Report of a Study in the Employment of Women's Royal Naval Service (WRNS) Personnel in the Royal Navy,* March 1989.

Royal Netherlands Navy Department of Social Research. *Sailing with Women,* 1985.

Sharp and W. C. Westmoreland. *Report on the War in Vietnam.* Washington, DC: Government Printing Office, 1968.

Sherman, J. A. and E. Fennema. "Distribution of Spatial Visualization and Mathematical Problem Solving Scores." *Psychology of Women Quarterly* 3 (1978): pp. 157-167.

Sheufele, LT, USN. Testimony before the Commission, 6 August 1992.

Shils, Edward A. and M. Janowitz. "Cohesion and Disintegration in the Wehrmacht in World War II." *Public Opinion Quarterly*, 1948.

Sinclair, T. W. "Perceptions of U.S. Coast Guard Women Concerning Their Integration into Active Service." Naval Postgraduate School, 1977.

Stegmeyer, SGM, U.S. Army. Testimony before the Commission, 5 May 1992.

Stone, Maj, W., USAF. Testimony before the Commission, 9 June 1992.

Stouffer, S. A., et al. *The American Soldier.* Princeton, NJ: Princeton University Press, 1949.

Summary Report on Fact-Finding Trip to Nellis AFB, 5-7 July 1992.

Summary Report on Fact-Finding Trip to Canada, 26 August 1992.

Summary Report on Fact-Finding Trip to NSB Kings Bay and NTC Orlando, 15 October 1992.

Taylor, John and Donald S. Strassberg. "The Effects of Sex Composition and Interpersonal Learning in Short-Term Personal Growth Groups." Journal of the Division of Psychotherapy (1986): pp. 267-273.

U.S. Air Command and Staff College. "Cost Effectiveness of the Enlisted Female." October, 1978.

U.S. Air Force B-1 Crew. Testimony before the Commission, 15 July 1992.

U.S. Air Force Missile Crew. Testimony before the Commission, 14 July 1992.

U.S. Air Force Personnel Survey Branch. "Opinion on Women in Combat." 1992.

U.S. Air Force Research Laboratory Institute For Environmental Medicine. *Air Force Female Pilots Program: Initial Performance and Attitudes*. 1967.

U.S. Air Force Systems Command. "Cockpit Accomodation." October, 1991.

U.S. Air Force Systems Command Aeronautical Systems Division. Report of the Study Group on USAF Female Aircrew Requirement for Life Support and Protective Clothing. October 1977.

U.S. Air Force Systems Command. Aerospace Medical Research Laboratory. "Height/Weight Programs for Women's Protective Garments." June, 1979.

U.S. Army. "Validation of the Military Entrance Physical Strength Capacity Test." 1984.

U.S. Army Combat Support. Testimony before the Commission, 28 August 1992.

U.S. Army Human Engineering Laboratory. "The Female in Military-Equipment Design." April, 1976.

U.S. Army Natick Research and Development Laboratories. "Anthropometric Sizing Systems for Army Women's Field Clothing." March 1981.

U.S. Army Research Institute For Environmental Medicine. "An Analysis of Aerobic Capacity in a Large United States Population." 1985.

U.S. Army Research Institute For Environmental Medicine. "Cerebral Laterality and Handedness in Aviation: Performance and Selection Implications." 1988.

U.S. Army Research Institute For Environmental Medicine. "Assessment of Muscle Strength and Prediction of Lifting in U.S. Army Personnel." 1985.

U.S. Army Research Institute For Environmental Medicine. "The Nature and Cause of Injuries in Female Recruits Resulting from an 8-Week Physical Training Program." 1979.

U.S. Army Research Institute For Environmental Medicine. "Incidence of and Risk Factors for Injury and Illness among Male and Female Army Basic Trainees." 1988.

U.S. Army Research Institute For Environmental Medicine. "Performance on Selected Candidate Screening Test Procedures Before and After Army Basic and Advanced Individual Training." 1985.

U.S. Congress. House. Subcommittee on Military Personnel and Compensation. Statement by Dr. Edwin Dorn. 29 July 1992.

U.S. Embassy, Saigon, "Diary of an Infiltrator." Document No. 102, Vietnam Documents and Research Notes, 1967: pp. 43-44.

U.S. General Accounting Office. NSAID Defense Force Management. DoD Service Academies: Sexual Harassment. 1992.

U.S. Helicopter Support Crew. Testimony before the Commission, 28 August 1992.

U.S. Naval Aviators. Testimony before the Commission, 6 August 1992.

U.S. Naval Health Research Center. "A Comparison of the Effects of Circuit Weight Training on Navy Men and Women." Report 85-13. n.d.

U.S. Naval Personnel Research and Development Center. "Documentation of Muscularly Demanding Job Tasks and Validation of an Occupational Strength Test Battery (STB)." San Diego, CA, 1985.

U.S. Navy Personnel Research and Development Center. "Men and Women in Ships: Attitudes of Crew After One to Two Years of Integration." November 1983.

U.S. Naval Ship Engineering Center. Ship's Physical Evaluation Form. March 1973.

U.S. Naval Training Center Orlando. "Gender Integrated Recruit Training Pilot Program Final Report." July 1992.

U.S. Navy Enlisted. Testimony before the Commission, 6 August 1992.

U.S. Navy Personnel Research and Development Center. "Integration of Sexes at Sea: Attitudes and Expectations of Men and Women on Two Ships." October 1981.

U.S. Navy Top Gun Pilots. Testimony before the Commission, 6 August 1992.

Van Tien Dung. "On Experience in Building the Revolutionary Armed Strength of Our Party." Quoted in Turley, William S. "The Political Role and Development of the Peoples' Army of Vietnam." Paper Presented at the American Political Science Association Convention in San Francisco, September 1975.

Vogel, J. A. Testimony before the Commission, 7 August 1992.

Wagner, J. A., D. S. Miles, S. M. Horvath, and J. A. Reyburn. "Maximal Work Capacity of Women During Acute Hypoxia." Journal of Applied Physiology (1979): pp. 1,223-1,227.

Webe, Tom. "Rewarding Things that Count." Research Directorate (1982): pp. 3-7.

Weinberger, Casper. Secretary of Defense. Memorandum 20 July 1988.

Williams, Jean M. and Collen M. Hacker. "Casual Relationships Among Cohesion, Satisfaction, and Performance in Women's Intercollegiate Field Hockey Teams." Journal of Sports Psychology, 4 (1982): pp. 324-337.

Zehner, G., R. Mankin, J. Parker, L. M. Tanner. Testimony before the Commission, 29 August 1992.

# PANEL THREE BIBLIOGRAPHY

Adair, Lawrence R., LTC, USA.  Testimony before the Commission, 7 August 1992.

Ainsworth, Mary D. Salter.  "Attachments Beyond Infancy."  *American Psychologist* (April 1989):  pp. 709-716.

Ainsworth, Mary D. Salter and John Bowlby.  "An Ethological Approach to Personality Development."  *American Psychologist* (April 1991):  pp. 333-341.

"Attitudes Regarding the Assignment of Women in the Armed Forces:  The Military Perspective."  The Roper Organization Inc., September 1992.

"Attitudes Regarding the Assignment of Women in the Armed Forces:  The Public Perspective."  The Roper Organization Inc., August 1992.

Beck, William J., Lt Col, USAF.  Testimony before the Commission, 14 July 1992.

Belsky, Jay and Michael J. Rovine.  "Nonmaternal Care in the First Year of Life and the Security of the Infant-Parent Attachment."  *Child Development*, 157-167.  n.d.

Belsky, Jay, Bonnie Gilstrap, and Michael J. Rovine.  "The Pennsylvania Infant and Family Development Project, I:  Stability and Change in Mother-Infant and Father-Infant Interaction in a Family Setting at One, Three and Nine Months."  *Child Development* 55, pp. 692-705.  n.d.

Belsky, Jay.  "Parental and Nonparental Child Care and Children's Socio-emotional Development:  A Decade in Review."  *Journal of Marriage and the Family* (November 1990):  pp. 885-903.

Belsky, Dr. Jay M.  Testimony before the Commission, 9 June 1992.

Beyer, Rev. Arthur.  Testimony before the Commission, 13 July 1992.

Bier, Gary, CAPT, USN.  Testimony before the Commission, 9 August 1992.

Binkin, Marty.  Testimony before the Commission, 4 May 1992.

Bowlby, John.  *Separation: Anxiety and Anger*.  New York:  Basic Books, Inc., 1973.

Bowlby, John.  *Attachment and Loss*.  New York:  Basic Books, Inc., 1980.

Bowlby, John. *A Secure Base: Parent-Child Attachment and Healthy Human Development.* New York: Basic Books, Inc., 1988.

Carlson, Dr. Allan. Testimony before the Commission, 13 July 1992.

DASD(MM&PP). Response to Question 1 from 25-26 March 1992.

DASD(MM&PP). Response to Question 4 from 25-26 March 1992.

DASD(MM&PP). Response to Question 117 from 12 September 1992.

DASD(MM&PP). Response to Question 167 from 23 September 1992.

DASD(MM&PP). Response to Question 171 from 23 September 1992.

DASD(MM&PP). Response to Question 175 from 23 September 1992.

DASD(MM&PP). Senior Enlisted Advisors. Testimony before the Commission, 26 June 1992.

DASD(MM&PP). Service Representatives. Testimony before Panel 3 Commissioners, 26 September 1992.

Deegan, Gene A., MajGen, USMC. Testimony before the Commission, 25 June 1992.

Dempsey, Robert E., Maj Gen, USAF. Testimony before the Commission, 14 July 1992.

Department of the Air Force. Personnel Plans and Policy. "Air Force Non-Deployability." Testimony before the Commission, 11 September 1992.

Department of the Army. Office of the Deputy Chief of Staff for Personnel. "Non-Deployability: Operation Desert Shield, Operation Desert Storm, August 1990 - March 1991." Testimony before the Commission, 8 August 1992.

Department of the Army. Office of the Deputy Chief of Staff for Personnel. "Enlisted Separations, DCSPER 598 Report." n.d.

Department of the Army. Office of the Deputy Chief of Staff for Personnel, Plans and Analysis Division, Human Resources Directorate. "Public Opinion on Women in the Military and in Combat." Review by Elena Verdugo of civilian surveys, 8 May 1992.

Department of the Navy. "Navy Lost Time Briefing." Testimony before the Commission, 1 October 1992.

Department of the Navy. Bureau of Naval Personnel. "Navy Women in the Gulf: Operations Desert Shield and Desert Storm." Testimony before the Commission, 11 September 1992.

Department of the Navy. United States Marine Corps. Headquarters, United States Marine Corps. "Non-Deployability: Operation Desert Shield, Operation Desert Storm, August 1990-March 1991." Testimony before the Commission, 11 September 1992.

Downing, Tom, LT, USN. Testimony before the Commission, 9 August 1992.

Dworetzky, John P. and Nancy J. Davis. *Human Development: A Lifespan Approach.* Annaheim, CA: West Publishing Company, 1989.

Fanning, Rev. Buckner. Testimony before the Commission, 27 August 1992.

Foote, Evelyn, BG, USA. Testimony before the Commission, 25 June 1992.

Friedman, Dr. Sonya. Testimony before the Commission, 9 June 1992.

Frost, George E., BMCM (SW), USN. Testimony before the Commission, 9 June 1992.

Giffin, Mary, M.D., and Carol Felsenthal. *A Cry For Help.* Garden City, New York: Doubleday and Company, Inc., 1983.

Glosson, Buster C., Lt Gen, USAF. Testimony before the Commission, 8 June 1992.

Graham-Mist, Peter, CDR, USN. Testimony before the Commission, 9 June 1992.

Horowitz, David. Testimony before the Commission, 6 August 1992.

Hunter, Dr. Brenda M. Testimony before the Commission, 9 June 1992.

Jacobs, Marianne Scherer. "The Best of Times, The Worst of Times: The Vietnam Experiences of and Post-Traumatic Stress Disorder Among Female Nurse Veterans." PhD dissertation, University of Washington, 1990.

Kennedy, Senator Edward M. (D-MA) Testimony before the Commission, 25 June 1992.

Krulak, Charles, MajGen, USMC. Testimony before the Commission, 25 June 1992.

Lepowsky, Dr. Maria. Testimony before the Commission, 13 July 1992.

Loughran, Michael P., Col, USAF. Testimony before the Commission, 28 August 1992.

Manning, Dr. Richard, COL, USA. Testimony before the Commission, 9 June 1992.

Mattox, William R. Testimony before the Commission, 9 June 1992.

McLane, Robert L., CDR, USN. Testimony before the Commission, 9 August 1992.

Military Child Care Act of 1989, P.L. 101-189, 29 November 1989.

Military Selective Service Act, 50 U.S.C. App. 453. n.d.

Miller, Laura and Dr. Charles C. Moskos. *1992 Survey on Gender in the Military.*

Morris, Ailneal, Capt, USMC. Testimony before the Commission, 7 August 1992.

Morrison, Robert. Testimony before the Commission, 25 June 1992.

National Opinion Research Center. National Survey of Adults, February - April 1982-1984.

Newton, Lloyd W., Brig Gen, USAF. Testimony before the Commission, 28 August 1992.

P.L. 65-12, 18 May 1917.

P.L. 90-40, 30 June 1967.

P.L. 82-51, 19 June 1951.

P.L. 101-189, n.d.

P.L. 102-25, n.d.

Raaz, Richard Dean, CAPT, USN. Testimony before the Commission, 9 August 1992.

Rinn, Paul X., Capt., USN. Testimony before the Commission, 9 June 1992.

Roach, Father Richard. Testimony before the Commission, 13 July 1992.

Roggero, Michael, Col, USAF. Testimony before the Commission, 14 July 1992.

Segal, Dr. Mady. "The Military and the Family as Greedy Institutions." *Armed Forces and Society,* (Fall 1986): pp. 3-98.

Segal, Dr. Mady. Testimony before the Commission, 9 June 1992.

Seigle, Robert, COL., USA. Testimony before the Commission, 7 August 1992.

Selective Service Regulations of 1918.

Selective Service Regulations -- First Edition, Paragraph 364. 23 September 1940 to 1 February 1942.

Selective Service Regulations -- Second Edition, First Printing, Paragraph 622.31. 1 February 1942 to 1 February 1943.

Selective Service Regulations -- Second Edition, Second Printing, Paragraph 622.31-2. 1 February 1943 to 31 July 1945.

Selective Service Regulations -- Second Edition, Third Printing, Paragraph 622.32. 31 July 1945 to 31 March 1947.

Sigas, Dr. Ibis, Col, USAF. Testimony before the Commission, 9 June 1992.

Simpson, Kathleen, Capt, USAF. *1991 USAF Women in Combat Survey, 1992.*

Smith, Stephen Scott, LTC, USA. Testimony before the Commission, 7 August 1992.

Sroufe, Alan J. and Mary J. Ward, "The Importance of Early Care." *Women in the Workplace: The Effects on Families*, eds. D. Quarm, K. Borman, and S. Gideonese. Norwood, NJ: Ablex, 1984.

Stewart, Rev. John. Testimony before the Commission, 6 August 1992.

Summary Report on Fact-Finding Trip to Parris Island Marine Corps Recruit Depot and Fort Bragg, NC, 15-16 June 1992.

Thomas, Patricia. "The Impact on Navy Systems." February 1992.

Thomas, Patricia and CAPT Martha Whitehead, USN. "Lost Time of Enlisted Men and Women." Testimony before the Commission, 1 October 1992.

Tystad, Douglas, LTC, USA. Testimony before the Commission, 7 August 1992.

U.S. Air Force.  "A Study of the Effectiveness of Family Assistance Programs in the Air Force During Operation Desert Shield/Desert Storm."  n.d.

U.S. Army Research Institute.  *Longitudinal Research on Officer Careers*, 9 October 1991.

U.S. Coast Guard.  *Commandant Instruction 1040.5*, 12 June 1991.

U.S. Congress.  Senate.  Committee on Armed Services.  Subcommittee on Manpower and Personnel. Testimony of GEN Carl Vuono, USA, 18 Jun 1991.

U.S. Department of Defense.  Defense Manpower Data Center.  "Discharge/Separation of Enlisted Members by Character of Service and Reason for Separation."  March 1992 and September 1992.

U.S. Department of Defense.  Defense Manpower Data Center.  "Fact Sheet:  Women in the Military."  20 August 1992.

U.S. Department of Defense.  DoD Directive 1315.7, Change 1, 21 August 1991.

U.S. Department of Defense.  DoD Instruction 1342.19, "Family Care Plans," 13 July 1992.

U.S. Department of Defense.  "DoD Report on Title III of the Persian Gulf Conflict and Supplemental Authorization and Personnel Benefits Act of 1991:  P.L. 102-25."

U.S. General Accounting Office.  *Operation Desert Storm:  War Highlights Need to Address Problem of Nondeployable Personnel.*  31 August 1992.

U.S. Naval Health Research Center.  "Sex Differences in Health Care Requirements Aboard U.S. Navy Ships."  Report No. 90-2.  20 March 1990.

U.S. Navy Personnel Research and Development Center.  "Navy-Wide Personnel Survey (NPS)" *1990.*

U.S. Navy Personnel Research and Development  Center.  "Navy-Wide Personnel Survey (NPS)" *1991.*

Ursano, Dr. Robert.  Testimony before the Commission, 9 June 1992.

Wine-Banks, Jill.  Testimony before the Commission, 13 July 1992.

I-37

# PANEL FOUR BIBLIOGRAPHY

"Administration Against Women in Combat Roles." *Air Force Times*, 5 December 1983.

Alexander, Robert M., Lt Gen, USAF. Prepared statement before the Defense Subcommittee, Senate Appropriations Committee, *Defense Issues*, 26 March 1992.

ASD(FM&P). "Population Representation in the Military Services, FY 90." July 1991.

ASD(FM&P). "Military Women in the Department of Defense." July 1990.

"Attitudes Regarding the Assignment of Women in the Armed Forces: The Public Perspective." The Roper Organization Inc., August 1992.

"Attitudes Regarding the Assignment of Women in the Armed Forces: The Military Perspective." The Roper Organization Inc., September 1992.

Barrow, Robert H., Gen, USMC (Ret.). Congressional Testimony, June 1991.

Beck, Melinda, et al. "Women in the Armed Forces." *Newsweek*, 18 February 1980.

Belsky, Dr. Jay. Testimony before the Commission, 19 June 1992.

Bier, Gary, CAPT, USN. Testimony before the Commission, 6 August 1992.

Bird, Julie. "AF Women Filled Many Roles in Panama Mission." *Air Force Times*, 29 January 1990.

Boening, Suzanne S. "Woman Soldier, Quo Vadis?" *Parameters*, (June 1983): pp. 58-64.

"Bring Back the Draft?" *U.S. News and World Report*, 14 February 1977.

Burke, Yvonne Brathwaite. "Let's Play Taps for an All Male Army!" *Saturday Evening Post*, October 1977.

Bushey, Duane R., MCPO, USN. Testimony before the Commission, 26 June 1992.

Carey, Dr. Sandra. Testimony before the Commission, 26 March 1992.

"Carter: Women Won't Serve in Combat." *Air Force Times*, 25 February 1980.

Chapman, Michael E., Sgt, USMC. et. al. Testimony before the Commission, 26 June 1992.

Chappell v. Wallace, 462 U.S. 296, 301 (1983).

Chastain, Jane. Testimony before the Commission, 26 June 1992.

"Chiefs Discuss Military Women, Discrimination, Harassment." *Defense Issues*, 18 August 1992.

Conant, Jennet and John Barry. "Women in Combat?" *Newsweek*, 11 November 1985.

Craig v. Boren, 429 U.S. 190 (1976).

DASD(MM&PP). Air Force Response to Question 19 from 25-26 March 1992.

DASD(MM&PP). Army Response to Questions 3, 7, 11, 12, 13 from 25-26 March 1992.

DASD(MM&PP). Army, Navy, Air Force Responses to Question 6 from 25-26 March 1992.

DASD(MM&PP). Individual Service Responses to Question 11 from 4-6 April 1992.

DASD(MM&PP). Marine Corps, Air Force, and Navy Responses to Question 3 from 25-26 March 1992.

DASD(MM&PP). Response, DoD Risk Rule, 24-27 June 1992.

DASD(MM&PP). Response, 13-15 July 1992.

DASD(MM&PP). Response to Question 1, copy of H.R. 4084. n.d.

DASD(MM&PP). Response to Questions 124-125 from 10-12 September 1992.

DASD(MM&PP). Senior Enlisted Advisors' Replies to OSD Question 27, 24-27 June 1992.

Deegan, Gene A., MajGen, USMC. Testimony before the Commission, 15-16 June 1992.

DeLay, Congressman Tom. Testimony before the Commission, 25 June 1992.

Department of the Air Force. "Combat Exclusions for Women." 18 August 1989.

Department of the Navy. SecNAV Instruction 1300.12A, 20 February 1989.

Dillingham, Wayne E., Maj, USAF. "The Possibility of American Military Women Becoming POWs: Justification for the Combat Exclusion Rules?" *Federal Bar News & Journal*, (May 1990): pp. 223-229.

Donnelly, Elaine. "Politics and the Pentagon: The Role of Women in the Military." May 1991.

Drogin, Bob. "Adam and Eve and the Army." *The Progressive*, March 1979.

Durney, Robert. "Women in Combat: Closer Than You Think." *U.S. News & World Report*, 3 March 1980.

Eaker, Ira C. "Combat Duty for Women." *Air Force Times*, 10 April 1978.

Foote, Evelyn, BG, USA (Ret). Testimony before the Commission, 25 June 1992.

Friedman, Dr. Sonya. Testimony before the Commission, 9 June 1992.

Frontiero v. Richardson, 411 U.S. 677 (1973).

Gilbert, Michael H., Maj. "Women in Combat: Who Should Make the Policy." *Minerva: Quarterly Report,* (Summer 1992): pp. 1-4.

Gilder, George. "The Case Against Women in Combat." *New York Times Magazine*, 28 January 1979.

Gilliat, Robert L. Testimony before the Commission, 25 March 1992.

Gilligan v. Morgan, 413 U.S. 1, 10 (1973).

Goldman v. Weinberger, 475 U.S. 503, 507 (1986).

Green, Brian. "Women in Combat." *Air Force Magazine*, June 1990.

Gropman, Alan L., "The Korean War and Armed Forces Racial Integration." Industrial College of the Armed Forces Essay, n.d.

Halloran, Richard. "Military Women: Increasingly Indispensable." *New York Times*, 13 March 1988.

Hammond, Judith D., CDR, USCG. Testimony before the Commission, 26 March 1992.

Heck, Karen, Maj, USMC. Testimony before the Commission, 26 March 1992.

Henderson, W. Darryl, LTC, USA (Ret). "Can-do NCOs -- With Clout -- Can Help Cohesion Problem." *Army*, March 1982.

Hines, Charles A., MG, USA. Testimony before the Commission, 8 June 1992.

Holm, Jeanne, Maj Gen, USAF (Ret.). *Women in the Military: An Unfinished Revolution.* Washington, DC, 1982.

Hooker, Richard D., Jr. "Affirmative Action and Combat Exclusion: Gender Roles in the US Army." *Parameters*, (December 1989): pp. 37-49.

Horowitz, David. Testimony before the Commission, 6 August 1992.

Hosek, James R. and Christine E. Peterson. "Serving Her Country: An Analysis of Women's Enlistment," RAND National Defense Research Institute, January 1990.

Jones, Paul E. Testimony before the Commission, 26 March 1992.

"Judicial Review and Soldiers' Rights: Is the Principle of Deference a Standard of Review?" 17 Hofstra L. Rev. 465, 475, (1989).

Kennedy, Senator Edward M. (D-MA) Testimony before the Commission, 25 June 1992.

Kessler and Gabriel. "Women in Combat? Two Views." *Army,* March 1980.

Kitfield, James. "Total Force." *Government Executive*, March 1991.

Klein, Steven, et. al. "Why Recruits Separate Early." RAND National Defense Research Institute, 1991.

Lawrence, William, VADM, USN (Ret.). Testimony before the Commission, 26 June 1992.

Lien, Maurice L., Lt Col, USAF (Ret.). "Women in the All-Volunteer Force." *The Retired Officer,* October 1982.

Lind, William S. Testimony before the Commission, 25 June 1992.

"Lord: Repeal Hill Ban on Women in Combat." *Air Force Times*, 11 January 1982.

Mack v. Rumsfeld, 609 F.Supp.1561 (1985).

Mariner, Rosemary Bryant, CDR, USN. "A Soldier is a Soldier." National War College Essay, 1992.

Mariner, Rosemary Bryant, CDR, USN. "'Jane Crow' Policies Keep Women Out of Combat Cockpits." *Armed Forces Journal*, (May 1992): p. 46.

Mariner, Rosemary Bryant, CDR, USN. Testimony before the Commission, 25 June 1992.

Markley, Greg. "Grenada Mission Provides Female MPs Valuable Combat Experience." *McClellan News*, 15 May 1992.

Marlowe, Dr. David, and Dr. Owen Jacobs. Testimony before the Commission, 5 May 1992.

Martindale, Dr. Melanie. "Sexual Harassment in the Military: 1988." Defense Manpower Data Center, September 1990.

Mattox, William R. Testimony before the Commission, 9 June 1992.

Maurmann, Steve, Maj, USAF. "DoD Definition of Fraternization." Testimony before Panel 4, 5 May 1992.

Mayer, Caroline. "We Can Do Anything -- Women Speak Out." *U.S.News & World Report*, 5 June 1978.

McDaniel, Eugene B., Capt, USA (Ret.). Testimony before the Commission, 25 June 1992.

McDonald, Richard A., Lt Col, USAF. "Women in Combat: When the Best Man for the Job is a Woman." Air Force Air War College Essay, May 1991.

McKart v. United States, no. 403 (1969).

Miles, Donna. "The Women of Just Cause." *Soldiers*, March 1990.

Military Selective Service Act, 50 U.S.C. App. 453. n.d.

Miller, Laura and Charles C. Moskos. *1992 Survey on Gender in the Military.*

Mongiovi, Kathleen, Lt Col, USAF. "Women in Combat: The Policy Aspect." Industrial College of the Armed Forces Essay, 1991.

Moskos, Charles C. "Army Women." *The Atlantic*, August 1990.

Navy Women's Study Group. "Update Report on the Progress of Women in the Navy." 1990.

Novak, Michael. "Woman as Soldier: Reality Defied." *Chicago Tribune*, 21 February 1980.

Owens v. Brown, 455 F. Supp. 291 (1978).

Passmore, George, VADM, USN. Testimony before the Commission, 26 March 1992.

Pfingston, Gary R., CMSgt, USN. Testimony before the Commission, 26 June 1992.

Pickavance, Bill, CAPT, USN. et. al. Testimony before the Commission, 6 August 1992.

Quester, Aline O. "Enlisted Women in the Marine Corps: First-Term Attrition and Long-Term Rentention." Center for Naval Analyses, August 1990.

Quester, Aline O. "Factors Associated with Navy First-Term Female Attrition Losses." Center for Naval Analyses, June 1990.

Quester, Aline O. "Non-prior-service Male and Female Recruits: Historical Comparisons of Continuation, Promotion/Demotion, Desertion Rates." Center for Naval Analyses, July 1988.

Rapoport, Daniel. "Women in the Military -- The Barriers to Full Equality." *National Journal*, (5 April 1980): pp. 565-567.

Reed, Fred. "Women in Combat: A Real Bad Idea." *Army Times*, 29 January 1990.

"Reopening an Old Debate." *Time*, 11 February 1980.

Ritter, Professor Stephanie. Testimony before the Commission, 5 May 1992.

Rogers, Robin. "A Proposal for Combatting Sexual Discrimination in the Military: Amendment of Title VII." California Law Review, 1990.

Roggero, Michael J., Col, USAF. et. al. Testimony before the Commission, 14 July 1992.

Rostker v. Goldberg, 453 U.S. 57, 70 (1981).

Roush, Dr. Paul E. Testimony before the Commission, 9 June 1992.

Ruddick, Sara. "Drafting Women: Pieces of a Puzzle," Point Paper, 19 June 1982.

Ryan, Michael. "A Woman's Place is at the Front." *People Weekly*, 22 January 90.

Schlafly, Phyllis. Testimony before the Commission, 9 June 1992.

Schlesinger v. Ballard, 419 U.S. 498, 510, (1975).

Secretary of Defense. "DoD Definition of Sexual Harassment." 20 July 1988.

Segal, Mady Wechsler. *Female Soldiers - Combatants or non-Combatants? Historical and Contemporary Perspectives.* "The Argument for Female Combatants." Westport, CT: Greenwood Press, 1982.

Segal, Mady Wechsler. "The Military and the Family as Greedy Institutions." *Armed Forces and Society,* Fall 1986.

Seigle, Greg. "Women Present Case for Combat." *Army Times,* 6 July 1992.

Seigle, Greg. "Women-in-Combat: Supporters Present Their Case." *Air Force Times,* 6 July 1992.

"Selective Service System, Information for Registrants." October 1988.

Sellman, Dr. Wayne S. Testimony before the Commission, 6 April 1992.

"Should Women Fight in War? Pro and Con" *U.S. News and World Report*, 13 February 1978.

Simpson, K., Capt, USAF. Testimony before the Commission, 13 July 1992.

Smith, Ellen O. Testimony before the Commission, 25 June 1992.

SRA Corporation. "Organizational Assessment Study: An Analysis of the Effects of Varying Male and Female Force Levels." February 1985.

Stanley, Sandra Carson and Mady Wechsler Segal. "Women in the Armed Forces." 1992.

Steele, William M., BG, USA. Testimony before the Commission, 7 August 1992.

Stiehm, Judith H. "Women and the Combat Exemption." *Parameters*, (June 1980): pp. 51-59.

Summary Report on Fact-Finding Trip to Seymour-Jounson AFB and Camp Lejeune Marine Base, 2 June 1992.

Summary Report on Fact-Finding Trip to Parris Island Marine Corps Recruit Depot and Fort Bragg, NC, 15-16 June 1992.

U.S. Coast Guard. Commandant Instruction 1040.5, 12 June 1991.

U.S. Coast Guard. "Women in The Coast Guard." 10 July 1990.

U.S. Congress. House. Subcommittee on Military Personnel and Compensation. Statement by Maj Gen John Singlaub, USAF (Ret.). 5 March 1980.

U.S. Congress. House. Subcommittee on Military Personnel and Compensation. "Implementation of the Repeal of the Combat Exclusion on Female Aviators." 29 January 1992.

U.S. Congress. House. Subcommittee on Military Personnel and Compensation. Statement by Lawrence J. Korb. 17 November 1983.

U.S. Congress. Senate. Manpower and Personnel Subcommittee of the Senate Armed Services. Testimony of Christopher Jehn. 18 June 1991.

U.S. Congress. Senate. Manpower and Personnel Subcommittee of the Senate Armed Services. Testimony of Barbara Spyridon Pope. 2 June 1992.

U.S. Congress. Senate. Manpower and Personnel Subcommittee of the Senate Armed Services. Testimonies of Service Chiefs. 18 June 1991.

U.S. Department of Defense. Directive 1350.2 "The Department of Defense Equal Opportunity Program." 23 December 1988.

U.S. Department of Defense. "The Military Selective Service Act." Point Paper prepared by the Office of the General Counsel, 1992.

U.S. Department of Defense. "Report: Task Force on Women in the Military." January 1988.

U.S. Department of Justice. Memorandum for Honorable John White from John M. Harmon, 31 January 1980.

U.S. General Accounting Office. "Women in the Military: Impact of Proposed Legislation to Open More Combat Support Positions to Women." July 1988.

U.S. General Accounting Office. "Women in the Military: More Military Jobs Can Be Opened Under Current Statutes." September 1988.

U.S. General Accounting Office. "Women in the Military: Career Progression Not a Current Problem but Concerns Remain." September 1989.

U.S. General Accounting Office. "Women in the Military: More Military Jobs Can Be Opened Under Current Statutes." September 1988.

U.S. General Accounting Office. "Women in the Military: Attrition and Retention." July 1990.

U.S. General Accounting Office. "Women in the Military: Air Force Revises Job Availability but Entry Screening Needs Review." August 1991.

U.S. Marine Corps. Marine Corps Order 1300.8P, 12 August 1988.

Warner, Senator John. (R-VA) Testimony before the Commission, 25 June 1992.

Webster, Alexander F.C. "Paradigms of the Contemporary Soldier and Women in the Military." *Strategic Review,* (Summer 1991): pp. 22-30.

Weinraub, Bernard. "Pentagon Asks Congress to End Ban on Women in Combat Units." *New York Times*, 4 March 1978.

Weiss, Laura B. "Debate in House Panel Focuses on Legal Questions, Combat Role." *Congressional Quarterly Weekly*, 21 May 1991.

Whitehead, Martha L., CAPT, USN. Testimony before the Commission, 6 April 1992.

Williams, Dr. and Mr. Garvey. Testimony before the Commission, 5 May 1992.

Willis, Grant. "Senate to Test Women in Combat." *Air Force Times*, 3 March 1992.

Willis, Grant. "Promotions: Women Gaining, DoD Says." *Air Force Times*, 5 November 90.

Willis, Grant. "All-or-None." *Air Force Times,* 17 August 1992.

Willis, Grant. "Women's Assignment Rules Simplified." *Army Times*, 29 June 1992.

Willis, Grant. "Women Barred From Humanitarian Missions." *Navy Times*, 29 June 1992.

Wine-Banks, Jill. Testimony before the Commission, 13 July 1992.

Winters, Kathleen, Capt, USAF. "Women in the Military -- Yesterday and Today." *Air Force Journal of Logistics.*

Wolffe, Jim. "Men, Women Enlist for Similar Reasons, Study Finds." *Air Force Times*, 19 March 1990.

Woods, Dorothea E.   "The Conscription of Women for National Defense, the Militarization of Women, and Some Ethical Perspectives on Women's Involvement in the Military."   Current Research on *Peace and Violence,* Spring 1983.

## APPENDIX J

COMMISSIONER BIOGRAPHIES

The Presidential Commission on the Assignment of Women in the Armed Forces was created by Congress on December 5, 1991 in Public Law 102-190. The law required the Commission's 15 members to be "diverse with respect to race, ethnicity, gender, and age," with the President appointing the Commissioners in consultation with the chairman and ranking minority members of the House and Senate Armed Services Committees.

Appointees were also required to have "distinguished themselves in the public or private sector" and have "significant experience" with a number of matters, including social and cultural issues affecting the military and civilian workplace, the law, combat service, military personnel affairs, women in the military and civilian sectors and women's issues.

Commissioners were appointed by the President on March 17, 1992. United States Solicitor General Kenneth W. Starr swore them in on March 25, 1992.

**General Robert T. Herres, USAF (Retired),** Commission Chairman, is Vice Chairman, President and Chief Operating Officer of USAA, which he joined after 36 years of military service involving assignments in fighter interceptor aircraft, technical intelligence, military space activity and strategic offensive operations. His command experience includes two strategic wings, the Air Force Communications Command, the Eighth Air Force, and the Air Force Space Command. He was the first commander-in-chief of the U.S. Space Command and retired after three years as the first Vice Chairman of the Joint Chiefs of Staff. General Herres is a member of the Vice President's Space Policy Advisory Board and serves on the National Board of Directors for Junior Achievement, the Air Force Academy Falcon Foundation, the U.S. Naval Academy Foundation and the Air Force Historical Foundation. He is also a member of the National Leadership Council of the Center for Strategic & International Studies and is on the Board of the Atlantic Council of the United States.

**Major General Mary Elizabeth Clarke, USA (Retired),** left the Army after more than 36 years of military service. She commanded Fort McClellan, AL and was Commandant of the Military Police Corps and Chemical Corps. General Clarke assisted in making major policy decisions concerning military women, including changing the length of women's overseas tours to match those of men and making weapons training mandatory for women recruits and officers. She was also the Army's chief advisor on numerous studies regarding the assignment of women to locations where they had never served. She was Director of the Women's Army Corps for three years. General Clarke was Vice Chairman of the Defense Advisory Committee on Women in the Services (DACOWITS) in the 1980s and is presently a member of the Council of Trustees of the Association of the United States Army (AUSA).

**Brigadier General Samuel G. Cockerham, USA (Retired),** is a combat veteran of the Korean and Vietnam Wars. He planned the development of the APACHE and was the first military pilot to fly this attack helicopter. He has served in the Office of the Joint Chiefs of Staff in Strategy and Mobility and in the Office of the Secretary of the Army as a contracts specialist with the Directorate of Procurement. General Cockerham also served in the Office of the Army Chief of Staff and the Office of the Deputy Chief of Staff for Plans and Operations. General Cockerham is a 1948 graduate of West Point and holds advanced degrees from Purdue and George Washington Universities. He is now an advisor in defense, aviation and strategic mobility systems.

**Elaine Donnelly** is a former member (1984-86) of the Pentagon's Defense Advisory Committee on Women in the Services (DACOWITS). She has researched and written extensively on issues concerning women in the military, including a lengthy monograph for academic credit entitled Politics and the Pentagon -- the Role of Women in the Military. Mrs. Donnelly's articles on this and many other subjects have been published in *The National Review, The Detroit News, Cleveland Plain Dealer, Human Events,* and several major daily newspapers nationwide.

**Brigadier General Thomas V. Draude, USMC,** is the Director of Public Affairs at Marine Corps Headquarters in Washington, D.C. He served three times in Vietnam. He was the first Director of the Defense Management Report Implementation Coordination Office under the Deputy Secretary of Defense and was the Assistant Division Commander, First Marine Division, during Operations Desert Shield and Desert Storm. He has received ten personal awards for combat including two Silver Star Medals. Two of his children are Navy officers: a daughter who is a jet pilot and a son who is an intelligence officer.

**Captain Mary M. Finch, USA,** is a graduate of West Point and the Signal Officer's Basic Course, as well as the Aviation Officer's and Military Intelligence Officer's Advanced Courses. A helicopter pilot, she is qualified in the UH-1 and OH-58. Captain Finch has held various positions of responsibility in aviation units in Germany, where she was Commander of a separate aviation detachment and Battalion Adjutant. Captain Finch served as a Tactical Officer at West Point (1989 - 1992) and is currently pursuing a graduate degree in Business Administration at George Mason University.

**Dr. Wm. Darryl Henderson** holds a PhD in Comparative Systems and International Relations from the University of Pittsburgh and is an honored graduate of the Army's Command and General Staff College and the National War College. His publications include: The Hollow Army; Cohesion: The Human Element in Combat; and Why the Vietcong Fought: A Study of Motivation and Control in a Modern Army of Combat. He was an infantry company commander for three years, including a tour in Vietnam. Dr. Henderson's most recent assignment before retiring as a full Colonel in 1988 was Commander of the US Army Research Institute in Washington, D.C., where he led efforts to study combat effectiveness through research on the accession, development, training and utilization of soldiers. He wears the Legion of Merit, Bronze Star, Purple Heart, and Combat Infantryman's Badge.

**Admiral James R. Hogg, USN (Retired),** served in the Navy for 35 years, retiring in 1991 following a three year appointment as U.S. Representative to the NATO Military Committee. Previous service assignments included command of the Seventh Fleet, Director of Military Personnel Policy, and Director of Naval Warfare. Admiral Hogg graduated from the Naval Academy and the Air Force Command and Staff College; he also has an advanced degree from George Washington University. He is President and Chief Executive Officer of the National Security Industrial Association with headquarters in Washington, D.C.

**Newton N. Minow** is Counsel to the law firm of Sidley & Austin in Chicago. Mr. Minow has served as Chairman of the Federal Communications Commission, Chairman of the RAND Corporation and Chairman of the Public Broadcasting Service. Mr. Minow served in the Army during WWII in the China-Burma-India Theater. He is a member of the board of directors of Aon Corporation, Foote, Cone & Belding Communications, Inc., Encyclopaedia Britannica, Inc., Manpower, Inc., Sara Lee Corporation and Tribune Company.

**Charles C. Moskos,** a former draftee, is a Professor of Sociology at Northwestern University. He also serves as Chairman of the Inter-University Seminar on Armed Forces and Society. Dr. Moskos has been a Fellow at the Woodrow Wilson International Center for Scholars and has also been awarded fellowships from the Ford, Rockefeller, and Guggenheim Foundations. His writings on military sociology have been translated into eleven languages.

**Meredith A. Neizer** is a Trade Manager with Sea-Land Services, Inc. She has served as a Business Manager for the New York & New Jersey Port Authority and as a White House Fellow to the Secretary of Defense. In 1990, Defense Secretary Cheney awarded her the Secretary of Defense Medal for Outstanding Public Service for her role as Chair of the Defense Advisory Committee on Women in the Services (DACOWITS). Ms. Neizer graduated from the U.S. Merchant Marine Academy in 1978 and earned an MBA from Stanford Graduate School of Business in 1982.

**Kate Walsh O'Beirne** is Vice President of Government Relations at the Heritage Foundation in Washington, D.C. Before joining Heritage, she served as Deputy Assistant Secretary for Legislation at the Department of Health and Human Services. Mrs. O'Beirne is a Contributing Editor to National Review and is a member of Goodwill Industries of America's National Business Advisory Council. Married to a retired career infantry officer, she has lived on military installations here and abroad. Mrs. O'Beirne is a panelist on a weekly PBS public affairs talk show, "To The Contrary," and is a graduate of St. John's University Law School.

**Ronald D. Ray** is an attorney with his own firm in Louisville, Kentucky. From 1984 to 1985, he served as the first Deputy Assistant Secretary of Defense for Guard/Reserve Readiness and Training. A Vietnam combat veteran, Mr. Ray was awarded two Silver Stars, the Bronze Star with V Device and the Purple Heart. In addition to practicing law, he is a Reserve Colonel and Historian at the Marine Corps Historical Center in Washington, D.C. and a Commissioner on the American Battle Monuments Commission. Mr. Ray graduated magna cum laude from the University of Louisville School of Law.

**General Maxwell Reid Thurman, USA (Retired),** served more than 37 years in the Army before retiring in 1991. General Thurman was the Army's Chief of Recruiting and served as the Army Deputy Chief of Staff for Personnel. Appointed General in 1983, he served four years as the Vice Chief of Staff, U.S. Army. In 1987, he became the Commander of the U.S. Army Training and Doctrine Command, and in 1989, was appointed Commander-in-Chief of the U.S. Southern Command, an assignment which put him in command of all U.S. military forces during Operation Just Cause. General Thurman graduated from North Carolina State University, the United States Army Command and General Staff College and the United States Army War College. He is a Senior Fellow at the Association of the U.S. Army, and is a Presidential appointee as U.S. Representative on the Panama Canal Consultative Committee.

**Sarah F. White** is a Master Sergeant in the U.S. Air Force Reserve, assigned to the U.S. Air Force Intelligence Command, with 17 years of service. She is an Executive Assistant with Science Applications International Corporation. She has received the Airman of the Year Award (Westover AFB, 1976) and the Air Force Commendation Medal. Her current assignment is with a unit that supports special studies and assessments for the Air Force Chief of Staff for Intelligence (ACS/I) in the Pentagon. While serving as a legislative analyst with Concerned Women for America (CWA), Miss White published several articles in CWA's monthly magazine, and was author of their monthly Capitol Hill Report.

## ACKNOWLEDGEMENTS

*Over the past eight months, the Commission asked innumerable questions and requested reports, documents, evidence, and testimony from the Office of the Secretary of Defense and the Army, Navy, Marine Corps, Air Force, and the United States Coast Guard. The Commission expresses special appreciation to:*

*Major Steven F. Maurmann, USAF, Deputy Director, Personnel Utilization, Office of the Assistant Secretary of Defense for Force Management and Personnel*

*Captain Jeffory Smith, USA, Office of the Assistant Secretary of Defense*

*Colonel Terry M. Hulin, USA, Chief, Soldier Policy Division, Human Resources Directorate, Office of the Deputy Chief of Staff For Personnel, Headquarters U.S. Army*

*Captain Martha L. Whitehead, USN, Special Assistant for Women's Policy to the Chief of Naval Personnel, Headquarters U.S. Navy*

*Lieutenant Colonel Eugene Brindle, USMC, Head, Manpower Policy Section, Headquarters U.S. Marine Corps*

*Lieutenant Colonel James M. Lynch, USAF, Chief, Officer Accessions Plans and Policy, Directorate of Personnel Plans, Deputy Chief of Staff for Personnel, Headquarters U.S. Air Force*

*Commander Judith Hammond, USCG, Women's Policy Advisor, Workforce Planning, Office of Personnel and Training, U.S. Coast Guard*